# Which edition of the bible is from God?

By Gregory Heary

Originally there were many different gospels written by many different people and each early church had their own collection of scripture. Every church practiced Christianity differently because they didn't all have access to the same scriptures. Before the version of Christianity practiced in Rome became the state religion of the Roman Empire by Theodosian decree in 380 CE many Christian denominations existed, there were the Adoptionists, Agnoites, Alogians, Apellaeans, Apocarites, Apollinarianists, Aquarians, Archonticks, Artemonites, Artotytrites, Asclepidoteans, Ascodrogites, Ascodrutes, Bardesanistes, Basilidians, Beryllians, Bonosians, Cainians, Carpocratians, Cerdonians, Cerinthians, Chiliasts, Colluthians, Collylyridians, Docetists, Donatists, Ebionites, Elcesaites, Encratites, Eudoxians, Eusebians, Eustathians, Eutuchites, Eutychians, Florinians, Gacianitae, Gnostics, Helsaites, Heracleonites, Hermogenians, Heterousians, Hieracites, Lucianists, Luciferians, Macedonians, Manicheans, Marcellians, Marcosians, Maronites, Massalians, Melecians, Melchizedichians, Menanderians, Monarchianists, Monophysites, Montanists, Nazareans, Neonomians, Nestorians, Nicolaitians, Noetians, Novations, Ophites, Originists, Ossenians, Patricians, Paulianists, Pelagianists, Photinians, Priscillianists, Proclianites, Psaytrians, Ptolemattes, Proto-Coptics, Quartodecimani,Quintillians, Sabellians, Sachophori, Satanians, Saturnians, Secundians, Seleucians, Semi-Arians, Semi-Pelagians, Serverians, Sethians, Simonians, Soldins, Stilites, Subordinationists, Tatianites, Theopaschites, Trisormiani, Tritheists, Valentinians, Universalists, Zacheans, and that's just to name a few. I'm not being sarcastic either, that is only a few of the many which existed. All the diverse early Christian groups each had their own gospels supporting their views. This is biblically evident with Paul's numerous letters to the different churches that were practicing different forms of Christianity. It is important to note that Paul himself founded all those churches he wrote to. Despite that Paul wrote many letters because there were so many different forms of Christianity being practiced and so many different "scriptures" were being used to justify the drastically different ancient Christian denominations. Not everyone believed Saul/Paul was genuine, nor did they accept his new doctrine because they had their own gospels, alleged to have been written by Thomas, James, Peter, Barnabas and many others. They taught a very different version of Jesus than the one preached by Paul; who never met Jesus while he was on earth. Although not all of these gospels were actually written by the one whom the texts claim, often they were written pseudonymously. Some were forgeries and others were changed after being written by the copiers, intentionally and unintentionally. Essentially every church had a different understanding of Jesus based on different scriptures and there was little uniformity among early Christians. This continued for some time with different denominations denouncing the others as heretics. Everyone was claiming to be followers of Jesus, frequently their arguments would turn violent and blood would be shed. This continued until Constantine became the emperor of Rome and wanted the chaos to stop in order to rule over a unified empire. Constantine called for the Council of Nicaea in 325 CE inviting the leaders of different denominations to end the bickering and agree, hoping that one day Christianity could potentially unify the expansive Roman empire and be used as a political tool for control. Many bishops from all over the world with different theologies attended this council. The various bishops all brought their own scriptures with them in order to support their religious beliefs. Some bishops had all their expenses paid for by Constantine before they were "convinced" they should attend. A pagan at the time, Constantine was no theologian, he was a politician who had no patience for further arguing. The bishops adjourned for the day and were ordered to leave all their gospels behind them in a big pile in the center of the room. The doors were locked and the bishops were told to pray that God would sort it all out. There were between 270-4,000 different gospels in there such as the Gospel of Phillip, the Gospel of Peter, the Gospel of Thomas, the Gospel of Judas, the Gospel of Truth, the Gospel of Mary, the Gospel of Mary Magdalene, the Gospel of the Nazarites and many others we don't know the titles of. When they opened the doors the next day, under the impression that no one had been inside since the day before, it was discovered that all but 4 books were thrown about and scattered across the room making it completely disorganized while the 4 gospels of Matthew, Mark, Luke and John were neatly placed on the long meeting table. The bishops were told it was a sign from God that no one could doubt, even though there were no witnesses and it is unknown who had the keys to the doors on that night. Irenaeus says there had to be exactly 4 gospels no more and no less, because there are 4 winds of the earth and 4 corners of the earth. (thus, people thought the world was flat) Why did they think there were 4 corners of earth? Because in the bible Isaiah 11:12 says, "*He will set up a banner for the nations, and will assemble the outcasts of Israel, and gather together the dispersed of Judah from the four corners of the earth.*" Likewise the verses of Job 38:13, Jeremiah 16:19, Daniel 4:11 and Isaiah 40:22 mentioning the "ends of the earth" and God sitting upon the "circle of the earth" was interpreted to mean that "the earth" is flat on the bottom with 4 corners but in the middle it has a half-dome shape giving it some vertical depth as though it were a 3-d object resting on a flat surface with the whole model being called earth instead of just the half-dome part. Earth was thought by those who believed in the bible to have a flat bottom with land only being on the top parts of the dome and the water filling in the rest of the flat earth structure so that way instead of just falling off the dome to the bottom of the map water levels rose in order to be even with the land in all places. Think of it as though you had a half slice of apple in a tank filled with water just high enough so that some parts of the dome part of the apple were visible. Those dry parts were called land, the whole tank and its contents were called "earth". Of course it sounds crazy, but if you actually look at early Christian maps of the world you will see how they depicted a flat circular 4-cornered world, from the bird's eye view that doesn't show the dome outdentation. Jerusalem was thought to be at the center of earth on top of the dome, hence the middle east was logically the driest since it was furthest from the water of the tank. Anyways since the bible taught the world had 4 corners then there were to be 4 gospels, no more no less. At that time instead of being called Sacred Scripture the 4 chosen books were called "*Memoirs of the apostles*". Thereafter the 4 gospels of Matthew, Mark, Luke, and John became popular though a bible would not exist until much later. Although these versions of Matthew, Mark, Luke and John are not the same as we have today, none of them were in English. They consisted of gospels written in Hebrew, Aramaic and Syriac with the oldest versions being written in Greek. It was ordered that all the other gospels, which people still considered authentic scriptures, were to be burned and banned throughout the Roman Empire and those found with such gospels were killed on the spot. Millions were killed. Thus, many of these gospels have been lost to us forever, with only a few surviving the mass-burnings. People risked their lives hiding second hand copies of the originals of these banned gospels that were to be found by later generations. Many were rediscovered at Nag Hammadi. Some gospels have been excavated from graves like the Gospel of Barnabas found in Barnabas' grave in 478 CE. In the end, might decided what was right and which books were to be put in the yet to be completed Bible, that would gradually become accepted as scripture. Unfortunately, none of the original versions of Matthew, Mark, Luke and John exist today. Time has caused them to decompose destroying them. Instead of the originals, translations were used when creating what we today know of as the New Testament. One can only hope they were translated honestly with integrity having as few mistakes as possible without the translator intentionally changing the texts, as ancient translators had a tendency to do. It's not as though copyists or translators always intentionally made errors, but keep in mind every letter was copied and/or translated by hand. You can try this yourself to see how difficult it is to copy a gospel by hand accurately. Try writing on a separate piece of paper an entire gospel from the bible, letter by letter making sure what you write is exactly the same as what is written. Even though you are far more literate and your source of copying is easier to read than what the ancient copyists and translators would have used, you will still make many mistakes. If the 1st copyist of the gospel were to make a mistake, then the 2nd copyist copying the 1st's copy of the gospel would copy the mistake, unless they corrected it realizing it was a mistake. Although the 2nd copyist could also "correct" something that is not a mistake, making a new mistake while not correcting the real mistakes, thereby adding more mistakes. The 3rd copyist would have an even greater dilemma and harder job to do than the previous copyists. Since all were handwritten, every single copy would have been unique, different from the rest in different handwriting. Everyone knows that different types of handwriting can be interpreted in different ways. Depending on who is reading the words they will think different words were written, solely because of the handwriting style. A copyist could also make a mistake by thinking a note in the margins by an earlier copyist was actually a part of the text, so in their copy they would mistakenly add the previous copyist's notes into the scripture. Sometimes alterations were intentionally made to make the texts say what people wanted them to say. It also doesn't help that we don't know who copied and translated these documents, which casts doubt on the reliability of the translations. Let's assume that they were translated from accurate copies without malicious intentions as best as is humanely possible. A translation, no matter how good it is, can never mean the same as the text did in its original form. This is because rhythm, double meaning, idioms, informalization, rhetoric and puns are not translatable. Take "William Shakespeare" for example, who is regarded to be the best English playwright of his time if not all time; according to the popular belief of the majority. If you translate Shakespeare's works into Swahili the translated works will not have the same effect nor the same meaning. Some words simply can't be translated so the character dialogues in his translated stories will be of a different quality, making any plays performed in Swahili have a different plot than the same play would have had it been done in English. But the English bible we have today was not translated from the original texts, because the originals didn't exist by the time Christianity came to English speaking people. Even if the originals still existed there is another problem because the gospels and epistles were first written in Greek. Jesus and his apostles didn't speak Greek. This means the original New Testament was translated before it was ever written down, so the originals were actually translations, but for the sake of argument let's assume the oral tradition the Greek texts came from were translated correctly, even though when translating from a semitic languages such as Hebrew or Aramaic into non-semitic languages like Greek 80% of the meaning is automatically lost. Next, they were translated from Greek into Latin, then translated from Latin into German, then translated from German into French, then translated from French into English.  Now early Church fathers like Tertullian and Augustine did not know Greek, they relied on Jerome's Latin translation.  Which means the leading scholars of the early Christian Church were relying on texts that were translated a minimum of 2 times.  Meaning it would be like you reading Shakespeare for the first time ever in a Chinese translation, but not a direct Chinese translation from English rather a Chinese translation of the Swahili Shakespeare.  Do you think you'd get the same meaning as you would by reading the original English?  Today nobody denies that the English bibles are translations.  Yet they rarely admit their Bible to be a translation of a translation of a translation of a translation of a translated oral tradition.  If you were to translate Shakespeare into French, then take the French Shakespeare and translate it into German, then take the German Shakespeare twice translated and translate it to Latin, then the Latin Shakespeare thrice translated and translate it into Greek, then take the Greek Shakespeare 4 times translated and translate it back into English, you would find that the English Shakespeare that went through so many translations would be very different than the original writings of Shakespeare.  Therefore, the Shakespeare that was translated many times would no longer be considered to be the actual words of Shakespeare.  The translated Shakespeare compared to the actual words of Shakespeare would be obviously different.  You can try this yourself with basic free internet translation tools, or try with an expensive professional translation service.  A translation can never be the actual words of the original.  Which is why if you are reading this book in a language other than English as the author, I can assure you that you are not getting the same meaning as you would if you were reading it in its original English.  At the outset during 382 CE soon after Roman Catholicism was declared the official religion of the Empire, Pope Damascus forbid those who weren't priests from reading the bible and priests were not allowed to teach the bible either. Bible translations were expressly prohibited and considered sinful. In 860 CE Pope Nicholas I banned the bible from being used in public by any who weren't Catholic priests. Another Pope Gregory renewed and supported the ban in 1073 CE. My former role model, Pope Innocent III in 1198 CE ruled that anyone caught reading a bible who wasn't a Catholic priest would be stoned to death by "soldiers of the Church". In 1229 CE it was prohibited for laymen to even possess the Old or New Testament. Eventually by the 14th century CE if you were found with a bible and were not a Catholic priest you would be whipped, have all your property confiscated and then would be burned to death at the stake. Why would the Christian leaders go to such an extreme extent and mete out such severe punishment to those who possessed what they say is "*the word of God*"? Keep in mind being burned at the stake was for possession of the bible, one cannot even imagine what they would have done if a person was caught committing the crime of reading the bible. In fact, the first man to translate the full bible into English was William Tyndale and because of committing such a "heretical blasphemous deed" he was burned to death in 1536 CE. Isn't this suspicious? What was in their bible that they didn't want the world to know? Is that dangerous information still in the bibles we know of today? Have you ever heard of anything more hypocritical than Christian religious leaders prohibiting people from possessing a bible? This period where the bible was prohibited throughout Europe is known as the golden age of Christianity. How could that be if Christianity is based on the bible? This isn't ancient history either, because of a law passed by King Henry VIII it was illegal for women in England to read the bible until 1850 CE. Now this Henry VIII died in 1547. However, in 1535 CE, 12 years before his death, he commissioned the Church of England, which he created, to translate the bible into English in order to have a bible that agreed with his personal theology. This bible became what is known as "The Great Bible" and was published in 1539 CE. Then Queen Elizabeth reigned and created the state-sponsored Angelican church in 1559 CE. Since the bible of King Henry VIII was rather anti-clerical, in 1568 CE the Angelican Church of England published the "Bishop's Bible" and this bible gave more authority to clergy than King Henry's version. But then the clerical tug of war shifted back to the sovereignty and in 1611 CE the King James bible was printed. The King James bible was supposed to end the biblical tug of war where Protestant Episcopalians altered the bible to fit their theology, but in fact the tug of war got worse. The Calvinists/Puritans were outraged at this King James bible and left England to go to America, leaving the King James bible behind taking their Geneva Bible with them. Nobody outside of England believed in King James' bible because it was an Angelican bible and only England was Angelican because the state invented Angelicanism and said English people had to be Angelican officially making it a legal requirement in 1628 CE. Plus, the rest of Europe didn't really speak English so they didn't use the Angelican English King's bible printed in English. However other Kings took note of this process where Kings were writing their own bible to suit themselves and make their desires become doctrines believed to have come from God. Therefore, many kings wrote their own bible that promoted their state policies. In England, they didn't want to cause religious instability or doubt by having every king make his own bible since that would make the bible be seen as the King's book instead of sacred scripture. So, in England future Kings and Christian clergy members decided they would simply change the biblical text but keep the same general name as "King James' bible" so the public would be none the wiser. Unfortunately, this ruse has worked and many today think the King James Bibles they have are old books when they are very modern. The trick is they have "The Authorized King James Version", "The King James Version", "The King James Bible", "The New King James Bible", "The Revised King James Bible", "The New Revised King James Bible", "The standard King James Bible" and many other completely different bibles, but because of their names being so similar all saying "King James" the average person is unaware that each of those bibles say very different things with different theological teachings. There are more bibles associated with King James than there have been Kings who were named James. To further complicate the situation, rather than changing the name every time they changed the bible, they started simply changing the date of publication. For instance, "X bible" published in 1953 is a very different book than "X bible" published in 1961, yet on the bookshelf they have the same exact name and extremely similar covers. So, these various "King James bibles" that exist were never read by King James nor have anything to do with him. Honestly if you get someone a copy of the original 1611 CE text published by King James I, which wasn't even called the King James bible until 1715 CE, an English person today can't even read it or understand what it says because it's written in 17th century olde olde English. Most who do manage to actually think they've seen the infamous real King James bible ask what language it is when they read it, because they don't even consider the true "King James Bible" to be English since by modern English standards it's not. However, nobody even knows which bible published by King James in 1611 CE is "the original" because even in 1611 CE they had different versions right off the presses. To put this chaos in a modern perspective, imagine if every single book you've ever seen whether it be in a library, in a school or at a store, was a one of a kind which said things no other book did even if it was supposed to be the same book. For instance, imagine if every student in a classroom had their textbook teach different things. That's what happened when the bibles were printed throughout Europe, except ordinary folk weren't allowed to read them, only clergymen were. Thus, it's no wonder they denounced each other for not following the bible, their bibles literally said different things but rather than blame the publishers they blamed the preachers. Even with one standard text being used by certain Christian denominations, differences still existed among the bibles of the very same version and edition because of the European process of printing a book itself, whereby every machine churned out a book with different words because of the mechanical differences of machines which existed even after machines became standardized having the same parts because not everybody kept their book machines in factory conditions or kept them at factory settings. Afterall as a book printer if you were printing on the same machine as your competition then in order to make your products stand out you had to do some tinkering, and even if you didn't because other people did then your books would still be different because of your competition tinkering with their printing press. Also because of the manual labor involved in typesetting, humans still deeply affected the printing process of each individual book. Because of human involvement, up until the 1800s you could've in theory had everyone using the same script, printing on identical machines with identical settings but because the machines were operated by different people they would produce different results. It used to be even worse in that the same person wouldn't have been able to copy themselves from book to book because each book used to be done all at once, so it was similar to copying books by hand except they were printed by hand set type. Fortunately for Europeans and Americans the photostat was invented in 1907 CE which was a type of printing that utilized a camera to take a photo of the script, books printed this way were basically picture books of pages of a book's manuscript. Unfortunately, however the moveable type remained popular until the 1960s CE and it wasn't until the late 1960s CE that universal standards in book publishing were set throughout the industry; so that every copy of a book would actually be the same regardless of where it was printed at, what machine was used and who used the machine and when they used it. Yet perhaps the funniest part about all these King James advocates who passionately stress "the King James bible is the best" is that when King James was King and published his olde olde English version, women were forbidden to read it. King James actually said women were not allowed to read his bible. Thus, it's humorous when people have the notion King James was inspired by God to write a bible, even though he didn't even write the book or translate it, when this very same King would punish women if they read his bible. Realistically if one says God inspired King James to put out a reliable bible then one would also have to say that God must not want women to read the bible, because the guy he allegedly inspired forbid women from reading it and punished any who did. King James even said that God told him that God doesn't want women to read his King James bible and that it was sinful for them to do. King James taught that a Christian woman would burn in hell if she read the King James Bible. I repeat that King James would physically harm women if they read his bible, or any bible, even more if they read other bibles because those bibles were forbidden by James. Yet sadly the majority of Christians don't have a clue who King James was, but most Protestant denominations love the bibles printed in his namesake, which they think are the same as his, even though in his own lifetime only Angelicans accepted it. The reason the King James biblical namesake became popular was only because the British Empire made lots of colonies and that was "The English bible". Since the fall of the British Empire many other English bibles have been printed, but each one is printed with a certain perspective due to particular denomination's beliefs and to this date there has yet to be one officially recognized bible which all Christians accept as authoritative or authentic. To this day bibles have different books and different verses depending on which version you read. Yet it still remains that even though it is no longer a death sentence for non-clergy and for women to read a bible, very few Christians bother to read it even though they popularly believe it's contents; the majority of which remain unknown to the "believer". After all those laws that have been overturned to give people the opportunity to safely read what they believe is sacred scripture, the vast majority still don't.

If you open any bible and look at the list of authors nowhere will you find the exact words "*written by God*", it was not published by God either. The Book of Esther doesn't even have the word "God" in it. However could the bible still be the divinely inspired words even if it is not verbatim? In 367 CE the Bishop of Alexandria, Athanasius, created a 27-book compilation in his 39th Festal letter, this would become what we know today as the "New Testament". However not every Christian agreed with Athanasius' compilation and it was heavily disputed and continues to be disputed until today. At the Council of Carthage in 397 CE the Catholic Church decreed what the books of the bible would be, certain books were declared scripture by a vote of 568 in favor with 563 against. Meaning that the bible was created via democratic elections and not direct divine revelation. 49.7% of those priests present voted against the bible being considered

Sacred Scripture. Yet even after this "decisive vote" the apocalyptic "*Book of Revelation*" wasn't included until 419 CE at another Council of Carthage. Meaning for 24 years after democracy declared the bible to be completed and authoritative, the famous "*Book of Revelation*" was not part of the bible. Thus when we discuss which edition of the bible is the "word of God" we have to keep in mind that different parts of the bible were added to it at different times. For all we know a new book might be added to the bible tomorrow. So, we must look at each piece separately for what it is. The bible is an anthology, which is a collection of literary works of various authors chosen by a certain compiler. Without a doubt it was humans who compiled the bible and humans also wrote the bible, but did God inspire all the authors, compilers and translators?

It is significant that the first official bible as we know it came into being well over 360 years after Jesus was on earth. Jesus never read the bible and neither did he approve what it said about him. In the bible 21 out of 27 of the books of the New Testament are in the form of epistles otherwise known as letters. These letters are written by humans to other humans. If a human being is writing a letter, then clearly that is not the words of God in the letter, they would be the words of a person. So, considering those biblical or "apostolic" letters as "divine revelation" would be like considering an email to be "divine revelation". Whereas to have an email be divine revelation that would have to be an email sent by God's personal email address, if he has one that is, of which I don't know of any proof to suggest he does so I cannot say either way. Although since God is not comparable to his creation, then a divine email would be unlike anything we can imagine. Also, if God did have email and sent you an email then that would make you a Messenger of God, like Moses, because only

Messengers of God can receive divine revelation. Now remember 77% of the material in the New Testament portion of the bible consists of letters created and written by humans. It is mind-boggling how a simple letter from a non-prophet known for persecuting the followers of Jesus becomes Divine Revelation. Even letters that genuine prophets like King David or King Solomon wrote are not considered divine revelation but Paul's letters are? That's like getting X number of spam emails from suspicious senders in your inbox and then someone else tells you those are not considered as emails but divine revelation sacrosanct holy scriptures. Yet to be divine revelation they must be from God himself, letters from other beings are other things. For instance, the letter Solomon sent to the Queen of Sheba is not divine revelation but simply a letter from a human, a human prophet but a human nonetheless. However, even these letters in the bible, or epistles as they are called, cannot be 100% verified as to which person wrote them. 14 letters in the New Testament canon are believed to have been written by Paul. Of these 14 Pauline epistles, Christian scholars are heavily disputing 6 of them as to whether Paul was the actual author. The epistles Ephesians, Colossians and the 2nd Thessalonians are debated concerning authorship and it is doubtful Paul was the one who wrote them. Aside from textual reasons themselves Paul is thought to have died in 67 CE yet Ephesians was written between 80 and 100 CE, Colossians thought to have been written in 80 CE and 2nd Thessalonians is thought to be written between 80 and 115 CE. So, it's rather hard to think Paul wrote decades after he died. While Timothy 1, Timothy 2 and Titus have been declared 100% forgeries by Christian scholars. This is not coming from me, this is according to Christian scholastic intellectuals who go to church and believe in the bible and have studied the language and manuscripts who are recognized biblical experts; they say

Timothy 1, Timothy 2 and Titus were NOT written by Paul. Without a doubt about it. They still agree with the doctrines contained in the books but they say Paul did not write it, they wish he did but they publicly admit that he didn't. If you read the letters, they say they are written by Paul but they're not, so they are forgeries. Meaning someone wrote them and pretended they were written by someone else. A person might do this for money, but since this is a religious text it was likely done in order for someone to have their doctrine gain more attention and credibility than it could have if published under their own name. The true author's name was less known and if they published it in their own name it would not have been believed or as widely circulated. Maybe you think that can't be true and even if Paul didn't write them, they were still inspired by God or are the words of God, right? Well, if that's the case let's look at what they say. In 1 Timothy 2:9-12 the bible says Paul wrote: "[9] *I also want the women to dress modestly, with decency and propriety, adorning themselves, not with elaborate hairstyles or gold or pearls or expensive clothes,* [10] *but with good deeds, appropriate for women who profess to worship God.* [11] *A woman should learn in quietness and full submission.* [12] *I do not permit a woman to teach or to assume authority over a man; she must be quiet."* If you believe that this epistle is the word of God, or inspired by God, then you are claiming that God instructs us that women are not permitted to teach men or to have any position of authority over them and must be quiet. Keep in mind Islam doesn't teach that, Islam has many prestigious female scholars who teach men, Aisha bint Abu Bakr is even the #1 Muslim Scholar out of all Muslims after Muhammad. A woman is the top Muslim Scholar, and no man to come after her can ever be more learned than she was. If not for women teaching men, Islam would not exist today. Whereas on the other hand the bible prohibits female teachers. If you believe these words are of divine origin then you would be punished for not following these instructions in the way you conduct your life. This is what Christians claim to believe, in reality the majority don't practice this nor believe it and will try to use apologetics attempting to justify not following or believing what they say God instructs or inspired people to write. The dilemma is that if this letter to Timothy is not divine or divinely inspired, anyone who says it is would be damned for having attributed something to God that he is innocent of, such a person would be lying about God and God hates liars. On the other hand, if you agree with the Christian scholars, who say it is a forgery that's not even written by Paul, then why is it in the bible and considered to be scripture, or divinely inspired? If it isn't from divine origins then those who follow it would be doing something that God didn't instruct them to do. Either way according to this alleged letter from Paul to Timothy the majority of Christians today are damned if they believe it's true and damned if they believe it's false. Most Christians who will testify in court that they believe the bible to be the word of God or divinely inspired don't even know these verses are in there. It's very dangerous to say something is the word of God or inspired by God if one hasn't even read it.

      Ok if it's a forgery let's just remove it from the bible and admit mistakes have been made and all those who died before the bible was fixed were unknowingly duped and lied to about God instructing things he never inspired, no harm done right? Of course, Christian leaders would not risk the embarrassment such a correction would cause. Although let's pretend they did and the forged letters were removed so only those authentic letters written by Paul remain. What do those say? In the English translation of the New International Version of the bible in the New Testament 1 Corinthians 14:34-35 Paul allegedly writes: "[34] *Women should remain silent in the churches. They are not allowed to speak, but must be in submission, as the law says.*[35] *If they want to inquire about something, they should ask their own husbands at home; for it is disgraceful for a woman to speak in the church."*

That's even more misogynist than the forged letter to Timothy. However, the Christian scholars have said this verse was not actually written by Paul, but was written in the margins of the original letter by a scribe. Yet some Christians ignore their scholars and maintain that Paul wrote the entire letter and was divinely inspired to write those exact words. Despite that belief, few women remain silent in church today and see it as a disgrace if they speak in church. Most of the time women in church are singing and saying the same prayers and words aloud as the men at the same time, oftentimes even louder than the men. Some churches even have women preachers or bible readers giving them a platform from which to speak. While at the same time they claim the word of God, or the inspired word of God, instructs women to remain silent in church. In the 16th century CE King Henry VIII of England even went so far as to prohibit women from reading the bible. He's not the only one who had such a Christian view either, I say "Christian view" because that's what Christianity taught. As the following "saints" have said regarding women:

> *"Woman is the instrument which the devil uses to gain possession of our souls"* -"St." Cyprian
>
> *"Woman is the fountain of the arm of the devil, her voice is the hissing of the serpent"*- "St." Anthony
>
> *"Woman is a daughter of falsehood, a sentinel of Hell, the enemy of peace; through her Adam lost paradise"*     "St." John Damascene

*"Woman has the poison of an asp, the malice of a dragon"*
  -"St." Gregory "the great"

*"What is the difference whether it is in a wife or a mother, it is still Eve the temptress that we must beware of in any woman."*
  -"St." Augustine

*"As regards the individual nature, woman is defective and misbegotten, for the active force in the male seed tends to the production of a perfect likeness in the masculine sex; while the production of woman comes from a defect in the active force or from some material indisposition, or even from some external influence."*-
"St." Thomas Aquinas

Even Tertullian said this to women: *"Do you not know that you are each an Eve? The sentence of God on this sex of yours lives in this age: the guilt must of necessity live too. You are the Devil's gateway: You are the unsealer of the forbidden tree: You are the first deserter of the divine law: You are she who persuaded him whom the devil wasn't valiant enough to attack. You destroyed so easily God's image, man."*

These sexist religious views were held by the very "saints" many Christians adore, some of them even get prayed to. I was even named after one of those jerks. But it's not Christians who started this anti-woman view the Jews preached it too. Since the Jewish Talmud forbids women from learning the Torah, Rabbi Eliezer in the 1st century CE explained the reason why: *"If any man teaches his daughter Torah it is as though he taught her lechery"*. Jewish women are not allowed to pray in synagogues either. Although it's even worse in that Orthodox Jewish men recite in their daily morning prayer, *"Blessed be God King of the universe that Thou has not made me a woman."* While in the Jewish woman's daily morning prayers they thank God for *"making me according to Thy will"*. So, the anti-woman sentiment taught by Paul in the bible, (not Jesus mind you) is actually part and parcel of Judeo-

Christian doctrines. Ironically some Christian women even pray to Paul audibly in churches thinking he's a saint despite their belief that he wrote women should be silent in church. How can women pray to Paul in church out loud when they believe he basically wrote *"Women should shutup in church!"* and was inspired by God to write so? Some say there are no stupid questions, the bible says there are no female questions allowed in church and that women should ask their husbands at home if they want to learn something, while if they aren't married then they are to remain silent and dumb; but not deaf. This is what the bible says. Just because it might be contrary to our culture, or not practiced, doesn't mean it is not instructed by God. Personally, I do not believe these bible verses were divinely inspired by God. Personally, I do not think Paul was honest and I believe he distorted the message of Jesus and led many people astray, the complete opposite of a saint, rather a Satan. Whether Paul was intentionally malicious in hating Jesus or was just confused himself, I do not know. Although it is interesting that Paul never once mentions Mary the mother of Jesus or his virgin birth, yet he claims to love Jesus so much. Also, Paul never had one nice thing to say about the prophet John who was a contemporary, colleague, relative and friend of Jesus. However, if people believe Paul was inspired by God and consider his writings to be scripture this raises a second question. If the bible is the word of God or inspired by God as some claim, then why don't they practice it before they preach it?

    For instance, Deuteronomy 23:1-2 says: *"No one who has been emasculated by crushing or cutting may enter the assembly of the LORD. 2 No one born of a forbidden marriage nor any of their descendants may enter the assembly of the LORD, not even in the tenth generation."* These verses mean any man who has lost their reproductive organs by crushing or cutting cannot enter church. Although it is well known that many of the early Church fathers castrated themselves to avoid sexual desires. Meaning they cut their own privates off because it distracted them from religion and they wanted to follow the bible verse of Matthew 19:12 which says: *"For there are eunuchs who were born that way, and there are eunuchs who have been made eunuchs by others – and there are those who choose to live like eunuchs for the sake of the kingdom of heaven. The one who can accept this should accept it."* So many early Christians castrated themselves that the Council of Nicaea in 325 CE actually had to forbid clergy from castrating themselves. It was that big of a problem. Makes you wonder about the mental sanity of early Christian leaders if such decrees had to be passed. According to the Old Testament the early Christian leaders, who cut their privates off attempting to follow Matthew 19:12, wouldn't be allowed in church. This also means any who have operations to induce sterility are forbidden from going to church according to the bible. While the second verse of Deuteronomy 23 says no one born out of wedlock or from illegitimate marriages can enter a church either, not even in the 10th generation. These are biblical rules and advices which aren't followed today. Other less known biblical commands on par with the 10 commandments are found in Deuteronomy 22, the verses are all from an English translation of the New International Version of the bible.

> Deuteronomy 22:5 " *A woman must not wear men's clothing, nor a man wear women's clothing, for the LORD your God detests anyone who does this.*"

How many women today wear pants or men's clothes? According to the bible, God detests them. That's the reason why Joan of Arc was burned alive, because she wore pants and men's clothes which meant disbelief in and rejection of the bible. Seriously that's the reason, on May 24th, 1431 CE she was sentenced to life imprisonment after she promised to stop wearing men's clothes. But when she started wearing female clothes in prison, the prison guards tried to rape her. So, on May 28th, 1431 CE she refused to wear females dress insisting upon wearing men's clothes, as a result she was said to have "relapsed back into heresy" and got burned to death 2 days later on May 30th, 1431 CE. Of course, there are rare exceptions that permit Christian women to wear pants if they literally have nothing else to wear or buy, and it's either they wear pants or go naked; then biblically they have an excuse. But most modern Christian women would get burned alive 600 years ago just because of the clothes they choose to wear. That's the biblical and Christian teaching, fortunately Islam doesn't say to kill women if they don't dress the way Allah told them to dress. The bible also teaches that women should wear veils, aka niqab or burqa, when they are around men they aren't married or related to so the men can't see them. As the verses in Genesis 24:63-67 relate:"[63] *He went out to the field one evening to meditate, and as he looked up, he saw camels approaching.* [64] *Rebekah also looked up and saw Isaac. She got down from her camel* [65] *and asked the servant, "Who is that man in the field coming to meet us?" "He is my master," the servant answered. So, she took her veil and covered herself.* [66] *Then the servant told Isaac all he had done.* [67] *Isaac brought her into the tent of his mother Sarah, and he married Rebekah. So, she became his wife, and he loved her; and Isaac was comforted after his mother's death."* Rebekah was able to be seen by the servant because he was her slave as well as Isaac's, since he was the slave of the clan of Abraham to which she belonged. The very reason she was selected to be Isaac's wife was because Rebekah and Isaac were first cousins and Abraham wanted his son to marry from his father's side of the family. This is what the bible says. Thereby showing us the bible not only promotes first cousins getting married to each other, but it teaches us that male cousins aren't allowed to see their female cousins unless they are married to each other; obviously the same rule applies between men and women even more distant regarding blood relation.  This is the actual biblical teaching too as Rabbi Menachem M. Brayer (Professor of Biblical Literature at Yeshiva University) explained that the custom when Jewish women went out in public was to wear a head covering, which sometimes even covered their whole face leaving only one eye visible for them to see with.  In his books he quotes famous ancient Rabbis saying, *"It is not like the daughters of Israel to walk out with heads uncovered"* and *"Cursed be the man who lets the hair of his wife be seen…. a woman who exposes her hair for self-adornment brings poverty."*  Contrary to what people may think or practice today, Rabbinic law forbids the recitation of blessings or prayers in the presence of a bareheaded married woman since uncovering the woman's hair is considered nudity.  Rabbi Menachem M. Brayer also states that, *"During the Tannaitic period the Jewish woman's failure to cover her head was considered an affront to her modesty. When her head was uncovered she might be fined four hundred zuzim for this offense."*  On top of this the bible says Isaac brought Rebekah into his mother's tent, thereby demonstrating that male and female strangers weren't allowed to be alone together.  Keep in mind they were engaged and she still covered herself so her fiancé couldn't see her.  Furthermore, when Moses assisted the daughters of Shuaib watering their flock of sheep and then was requested to visit their father to be rewarded the way he traveled with those women further prove this point.  Despite not knowing which way to go and when/where to turn Moses walked in front of the women and instructed them to toss a stone in front to his left or right when it was time to take a certain turn.  This was because Moses knew that it's improper for a man to walk behind a woman he is not married or related to, for obvious reasons, and keep in mind this was Moses.  In that circumstance he technically had a legitimate reason to justify walking behind them yet he still didn't because it's such a bad thing to do and violates modesty. So since in such circumstances it was improper for a guy like Moses to do, then the guys today got no excuses. Thus, we can conclude with certainty that modern "dating" is totally forbidden according to the bible. But since that's the Old Testament Christian women tend to think that the New Testament or God doesn't care about their clothing or who sees them. However, even Paul, who rejected the other divine laws, commanded Christian women to wear the hijab in 1 Corinthians 11:5-6,"But *every woman who prays or prophesies with her head uncovered dishonors her head* – *it is the same as having her head shaved. 6 For if a woman does not cover her head, she might as well have her hair cut off; but if it is a disgrace for a woman to have her hair cut off or her head shaved, then she should cover her head."* This is why some women in church put tissues or hats on their head. But the verse is about covering the hair on the head. Paul gives women 2 options, either they can cover their hair or they can shave it all off. The New Testament of the bible teaches that the prayers of women who pray without covering their head, including all their hair, are invalid. That's no joke, if a woman wants to follow the bible, she has to have all of her hair covered every single time she prays or else biblically it doesn't count. Although Christian woman are also required to cover their hair outside of prayer as well. This was so well known by early Christians that they didn't even dispute or comment on it. This is evident in Tertullian advising, *"Young women, you wear your veils out on the streets, so you should wear them in the church, you wear them when you are among strangers, then wear them among your brothers..."* Notice Tertullian said women must cover themselves with veils in Church because they do so in public. Christian women veiling in public wasn't even up for a debate. The debate was if Christians are brothers and sisters in faith then do women have to veil in front of

Christian men, since they are "brothers"? The early Christian practice and teaching was that Christian women indeed had to cover themselves for all except true blood relatives or spouses. It was actually scandalous because some of the Christian women would veil in public but then in Church, since they didn't know what the bible said, they'd unveil and show their beauty to their "brothers". Thus, after quoting textual reasons Tertullian refuted this notion saying: "<u>they veil their head in presence of heathens, let them at all events in the church conceal their virginity, which they do veil outside the church.</u> *They fear strangers: let them stand in awe of the brethren too; or else let them have the consistent hardihood to appear as virgins in the streets as well, as they have the hardihood to do in the churches. I will praise their vigour, if they succeed in selling aught of virginity among the heathens withal. Identity of nature abroad as at home, identity of custom in the presence of men as of the Lord, consists in identity of liberty.* <u>**To what purpose, then, do they thrust their glory out of sight abroad, but expose it in the church? I demand a reason. Is it to please the brethren, or God Himself? If God Himself, He is as capable of beholding whatever is done in secret, as He is just to remunerate what is done for His sole honour. In fine, He enjoins us not to trumpet forth any one of those things which will merit reward in His sight, nor get compensation for them from men.**</u> *But if we are prohibited from letting "our left hand know" when we bestow the gift of a single halfpenny, or any eleemosynary bounty whatever, how deep should be the darkness in which we ought to enshroud ourselves when we are offering God so great an oblation of our very body and our very spirit----when we are consecrating to Him our very nature! It follows, therefore, that what cannot appear to be done for God's sake (because God wills not that it be done in such a way) is done for the sake of men,----a thing, of course, primarily unlawful, as betraying a lust of glory.*" It's crystal-clear Tertullian couldn't even contemplate that Christian women wouldn't be veiled in public. The bit about virginity and virgins is because these quotes are from his treatise "On the Veiling of Virgins". His definition of a virgin women was basically a pure woman free from sin as Mary was a virgin who wasn't sinful. He knew the term was confusing as well and he gave a separate refutation of women who might use the excuse of saying how since they're married and aren't virgins then they don't have to veil, in church; because even then nobody imagined Christian women in public wouldn't be veiled. Tertullian explained his definition and said that even if they try to take his words and give them different meanings, they still have no excuse not to veil in church because if married women didn't veil, they'd be distinguishing themselves from genuine virgins who aren't married and thus it would hurt the feelings of unmarried virgins, be arrogant and defeat the very purpose of veiling to begin with. Plus, if the guys in church only saw married women, then adultery would spread, since married women who didn't veil would be more tempting to men than veiled non-married women. Needless to say, Tertullian would be appalled by most Christian women today. A few Christian women do still partially cover themselves like the Amish, Mennonites and Russian Orthodox Christians, but even then, they still fall far short of the biblical and Christian dress code. The Christian female dress code also meant no new dresses as the "saint" Bernard of Clairvaux (founder of the Templar Knights) stressed to his sister when she visited him at a monastery while wearing a "new dress". This "saint" called his sister a filthy whore and a clod of dung. Thus personally, nuns included, I have not met a single Christian woman who follows the biblical or Christian teachings in dressing modestly. Yet most all of them think and will claim that they're modest. Whereas the modest woman doesn't need to say that she's modest and she's actually too modest to ever claim that she's modest. So, if any woman tells you they're modest you can tell them they're not and you know for certain they aren't because they told you they were and that means they're not, because the modest woman is modest in everything from her dress, to her speech, to her gaze, to her thoughts.  Forget about going back to the time of Jesus, if Christian women just went back 1,000 years, they'd all be denounced as slutty harlots; including the nuns because even the nuns dress code got sexier.  The only time Christian women are recorded as having dressed semi-biblically of their own choice is in post-Muslim Spain the mid-1400s to the late 1500s CE.  During that time under Christian rule Spanish Christian women voluntarily choose to wear stiff flat corsages and veils that covered all of their body from head to feet, leaving only their eyes uncovered.  Their color was black because black was the most expensive/luxurious dye.  So, when zealous Christians with a Crusader mentality dream of a post-Reconquista world, that super-Christian world had all the non-Muslim women wearing black niqab because of Christian modesty.  The problem is that since Christianity is a devolving religion modesty is always devolving with the times and "Christian modesty" truly has no officially recognized definition to most denominations aside from "common sense".  Which means generally most Christians think women can dress however they want just as long as they aren't dressed as promiscuously as the promiscuous non-Christians, basically they have to stay 1 fashion trend behind in the sexiness department.  Thus, what's considered immodest by Christian adults to wear today, will not be immodest for their daughters to wear but normal and their granddaughters will consider their grandparents sense of modesty to be extreme overkill.  Yet each generation will think and be told that they are dressing modestly according to Christian doctrines, despite each generation wearing vastly different styles.  In case you think I'm extreme or making stuff up, following is what Tertullian ended his treatise with giving specific details on exactly on how married Christian women are required to dress. *"But we admonish you, too, women of the second (degree of) modesty, who have fallen into wedlock, not to outgrow so far the discipline of the veil, not even in a moment of an hour, as, because you cannot refuse it, to take some other means to nullify it, by going neither covered nor bare. For some, with their turbans and woollen bands, do not veil their head, but bind it up; protected, indeed, in front, but, where the head properly lies, bare. Others are to a certain extent covered over the region of the brain with linen coifs of small dimensions----I suppose for fear of pressing the head----and not reaching quite to the ears.* <u>*If they are so weak in their hearing as not to be able to hear through a covering, I pity them. Let them know that the whole head constitutes "the woman." Its limits and boundaries reach as far as the place where the robe begins. The region of the veil is co-extensive with the space covered by the hair when unbound; in order that the necks too may be encircled.*</u> *For it is they which must be subjected, for the sake of which "power" ought to be "had on the head: "the veil is their yoke.* <u>*Arabia's heathen females will be your judges, who cover not only the head, but the face also, so entirely, that they are content, with one eye free, to enjoy rather half the light than to prostitute the entire face. A female would rather see than be seen. And for this reason a certain Roman queen said that they were most unhappy, in that they could more easily fall in love than be fallen in love with; whereas they are rather happy, in their immunity from that second (and indeed more frequent) infelicity, that females are more apt to be fallen in love with than to fall in love. And the modesty of heathen discipline, indeed, is more simple, and, so to say, more barbaric. To us the Lord has, even by revelations, measured the space for the veil to extend over.*</u> *For a certain sister of ours was thus addressed by an angel, beating her neck, as if in applause: "Elegant neck, and deservedly bare! it is well for thee to unveil thyself from the head right down to the loins, lest withal this freedom of thy neck profit thee not!"* And, of course, what you have said to one you have said to all. **But how severe a chastisement will they likewise deserve, who, amid (the recital of) the Psalms, and at any mention of (the name of) God, continue uncovered; (who) even when about to spend time in prayer itself, with the utmost readiness place a fringe, or a tuft, or any thread whatever, on the crown of their heads, and suppose themselves to be covered? Of so small extent do they falsely imagine their head to be!** *Others, who think the palm of their hand plainly greater than any fringe or thread, misuse their head no less; like a certain (creature), more beast than bird, albeit winged, with small head, long legs, and moreover of erect carriage. She, they say, when she has to hide, thrusts away into a thicket her head alone----plainly the whole of it, (though)----leaving all the rest of herself exposed. Thus, while she is secure in head, (but) bare in her larger pans, she is taken wholly, head and all. Such will be their plight withal, covered as they are less than is useful.* **It is incumbent, then, at all times and in every place, to walk mindful of the law, prepared and equipped in readiness to meet every mention of God; who, if He be in the heart, will be recognized as well in the head of females."** The Islamic Niqab doesn't even comply with the Christian female dress code. Yet Tertullian says he gets this specific dress code from *"the Lord, even by revelations"*. So for anyone who says "well the New Testament doesn't say this", then you gotta ask what "revelation from the Lord" was Tertullian getting this specific measurement for the veil from? He says the "Arabian heathens" who modestly dressed only showing one eye are "barbaric" compared to the modesty required by Christian women. As for the comment on Arabian heathens, during the time of Muhammad the Arabian women had been corrupted to the point where they nearly dressed in less than promiscuous women do today. Then Allah revealed verses in the Quran explaining what parts Muslim women should cover and who they don't have to cover for. While authentic hadith relate how the Muslim women applied the verses and immediately changed their dress into black niqab. Unfortunately, some anti-Islamic people will claim the niqab is pagan but this is false. As you can see the "Arabian Heathen" women during Tertullian times actually dressed more modestly than Islam requires. So, the claim that Muhammad just got the dress code from pagan Arabia is completely farcical, because modesty was long outdated and the ancient pagan dress code was even stricter than the Islamic. Whereas the Christian and Jewish dress code is even stricter than all of them. The difference is that no Christian women practice their religion and its part and parcel of Judaism to change their religion. Essentially the main reason Christians may think the Niqab or Hijab is strict, is because they don't follow or have a clue about what Christianity teaches regarding female clothing and interactions with the opposite gender. The maximum Muslim female dress code is less strict than the minimum obligatory Christian female dress code. Yet there is another interesting dress code from ancient Assyria for those who don't care about Judaic, Christian or Islamic dress codes for females. In 1075 BCE Assyrian law in the Code of Assura distinguished prostitutes from other women by dress. "*If the wives of a man, or the daughters of a man go out into the street, their heads are to be veiled.* **_The prostitute is not to be veiled_**. *Maidservants are not to veil themselves. Veiled harlots and maidservants shall have their garments seized and 50 blows inflicted on them and bitumen [a tar like substance] poured on their heads.*" The Assyrian law indicated all wives and all daughters must be veiled in public. Only female slaves and prostitutes could be seen in public unveiled. The way to identify a female slave or a prostitute was by seeing them unveiled. Think about that. For a woman in the past to show her hair and face in public meant she was legally a prostitute or a slave (sex slave). While if such a prostitute or sex slave dared to cover their hair or face, they would be physically hit 50 times and have bitumen poured on their heads. This is because a veil is honor for a female and for prostitutes or sex slaves to wear a veil was false advertising. Meaning that any female who doesn't veil themselves in public according to Assyrian law is advertising themselves as a prostitute or letting it be publicly known they are a sex slave. The sex slaves had to be unveiled so that they could be bought if desired by a passerby. To not veil meant you were on the sex market available to be bought or rented. It is also interesting that the law required such severe punishment for prostitutes and sex slaves who covered their face or hair. This means thousands of years ago women wanted to cover their hair and faces so much that they were willing to risk getting beaten and tarred just to veil themselves. Back then governments forced women to not wear veils and women broke the law risking their lives to wear them. Yet today many "civilized" women want to dress like ancient Assyrian prostitutes. Is it not perplexing that the uncivilized governments forced women to not wear veils but today "freedom" causes women to "choose" not to wear veils? Its unanimous among Judaism, Christianity and Islam that women either wear a veil or go to hell for some time to pay the price for not veiling. Yet how many women today practice this core tenet?

> Deuteronomy 22:8-9, *"When you build a new house, make a parapet around your roof so that you may not bring the guilt of bloodshed on your house if someone falls from the roof. ⁹ Do not plant two kinds of seed in your vineyard; if you do, not only the crops you plant but also the fruit of the vineyard will be defiled."*

Who builds a parapet around their roof today?

How many farmers and gardeners follow this command?

Deuteronomy 24:19-22, "*When you are harvesting in your field and you overlook a sheaf, do not go back to get it. Leave it for the foreigner, the fatherless and the widow, so that the LORD your God may bless you in all the work of your hands. 20 When you beat the olives from your trees, do not go over the branches a second time. Leave what remains for the foreigner, the fatherless and the widow. 21 When you harvest the grapes in your vineyard, do not go over the vines again. Leave what remains for the foreigner, the fatherless and the widow. 22 Remember that you were slaves in Egypt. That is why I command you to do this.*"

When was the last time you saw somebody harvesting and leave the produce from their plants for the foreigners, orphans and widows to eat for free? Well, the biblical God commands this.

1 Thessalonians 5:6 "<u>Greet all God's people with a holy kiss</u>. 27 I charge you before the Lord to have this letter read to all the brothers and sisters."

Romans 16:16 " **<u>Greet one another with a holy kiss</u>**. All the churches of Christ send greetings.

1 Corinthians 16:19-21, "*The churches in the province of Asia send you greetings. Aquila and Priscilla greet you warmly in the Lord, and so does the church that meets at their house. 20 All the brothers and sisters here send you greetings. <u>Greet one another with a holy kiss.</u> 21 I, Paul, write this greeting in my own hand.*"

2 Corinthians 13:12 -13, "<u>Greet one another with a holy kiss</u>. 13 All God's people here send their greetings."

What these New Testament bible verses mean is that every Christian must give all other Christians a "holy kiss" when they greet them. I'm not perverting the bible verses with my own interpretation that's actually what early Christians did because of these verses. Every time a Christian greeted another Christian, they would give them the "holy kiss". As regards Christians today every time in Church when Christians turn around and greet each other shaking hands and saying "Peace" they are actually all supposed to kiss each other at that time. They even used to do this too directly after saying the "Our Father" prayer before getting the Eucharist, the "St." Augustine even considered it part of the sacrament of Eucharist. Augustine said the lips kissing were the "sign of peace", in that if there was no kiss then you didn't really show them peace. Fortunately, Christians changed this aspect of the religion but biblically they are instructed to kiss when they greet. Paul taught Christians they are all brothers and all sisters and must kiss each other with compassion. Oh, and before, during and after the time of "St." Augustine this kiss was on the lips, and Augustine gave sermons praising the Christian practice of lip-locking. So even though priests were celibate they were still getting their kisses, so don't feel too bad for them. For over a thousand years Christians would kiss each other when they greeted each other and it only stopped in the Middle Ages, this is well recorded. They kissed so much they had names for special kisses with the kiss during church called the "kiss of peace". The "St." Cyril even wrote, "*this kiss is the sign that our souls are united, and that we banish all remembrance of injury*". The "kiss of peace" was done to display forgiveness because Christians said and still say during the "Our Father" prayer, "*Forgive us our trespasses (or sins) as we forgive those who trespass (or sin) against us*". The kiss was the sign of their forgiving their trespassers and it wasn't just restricted to Church either, Christians kissed each other at secular events and knights would even kiss each other before entering combat at a tournament to show they held nothing against each other. Technically the case could be made that Christians saying the "Our Father" wanted a kiss from God "their father", but personally I don't think the "Our Father" is about God because God doesn't trespass anybody or sin against people as the prayer says the

"Father" does. The "holy kiss" was mandatory so people were forced to do it whether they wanted to or not because the bible said they had to do it and after a few centuries the kiss on the lips was changed to be a kiss on the cheek. Keep in mind men could only kiss men and women could only kiss women. Yeah, I know you were probably thinking *"Wait so the bible says all Christian guys and girls have to kiss each other on the lips when they meet? Sounds great, Sign me up!"* Well, if you had such perverted thoughts, you should know that it was not like that at all. Guys could only kiss guys and girls could only kiss girls, so as we'd say today *"that's kind of gay"* but that's what the New Testament teaches. Keep in mind this means Paul kissed many guys during his ministry, or he didn't practice what he preached. But what about when in church, how would they kiss with all the guys and girls sitting together? What if a guy couldn't find a guy or a girl found no girl nearby to kiss? Well, there was no problem because men and women sat in separate areas in church so a guy never would have an opportunity to kiss a girl and vice versa. The genders sat separately and didn't touch or look at each other. When the seating arrangements changed the kissing changed too, or maybe the kisses were changed first I don't know. This is the problem with making changes to religion, if one tiny thing gets changed the whole system has to change as well. Thus, when people admit that changes were made that means the whole system has been changed. Sadly, people think changes can be kept to just a few but with religion it's always either many changes took place or none. If any changes happened that means many changes happened. Some may say that a handshake is equivalent to the "Holy Kiss", but have you ever heard of a "Holy Handshake"? I haven't. The whole biblical and Christian tradition of the "Holy Kiss" is why Judas, who was thought to have betrayed Christ with a kiss, was seen as such a bad guy. The "Holy Kiss" was like a sacrament, so for early and medieval Christians betrayal via the "Holy Kiss" would be like betraying someone by giving them communion or baptism. To them they thought Judas basically said "Kill the guy I baptize or give communion to". Even though biblically, depending on which gospel you read, Judas didn't even betray Jesus with a kiss, but Christians were forbidden from reading the bible so they thought he did and still do. Yet this "Holy Kiss" is a good test to prove to a Christian that they don't follow the bible. You can ask some fun questions like "*How many people do you kiss in church on average?*" or "*What's your personal kissing record in Church?*", or "*Can you tell me how many Christians of the same gender you've kissed throughout your lifetime?*", "*What's your daily average?*" or "*Have you ever tried to kiss a random Christian in public only to find out they weren't a Christian?*" or "*Do you tend to kiss strangers first or do they kiss you first?*", "*When you do all this kissing do you do it on the lips or elsewhere?*" Most likely they will be completely confused and outraged so you will have to apologize for seeming perverse, they'll probably think you're a crazy pervert so it's best if you know the person a bit before you ask this stuff. Don't ask this stuff to a Christian stranger or you might get in trouble, unless they are a minister or priest; in that case it'll be very fun to ask them and will be a great way to introduce yourself and their ignorance. Then just explain you thought they were Christian and followed the bible, so you were interested in what life was like for someone who followed the bible because in the New Testament the bible says Christians have to kiss other Christians of the same gender in public and in church every time, they greet each other. Then they'll try to tell you the bible doesn't teach that and you don't know what you are talking about, but in reality, they don't know their bible or Christianity and they don't follow their bible or Christianity. Religiously if they aren't kissing random Christians whenever they greet them then their "Our

Father" prayers don't count. Warning if you are a Christian don't go out kissing people and then blame it on me. I don't think people should do this, especially with sodomites and lesbians around, this kissing is just what the bible teaches and what Christianity used to teach. Ironically the Amish still do the "holy kiss" on the lips, their guys kiss their guys and their girls kiss their girls, and you probably thought the Amish were just boring farmers when in reality they are experts at kissing their own gender on the lips.

> Deuteronomy 22:13-29, "*If a man takes a wife and, after sleeping with her, dislikes her* [14] *and slanders her and gives her a bad name, saying, "I married this woman, but when I approached her, I did not find proof of her virginity,"* [15] *then the young woman's father and mother shall bring to the town elders at the gate proof that she was a virgin.* [16] *Her father will say to the elders, "I gave my daughter in marriage to this man, but he dislikes her.* [17] *Now he has slandered her and said, 'I did not find your daughter to be a virgin.' But here is the proof of my daughter's virginity." Then her parents shall display the cloth before the elders of the town,* [18] *and the elders shall take the man and punish him.* [19] *They shall fine him a hundred shekels of silver and give them to the young woman's father, because this man has given an Israelite virgin a bad name. She shall continue to be his wife; he must not divorce her as long as he lives.* [20] *<u>If, however, the charge is true and no proof of the young woman's virginity can be found,</u>* [21] *<u>she shall be brought to the door of her father's house and there the men of her town shall stone her to death.</u> She has done an outrageous thing in Israel by being promiscuous while still in her father's house. You must purge the evil from among you.* [22] *<u>If a man is found sleeping with another man's wife, both the man who slept with her and the woman must die.</u> You must purge the evil from Israel.* [23] *<u>If a man happens to meet in a town a virgin pledged to be married and he sleeps with her,</u>* [24] *<u>you shall take both of them to the gate of that town and stone them to death</u> – the young woman because she was in a town and did not scream for help, and the man because he violated another man's wife. You must purge the evil from among you.* [25] *But if out in the country <u>a man happens to meet a young woman pledged to be married and rapes her, only the man who has done this shall die.</u>* [26] *Do nothing to the woman; she has committed no sin deserving death. This case is like that of someone who attacks and murders a neighbor,* [27] *for the man found the young woman*

*out in the country, and though the betrothed woman screamed, there was no one to rescue her. <u>²⁸ If a man happens to meet a virgin who is not pledged to be married and rapes her and they are discovered, ²⁹ he shall pay her father fifty shekels of silver. He must marry the young woman, for he has violated her. He can never divorce her as long as he lives.</u>"*

This means any girl who wasn't a virgin when she got married is liable to be stoned to death. How many Christian women aren't virgins when they get married? The bible says they should be stoned. Likewise male rapists should be killed according to the bible, as should adulterers and those who have sex with engaged women. Unless a man happens to rape a virgin, who isn't engaged, in that case if they're caught the bible says he has to pay her father 50 shekels of silver and then the girl he raped becomes his wife. So, does the bible discourage premarital sex and rape or encourage rape and premarital sex? Just imagine what would happen if countries decided to rule by biblical law today. We wouldn't have "Date rape" we'd have rape weddings. Biblically speaking if a guy wants to get married all he has to do is go rape some virgin girl who isn't currently engaged. The bible is practically a manual on how to rape virgins and make them your wife against their will. But don't worry the rapist has to pay her dad 50 shekels of silver which is 0.35 ounces or 11 grams; which at today's silver prices is equal to $11.52. I mention this so Jews and Christians watch out since biblically if someone rapes their virgin unbetrothed daughter, the rapist just pays the father $12 and he becomes her husband and a member of the family with inheritance rights and everything. Then imagine having to tell the story of how your daughter met her husband to your grandkids or strangers. Oh, and remember Christian weddings are "til death do we part". Sorry, but the biblical rapist wedding doesn't seem to be the recipe of success that will lead to a "happy ever after". Dumb kids today say "first come love, then comes marriage" well the bible teaches "*first comes rape, then comes marriage with no divorce*".

In contrast to this biblical ruling of forcing the raped woman to marry her rapist for life, there is the teaching of Muhammad. As related in a Hasan hadith in Jami` at-Tirmidhi hadith #1454 what in English means: *Narrated 'Alqamah bin Wa'il Al-Kindi: From his father: "A women went out during the time of the Prophet (ﷺ) to go to Salat(Prayer), but she was caught by a man and he had relations with her, so she screamed and he left. Then a man came across her and she said: 'That man has done this and that to me', then she came across a group of Emigrants (Muhajirin) and she said: 'That man did this and that to me.' They went to get the man she thought had relations with her, and they brought him to her. She said: 'Yes, that's him.' So, they brought him to the Messenger of Allah (ﷺ), and when he ordered that he be stoned, the man who had relations with her, said: 'O Messenger of Allah, I am the one who had relations with her.' So, he said to her: 'Go, for Allah has forgiven you.' Then he said some nice words to the man (who was brought). And he said to the man who had relations with her: 'Stone him.' Then he said: 'He has repented a repentance that, if the inhabitants of Al-Madinah had repented with, it would have been accepted from them.'"*

Muhammad let the raped woman go free and the rapist confessed, repented and was stoned to death. The rapist is not condemned to hell, yet justice is served. The immoral oppression was eradicated from the community and deterred. Personally which law do you think is better? The law of the bible or the law taught and implemented by Muhammad?

It's also interesting that the biblical fee for falsely accusing a virgin wife for not being a virgin is double the cost of the fee for raping a virgin! Biblically it's 50% cheaper to rape a virgin than it is to lie and say your wife wasn't a virgin when you got married.

Although how is a man supposed to know if his wife really was a virgin when she married him? Well, the bible says the bed cloth will prove her virginity, referring to the blood from the female hymen being torn as a result of her "first time". This is how most men think one can tell whether a woman is a virgin or not but this "hymen test" is not accurate. The female hymen is a membrane on the female private part but there is no rule that it breaks and bleeds the first time a woman has sex. Many sexually active females have hymen's that aren't torn or broken despite not being virgins. Frequently the hymen will simply stretch during intercourse and never ever tear, or it could tear due to disease, a cut or even masturbation. Basically, bloody sheets or cloth cannot prove one's virginity, women know this and God knows it since he made it. However, the bible was written by men who didn't know much about the female hymen. Thus, they wrote in the bible this law where a woman would be stoned to death if she didn't bleed the first time she had sex with her husband. In reality lots of women don't bleed the first time or anytime because bleeding from a torn hymen has nothing to do with virginity and some hymens never ever get torn. This proves the men who wrote the bible were NOT inspired by God to write what they wrote and that the biblical laws are NOT God's laws. Virgin women don't stain the sheets 100% of the time when they lose their virginity and God would never make a law saying to kill all women who don't as the bible says to do. It's a scientifically erroneous misconception in the bible being passed off for centuries as having come from God. What's sad is that many women have been killed or divorced because of this male error in the bible which tricks Jewish and Christian females into thinking they have to bleed during their "first time" or else. Women throughout history were forced to either say they weren't a virgin because they didn't bleed or to say the bible is wrong, both of which were dangerous. Thus, many Jewish and Christian women were forced to make themselves bleed during sex in order to survive and utilized their period, trickery or self-mutilation. Although after seeing the bible's teachings on rape leading to marriage, maybe Jew and Christian women bled their first time because it was rape? Afterall that is how the tradition of the groom carrying the bride over the threshold started, guys would literally carry a girl into his house against her will to rape her after which they'd biblically get married, yet today when people do it, they think it's "romantic". When will Jewish and Christian women stand up and say, "*Hey guys the bible is wrong about the female body and virginity! If God inspired the bible, he doesn't know anything about the hymen which he gave me!*" So, answer me this, did God create the hymen or inspire the bible?

Yet let's not ignore the instructions of the New Testament where the English New International Version of the bible says in Mark 16:17-18, "And <u>these signs will accompany those who believe</u>: *In my name they will drive out demons; they will speak in new tongues;* <sup>18</sup> <u>*they will pick up snakes with their hands; and when they drink deadly poison, it will not hurt them at all;*</u> *they will place their hands on sick people, and they will get well.*"

"Mark's" gospel instructs readers of the bible to "*pick up snakes with their hands*" to "*drink deadly poison*" and that only "*those who believe*" will do this. According to this biblical text the only believers on earth are snake handlers, yet even they don't fit the bible's criteria because contrary to the bible they claim to follow they do get hurt by the snakes they handle and the poison they drink. Strictly speaking if you're harmed "*at all*" when drinking deadly poison then according to the New Testament you're a disbeliever, especially if you don't drink deadly poison at all. The same applies if you don't pick up snakes with your hands, the bible says that means you don't believe. Alcoholics might try to say how they follow this since they drink deadly poison, but elsewhere in the bible alcohol is prohibited. But this isn't just the bible telling people to pick up snakes and drink deadly poison if they believe, in context the bible says Jesus said this after he had allegedly risen from the dead after the alleged crucifixion. So, this instruction comes from the biblical post crucifixion post risen apparition of Jesus. If Christians insist Jesus was crucified and rose from the dead then why don't they do what the bible says this risen Jesus said those who believe will do? Personally, I don't think they should because I think this biblical post crucifixion Jesus either didn't exist, which is why the oldest manuscripts of Mark don't include these bible verses, or he was a Jinn/Devil impersonator trying to trick people to sin, disbelieve and kill themselves. The point is that according to the biblical post death Jesus most Christians don't believe because they disobey these verses. A pre-death biblical Jesus instructs us in Luke 10:19 "*I have given you authority to <u>trample on snakes and scorpions</u> and to overcome all the power of the enemy; <u>nothing will harm you</u>.*" The bible tells us Christians have legal authority from Jesus to trample on snakes and scorpions and nothing will harm them. Yet when was the last time you saw Christians trampling snakes and scorpions because the bible says to? Also, when have you ever seen the invincible Christian which nothing can harm? (including the snakes and scorpions they trample) Remember that just because it's not being practiced doesn't mean it's not supposed to be, or that it's not divine revelation. The word of God is the word of God, whether it is practiced or not. Just because modern cultures might see it as harsh or barbaric doesn't mean it's not really commanded by, written by or inspired by God. Personal opinion does not disqualify divine revelation. Personal opinion cannot make something divine revelation either. Whether you like it, hate it, believe it, or reject it, personal opinion has nothing to do with whether it is the word of God or not.

More material remains to be reviewed before any decision on whether the bible is the word of God or not can be made. Again, to be fair I am using the opinions of learned Christian scholars who have studied the bible and their manuscripts, who have much more authority than me when it comes to discussing the bible. According to Christian scholars the books of Hebrews and James were written anonymously, they weren't written to Hebrews or by a guy named James. If you don't know the writer then how can you say he was divinely inspired and that what was written is the word of God? For all we know the authors of Hebrews and James could've been a pagan, or Jew, playing a joke seeing whether they could fool Christians into believing what they wrote. Maybe it was written by the world's biggest liar, or a psychopath, or was inspired by Satan. We simply don't know who wrote these, this is what Christian scholars are saying. Nobody knows who wrote the books of Hebrews or James. Now who would base their lifestyle and behavior upon the writings of an unknown person? Such a person is risking eternal punishment and potentially sacrificing eternal pleasure based on an anonymous source. If someone gives me advice, I want to know who it is, because if it's someone mysterious it may be Satan trying to lead me astray. This is even riskier and more dangerous when you are following anonymous authors because they have zero credibility. Everyone knows you don't trust someone who refuses to tell you their name, yet this is the case with the biblical books of Hebrews and James. Christian scholars also mention Peter 1 and Peter 2. The first book of Peter is still disputed as to whether it was written by him while the second book of Peter is proven to be a forgery done in his name. Meaning someone pretending to be the apostle Peter used that name to spread what would be rejected as heresy if written under their own name. However, the scholars do agree that whoever wrote Peter 1 was definitely a different person than the one who wrote Peter 2. If we don't know who wrote it then we cannot say it was inspired by God, because we don't know the character of the author of the second book of Peter. Yet biblically neither Peter nor John could write anything as Acts 4:13 says: "*When they saw the courage of <u>Peter and John</u> and realized that they <u>were unschooled, ordinary men</u>, they were astonished and they took note that these men had been with Jesus.*"

But what do the words "unschooled" and "ordinary" actually mean? Well let's look at the Greek New Testament manuscript which this was allegedly translated from:

Acts 4:13- Θεωροῦντες δὲ τὴν τοῦ Πέτρου παρρησίαν καὶ Ἰωάννου καὶ καταλαβόμενοι ὅτι ἄνθρωποι ἀγράμματοί εἰσιν καὶ ἰδιῶται, ἐθαύμαζον, ἐπεγίνωσκόν τε αὐτοὺς ὅτι σὺν τῷ Ἰησοῦ ἦσαν,

ἀγράμματοί is pronounced **Agrammatos** (*ag-ram-mat-os*) and means: *illiterate, unlearned.*

ἰδιῶται is pronounced **Idiotes** (*id-ee-o'-tace*) and means: *an unlearned, illiterate, one who is unskilled in any art.*

      The Greek manuscripts call Peter and John "*Agrammatos Idiotes*" *which* basically means they were grammatical idiots or in english we'd say illiterate idiots. The English word "idiot" actually comes from this Greek biblical word used to describe Peter and John. Personally, I think that's nasty, but these are the words the ancient biblical Greek texts use to describe them, the bible says what it says I'm just sharing what the bible says. Unfortunately, these words tend not to get translated correctly, because let's face it if people read in their English bible that John and Peter were illiterate illiterates (or Idiotes) they will no doubt wonder who the heck wrote the biblical books of John and Peter if the bible says they couldn't? Biblically these two men never wrote or read anything and historically 97-98.5% of Jews at that time were illiterate, the rate for gentile illiteracy was even higher. The bible tells us that Peter and John never learned how to read or write; there were no secretaries then either. Peter and John were poor illiterate fisherman, never went to school and couldn't read or write their native language Aramaic, or Hebrew, let alone author letters and books in foreign Greek.

Nearly every Christian knows the verse of John 3:16, even non-Christians know it and it has many memes. However, according to Christian scholars, the 1st 2nd and 3rd books of John were NOT written by John of Zebedee. Also, the book of Revelation was written by a different author than the gospel of John. Many are often confused because the authors didn't use their last names, perhaps they didn't use them intentionally in order to cause this confusion. Even though John 3:16 wasn't written by an apostle, it was written pseudonymously (meaning written in someone else's name, also known as forgery), I will mention the profane translation Christian scholars agree upon. In the English translation of the New International Version of the bible John 3:16 says, "*16 For God so loved the world that he gave his one and only Son, that whoever believes in him shall not perish but have eternal life.*" Many people mistakenly believe or have mistranslations that read "begotten son". The word beget refers to the act of procreation. The word that is mistranslated as begotten is μονογενῆ (monogenes). The word "monogenes" is in the bible 9 different times, 3 times in Luke 7:12, 8:42 and 9:38, once in Hebrews 11:17, 4 times in the gospel of John 3 and once in John 1. But only in John 3:16 has it ever been mistranslated as begotten. It is impossible for God to procreate because there is only one Creator. Only the creation can procreate or beget and Christian scholars and scholars of the Greek language have agreed that begotten is an incorrect blasphemous translation. Anyone who claims God has begotten is a disbeliever according to Christian scholars, Greek scholars and the bible. The New International Version of the bible was translated by over 100 internationally known Christian scholars of different Christian denominations but hundreds of bibles have removed the word "begotten". This means the intellectual elite of the Christian world says "God does not beget". If any Christian tells you God begot a son you can tell them they are lying according to the top 100 Christian scholars and many others as well as lying about the Greek language. But so what if beget isn't the correct term, the message is still the same right? Generally speaking, the point Christians like to make is the same in the New International Version of John 3:16, but let's see if it's a valid point to make from a biblical perspective. John 3:16 says: "16 *For God so loved the world that he gave his one and only Son, that whoever believes in him shall not perish but have eternal life.*"

Compare John 3:16 to what the bible says was revealed to the prophet David, as Psalm 2:7-10 says: "*I will proclaim the Lord's decree: <u>He said to me, "You are my son; today I have become your father.</u> 8 Ask me, and I will make the nations your inheritance, the ends of the earth your possession. 9 You will break them with a rod of iron; you will dash them to pieces like pottery." 10 Therefore, you kings, be wise; be warned, you rulers of the earth.*"

This has David saying he was called the son of the Lord with the Lord being his father. He relates this so that the kings of the earth are warned not to mess with him or they will be destroyed. This is a biblical contradiction within the same English New International Version, one part of the book says Jesus is the one and only son of God and another part says that God told the prophet David *"You are my son; today I have become your father."* God does not lie and God does not beget, so these terms son and father cannot mean biologically. David never claimed divinity and everyone knew he had human parents. Rather the "son of God" is a title which refers to someone pious and liked by God. Like how elders call children they are fond of son or sonny. Catholics even call priests "Father" yet they never consider them to be their fathers in a literal or biological sense. In fact, these "Fathers" claim to be celibate, so why are they called "Father" if they don't have children? Just as calling a priest "Father" doesn't mean he has children, calling God "Father" doesn't mean God has children. It is important to remember when reading ancient text that we have to interpret it as the ancient people did because they had different ways of saying things than we do today. If we judge what we read based on our own vocabulary we may misunderstand what we read. For example, when parents are displeased, they may say to their child *"I have no son"*, but the word son is never meant literally. Similarly, people will call each other a *"son of a gun"* or a *"son of a female dog"* although not for a second do the speakers actually believe the person had un-human parents. Yet if someone 2000 years later heard an audio clip and didn't understand the vernacular then they may actually think a dog gave birth to this person or that this child must have had a gun as their parent. They would be adamant and say, *"It's clear that "son of a gun" must have meant son of a gun there is no other explanation. I don't know how, but without a doubt this person had a gun as their parent, with gun in their DNA, they were half human- half gun, even though they looked and acted completely human. Don't tell me it's impossible for a gun to have a human child, anything is possible, it was a miraculous birth, so the miracle must have been that he was the only son of a gun."* Such a person might even wear a bullet around their neck to symbolize the one born of a gun. The bible has "sons by the tons" and many times God is mentioned to have a son and never has it historically been interpreted literally. Except unfortunately when Christians read John 3:16, which I repeat Christian scholars have said was NOT written by the apostle John the son of Zebedee. The famously mistranslated misinterpreted verse comes from a person unknown, with unknown honesty, spirituality, memory and motive. If an author is unknown, it is impossible to claim their writings to be authentic or truthful, because they could have just made it all up and used someone else's name to get away with it. To say a pseudonymous writing is the word of God or divinely inspired is dangerous and risks blasphemy regardless of what it says. But not only do Christian Scholars say John 3:16 wasn't written by John of Zebedee since he was dead, but they say even if he hadn't been dead, it would have been impossible for the entire gospel to have been written by him. This is because the gospel of John says Bethsaida was in Galilee. Whereas there is no such place called Bethsaida in Galilee and there never ever was, Bethsaida was on the Eastern side of Tiberias while Galilee was on the Western side. For most people this would be an excusable mistake, but not for God to make, or a man "inspired by God", nor could John of Zebedee be excused. Because John of Zebedee was born in Bethsaida, so if he wrote the gospel of John then it reveals that he doesn't know the geographical location of his own birthplace! If he doesn't even know where he was born or where that city is located and writes down false information about it, then how can you trust this guy to tell you the truth about anything? Either John of Zebedee was a fool who made one of the biggest published blunders of all time or else the gospel of John was written by someone else. Perhaps multiple mystery persons writing in a name other than their own. If you still believe the gospel of John is truly divinely inspired and that Jesus is the "only son of God" then what are we to make of the English translation's New International Version of the bible 1 John 3:1-10, "*See what great love the Father has lavished on us, that we should be called children of God! And that is what we are! The reason the world does not know us is that it did not know him.* [2] *Dear friends, now we are children of God, and what we will be has not yet been made known. But we know that when Christ appears, we shall be like him, for we shall see him as he is.* [3] *All who have this hope in him purify themselves, just as he is pure.* [4] *Everyone who sins breaks the law; in fact, sin is lawlessness.* [5] *But you know that he appeared so that he might take away our sins. And in him is no sin.* [6] *No one who lives in him keeps on sinning. No one who continues to sin has either seen him or known him.* [7] *Dear children, do not let anyone lead you astray. The one who does what is right is righteous, just as he is righteous.* [8] *The one who does what is sinful is of the devil, because the devil has been sinning from the beginning. The reason the Son of God appeared was to destroy the devil's work.* [9] *No one who is born of God will continue to sin, because God's seed remains in them; they cannot go on sinning, because they have been born of God.* [10] *This is how we know who the children of God are and who the children of the devil are: Anyone who does not do what is right is not God's child, nor is anyone who does not love their brother and sister.*"

    According to "John" in a different book he says "we" are children of God, completely contradicting John 3:16 which says God has only one son. This part of the bible repeatedly stresses that every Christian is a child of God. Does this mean literally that God is the biological parent of everyone who is righteous? However, no child of God can sin and no one who knows God or Jesus can sin. Therefore, according to the bible if you sin then you don't know God and are not a Christian. The bible has "John" saying, "*The one who does what is sinful is of the devil*" meaning the sinner is a child of the Devil, "*This is how we know who the children of God are and who the children of the devil are: Anyone who does not do *what is right is not God's child, nor is anyone who does not love their brother and sister."* According to "John" anyone who does what is right is the child of God and every sinner is the child of Satan. This gives us a whole different understanding on just what a "son of God" is and what the term means. According to this part of "John" if you sin, then you are the son of Satan. Now does this mean that sinners are literally biologically demonic with the devil as their actual parent?

But let's forget about "John" and see what the bible says Jesus himself said concerning the *"children of God"*. Yes indeed, contrary to John 3:16 the biblical Jesus says God has more than one child! In Matthew 5:9 the bible says Jesus said, *"Blessed are the peacemakers, for they will be called children of God."* Thus, it's obvious that since nobody is permanently a peacemaker from the day they are born then nobody can be a child of God since the day they are born. Also, because a peacemaker can turn into a warmaker the term child of God according to Jesus is not literal but figurative. If it's literal then that means God can lose his children if they stop being peacemakers. Meaning when Jesus unpeacefully whipped people in the temple or will unpeacefully kill the antichrist, those actions biblically disqualify Jesus from being a child of God according to what the bible says Jesus said was the standard of who a child of God is. A God that gains or loses kids is not eternal so it's impossible for Jesus to have been literal and yet nowhere does he clarify in any way that he is an exception as a literal son of God, because he wasn't. Furthermore, the verses of Matthew 5:43-48 say Jesus said: 43 *"You have heard that it was said, 'Love your neighbor and hate your enemy.'* 44 But **I tell you, love your enemies and pray for those who persecute you,** 45 **that you may be children of your Father in heaven.** *He causes his sun to rise on the evil and the good, and sends rain on the righteous and the unrighteous.* 46 **If you love** *those who love you, what reward will you get? Are not even the tax collectors doing that?* ⁴⁷ *And if you greet only your own people, what are you doing more than others? Do not even pagans do that?* ⁴⁸ **Be perfect, therefore, as your heavenly Father is perfect."**

Once more demonstrating a "child of God" is someone who obeys God's laws, with Jesus telling his audience to *"be perfect" "as your heavenly Father is"*. Jesus didn't consider his audience to be literal "sons of God" yet he called God their Father because God is the one whom they obey. These bible verses also tell us that Jesus told people to *"be perfect"*, he never taught that he was the only perfect person or only son of God who was going to die on the cross for mankind's sins to be forgiven. The biblical Jesus teaches the exact opposite of Christianity. Biblically Jesus teaches God is *"your Father"* and he wants you to be perfect, like God is. Everywhere the bible mentions God having a son is in the figurative sense with this understanding of a *"son of God"* being a righteous perfect person who doesn't sin. Every time the bible labeled someone as a son of God it has always been understood to mean that the person was very righteous.

> Genesis 6:1-4 *"When human beings began to increase in number on the earth and daughters were born to them,* ² *the sons of God saw that the daughters of humans were beautiful, and they married any of them they chose.*³ *Then the LORD said, "My Spirit will not contend with humans forever, for they are mortal; their days will be a hundred and twenty years."* ⁴ *The Nephilim were on the earth in those days – and also afterward – when the sons of God went to the daughters of humans and had children by them. They were the heroes of old, men of renown."*

The Nephilim are considered to be either humans of giant proportions descended from the prophet Seth, or considered to be a name for disbelieving sinners. The verse about 120 years could be a prophesy that sinful people who are not righteous "sons of God" will only live a hundred and twenty years maximum. However, it seems more likely that this was specifically concerning those particular people addressed at that time who were on earth. This interpretation makes more sense as a reference to the human daughters who are sinners not being with their righteous husbands, or "sons of God" forever. With the verse likely meaning that their days with their husbands will amount to 120 years before they either die or are separated. This also shows how disbelieving sinful wives will not accompany righteous husbands eternally in paradise. No one can get into heaven via marriage, which is demonstrated by the examples of the wife of Noah and the wife of Lot. I mistakenly use to misunderstand this bible verse to mean that I could potentially live for a maximum of 120 years and that good people would naturally live for 120 years. Interestingly 14 of Muhammad's companions lived to be 120 years old. Although this 120-year rule from the bible is wrong because even the bible mentions people after this verse living well beyond 120 years, Genesis 11:10-32 provide such examples.

> Exodus 4:22-23 "²² *Then say to Pharaoh, 'This is what the LORD says: Israel is my firstborn son, and I told you, "Let my son go, so he may worship me." But you refused to let him go; so I will kill your firstborn son.'*"

According to the book of Exodus it is impossible for Jesus to have been the firstborn son of God, or his only son because Israel was the firstborn son according to the bible. However, this verse is clearly corrupted because the earlier book of Genesis mentions sons of God, so this is obviously a Jewish insertion to make Jews seem special despite the very notion contradicting their earlier Scripture. Also, the word "firstborn" denotes that there will be more to come so biblically speaking there can never be an only son unless it is the first, but Jesus is not the first since Genesis and Exodus have already mentioned numerous sons with Israel being the first. It's also biologically literal since in context it has God allegedly comparing his "firstborn son" with Pharaoh's literal "firstborn son". Or at least that is how Jews and Christians interpret it, but historically Pharaoh didn't have kids and that's why he adopted Moses. Biblical scholars have said the Jews invented this story about God killing the firstborn sons of Egyptians because they wanted to hide the shame of their own firstborn sons being killed, which some biblical scholars said the Jews killed their own kids as a sacrifice to God hoping for improved working conditions but that is incorrect as well. Some may have killed their own sons simply to avoid Pharaoh's soldiers killing them but Pharaoh never had kids, so then what does God mean when the bible says he said "son"? But we have more trouble when Jeremiah 31:9 says that God said Ephraim will be his "firstborn son". So not only does the bible teach that God has many sons, but that he himself says he has many "firstborn sons of God" as well. Yet something must be false because by definition there can only be one "firstborn son" unless a "son " doesn't mean son in the literal sense and "firstborn" doesn't mean "firstborn" but if all this stuff in the bible doesn't actually mean what it says then why would anyone think it means what it says when it says similar stuff about Jesus?

> Psalm 89:24-34 *"My faithful love will be with him, and through my name his horn will be exalted. 25 I will set his hand over the sea, his right hand over the rivers. 26 He will call out to me, 'You are my Father, my God, the Rock my Savior.' 27 And <u>I will appoint him to be my firstborn</u>, the most exalted of the kings of the earth. 28 I will maintain my love to him forever, and my covenant with him will never fail.29 I will establish his line forever,his throne as long as the heavens endure. 30 "<u>If his sons forsake my law </u>and do not follow my*

*statutes, <sup>31</sup> if they violate my decrees and fail to keep my commands, <sup>32</sup> <u>I will punish their sin</u> with the rod, their iniquity with flogging;<sup>33</sup> but I will not take my love from him, nor will I ever betray my faithfulness. <sup>34</sup> <u>I will not violate my covenant or alter what my lips have uttered</u>."*

   Here the Psalms contradict Genesis, Exodus and Jeremiah by saying this person will be appointed as God's firstborn. If Israel is indeed the firstborn then either God is lying in the Psalms or the Psalms are not authentic revelation. These verses from the alleged Psalms of David are particularly interesting because it says "He", denoting a human male, will call out "*You are my Father, my God, the Rock my Savior*". Some Christians may try to say this is all referencing Jesus, but if that's the case then how can Jesus be a savior if he considers God to be his savior? Some Christians will even blasphemously claim Jesus is God! Psalms also says "He" will be appointed to be "*the most exalted of the kings of the earth.*" whereas Israel was never a king. Since the Psalms are said to be revealed to David then it is unlikely David is the "he". If we examine who was "*the most exalted of the kings of the earth.*" we will recognize Solomon, the prophet king son of David, as having the strongest kingdom of all time. Solomon was given authority by God over the wind and was able to use it to make ships in his army travel faster than naturally possible which fulfills the prophesy in verse 23. Solomon is also renowned for his architecture which would make him the most exalted who has been known to man ever since. The army of Solomon included animals big and small, such as lions and elephants, to birds who would spy for him and drop stones on enemies from above. Although one thing Solomon had which none before him had nor any after him will ever have was the special ability given by God to have authority over the Jinn. Solomon was able to command the Jinn to do what he wanted. Some have said his authority over the Jinn means he was satanic, or a magician, but this is a false slander because Solomon actually outlawed magic throughout his kingdom since it is dangerous and makes its users disbelievers. Angels even descended from Heaven to teach magic to people as a test in response to the allegations that Solomon was a magician. Because since Solomon eradicated magic the people didn't know the difference between magic and a miracle. Once the people saw the angels demonstrate what magic was, they knew the difference between miracles done by a prophet like Solomon and the magical spells done by sorcerers. Unfortunately, some didn't heed the warning of the angels that practicing magic is disbelief and will eliminate the chance of paradise for those who practice it and don't repent. Since then, magic has continued to be practiced in the world and out of jealousy for his superiority the magicians have tried to slander Solomon and reduce him to the level of a petty magician, instead of the prophet who was "*the most exalted of the kings of the earth.*" But you don't have to believe me, because an English translation of the New International Version of the bible 1 Chronicles 22:9-13 says God told David: "*But you will have a son who will be a man of peace and rest, and I will give him rest from all his enemies on every side. <u>His name will be Solomon</u>, and I will grant Israel peace and quiet during his reign.* <sup>10</sup> *He is the one who will build a house for my Name. <u>He will be my son, and I will be his father</u>. And I will establish the throne of his kingdom over Israel forever.'* <sup>11</sup> *"Now, <u>my son, the LORD be with you</u>, and may you have success and build the house of the LORD your God, as he said you would.* <sup>12</sup> *May the LORD give you discretion and understanding when he puts you in command over Israel, so that you may keep the law of the LORD your God.* <sup>13</sup> *Then <u>you will have success if you are careful to observe the decrees and laws that the LORD gave Moses for Israel</u>. Be strong and courageous. Do not be afraid or discouraged.*"

Another reason the Psalms cannot be referring to Jesus is because it explicitly mentions what will happen *"If his sons forsake my law"*, at this time Jesus does not have any sons and Christians claim he never will. Ironically some support that claim by saying Jesus is God and God can't have sons, yet then when you ask them why Jesus is God they say because he is the son of God with them uttering contradicting blasphemy not realizing these statements contradict the same bible they claim is the word of God, or inspired by God. This is called double think when a person holds 2 contradictory beliefs simultaneously while accepting both of them to be true at the same time. I'm not mentioning this to make fun of or insult anybody, I just don't want people to slander God or Jesus and make themselves disbelievers by uttering such blasphemy or lies while they think they are correct or doing good. If God is God and Jesus is God then how can there only be one God? Jesus cannot possibly be the son of himself. Mathematically the trinity theory doesn't add up, 1+1+1=3 not 1. In reply some may say if you multiply 1x1x1 it =1, which is true but where did the two 1's that are being multiplied come from? We could make the same case that 1x1x1x1x1x1=1 so no matter how many 1's there are we would still get 1. Why stop and say there are three 1's if any number of 1's will do the trick? Also, the trinity is not a multiplication but is always described in additive terms such as *"The father, the son AND the holy spirit"* nobody believes in *"the father times the son times the holy spirit"*. So, such Christians are just changing the formula because it doesn't add up, similar to how on a first-grade math paper I once changed all the subtraction signs into addition signs because I didn't know how to do subtraction well, so I just changed the formula into addition so that my answers would be right. Although because the paper was a color-coded picture my answers didn't correlate with what was right and my picture was visibly colored wrong even though the math was right. The problem wasn't with my math, it was that I changed the paper in order to do the math however I wanted so my answers would be right. Rather than treat it for what it was I simply did whatever I could to avoid being wrong even if it meant inventing my own math problems and then trying to tell the teacher that I did the paper I was given correctly. Many people do this with religion and religious texts. It reminds me of the game children would play, they ask you "*What's 1+1?*" If you say 2 then they say "*No 1+1=11 are you stupid?*" Then they ask you again "*What's 1+1?*" if you then say 11, they say "*No 1+1=2 are you stupid?*" so no matter what you answer the response would be the same. They were right and you were wrong and stupid, because you didn't agree with their special methodology. But how can you agree with their methodology in order to come up with the right answer when it remains a mystery? Has Satan been trying all this time to misguide people away from a mystery? If a mystery is something you don't know, then what is the difference between not knowing it and not believing it? Is the road to paradise full of religious mysteries? Is it even possible to be "guided by a mystery"? Just imagine someone asks you for traveling directions and you responded, "*I got something even better than directions, I got a mystery for you*". Did those who disbelieved in the prophets of God say it was because they "*refuse to believe in a mystery*"?

    There are many ways the trinity is explained, a famous one is that a priest named Patrick would use a shamrock to show how 3 leaves can be part of one plant. If this is true then polytheists can make the same claim and say how a tree has many branches and many leaves but it's still one tree. Unknown to most Christians is that before Patrick, the Druids in Ireland used the shamrock as a depiction of their trinity in 3,025 BCE. Which means the shamrock was a pagan symbol for their god over 3,000 years before Jesus was born. One glaring problem with this belittlement of comparing God to plants is that plants die and can get eaten by bugs or lose their leaves, they are not eternal and one day you can have a 4 leaf clover and then a bug eats a leaf and it becomes a 3 leaf shamrock, then a child picks a leaf off and it has 2 leaves left, then the wind blows a leaf off and only 1 leaf is left, then the field is burned and nothing but the stem remains and the plant has no leaves left, but then it grows back from the dead in the spring after the winter snow melts and has 4 leaves once more; or who knows maybe even 5 depending on the fertilizer. Does God go through such stages of gaining and losing parts? No. The shamrock explanation of God has a shameful pagan origin and is a downright sham. Maybe the trinity could be like an egg, a shell outside, white inside and a yolk, 3 parts 1 egg. However, the shell can be separated, as can the inside and there might even be a double yolk making it 4 parts in 1 egg. Let's not forget God doesn't get eaten, or come out of the butt of a bird. Also, the parts of the egg are not equal to each other and neither are the leaves of a plant. Maybe the trinity is like water, water can be solid, liquid and gas so that's 3 different stages of 1 thing. Well water can become salt water or dirty water or fluoride water. Also, there is no water molecule that I know of that can be ice, liquid and gas all at the same time, a water molecule can only be in one form at one time. Likewise, God cannot be human and divine or the Father and the son. Ok, what about geometry maybe the trinity can be compared to a triangle? 3 sides or 3 points all in one shape. Many pagans used geometric symbols to explain their Trinitarian belief such as the Merovingian Fleur de lis in 4,540 BCE, the Italian trinicarian during 3,640 BCE, the Norse Odin's Horn in 2,540 BCE, the Celtic Triquetra in 2,049 BCE, and the Germanic Trefot in 2,025 BCE. Although let's stay simple and use a triangle as an example of the trinity. However, there are different types of triangles, there are right triangles, obtuse triangles, acute triangles of which all have different angles. But let's assume the Trinitarians use an Equilateral triangle, which has 3 sides of equal length with 3 sixty-degree angles. Could this work? Now let's remember all the prophets believed in God and this triangle theory would be easy to explain since they wouldn't need to grow shamrocks in Palestine, or rely on water sources, or birds menstruating to explain it, just draw a triangle on the ground and presto there is your explanation of god. It just so happens that there were people who did this with an equilateral triangle. Except they called it the Thaumaturgic Triangle and instead of being believers they were witches and wizards who professed to be Satanists who were recorded to cast spells during the time of King Solomon. Some considered the symbol to represent the Earth, Sky and Water. Others thought the three angles or points represented the 3 in 1 magical trinity. The lower left symbolized the Arcane, the lower right symbolized the Divine, and the top symbolized Witchcraft. The Trinitarian idea of 3 parts in one entity actually originated from disbelieving magicians. Now Moses was experienced in combating magic and likely would have known of this 3 in 1 triangle of the magicians. He could have said to the Israelites that God was like a triangle with a Father, Son and Holy Spirit, but he didn't. The Israelites would have been particularly familiar with triangles and could have even come to that conclusion themselves had they believed in a trinity; after all they saw the pyramids of Egypt. Some may say *"but Jesus wasn't known to Moses so of course he couldn't have known about the trinity so that's why he didn't teach it"*. That is true Moses didn't know Jesus personally, but Moses did talk to God and have conversations with him. Moses knew God and was closer to God than anyone I know to be on earth today. If God was a trinity Moses would definitely have known.

The pagan Egyptians believed in a trinity themselves and worshiped a trinity. Therefore, if God were a trinity, it would have been easy to explain to Moses since Israelites would already have known the concept of Trinitarian belief, yet they left Egypt and considered their trinity to be a false god of paganism. God affirmed that the trinity of the Egyptians was false and instructed Israelites to worship him alone. If God were a trinity, why would he refer to the concept of a trinity as blasphemous only to reveal himself as a trinity later? This would be extremely hypocritical. When giving the first commandment which says: there is only one God and to worship him only, wouldn't God have said that one God actually means 3 parts in one and that there is a Father and Son but the son will come later and die for the sins of everyone so be ready for his coming? Also saying that you should worship or pray to the son after he comes and he will tell you how you won't have to follow any of the laws now being given to Moses which you are expected to follow? Of course, this may prompt Moses to ask why not send the son now and whether he also has to worship the son, or teach people about the concept of salvation through crucifixion, or if he should get baptized, or baptize people. Moses may then ask why bother sending him these laws if they will just be made null and void, also asking why not just give the laws that people will live by later. Satan likely didn't even try to mislead Moses with this trinity doctrine out of fear that Moses would refute it so future generations were not led astray as they are today. But let's go back to before Moses. Because God existed before Moses and did many things. Now if God were a trinity and Jesus is part of that trinity then that means Jesus would've done those things as well. Meaning that if the trinity is true, Jesus would've caused the flood that killed everything on earth except for the creatures in Noah's ark, Jesus would've killed the sodomous people of Lot, Jesus would've killed the Egyptian military and sent all those plagues upon the people of Egypt. Jesus would've been responsible for every act and order of violence in the Old Testament if the trinity were a true concept. Also, if Jesus were God, then all those rules God made in the Old Testament would've actually been the rules of Jesus. If the trinity were true, that means Jesus would've created Satan and the hellfire. If Jesus were God, then that means Jesus would've kicked Adam and Eve out of paradise.

Unfortunately, many people have been brainwashed to think they cannot learn by reading and are *"visual learners"*. Therefore, to accommodate such people I have included graphs so they can visually see the trinity doctrine for what it is. As they say "seeing is believing", well let's see just what Trinitarian Christians believe. On the following pages are representations of the Christian trinity as it is believed to have been *"Before Jesus"*, *"During Jesus' time on earth"* and *"After Jesus"*.

    This is how Trinitarian Christians believe God was all the way up until Jesus was created in the womb of his mother Mary. Notice that people are distinctly not a part of God, have any part of God overlapping them, or within them and that God is represented as 1 general thing with 3 contained parts. The Father, Son and Holy Spirit are all of the same substance in this depiction. Some people might consider this monotheism but it is actually Henotheism. Henotheism is the religious belief that elevates one deity above others. For instance, most Trinitarian Christians will state that God is on a higher level than Jesus or at least the Holy Spirit, yet they will claim that all three are divine. Thus, because there is a pecking order of different beings who are divine (even though Trinitarian dogma states they are all equal) this disqualifies such a belief from being considered monotheism, both religiously and linguistically it is called Henotheism. Henotheists have always been considered polytheists, but unfortunately Henotheists themselves tend to consider themselves monotheists because they don't know the difference and because it is part of human nature to know that polytheism is wrong. Thus, henotheists claim to be monotheists because most think and were told that they are and if they ever admitted to being henotheists, they'd be admitting to being polytheists, thereby admitting their error. Therefore, the religious category of henotheism isn't taught in Christian regions. In secular countries that promote the doctrine of "freedom of false religions from being proven wrong" the authorities play along with the deception of the henotheist religious leaders and let the masses of henotheists believe, teach and falsely lay claim to being monotheists. This is because they don't care what people call themselves and they don't want people to be monotheists anyways, so to them the mislabeling of henotheism as monotheism helps them destroy monotheism.

As Jesus is on earth God allegedly changes. The Father and Son are of distinctly different substances with the Holy Spirit tying them together being similar to both. On the other hand, since Jesus is a person it means people now have a part of God overlapping people, with one of the people being the son of God. The son is both human and divine, but the Father and Spirit are only divine and not human at all. This is called anthropomorphism where God is given a human form and/or human attributes. Basically, anthropomorphism is a class of man-made religions where humans invent a god which is humanesque, or has some percentage of human biology or abilities/flaws instead of being 100% God. Without the graph it would be very confusing to explain. Another important aspect of this chart is it shows Jesus is partially the Holy Spirit, which was traditionally called the "Holy Ghost". How much % of Jesus is ghost? If it's 0% or less the Holy Ghost/Spirit cannot be part of the trinity and this chart would be a false doctrine. If it's more than 0% as the chart indicates then the trinity is false because Jesus is a prophet and God does not send ghost prophets.

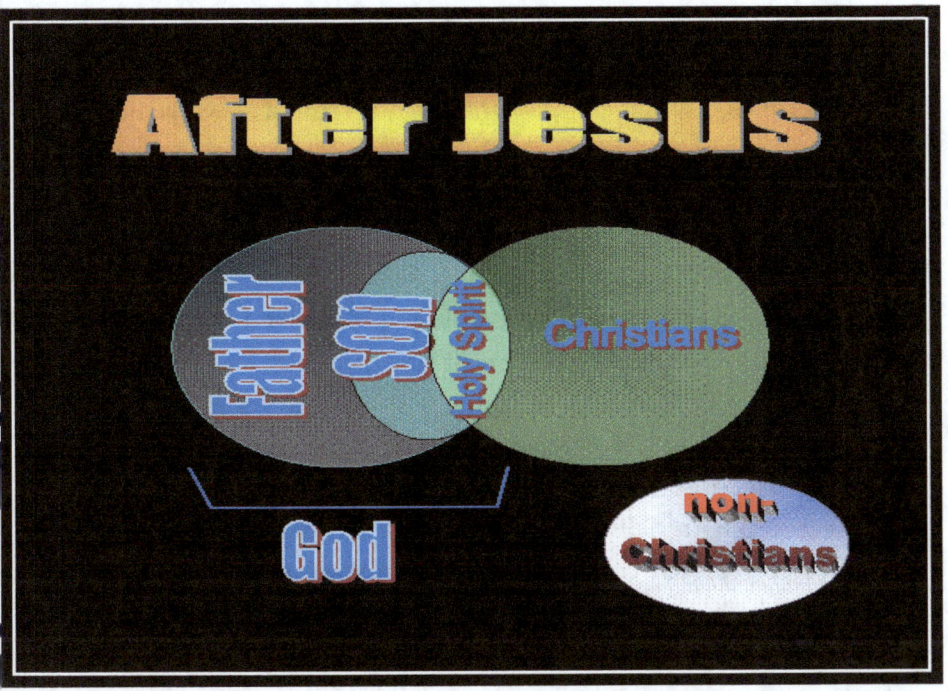

After Jesus leaves earth the dynamic of God changes yet again. At this time the Father, Son and Holy Spirit are thought to be entirely divine and there are different types of people as well. The people are in two categories, Christians, specifically Trinitarian Christians, and non-Christians. Since Trinitarian Christians believe they have been baptized in Christ and blessed/confirmed with the Holy Spirit those elements of God are now in them and are overlapping. For Catholics they believe the son (Jesus) is physically present in them as long as the Eucharist is being digested, until it reaches the toilet. Yet since the Son, Father and Holy Spirit are one, the Father is automatically overlapping as well with the Christians. This makes the Father both divine and human and the entire God-head is overlapping with Christians. Thereby making Christians semi-divine since the divine holy spirit is believed to be in them. If you refer to the first graph of *"Before Jesus"*, originally people had nothing to do with God. Although now Trinitarian Christians believe they have something to do with God, while people who are not Trinitarian Christians have nothing to do with God. On the other hand, Christians have parts of God within them elevating them to deity status while one special Christian, called Jesus, is believed to actually be God incarnate; or at least 2/3rds of God. How Christ can be a follower of Christ (Christian) is a question often left unasked. When a Christian filled with the Holy Spirit sins it essentially means God is sinning, unless the Holy Spirit were to leave every time before a sin was committed. However, if the Holy Spirit left then Christians would have to be reconfirmed every time, they sinned so it could re-enter. Even with the graph the idea of the trinity after Jesus is utterly confusing and reminiscent of the pagan trinities which were worshiped thousands of years before Christ, when the true believers believed in one God with one part. Perhaps the reason the trinity is so confusing is because Jesus never taught it to people. But if he is the most important part of the trinity and it is obligatory to believe in the trinity or else one is punished, then it would have been repeatedly mentioned over and over again by Jesus. Not only does Jesus never mention a trinity, but he repeatedly stresses that worshipping God alone without any intermediaries is the key to salvation. Jesus never teaches his execution is the means of salvation, or that believing he is God, or the son of God is necessary. Instead of teaching a confusing trinity, Jesus taught that God was simply one, unchanging, without beginning or end, all powerful and all knowing, who was the same God that Moses worshiped, who is unlike any of the creation. Jesus also stressed that he himself didn't know the hour of the Day of Judgment (Mark 13:32) and that by himself he couldn't do anything (John 5:30).

Yet people still claim Jesus is divine and part of a Trinitarian God. Not only do they make Jesus into God, but they claim as part of the trinity Jesus died as well. What this means, according to the trinity, is that at a certain point in time 33% of God was dead. This is one of the most blasphemous concepts I have ever heard. The belief that Jesus was part of a trinity and died implies God was only 66.6% alive. This is not an immortal God who never changes, imagine how insulted God is when people say 33% of him died. Even according to the equality trinity ideology this is impossible because what happens to one must happen to the others since they are equal parts or else it would cause imbalance and the trinity would no longer be equal. For instance, trinitarians may say that the trinity is like God having different titles, for instance Bob can be a Father, a Son and a husband while still being just one person. However, if the son Bob dies that means Bob the father dies as well as Bob the husband. It's impossible for Bob's mother to lose her son without Bob's daughter becoming an orphan and Bob's wife becoming a widow. Thus, if Jesus was part of the trinity and died, then all parts of the trinity would have had to die 100%. Although then it is not an immortal god if it died. So, if Jesus is part of the trinity, it is impossible for him to have died for even one millisecond and it is impossible for him to have been human for even one millisecond. But we both know that Jesus had a human mother and was human and as a human he must die at some point in time. This means Jesus cannot be part of a trinity and God cannot be a trinity. Also, if Bob the Son were on earth, then Bob the Father cannot be on the moon, they have to be in the same place at the same time and be the same in everything. Meaning when Bob the Husband is getting naked to have intercourse with his wife, Bob the Son is doing that as well as Bob the Father. Bob the Son can't have clothes on if Bob the Father is naked and vice versa. Bob the Son can't be sleeping while Bob the Father is killing people and Bob the Husband is making babies. Likewise if Bob the Son has a beard then Bob the Father has a beard too. Also, with eating when Bob the son is eating some food and puking or pooping then Bob the Father is having the same experience at the same time. Plus, Bob the Son has a mother as does Bob the Father and Bob the Husband, they all got that Mother at the same time. So, if Mary is the mother of Jesus and he is part of a trinity then she would've had to be the mother of God. But when did God ever get a Mother? God has always existed so his mother would have to be even older but that's not possible, especially for a human like Mary. Whereas when Bob the Son gets spanked by his mother then Bob the Father would also get those spankings too. When Bob the Son gets sick then so does Bob the Father. Thus God is not like Bob, God does not have split personalities. The trinity is almost like dissociative identity disorder depicting a God that has multiple personas, except it's worse than that because they say God doesn't just have multiple personas but actually has multiple persons/bodies. And they'll say *"It's just like how you can be a Father and Son too."* Yet such people don't even know what it means to be a Son nor a Father and aren't good parents or good children themselves. Whereas Jesus is a prophet. So, is God a prophet? A prophet of who? Is the Holy Spirit a prophet? God cannot be a Messenger of himself just like you don't send yourself as a messenger of yourself. Also remember that John was a prophet on earth while Jesus was alive. So, if God is a prophet, then how can he have another prophet called John on earth at the same time? When John saw Jesus did he say "What's up Boss?"

did John ever go around telling people that he was a "prophet of Jesus"? Did John ever ask his relative Mary what it was like giving birth to his God? Or did John ever say Mary was the Mother of the guy who he was a prophet of or who he worshipped? Really did John ever say *"I worship so and so and tell everyone to do so and Mary is his mother. Oh and she's a relative of mine too. She gave birth to the guy I worship. Wanna join my religion? It's easy I just gotta dunk you in the river to wash off the sins you got because your ancestors did a bad sin a long time ago. Although Mary didn't get it so I won't dunk her and Jesus don't have it either but I'm gonna dunk him anyways. Yet if I dunk you for some reason the dunking only works for you, whereas if you have kids, I'll have to dunk your kids too because they'll catch the sin even though after I dunk you the sin will be gone. Whereas even if you let me dunk your wife before you have kids, which I hope you let me do, I'll still need to dunk the kids and their kids and for thousands of years because somehow these sins which water washes off never get diluted through the ages. Earlier people had it too but they didn't get dunked and I'm not going to dunk my daddy Zachariah either. Oh and by the way nobody ever dunked me."* However, the trinitarian may still not be satisfied so let's say that God has 3 equal parts, with 33.333% Father, 33.333% Jesus and 33.333% Holy Spirit. Since according to the trinity theory that all 3 are equal then they must all deserve equal worship in time and quality. Meaning if God were a trinity, in order to properly worship such a deity, one would have to worship the Father 33% of the time, worship Jesus 33% of the time and worship the Holy Spirit 33% of the time. If you give any one of those 3 parts anything more or less than 33% of your time, enthusiasm or effort then you wouldn't be worshipping God correctly. For example, let's say you are saying a prayer to Jesus, if you do that then that means you are not saying that prayer to God or the Holy Spirit. Meaning you would be worshipping Jesus and not God or the

Holy Spirit which goes against trinitarian dogma. You see the trouble with being a trinitarian is that it's technically impossible to pray to a trinity. Worshipping a trinity would be like a guy with 3 wives saying "I love you" to all 3 at the same time. In such a scenario each one of the 3 would ask which one he was talking to hoping he meant them and them alone. If he then told them 1/3rd of that "I love you" goes to each one of you then they would be quite perplexed and likely hurt. Later when alone with one of them if he said "I love you" they would wonder whether he was giving them 100% of his love or just 33.3% as he had before when he said what he said. If he then said that he loved the 1 with all his heart they would wonder what about the other 2 persons and whether he really means it or if he is just saying that to everyone. Also, each one would always wonder if they are getting perfectly equal treatment. This is a similar to a trinitarian's alleged relationship with God. They'll say God is 1 of the 3 parts of the trinity and that they only worship God, but then they say God is all 3 parts of the trinity. That's the equivalent of the polyganist husband saying he only loves 1 of his 3 wives but the 1 wife which he loves is 3 people, but he only loves 1 person. That's literally exactly what trinitarian Christians say, they'll say "*I only worship 1 god his name is God. God is the 1st person in the trinity which has 3 persons in it total. Also, God is a trinity of 3 persons, so by worshipping the trinity I only worship 1 god, which is God the 1st person of the trinity.*" It's a statement that doesn't make coherent sense and cannot be true. Either God is the 1st person or God is all 3 persons combined. You can't say God is X and X = 1, then claim that 3X = God or that X + X + X equals 1. Ironically the trinitarian Christians think it's an ungodly abomination for a man to have 3 wives even though biblical prophets had more than 3. However as hard as it may be to love 3 wives equally it's even harder to pray to a trinity deity. You cannot pray to or worship 3 different beings at the same time, even if you tried. For the Christians who pray the "Our Father" prayer and believe in a trinity, for this to be non-contradictory then when they say Jesus prayed the "Our Father" prayer he must have been praying to himself just as much as he was to God. Meaning the "Our Father" prayer has to also be a prayer to "His Son" for the trinity to work. Otherwise, it's impossible to pray to a trinity. Whereas to believe that 33% of Jesus' prayers were to himself is insanity. How can Jesus worship himself 33% of the time he prays? The only way one can worship 3 beings or 3 persons is if they are a polytheist. But for the sake of argument let's pretend it were possible to pray 1 prayer that can be divided into 3 parts intended for and devoted to 3 different beings. Now if 1 being is God then 1 part of the prayer goes to God and 2 parts to the other beings. So 33% of the theologically impossible trinitarian prayer would in their theory go to God the 1st person of the trinity. But what about the other 67% or 66.6% if you want to be specific? Well, that portion would go to Jesus and the Holy Spirit. Meaning 67% of a trinitarian's prayer to "God the trinity" would not go to God the first person of the trinity. Thus, the majority of a trinitarian's prayer to a trinity would go to someone other than God. Meaning that the majority of the time they worship they would be worshipping beings other than the Creator. Now what do you think God thinks about someone who worships others 67% of the time? God is not okay with a paltry 33%, God accepts no less than 100%. The reason God can't be a trinity is because he can't share prayers. All prayers are supposed to be to and for God the Creator alone. Unfortunately, a trinitarian thinks God the Creator is only worth 33%. The most striking thing about this is that when trinitarians claim to not be worshipping other than God they really are by all accounts. Based on modern testing standards if you want to pass a test typically you need to get 65% right. Now the test of life has a different scoring system, but regarding the test of worshipping God alone you need 100% to pass and 33% is a failing grade. Yet putting God's criteria of 100% exclusive worship to pass aside, what if someone's goal was to worship something other than God? According to modern standards if you are worshipping others 65%+ that would mean successfully worshipping someone other than God. So, since the trinitarian deity they worship is 66.6% not God but composed of Jesus and the Holy Spirit, then the trinitarian is passing the test of worshipping something that is not God according to modern testing standards. If not worshipping God the Creator was their goal, then modern testing standards say the trinitarians succeed in that goal of NOT worshipping God and worshipping something else other than God the Creator. Although that 66.6% number isn't even accurate because not only do trinitarians tend to worship Jesus and the Holy Spirit, but they have the saints, Mary, the Popes, priests, angels, and many other extra beings they pray to either explicitly or implicitly plus if you add democracy then that's a much smaller percent than 33% going to God in theory. In reality 0% of their worship is going to God because God only accepts 100% pure monotheism, he doesn't take scrap percentages. To God worship is not divisible, it's either all for him or not, he doesn't share a prayer. Even according to the trinitarian's own standards of the trinity being 3 equal parts then they are over 66% worshipping others besides God when anything larger than 0% is enough to earn eternity in hell. Furthermore, if you ask any Christian if they love Jesus exactly as much as the Holy Spirit none will say they do. What's even worse is that most actually love Jesus more than they do the Creator and some even think he is the Creator despite that being completely anti-biblical and anti-trinitarian. However, is it just to treat Jesus as equal to the Father or the Holy Spirt or vice versa or vice vice versa when they all came into being at different times and they have all done different things?  If the Father isn't a prophet and Jesus is (and/or is a "son of God" and/or human) and the Holy Spirit is different than the other 2 then why treat them all the same?   That's unjust to all three.  To equate any part of the trinity to the others is to diminish the worth of some and overemphasize the worth of others.  Any kind of trinity deity is not a singular deity at all, it's more like a corporation with 3 different departments.  A trinitarian just worships different members of "team God" thinking that all 3 members equal 1 team.  <u>God is not a team of 3</u> equal members, he is 1 and there is no partner, equal or any to compete or compare with God.  Now how do you think God the 1 and only will feel about a person who believes in the trinity and publicizes this multi-blasphemous pagan belief dying upon it?  Do you think they will be served by angels in paradise for eternity or become barbequed without mercy?  Likewise, do you think those angels worship Jesus and/or the Holy Spirit?  Could an angel ever worship a human like Jesus?  Never.  Since the angels don't worship a trinity that means it's not God.  Truly no angel ever asked Jesus for help or prayed to him, nor do angels pray "in the name of Jesus" or the "Holy Ghost".  The trinity was not taught to people by angels but by devils.  And the devil Satan was never an angel he was, is and always will be a Jinn.  Satan made up the "fallen angel" backstory because he is a racist and thinks Jinn are better than humans.  So, by hiding his Jinn identity teaching the "fallen angel" lie he not only slandered the entire species of angels but protected his own Jinn race from public shame at the fact of him being a part of it.

  Traditionally while God and Jesus tend to remain in one form in the trinity depiction, the third part called the "Holy Spirit" is frequently mentioned in a variety of forms throughout the bible.

1. John 1:32 depicts the Holy Spirit as a dove
2. John 14:26 depicts the Holy Spirit as a person
3. John 20:22 depicts the Holy Spirit as breath
4. Luke 2:26 depicts the Holy Spirit as the author of revelation
5. Luke 3:22 depicts the Holy spirit as a tangible dove
6. Luke 4:1 depicts the Holy Spirit filling Jesus
7. Matthew 1:18 depicts the Holy Spirit as a force of impregnation
8. Mark 1:8 depicts the Holy Spirit as the element used in baptism replacing the use of water
9. Acts 2:2 depicts the Holy Spirit as wind
10. Acts 2:3 depicts the Holy Spirit as fire
11. Acts 2:4 depicts the Holy Spirit as linguistic fluency
12. Acts 8:17 depicts the Holy Spirit as a magnetic like aura transferred by the "laying on of hands"
13. Acts 10:38 depicts the Holy Spirit as if it were an ointment used for anointing
14. Acts 28:25 the Holy Spirit is depicted as the voice of the prophet Isaiah
15. Hebrews 6:4 depicts the Holy Spirit as a shareable commodity

According to Trinitarian belief God has 3 parts but remains 1, one part is eternal, immortal, unchanging and unseen, the second part is a human who experienced infancy, childhood, teenage years, adulthood and death, while the third part has so many different forms that you cannot count them on your fingers. However, all these 3 parts, of which some parts can shapeshift and take on many different forms, are all 1 eternal and never changing God despite the bible saying the Holy Spirit is frequently changing forms. Yet how can God be divine while at the same time being a human, while at the same time being a bird touching himself in human form, while speaking to himself from heaven? This is the portrayal of God Trinitarian Christians promote and believe in due to their biblical interpretations, although it is rarely described in such plain terms.

One of these depictions of the Holy Spirit is frequently glossed over without receiving proper attention, in Luke 4:1 it says: *"Jesus, full of the Holy Spirit, left the Jordan and was led by the Spirit into the wilderness"*. If one believes both the Holy Spirit and Jesus are two parts of God then this verse means that one part of God was inside of another part of God. This means we have a god within a god, yet all three parts are believed to be completely separate from one another. Not only is Jesus filled with the Holy Spirit, but he was led by "the Spirit". Who is "the Spirit"? Clearly it is a different thing than the "Holy Spirit" because the word Holy would have been used if they were both the same Spirits. Also, it would make no sense at all for the Holy Spirit to be internally within Jesus and then lead him externally. So, this bible verse is very strange, difficult to understand and believe in, especially if one believes in the trinity theory. If the trinity is true then this literally means the various parts of God can influence each other, if Jesus were God, then that would mean God was full of the Holy Spirit and if the parts are truly equal then they could be reversed and we could say the Holy Spirit was filled with Jesus or that God was filled with Jesus. This theory of the trinity is really getting freaky the more it's examined and this particular concept has made me feel ill just contemplating the implications. It is disgusting to consider God to be in such a way.

If according to the bible Jesus were truly God or the co-equal part of a trinity, then the names of each can be interchanged without altering the meaning of text. If both are divine then what is said about God can be said about Jesus and vice versa. The following table includes verses of the bible some which are even alleged to have been said by Jesus describing himself or God. In the second column they are as they exist in the bible, in the third column God is interchanged with Jesus. If Jesus is God or part of a trinity the change should be unnoticeable and the meaning should remain the same.

| Bible Verse | As is in the text. | If Jesus were God or part of a trinity. |
|---|---|---|
| John 14:28 | *You heard me say, 'I am going away and I am coming back to you.' If you loved me, you would be glad that I am going to the Father, for the Father is greater than I.* | You heard God say, 'God is going away and God is coming back to you.' If you loved God, you would be glad that God is going to Jesus, for Jesus is greater than God. |
| Luke 2:49 | "*Why were you searching for me?*" *he asked.* "*Didn't you know I had to be in my Father's house?*" | "Why were you searching for me?" God asked. "Didn't you know God had to be in Jesus' house?" |
| John 5:19 | [19] *Jesus gave them this answer: "Very truly I tell you, the Son can do nothing by himself; he can do only what he sees his Father doing, because whatever the Father does the Son also does.* | God gave them this answer: "Very truly I tell you, God can do nothing by himself; God can do only what he sees Jesus doing, because whatever Jesus does God also does. |

| | | |
|---|---|---|
| Matthew 20:23 | Jesus said to them, "You will indeed drink from my cup, but to sit at my right or left is not for me to grant. These places belong to those for whom they have been prepared by my Father." | God said to them, "You will indeed drink from my cup, but to sit at my right or left is not for me to grant. These places belong to those for whom they have been prepared by Jesus." |
| John 5:43 | I have come in my Father's name, and you do not accept me; but if someone else comes in his own name, you will accept him. | God has come in Jesus' name, and you do not accept God; but if someone else comes in his own name, you will accept him. |
| Matthew 27:46 | About three in the afternoon Jesus cried out in a loud voice, "My God, my God, why have you forsaken me?" | About three in the afternoon God cried out in a loud voice, "My Jesus, my Jesus, why have you forsaken me?" |
| John 1:18 | No one has ever seen God, but the one and only Son, who is himself God and is in closest relationship with the Father, has made him known. | No one has ever seen Jesus, but the one and only God, who is himself Jesus and is in closest relationship with Jesus, has made him known. |
| Luke 22:69 | But from now on, the Son of Man will be seated at the right hand of the mighty God. | But from now on, God will be seated at the right hand of the mighty Jesus. |
| 1 Timothy 2:5 | For there is one God and one mediator between God and mankind, the man Christ Jesus, | For there is one Jesus and one mediator between Jesus and mankind, the man God, |

| John 3:16 | For God so loved the world that he gave his one and only Son, that whoever believes in him shall not perish but have eternal life. | For Jesus so loved the world that he gave his one and only God, that whoever believes in him shall not perish but have eternal life. |
|---|---|---|
| Mark 13:32 | But about that day or hour no one knows, not even the angels in heaven, nor the Son, but only the Father. | But about that day or hour no one knows, not even the angels in heaven, nor God but only Jesus. |
| Ephesians 3:7-10 | I became a servant of this gospel by the gift of God's grace given me through the working of his power. ⁸ Although I am less than the least of all the Lord's people, this grace was given me: to preach to the Gentiles the boundless riches of Christ, ⁹ and to make plain to everyone the administration of this mystery, which for ages past was kept hidden in God, who created all things. | I became a servant of this gospel by the gift of Jesus' grace given me through the working of his power. Although I am less than the least of all Jesus' people, this grace was given me: to preach to the Gentiles the boundless riches of God and to make plain to everyone the administration of this mystery, which for ages past was kept hidden in Jesus, who created all things. |
| Ephesians 2:10 | For we are God's handiwork, created in Christ Jesus to do good works, which God prepared in advance for us to do. | For we are Jesus' handiwork, created in God to do good works, which Jesus prepared in advance for us to do. |
| Ephesians 1:3 | Praise be to the God and Father of our Lord Jesus Christ, who has blessed us in the heavenly realms | Praise be to the Jesus and Son of our Lord God, who has blessed us in the heavenly |

| | | |
|---|---|---|
| | *with every spiritual blessing in Christ.* | realms with every spiritual blessing in God. |
| Hebrews 5:4-5 | *And no one takes this honor on himself, but he receives it when called by God, just as Aaron was.*<br><br>*⁵ In the same way, Christ did not take on himself the glory of becoming a high priest. But God said to him, "You are my Son; today I have become your Father."* | And no one takes this honor on himself, but he receives it when called by Jesus, just as Aaron was.<br><br>In the same way, God did not take on himself the glory of becoming a high priest. But Jesus said to him, "You are my God; today I have become your Jesus." |
| 1 John 2:1 | *My dear children, I write this to you so that you will not sin. But if anybody does sin, we have an advocate with the Father — Jesus Christ, the Righteous One.* | My dear children, I write this to you so that you will not sin. But if anybody does sin, we have an advocate with the Jesus — God, the Righteous One. |
| Luke 6:12 | *¹² One of those days Jesus went out to a mountainside to pray, and spent the night praying to God.* | One of those days God went out to a mountainside to pray, and spent the night praying to Jesus. |
| John 6:38 | *For I have come down from heaven not to do my will but to do the will of him who sent me* | For God has come down from heaven not to do his will but to do the will of Jesus who sent God |
| John 20:17 | *Jesus said, "Do not hold on to me, for I have not yet ascended to the Father. Go instead to my* | God said, "Do not hold on to me, for I have not yet ascended to Jesus. Go instead to my |

| | | | |
|---|---|---|---|
| | | brothers and tell them, 'I am ascending to my Father and your Father, to my God and your God.'" | brothers and tell them, 'I am ascending to my Son and your Son, to my Jesus and your Jesus.'" |
| Philippians 2:9-11 | | *Therefore God exalted him to the highest place and gave him the name that is above every name, <sup>10</sup> that at the name of Jesus every knee should bow, in heaven and on earth and under the earth, <sup>11</sup> and every tongue acknowledge that Jesus Christ is Lord, to the glory of God the Father.* | Therefore Jesus exalted God to the highest place and gave him the name that is above every name, that at the name of God every knee should bow, in heaven and on earth and under the earth, and every tongue acknowledge that God is Lord, to the glory of Jesus the son. |
| Hebrews 2:9 | | *But we do see Jesus, who was made lower than the angels for a little while, now crowned with glory and honor because he suffered death, so that by the grace of God he might taste death for everyone.* | But we do see God, who was made lower than the angels for a little while, now crowned with glory and honor because he suffered death, so that by the grace of Jesus he might taste death for everyone. |

According to those who say Jesus was God the third column makes perfect sense and is hardly discernible from the second. Or at least that's what they claim to believe until they actually see that it's impossible. Honestly does the third column sound like God is godlike to you? Likewise does the second column sound like Jesus is godlike to you? The truth becomes clearer the closer one looks at it. Now do you seriously consider the third column to be true information? If Jesus and God are one almighty being as part of a trinity then it must be, haven't you ever heard some Christian tell you that Jesus said "*Before Abraham was, I am*"? Although "I am" is a sentence fragment and doesn't of itself mean anything, the authenticity of which is also dubious, the true meaning is simple to understand. It means that before Abraham physically existed Jesus existed in the knowledge of God, just as Moses existed in the knowledge of God, as did you and I. Before Abraham was physically alive, we existed. Biblically Jesus wasn't the only person after Abraham who existed before Abraham. In an English translation of the New International Version of the bible Jerimiah 1:4-5 say Jeremiah wrote: [4] *The word of the* LORD *came to me, saying,*[5] "*Before I formed you in the womb I knew you, before you were born I set you apart; I appointed you as a prophet to the nations.*"

Proverbs 8:23-27 say the prophet Solomon wrote:

[23] *I was formed long ages ago, at the very beginning, when the world came to be.* [24] *When there were no watery depths, I was given birth, when there were no springs overflowing with water;*[25] *before the mountains were settled in place, before the hills, I was given birth,*[26] *before he made the world or its fields or any of the dust of the earth.* [27] *I was there when he set the heavens in place, when he marked out the horizon on the face of the deep*"

Since some Christians use the statement of Jesus found in John saying he existed before Abraham was on earth to mean he is God, then according to the same methodology the humans Jeremiah and Solomon are also God too. So, does that mean God has 5 parts or 3 sons or what? Maybe these statements just mean what they say and don't mean what Christians want them to mean. The doctrine of the trinity, or of Jesus being a divinity, can never be accepted by a rational human being if they seriously think about it. Nor can it be accepted by anyone who actually reads the bible in context. Anyone who read the bible verses of Jeremiah and Proverbs and John would see that this alleged statement by Jesus is no different than what other 100% humans have said in the bible. The problem occurs because people don't read the bible, they get told Jesus is God because of X verse and don't realize lots of other humans in the bible said X too. Instead they will memorize the Jesus X verse, base their whole life on their incorrect understanding and expect that X verse is the reason why people believe Jesus is God forgetting that they already believed Jesus was God before they ever heard of the X verse of Jesus. Instead of having reasons to justify their belief, Christians use bible verses as excuses for why they believe something. The more you think about the trinity the less sense it makes and the more of a mess it is, that's why Christians are always strictly taught that *"the trinity is a mystery and is something we will never know, you just have to believe"*. However most every Christian has heard we are to *"know, love and serve the Lord with all your heart, mind and soul"*. If we had to believe in a trinity god and know, love and serve him with all our "heart, mind and soul" then Jesus being part of the trinity would have given detailed information so that the knowledge would be known. To know God means that God is not a mystery. If God is a mystery to you then that means you don't know God. How can you love or serve a being whom you don't know? You can't, which is why a Trinitarian religion is an ungodly form of disbelief created by Satan. Anyone who believes in a trinity doesn't believe in God, they may ardently say they do but to them God is a mystery; one who believes in a mystery is admitting that they don't know what they believe. If you don't know what you believe then you certainly don't know God. If you don't know God you cannot *"know, love and serve your Lord with all you heart, mind and soul."*

We must know the object of our affection, and service to the object of affection comes naturally to one in love. Plain logic dictates knowledge precedes love. What if I told you I was in love with a girl and you asked me "*who?*" and I said I don't know. Then what would you say? I'm guessing something like "*What do you mean you don't know who you're in love with?!*" What would be your response if I then told you, "*The reason I don't know who, is because it's a mystery.*" You would say that if that were the case then I'm not in love, because if I didn't know the person then that person cannot possibly know that I love them. Given what has been discussed thus far about the trinity and Christianity then I'm sure you would agree that if people actually had to serve God and know God then there would be a lot less people who called themselves Christians. Serving God means following the rules. People would prefer to get into paradise without following the rules if they can; they can't, but they like to think they can. A man-made religion would shape its doctrine to these desires of people who want to enter paradise without following any of the rules or suffering any of the hardships. Knowledge precedes action; you cannot serve something you don't know, unless you are doing so unknowingly. Although if you are unknowingly serving God then it's not being done out of sincerity and if you are not serving God sincerely then there is no reward for it. Simply put you must know your deity in order to worship it. It is impossible to worship a mystery. A being who desires to be worshiped would not shroud himself in mystery. Of course, we may not know every minute detail about God in this life, but God would provide enough for us to know just what it is we are worshipping. Thus, we know what God wants us to know and God has kept it very simple, God was never a mystery and Jesus never said he or God was unknowable.

1 Kings 8:60-61 *"so that all the peoples of the earth may know that the* LORD *is God and that there is no other. And may your hearts be fully committed to the* LORD *our God, to live by his decrees and obey his commands, as at this time."*

Isaiah 43:10-11 *"You are my witnesses," declares the* LORD, *"and my servant whom I have chosen, so that you may know and believe me and understand that I am he. Before me no god was formed, nor will there be one after me.*<sup>11</sup> *I, even I, am the* LORD, *and apart from me there is no savior."*

Isaiah 46:9-12 " <sup>9</sup> *Remember the former things, those of long ago; I am God, and there is no other;*
*I am God, and there is none like me.*
<sup>10</sup> *I make known the end from the beginning,*
 *from ancient times, what is still to come.*
*I say, 'My purpose will stand, and I will do all that I please.'*
<sup>11</sup> *From the east I summon a bird of prey;  from a far-off land, a man to fulfill my purpose.  What I have said, that I will bring about; what I have planned, that I will do.* <sup>12</sup> *Listen to me, you stubborn-hearted,  you who are now far from my righteousness."*

     God says there is none like him, meaning no shamrock, no egg, no water, no man, no woman, no triangle, no nothing. There is nothing like God and there is no other, apart from God the Creator of all there is no savior. The verses say God said, *"I will do all that I please"*. Biblically Jesus wanted to eat a fig from a fig tree, but it wasn't in season and had no figs, therefore he was unable to eat a fig as would have pleased him. God is not a liar and is not like any other. Jesus did not do all he pleased and is comparable to many other humans. Biblically speaking Jesus is not a savior, or the Lord, or God. Maybe he is the man, but he's not from a far-off land from the perspective of Isaiah. Who is this man from a far-off land? It is clearly a man that has been promised and planned for. The trouble is that many people don't think. When people are told something over and over since birth, they base their afterlife on what they're told without doing research. It is a well-known fact that more than 70% of people who call themselves Christians will never read the entire bible as long as they live. That means they believe something to be true when they haven't even read it. If any Christian seriously opened their bibles and read it through (if they even have one) they would never go to church again, because church teachings about God and Jesus contradict the bible except for a few select verses, which are the ones they say in church and in movies. I experienced this firsthand and stopped going to church, of which I was previously a daily visitor before I read the bible. Seriously if someone told you that someone else you never met bought you a ticket to heaven long before you were born and all you have to do is say and believe that they paid your way in order to enter eternal paradise, you could not dream up a better offer yourself. However, anyone would tell you it sounds too good to be true and probably isn't, but most people don't want to think that they've been scammed or duped. So, they never examine the details of the donor or if the tickets were really paid for as a third party not witness to the payment had told them. When they die believing their way has been prepaid, they will find out the gates of paradise are closed and that they had been deceived by Satan manipulating their desires.

  According to the bible Jesus is not the firstborn son of God, is not the one and only son of God and biblically the son of God is a figurative statement never to be understood in a literal sense. Some may play word games and try to say that there is a difference between "son of god" and "son of God". Although the examples given are unaffected by this trick, this excuse itself is incorrect because in Hebrew there are no capital or lowercase letters, there is only one case. Since there is only one form of God in the Hebrew language the bible allegedly came from there is no difference of case as such linguistic tricksters would suggest. If Jesus is the son of God, it is not literal, it is just an honorable title that can be and biblically has been attained by others as well. The Aramaic word for "son of God" is "bar dalaha" however this has many meanings and is typically used to refer to an orphan, a meek young man, a peacemaker, or a good kind pious individual, but never a divine son in the literal sense. Jesus never claimed to be "the only begotten son" because it contradicts the Torah and Zabur; this claim is exclusive to the mistranslated gospel of "John". The term "only begotten" is found as a translation of the word "monogenes" in the Greek gospel of John. "Monos" means singular "genos" means kind; it literally means one of a kind. In the Aramaic gospel of John the word is "Ehedaya" which means "beloved". So, when people say the gospel of John says "only begotten son" that's not true, because the ancient Greek, Aramaic and modern English versions don't as well as other bibles, so what source did they use to get *"only begotten son"* from when it is not in the ancient Greek or Aramaic translations? What gospel of "John" did they translate/mistranslate from? Biblically "sonship" of God was always a spiritual relationship between God and a human being based on love, respect and conditional upon doing the will of God, it actually meant the person was a *"friend of God"*. The Jews waiting for the Messiah had absolutely no inkling there was a trinity or that the Christ would literally be a son of God and such beliefs contradict Judaism, the Torah and Zabur. Many will take the Old Testament out of context and use verses trying to make it seem the Christian idea of Jesus was previously foretold. Yet biblically Jesus repeatedly quoted scripture, however Jesus never quotes previous scripture declaring his coming or his divinity, sonship of God or any of the verses Christians today use to try to justify their beliefs. If these oft quoted verses of previous scriptures actually meant what Christians claim then why didn't Jesus quote them as proof when he knew these very scriptures himself? Jesus did know these scriptures, didn't he?

Most every Christian has heard the famous bible story of Jesus fasting in the desert and being tempted by Satan which is found in the Gospel of Matthew 4:1-11,"*Then Jesus was led by the Spirit into the wilderness to be tempted by the devil.* ² *After fasting forty days and forty nights, he was hungry.* ³ *The tempter came to him and said, "If you are the Son of God, tell these stones to become bread."* ⁴ *Jesus answered,* **"It is written: 'Man shall not live on bread alone**, *but on every word that comes from the mouth of God."* ⁵ *Then the devil took him to the holy city and had him stand on the highest point of the temple.* ⁶ *"If you are the Son of God," he said, "throw yourself down. For it is written: "'He will command his angels concerning you, and they will lift you up in their hands, so that you will not strike your foot against a stone."* ⁷ *Jesus answered him,* **"It is also written: 'Do not put the Lord your God to the test."** ⁸ *Again, the devil took him to a very high mountain and showed him all the kingdoms of the world and their splendor.* ⁹ *"All this I will give you," he said, "if you will bow down and worship me."* ¹⁰ *Jesus said to him,* **"Away from me, Satan! For it is written: 'Worship the Lord your God, and serve him only."** ¹¹ *Then the devil left him, and angels came and attended him.*"

Interestingly this chapter begins by saying "*Jesus was led by the Spirit*" to be tempted by the devil. In Islam the "Holy Spirit" is the angel Gabriel. Whereas in Trinitarian Christianity "the spirit" is thought to be the spirit part of the trinity. However, this didn't use to be the case, for thousands of years Christians didn't believe nor did they claim to believe in a "holy spirit", instead they believed in a "holy ghost". Yes, a ghost was the third part of the trinity. All the Christian prayers which include the words "Holy Spirit" today used to say "Holy Ghost" but they just changed the words of their prayers when they changed their belief. The ghost was changed into a spirit because the masses began to realize God is not 33% ghost and bible verses like these which refer to a "spirit" could then be re-interpreted to promote the trinity doctrine. If this "spirit" is part of the trinity then that means God is leading Jesus to be tempted by the devil, despite the "Our Father" prayer which the bible says Jesus taught and that he prayed daily to God saying "*lead us not into temptation but deliver us from evil*". Also remember Trinitarians include Jesus as part of the trinity godhead, with their understanding this verse would mean that one part of God led another part of God to be tempted by the devil, despite that part of God praying to himself daily that his other parts "*lead us not into temptation*". Therefore, if Jesus were God, then God is acting against his own desires by leading himself into temptation while simultaneously praying to himself not to be led into temptation. This is a very confusing contradicting concept if you believe in the trinity. It is also significant to note that Jesus was fasting because the majority of people who claim to be Christians living today have never fasted a day in their life, but they claim that Jesus is their role model. Also, if Jesus were God, then why would he be sacrificing his appetite and suffering hunger and thirst? Who is he trying to please? Himself? On top of that how is it possible for God to even have an appetite? That would be a divine appetite, and there's nothing to suggest any prophet ever taught God ate or drank, or was able to get hungry or thirsty. Yet John 19:28 says "*Jesus said "I am thirsty"*". Nevertheless, in the story related in the gospel of Matthew, Satan approaches Jesus saying: "*If you are the Son of God, tell these stones to become bread._" Jesus answered, "It is *written: 'Man shall not live on bread alone, but on every word that comes from the mouth of God."* Satan knows God and knows whether God has children so if Jesus were a literal son of God Satan would be well aware of it and would not ask "If". However, "son of God" as has been previously explained doesn't mean "son of God" but means "friend of God". Now Satan doesn't know who the friends of God are, because as with any friendship it is liable to change. If a person does everything God loves then they could qualify to be a friend of God, but then if they start sinning and worshipping others than God the next day that friendship would be over and such an idolater would be hated by God unless they changed their ways. Thus, to be a *"friend of God"* is a high honor that must be constantly maintained and as long as one is alive it can potentially be lost. The friends of God are sometimes given special abilities by God, but being the pious people they are they tend to hide these special abilities. God also commands the angels to love those whom he loves.  So, the angels know who the friends of God are, but Satan being a jinni, who unlike the angels has the freewill to disobey God, would not be privy to this information. With this understanding it makes sense that Satan would ask Jesus to turn these stones to bread if he were the friend of God, because it would prove he was a friend of God to Satan yet at the same time it was a trap that could have led Jesus to become arrogant and get into the nasty habit of obeying Satan. If Jesus tried and failed Satan would make Jesus feel ashamed and think that he wasn't a friend of God and try to make him think God hated him so that Jesus would lose hope in the mercy of God, which is dangerous because only disbelievers lose hope in the mercy of God. This satanic question could go 2 ways. Either Satan would be able to make Jesus obey him and be arrogant and sinful potentially committing disbelief for knowingly performed a miracle to obey Satan (whom God explicitly told us not to obey and to treat as an enemy), or lead Jesus into disbelief by despairing of the mercy of God by thinking his inability to perform a miracle meant God hated him. Thus, whether Jesus successfully turns the stones into bread or not, if he tries to do so he would become a disbeliever. That is how tricky Satan is, he makes you think the test is about one thing when it really has nothing to do with that thing at all. Satan didn't care about stones or bread, he just said that because he knew Jesus was fasting and naturally would be hungry, thereby using his natural human and bodily desires as a tool in his war against a believer. In this there is a lesson in that Satan will not only use his own weapons against us, but he uses our own weaknesses and desires too. You see turning stones into bread technically was not a sin, so Satan wasn't asking Jesus to do something sinful, the sin was in doing something for the sake of Satan. From this we can learn that intentions themselves can make something sinful and even potentially turn a good deed into disbelief. Jesus answers, " It is written: 'Man shall not live on bread alone, but on every word that comes from the mouth of God ". If Jesus were a literal divine son his response makes absolutely no sense because it would have nothing to do with a divine being or the question being asked if "Son of God" meant son and not friend. Whereas if Jesus were 100% human, not God and not a divine literal son of God and "son of God" means friend of God, then this is a great practically flawless answer which is humble in that it implicitly shows Jesus considers himself a human with God as his sustainer, not the things of this world, while teaching and reminding Satan of the words of God, also not responding to Satan's attempts to find out whether Jesus is a friend of God or not. Also, that the bible says "*It is written*" may signify a mistake in the biblical text or it could be that Satan quoted an error so Jesus responded in kind, teaching how if Satan's quote should be followed then so should his quote.

Thus, Satan was taking text out of context that might have been man-made which doesn't even conform to another possibly man-made text. Or we could assume that these "*It is written*" phrases were the actual dialogue and didn't signify mistakes in the texts. However, by Jesus teaching man is to live on "*every word that comes from the mouth of God*" it teaches that according to Jesus divine revelation is something that comes from the mouth of God. Thus, technically it doesn't matter what is written, because if it's not God's literal speech then it's not divine revelation or at least this is the biblical Jesus' definition of divine revelation. Christians would disagree and say "*every word that comes from the mouth of God*" actually doesn't mean words from the mouth of God but words written by various humans allegedly inspired by a "Holy Spirit". Notice Jesus didn't feel pressure to clarify his relationship with God to Satan because he doesn't care what Satan thinks of him, he literally doesn't even respond to Satan's question; which is actually a genuine question asked out of Satan's ignorance. Also, it indicates Jesus didn't care about Satan worshipping God as there is no effort made to convert him, particularly to a Christian theology. However, Satan is persistent and never stops in his mission trying to mislead humans no matter how many times he fails.

"*Then the devil took him to the holy city and had him stand on the highest point of the temple.* ⁶ "*If you are the Son of God,*" *he said,* "*throw yourself down. For it is written:* '*'He will command his angels concerning you, and they will lift you up in their hands, so that you will not strike your foot against a stone.*" ⁷ *Jesus answered him,* "*It is also written: 'Do not put the Lord your God to the test.*'""

Next the gospel says "*the devil took him*". Some people think Jesus is God despite the "him", this means such people actually believe "*Satan took God*". This is a satanic idea in itself to think that Satan would have power over God to be able to physically take him, especially against his own will because Jesus did not ask Satan to take him anywhere, Satan did it without permission. Also, if Jesus were God, then how ridiculous is it for Satan to tell God to attempt suicide and that God will save him? Not even Satan is that stupid as to tell God to try to kill yourself because you will save yourself. God cannot die, he is immortal, therefore he cannot attempt suicide and likewise cannot save himself because he is never endangered. This also shows that Satan wanted Jesus to die. Again, Satan tries to get Jesus to prove he is the friend of God, this time by attempting suicide hoping God will command the angels to save him. This is because it is well known that when friends of God are in trouble God will save them if they aren't meant to die and enter paradise at that time, frequently God sends angels to save them. On top of that Satan disguises this test to make it seem like he's asking Jesus to fulfill a specific prophecy. In context Satan quotes Psalm 91:11 which is about how anyone who says God is their only refuge and desires to dwell in the Most High place of paradise will be protected by God and never fear anything whether it's their enemy, disease, poverty or animals. The verse Satan told Jesus to fulfill was one which said: "*He will command his angels concerning you, and they will lift you up in their hands, so that you will not strike your foot against a stone.*" Thus Satan goads Jesus making him think he is supposed to do this if he really is a friend of God, also by doing so everyone in the holy city will see this prophecy fulfilled and recognize him to be a friend of God and thus accept his prophethood. Thereby Satan uses his own ignorance of Jesus' status in God's sight as a tool against Jesus, trying to make him think Satan is unintentionally providing him a chance to fulfill his mission and guide all of Jerusalem into belief as God wants in the way God foretold. The reason I think this prophecy is actually about Jesus is because contrary to what Christians think, Jesus was literally lifted up to heaven by angels who were commanded to save Jesus from his enemies' plots to kill him without even having to run away, aka having his foot strike against a stone. Just look at what Psalm 91:14-16 say, "<u>Because he loves me</u>," says the LORD, "<u>I will rescue him; I will protect him</u>, for he acknowledges my name. 15 <u>He will call on me, and I will answer him</u>; I will be with him in trouble, <u>I will deliver him and honor him.</u> 16 <u>With long life I will satisfy him and show him my salvation</u>." But as usual Satan gives a false interpretation of this prophecy to Jesus himself, whom I believe these verses apply to. Ironically despite neither Muslims nor most Christians knowing about the context of Satan allegedly quoting Psalm 91:11 every single Muslim would completely agree that Jesus fulfills Psalm 91:14-16. Yet Christians would adamantly say Jesus doesn't fulfill those bible verses. Although Psalm 91:4 says God has feathers and wings so that part of Psalm 91 would be something Muslims don't believe is true, most Christians don't believe it's true either but that's because they don't know the bible, they claim to be the word of God says that God has feathers and wings. So that's why you got to be careful with the bible and can't hastily declare it to be true based on certain passages, because if you do then you might be saying God has feathers and wings without knowing that's what you are saying. As a reply to Satan, Jesus quotes scripture again citing a command of not putting "the Lord your God to the test". By saying this he is telling Satan that he is too humble to test God and prove his friendship with God and fears losing that friendship if he tests God. If the prophecy is about him it will come true how and when God decrees, Jesus isn't going to rush things and try to prove himself to the entire holy city, even though at the time they were stubbornly rejecting him. To Jesus it wasn't about whether people believed him or not, it was always about doing what God wanted, when and how God wanted, strictly for the sake of God. Jesus wasn't desperate to gain followers and wasn't concerned with how many he had. His response also indicates that Jesus either didn't know how the prophecy would be fulfilled, or it wasn't about him, personally I tend to think Jesus and Satan both knew it could be fulfilled by him but neither knew how it would be fulfilled. Yet Satan knew Jesus didn't know, thus he was exploiting that lack of knowledge about the future trying to bait Jesus taking advantage of Jesus knowing that God frequently uses Satan's plots against himself. So, you see Satan used his own extensive history of failures and plans that backfired as a weapon against Jesus. Thus, the response of Jesus is very potent by reminding Satan himself not to test the Lord using the words "your God" to remind Satan that God is his God too and shouldn't be tested. Which is what Satan is doing in that he is testing God's theory about humans, trying to prove to God that humans are ungrateful and will not worship or obey him despite all that God has done for us. Thereby Satan hopes to prove he is better than humans. After this if Jesus were God, then Satan would immediately stop testing him after being reminded, out of fear for the consequences. If Jesus were a literal son of God likewise Satan would stop testing him because the command of not testing God would also apply to any offspring. Also keep in mind this was a severe test for Jesus, in context he didn't have anything to eat or drink for 40 days! If you did that for 40 days and someone told you to jump off a building and God will send angels to save you, then you might actually consider it because of such a person's physical, mental and emotional state at that time. Many people would probably jump off a building even without being told angels would save them if they went just a week without food or drink. So, keep the physical state of Jesus in mind when he was being pestered by Satan, and no it doesn't mean that he was Superhuman or divine because the bible says he went so long without food or drink, and none of his followers made a big fuss about it either. Even today the Hindu Prahlad Jani has allegedly gone over 70 years without eating or drinking and claims the goddess Amba feeds him a special liquid elixir that drops down from an abnormal hole in his own palate. Scientists have even tested him and confirmed the guy doesn't eat or drink. Buddhists do the same going weeks, months and years in a trance-like meditative/hibernation state without food or drink. There is even an ideology called "Breatharianism" where people think humans don't need food or drink and can survive solely on air and sunlight. Yet some New Agers are even more extreme and believe in Sungazing, where they don't eat or drink but simply get energy by looking directly at the sun. They say you only need to stare directly at the Sun for 44 minutes a day to get "fully charged". Most cheat and some die trying it or go blind, but they publish so much material saying how powerful the "Sun of God" is, it makes me wonder whether Solar Power will eventually lead humans back to the pagan solar religions that worshipped the literal Sun of God that shines in the sky. Sungazers claim that humans will simply evolve and soon everyone will be getting their energy by staring at the sun instead of through food or drink. These "Sungazers" also have plans for global government based on "The Georgia Guidestones", aka America's Stonehenge, which say humanity should never exceed more than 500 million people so as to be in perpetual balance with nature and everyone should speak a new living language. So don't just dismiss Sungazers as crazy nutjobs, history is full of crazy nutjobs who did some serious damage. Anyways it is entirely possible that a 100% human Jesus literally went 40 days without food or drink. It doesn't mean Jesus isn't human, because both Elijah and Moses are said to have fasted 40 days too as 100% humans. It's not easy and none today should try it, I'm just saying Satan's tests are tricky enough but we often forget the physical aspect.

> *Again, the devil took him to a very high mountain and showed him all the kingdoms of the world and their splendor. 9 "All this I will give you,"* he said, *"if you will bow down and worship me."*

Yet since Jesus is not God, nor a son of God, Satan again takes Jesus without his permission to another place and offers him all the kingdoms of the world.  Keep in mind God created the universe and is already King of the universe.  If Jesus were God this offer wouldn't have been made.  Likewise, if Jesus were a son of God, Satan wouldn't offer it because the son of the king rules after the king and the kingdoms are hereditary.  Yet since God is immortal and doesn't perish there is none to inherit him, thus there is no need for any children.  Also since the world is the property and creation of God, then Satan doesn't even have the right to offer the world because it isn't Satan's property to begin with.  This is the way Satan works, he will offer you something that seems good which is temporary and not as good as it seems, yet he doesn't even own the thing he is offering, so you won't even get what he offers unless God wills you to get it through your own means.  This would be like me saying *"I'll sell you the sky"*, I don't own the sky so you'd be a fool to buy the sky from me just as we are fools to accept Satan's deceptive offers of pleasure through sin.  This time Satan isn't trying to get Jesus to prove he is the friend of God and is trying to offer him the world instead.  This is a trick that means Satan is trying to make Jesus think that Satan no longer thinks Jesus could ever be a friend of God and is being nice in offering him the world in order to compensate, trying to make Jesus feel better or be happy.  By doing this Satan is implying to Jesus that he thinks Jesus is doomed and has nothing waiting for him in the next life and must maximize his pleasure in this life. Satan plays the same trick with us when we sin, making us think God won't forgive us so we might as well keep sinning before we go to hell, in reality this is the attitude that makes one go to hell whereas if we repent correctly we'd be forgiven. In exchange for the world Satan asks Jesus to *"bow down and worship me"*. In previous divine laws it was permissible to bow to someone out of respect, but in the final law God sent it was prohibited. Regardless bowing to Satan has always been forbidden for us, since God declared him to be an enemy. If Jesus didn't bow down it wouldn't be the same, Satan knows that whoever one bows down to then that is who you worship. This is why Muslims do not bow down for anyone except Allah, we don't bow to kings, queens, celebrities, statues, flags, Asians, judges, popes, bishops, imams, scholars, spouses or anything except when we pray to the one who created everything. Jesus, like all the prophets, was known to bow down when praying. Satan hoped that those who followed Jesus would imitate him and would have bowed down and worshiped Satan as well, because he knew that believers imitate the prophets and worship the way the prophets do. This was a genius plan of Satan where if successful would've corrupted the entire religion, but the plans of Satan will never thwart the plan of Allah. If Jesus was God, it is inconceivable to think that Satan, who knows God, knows he was created by God, fears God, has been repeatedly thwarted by God, is awaiting eternal punishment by God, and knows God forbids any to be worshiped but him, would ever dare to ask God to worship him. But this is what people who believe Jesus was God are saying, whether they realize it or not they believe that Satan asked God to worship Satan. Not even a Satanist is that stupid to believe such a blasphemous abominable outrage! The same follows if Jesus were a literal son of God, Satan would not ask a son of God to worship Satan instead of his father, it would never ever work. Given the cleverness of Satan's previous tricky temptations this idea of tempting a son of God to worship other than God would have been the worst and dumbest trick Satan ever tried to pull off. Of course, Satan is stupid, but he's not that stupid, however Satan would love for us to believe that he is that stupid in order for us to let our guard down.

> *"Jesus said to him, "Away from me, Satan! For it is written: 'Worship the Lord your God, and serve him only."*
> *"Then the devil left him, and angels came and attended him."*

Jesus blatantly recognizes Satan's deceptive offer which he can't deliver and tells him to get away and cites the first commandment given to Moses. Thereby informing Satan that he is firm and refuses to worship any other than the Creator, whether directly or indirectly, publicly or privately, regardless of what he's promised. Jesus also reminds Satan that he should likewise worship God and serve him rather than disobeying God, as Satan does. This would have made Satan momentarily despair and want to leave, not because a human said to, but because he would see that the more, he tries to misguide Jesus then the firmer Jesus becomes while also reminding Satan of how wrong he is every time. Thereby making Satan feel bad for being disobedient and jealous that he is not a friend of God. Then being a friend of God, the angels came and attended to Jesus, proving that Jesus is a friend of God after all. Where if we take the first verse of this chapter that refers to "the spirit" leading Jesus to be tempted, as meaning the angel Gabriel then this story makes perfect sense. Jesus is the friend of God and as a result close to the angel Gabriel, God instructs Gabriel to lead Jesus to Satan and leave him to be tested. From the perspective of Jesus, not knowing why the angel Gabriel was leaving after having been on a good relationship since Gabriel announced the conception of Jesus in the womb of his mother Mary, this sudden departure could have made Jesus despair and think he had done something wrong and was no longer a friend of God. Satan then would take advantage of these doubts and antagonize him goading him to do miracles "if he were the friend of God". Which if Jesus tried then by obeying Satan, he would have lost the friendship and wouldn't have been able to do such miracles. Also, if Jesus realized this plan of Satan, then Satan would hope that Jesus would have been tricked into thinking that he actually couldn't do the miracles anyway because he wasn't a friend of God and that was why Gabriel had suddenly left and Satan suddenly appeared. From the perspective of Jesus to go from angelic to satanic company in a split-second would have been drastic and liable to make him come to the conclusion Satan wanted, that would then make Jesus despair and become a disbeliever. This story proves beyond a doubt that Jesus was not God. As James 1:13-14 states: "[13] *When tempted, no one should say, "God is tempting me." For God cannot be tempted by evil, nor does he tempt anyone;* [14] *but each person is tempted when they are dragged away by their own evil desire and enticed.*" Neither was Jesus a literal "son of God", he was 100% human, humble, intelligent, and a friend of God. It also shows that God allows us to be tested sometimes in order to make us stronger in faith and better worshippers which also has the effect of spreading reminders and warnings to the satanic forces testing and harassing us by the permission and plan of God. But doesn't that bible verse say God doesn't test/tempt anyone, yes but Genesis 22:1 specifically says "*God tested Abraham.*", so either Abraham had an evil desire that led him to be tested as James would say, or God specifically tests people as Genesis says. It's just one more biblical contradiction. Or one could say temptation isn't a test at all, but everyone knows that's a false claim, especially since the prophet Joseph was tempted to commit sinful sex and that temptation is considered as a test.

However, it could just be that the Old Testament God is a different being than the New Testament God but by coincidence they have the same names. Notwithstanding the biblical contradiction, this shows that the friends of God and those whom God loves are tested most severely, even by Satan directly. Yet the rewards for passing these tests are substantial. The fact that Satan tested and harassed him reveals that Jesus wasn't God or a divine being, because the Creator cannot be harassed by his own creation Satan. Satan never treats Jesus as though he were the Creator or the Creator's kid. If Jesus were a literal divine son of God, he would have just told Satan that he was the son of God so he better knock it off before he or God punished him. But he wasn't so he didn't.

    If people say this was all just to show humans that Jesus was tested like everyone else is, then it is interesting to note that for being something meant to teach people this story has zero human witnesses aside from Jesus. This made the test even harder because Jesus wasn't being observed by people so no one would have known if he had given in to Satan. As a lesson for us this shows that Satan attacks most fiercely when we are in private and no person is watching us and we think nobody will ever find out if we indulge in sin. This also proves that Jesus was capable of sin and could potentially have worshiped Satan. God is not capable of sin nor is any theoretically impossible offspring of God capable of sin, if it were impossible for Jesus to sin then the devil wouldn't have even tried since there would be nothing to gain by it and he could potentially be exposed. This biblical story only makes sense if Jesus is 100% human. If Jesus is anything else this bible story is illogical, impossible, glorifies Satan and defames God and the theoretically impossible offspring of God. If God wanted to show people a lesson as some Christians claim, he would have eyewitnesses present. Although no human could have seen the angels or the devil take Jesus to the holy city and then to a high mountain, the author of Matthew is not an eyewitness. Either this story is divine revelation, or the events were told by Jesus to combat the claims people made against him claiming he was divine, or this story is fabricated, or if it's true then it came to be known through some other means. Either way if this bible story is false, it means that the bible is not the word of God, although Psalm 91:4 saying God has wings and feathers might be proof enough. Yet there is one huge problem with Matthew's gospel account, it contradicts Luke 4:5-12 which has a similar story but in a different order. In Luke's tale it says the devil first took Jesus to a high place/mountain THEN to Jerusalem. So, which was it did the devil take Jesus to Jerusalem first or a mountain? Or did they have the same exact conversation two separate times, just changing the order of places they visited with both pretending they never had that conversation before? Both versions can't be true. If either is then it means Jesus is 100% human and that he is not God, nor a literal son of God, but a humble role model who was at least at that moment in time a friend of God. May Jesus continue to be a friend of God and die as a friend of God. May we also become a friend of God, live as a friend of God and most importantly die as a friend of God. If God is our friend, then who cares if anyone else is? Whereas if every human of all time is our friend and God isn't, then who cares about human friends if you're not friends with God?

  What about all those miracles such as healing the blind, curing leprosy, feeding the masses with meager rations, or raising the dead? Certainly, these must mean Jesus is special, but they do not mean he is divine in any way. In fact, these miracles are not even exclusive to Jesus and previous human prophets have done similar miracles which are mentioned in the bible. The prophet Elisha in 2 Kings 6:15-23 is written to have healed the blind by the will of God. In 2 Kings 5:10-14 Elisha is credited with instructing a leper on what to do to be healed by the will of God. While 2 Kings 4:42-44 has Elisha feeding 100 men with only 20 loaves of bread by the will of God. Two times the bible says the prophet Elisha is said to have raised a dead boy back to life by the will of God in 1 Kings 17:20-23 and 2 Kings 4:30-36. Not only does the bible say Elisha raised the dead while he was alive, but the bible even has the dead bones of Elisha bringing the dead back to life by the will of God. As explained in 2 Kings 13:20-22, "**Elisha died and was buried.** *Now Moabite raiders used to enter the country every spring. Once while some Israelites were burying a man, suddenly they saw a band of raiders; so, they threw the man's body into Elisha's tomb.* **When the body touched Elisha's bones, the man came to life and stood up on his feet.** *Hazael king of Aram oppressed Israel throughout the reign of Jehoahaz."* This miracle mentioned in the bible is even more miraculous than that of Jesus because Jesus was alive when he brought back the dead, but Elisha is already dead, decomposed and a skeleton yet his bones perform a miracle from the grave by the will of God. In comparison to the miracles of Jesus, Elisha does similar feats if not greater because none were ever brought back to life via the bones of Jesus. It is important to remember that all these miracles were done by the will of God. The point is that miracles do not make one to be God, because even the antichrist will raise people from the dead by the will of God. If someone is to believe a person is God because they read, he raised someone from the dead, then Elisha would qualify more than Jesus, but because the bones of Elisha were also a tool used by God to do a miracle then it is obvious that raising from the dead doesn't make a person God. Many will be fooled by the antichrist who will do this very feat and then think he is God because of it.

Miracles are not a sign of divinity they are tests. Tests for the people who witness the miracles to determine whether they will correctly understand the source of the miracle and to see whether they will worship God as a result, or if they will reject God, or go to extremes in worshipping the conduit of the miracle. Unfortunately, those who claim Jesus is divine or God's son have failed this test as will those who claim the antichrist is divine. For Christ his miracles were a sign to show he was a human prophet. For the antichrist his powers and abilities are a test to see whether people will worship a human who claims to be God. That is why he is called the antichrist because his message is the opposite of Christ's. Christ said he was a human and told people to worship God, the antichrist is a human and will tell people he is the Creator and order mankind to worship him. Many Christians essentially believe in the doctrine of the antichrist already, but worship Jesus instead of the antichrist. The religion of the antichrist is like Christianity with the antichrist swapped in for Jesus, just as Christianity is like Mithraism and many other pagan religions with Jesus swapped in for Mithras, Osiris, Dionysius and others. There is a famous saying found in the bible that "*in the land of the blind the one-eyed man is king*". Well Muhammad was the first prophet to inform mankind that the antichrist is "one-eyed", blind in his right eye which will look like a floating grape. Between the eyes of the antichrist will be the word كافر or the separate letters of the word as ك ف ر which will be read by all the believers literate and illiterate. The antichrist is a very severe test for mankind, which is why it surprises me that many people desire to experience him. Especially Christians, since they deify Jesus because of his miracles which they have only read/heard about. When the antichrist comes and does the same miracles in front of their own eyes while commanding them to worship him then how will Christians be able to resist? I've asked Christians this and they respond *"because the bible says the antichrist will do it"* so they think they won't be tricked, although I'm unfamiliar with these alleged passages in the bible that say the antichrist will raise the dead. Whereas these same Christians likely don't even know their bibles say Elisha healed the blind, cured leprosy, fed the masses and raised the dead while alive and while bones, by the will of God. The follow up question they find difficult to answer is *"What happens when you are reading those verses in the bible, which you say are in there, before the antichrist and he uses his power to replace your translation with a different translation saying that since he is God, he can change the words of God and makes your bible translation say to worship him?"* In that moment the bible translation they are reading, or have replaced in their hands, would say to worship the antichrist, so what is a believer in the bible to do then? Since a translation is never the word of God and the translations we have today of the bible are constantly being updated and changed it would be easy for the antichrist to change the bible before a Christian's eyes, he might not even need to use any special abilities to do so if the bible is on an electronic format. Bible publishers might have already changed the bible to say to worship the antichrist by his name in the latest editions and most Christians wouldn't know since they don't read the bibles. This is why it is important to memorize the word of God in its original language so it is in one's heart and mind. Although the bibles cannot be memorized because the translations are still being revised and changed. If one were to memorize the bible, which I doubt is possible, their memorized version would soon be out of date as soon as that version was revised. A perfect example is John 3:16, many have memorized it only to have Christian scholars say what they memorized isn't authentic. So not only is it impossible to memorize the bibles, but it is dangerous to even try because you might memorize a lie. Sadly, Christians don't know that the antichrist will tell the world that he is God in human form, which is exactly what Trinitarians already believe and those who believe Jesus is the son of God think so because of learning about Jesus' miracles and say: "*God can do anything so why can't he have a son?*" To which a follower of the antichrist will easily convert them by saying: "*Since God can do anything then he can become a human too and he came to us as a human because some people didn't believe when he sent his son. Can't you see his miraculous power? If he can do that, as we have seen, then he must be God.*" And if such people where to say "*but the bible says*" then the antichrist follower will simply "*Well since God can do anything then he can change the rules too.*" While those who say "*We just have to wait until after we die to find out which religion is true.*" or "*I'll believe it when I see it.*" are the very same types who will worship the antichrist. I've also read apocalyptic Christian writings and some of them think and believe that Jesus will come back and defend the Jewish state of Israel, thereby proving himself to the Jews and thereafter the Jews, Christians and everyone except the Muslims will worship him together and then they will fight the Muslims for being Muslims. Seriously they actually write that everyone will believe in "Jesus" except for the Muslims. Which is frighteningly ironic because the Muslims think everyone will worship the antichrist except for Muslims. So unintentionally everyone agrees that it will be Muslims following Islam on one side and everyone else on the other side worshipping a human being. The only difference is that Christians and Muslims disagree which human all non-Muslims will worship, but they all agree Muslims won't worship a human no matter if its Jesus or not. Such apocalyptic Zionist Christians tend to not even mention an antichrist coming before Jesus, but just say that Christians should support Israel and kill the Muslims because they say that's what Jesus will do. Which doesn't even make sense because the state of Israel is killing

Christians too. Fortunately, other Christians are less deceived and can see how the Zionist state of Israel is not a state Jesus would support and actually oppose it, claiming Israel is a precursor to the antichrist. Now regarding the state of Israel today being a "sign of the end" this is not something Islam teaches. The Islamic "signs of the end" are clear and Muslims cannot twist them try to make them seem as though they all foretell our current times. Many minor signs have come and some haven't, but at the time of this writing zero of the major signs have occurred. All the minor signs must come before the major signs, and then the major signs will rapidly take place. While such stuff is important to know, how you live is more important because for most of us our end is when we die and we will likely die before the end of the world, so we should live the same regardless. Seriously if someone proved to you 100% that the end of the world was guaranteed to happen in 45 days what would you do differently? Your lifestyle shouldn't really change at all. You should be doing good and avoiding evil all the time and this is why God hasn't revealed to us the exact time, because if we knew then we'd be lazy in life saying, "*Hey, relax, just enjoy your life and have lots of fun, stop acting like it's the end of the world.*" People who make such statements are the types who know they will be in big trouble when this worldly life does end. Whereas since our personal end is more likely to occur to us today than the end of the world, we should be acting on a daily basis like we are about to meet our maker by being repentant and pious, so we aren't in big trouble when it happens. Acting "like it's the end of the world" doesn't mean acting crazy, or uptight, it means being virtuous. As a sidenote, only the worst of disbelievers will be alive at the end of the world. This is because when the true religion is no longer available there will be no point for God letting the world continue since humans are created to worship him. Soon after God permanently removes guidance from the world it will be destroyed. So, if you plan on going to paradise and not going to hell, then you will die before the end of the world. Prepare for your end today, because today might be your day. Those who support Israel today think it is a sign of the end and do so for religious reasons, just as the popes told Christians to crusade because it was allegedly a sign of the end, although most pretend it's not for religious reasons because they want secular support. Most unislamic end times theories are specially crafted to lead one to think that certain people should be killed, or to promote political agendas, or that their religious books eerily and flawlessly predicted everything up until the present and thus must also predict the future, or that the end of the world will surely come in your lifetime so you must pay attention to them and join/ buy their stuff which has data you "*need to know*". What's most ironic regarding religious doctrines is that the religion of Christianity is the religion of the antichrist.

> Acts 2:22 has Peter say, "*Fellow Israelites, listen to this: Jesus of Nazareth was a man accredited by God to you by miracles, wonders and signs, which God did among you through him, as you yourselves know.*"

This verse in the English translation of the New International version of the bible has Peter, who is thought to have been the closest disciple of Jesus, preaching to the Israelites, not pagans, about Jesus. What does Peter, known as "*the rock of the church*", say about Jesus? Peter says that "*Jesus of Nazareth was a man*", this is straight from the bible allegedly said by Peter to the Jews. In order to prevent thoughts that it might be out of context Peter continues to say, " *accredited by God to you by miracles, wonders and signs, which God did among you through him,*" According to the bible Peter taught that Jesus was a man who was sent by God and given miracles by God to give him credibility. Peter explains Jesus did not do these miracles of his own power, but all the miracles were done by God through Jesus. No Muslim would disagree with this biblical description of Jesus, every prophet was like this, they were humans sent by God supported by miracles done by God through the actions of these prophets. According to biblical Peter, miracles do not make someone a God, or a son of God, or anyway more than a human. According to the bible, the top apostle of Jesus taught that *"Jesus of Nazareth was a man"*. The bible doesn't say Peter told Jews that Jesus was God or a son of God, but just that he was a man sent by God supported by God with miracles as proof which the Jews denied. Most Christians would say to think Jesus to be a mere man is blasphemous and such a person will burn in hell, but this is exactly what the bible says that Peter said. Also, if as people claim that the miracles of Jesus were meant to prove his divinity, then why are most of them done in private and not public with Jesus always instructing people not to tell? Of course he was humble, but if he were God and as God wanted people to worship him then he would be trying to generate as much publicity for his signs as possible so that people would believe. The same applies if Jesus were a son of God, he would be obligated to generate publicity for his miracles in order to communicate his divine lineage to the people. On the other hand, if Jesus were a man who only did miracles to genuinely help people, then he would want them to be kept a secret so that he didn't become arrogant, or have the publicity that might make people think he was more than human. Since all the pagan half-human deities were also thought to have done miracles Jesus would have been cautious of public miracles out of fear for being deified, especially since he didn't have a father. Some take the opposite interpretation that despite the bible saying Peter said Jesus was a man they say he was God incarnate who desires all to worship him and did miracles to prove he was God, but then didn't want people to tell others God had healed them in the form of Jesus because God didn't want people to worship him while he was on earth. This makes no sense even though it's recited in churches on a daily basis. Not only does it make no sense, but most of the bible says the opposite of what gets preached from Christian pulpits.

    The bible practically skips over 27 years of the life of Jesus. Now if this were God on earth, or even if it were the son of God, do you think "the word of God" would neglect to mention 27 years worth of the history of God or his son being on earth? A divinity on earth would be doing miraculous things every second! Everything he said would be "the word of God" and important to know. Yet some would have us believe that God was on earth for nearly 30 years and nobody knew it, even though God wants all people to worship him. Don't you think if Jesus were God that he would go to the pagans directly and tell them to stop what they were doing and worship him before they died? Yet Jesus is not once said to have instructed anyone to worship him anywhere in the bible. Not one verse. Large financial rewards have been offered for anyone who can bring one verse from the bible that has Jesus saying that he is God and should be worshiped, but these rewards have never been claimed because no bible has Jesus claiming to be God or telling people to pray to him. If Jesus were God, then what was he doing on earth in obscurity for so long? Jesus was so obscure to the people of his day that the bible says the Romans had to send one of his own disciples to identify him because they didn't know what Jesus looked like. Do you really think a man-God who wants to be worshiped would be so unpopular that even his mortal enemies don't know what he looked like? If Jesus was sent to the world in order for the world to worship him then he certainly did a very poor publicity campaign because the historians and philosophers of his time didn't even know he existed. Don't you think if God had become a man that he would go straight to the leaders of the world and prove his divinity to them and get the word out so all would know? The fact that Jesus during his own time on earth was humble and obscure of his own initiative shows he is not God or a literal son of God because God is not obscure and is glorified above all. If God were on earth, he would never suffer another being to be treated with more respect than him or to be ruled over. The verse about Jesus allegedly saying to give to Caesar what is Caesar's also proves Jesus wasn't God because God is the owner of everything; God wouldn't say that Caesar owned anything of what God had created. Some people go even further than this and claim that God in the form of Jesus was judged by Roman law. This is ludicrous! God is the law giver, remember the saying *"Only God can judge me"*? Well, that means nobody can judge God, or a "son of God" under any human legal system. If people say Jesus was judged under Roman law and sentenced then that would disqualify Jesus from being God or a literal son of God in any way, shape or form. Because for God to allow himself or his son to be judged by man-made laws would give the man-made laws legitimacy and be a relinquishment of God's own authority to make laws. It is absurd to imagine God or a son of God being put on trial and judged by the very beings God created. What kind of God would get judged and sentenced by his own creation? Not the God who created Paradise and Hell, who will judge all of humanity and sentence them to stay eternally in one of those two places which he created.

      What about modern-day statues speaking saying Jesus is God? Almost every Christian knows of at least one story of some Christian statue that cried, bled, opened its eyes, moved, spoke or some other "miracle", which they most likely haven't personally witnessed, but regardless they take it to mean Christianity is true. If this is a sign of the truth then what do we make of the undisputable documented fact that statues of Buddha miraculously speak and move without human involvement witnessed by many who recorded it on video? Does this mean Buddhism is true too? What about the Hindu statues of Ganesh who starting drinking milk and caused milk prices in New Delhi to rise by 30% on 9/21/1995 CE. This phenomenon reportedly happened to many Ganesh statues simultaneously around the world, where Hindus lifted milk up to their idol's trunk and it would go up into the statue. Several scientists have stated it was just a capillary action with surface action causing the milk to go up and then gravity sending it down. However, in Trinidad Hindu pictures actually drank milk! Yes, actual pictures were sipping milk from spoons. It happened throughout Hindu temples and homes with Hindus feeding milk to their pictures. Scientists are baffled as to how to explain it. Does this mean Hinduism is true because Hindu statues and pictures drink milk? What about those plants that grow and say the word "Jesus" on them or look like those famous statues? What about the Muslim vegetables that have the name of Allah on them? Remember not all these religions can be true. How can these unnatural occurrences concerning the statues of numerous faiths be explained? Well let's start with what is perhaps the most famous incident of a statue doing something unnatural. In the middle east a group of people in the desert had melted all their golden jewelry and made a statue of a golden cow. This happened during the time of Moses and the Israelites did this while he was away. The excuse they gave Moses for doing this was because when they left Egypt they had brought the peoples' ornaments with them. This shows the dangers of carrying "extra baggage" from a sinful life/environment along with you. At the time there were no mp3s, cds, radios, audio recording devices or electronics, yet this golden cow mooed. Scriptures testify to this unnatural incident by stating the golden cow the Israelites made emitted a mooing sound. As one might expect, people thought that since statues can't make sounds then this Cow must be a god and they began to worship it because it mooed. When Moses came back the idol was destroyed and the idolaters punished, however the fact still remains that the golden idol mooed. How did this happen? Scholars have explained that one of the Jinn went inside the golden cow and made the mooing sound purposely to mislead the people, anticipating the idolatrous effect making such a sound as a cow makes would have. This is a perfect example of Jinn misleading people with petty tricks, the statue was still a statue, it doesn't matter how many bells and whistles it has, a statue is not divine. When Moses returned, he even had a commandment that no statues or images of any animate beings were to exist, so from a Judeo-Christian-Islamic perspective, it is against the command of God to even have a statue in the first place. Since God prohibited statues and images then that means God is not going to use them to "prove his religion". Since Jinn can easily use these statues and pictures for tricks, God instructed them to be abolished to protect us from such deception. By a statue doing something "special and unnatural" it is not God using a statue he forbid to send a message, it is a Jinni using a statue God had prohibited to increase devotion to the forbidden object and mislead people into a false religion based on flimsy pretenses. We must remember the goal of Satan is to get us to follow the wrong religion, disobey God and worship other than the Creator. If all it takes for him to persuade a human to do that is to get a statue to bleed, talk, move, cry or whatever, then we are making Satan's job way too easy. If an unnatural statue is a proof of the true religion, then the idolatrous Israelites who worshiped the golden cow would have been practicing the true religion; but we know they were not. So don't be fooled by Satanic statues or pictures. That's actually where many of the pagan idols and mythologies originate from, because Jinn appeared in various forms doing supernatural things so pagans thought they were gods and worshipped them.

What about Christian exorcisms? Not the movies, I'm referencing actual real-life demonic possession where the demon leaves after a Christian minister intervenes. I once studied to be a Catholic Exorcist and read that this stuff happens. Does that mean Christianity is true? Well Muslims, Jews, Hindus, Buddhists and Pagans all have their rites of exorcism too. It may surprise you to learn that all types of exorcism work. But they work for different reasons. Remember the goal of a demon is to get a person to worship something other than God and follow the wrong religion, if they can harass a person then that's a bonus but their number one priority is to make someone believe in a false religion. So, let's say there is a pagan person who gets possessed by an evil Jinni, which would be considered a devil, science can't explain it and without a doubt it is a demonic possession. The person being a pagan goes to their pagan priest to be exorcised and have the demon cast out. After a dramatic encounter the demon finally leaves at the behest of the pagan priest. Then what? The person being freed from the demon credits this pagan religion as being what caused this demon to leave and he devotes himself wholeheartedly to this pagan faith for the rest of his life telling everyone his exciting story of being possessed and saved by the power of his pagan deity. Is this not the exact result the demon wanted? So, when a priest is standing over a person with a cross telling the demon to leave in the name of Christ, that demon has absolutely no reason to leave and the priest has no power over it no matter how much the demon may pretend to be hurt by whatever the priest says or does. Remember these demons can make statues talk and move; they can be quite theatrical when they want to be. The demon possessing this person wants the experience to be traumatic for the victim and everyone involved, especially if the people subscribe to a false religion. In that case the more publicity the demon can get the better, although they are careful to not make it seem like they are trying to get attention lest it betray their plot. The demon wants the person to follow a false religion, so when a priest puts up a cross the demon looks and thinks, *"If I leave right now and never return, this person will believe this cross saved them and the priest is truthful and that Christianity is true despite it being false. I want this person to follow a false religion and all who hear this person's story will think Christianity is true because I left. So I will leave."* The priest then credits Christianity with the victory just as the demon desired and as with other false religions people believe in the false doctrines even more, as a result of the formerly possessed sharing their story. Islamic exorcisms are different and the Jinn are revealed for who they are. The Jinn in a Muslim exorcism are treated for what they are, free-willed creations of God. Sometimes the Jinni is being forced against their will to possess someone because of a magician who is oppressing them. Sometimes the person unintentionally harmed a Jinni not knowing and the Jinni is just taking revenge. What is most remarkable about Muslim exorcisms is that the Jinn are encouraged to become Muslim. Since the Jinn have freewill, they have many religions of their own and not all follow the truth. Islam is the true religion and the only one the Creator will accept from both humans and jinn. Both humans and jinn are eligible for paradise and hell, and both were created to worship the Creator alone. Therefore, the Muslim exorcist isn't content with simply getting rid of the demon, but also guiding the Jinni to worship

God and become a good Muslim. Sometimes it actually happens where the Jinni becomes a Muslim, apologizes and leaves. Other times the Jinni refuses to become Muslim, but leaves because they don't want to hear Quran, or they fear the punishment of Allah for oppression. Sometimes the Jinni is stubborn and Allah doesn't will for it to depart at that time, so he allows it to remain and the person remains afflicted out of his wisdom. The point is that every religion can perform an exorcism that results in the demonic possession ending, so a successful exorcism alone doesn't constitute proof of that particular religion being true. Demonic possession usually happens to someone who isn't following the religion of Islam, because if Islam is practiced properly, it should protect one from jinn. But even if a practicing Muslim were afflicted it could be in order for God to use that person's suffering as an expiation for their sins, or a way for them to get a reward they couldn't earn any other way. However sometimes demonic possession of disbelievers results in death. Death comes by the will of Allah so we mustn't credit a demon with causing it, but if a demon is using exorcism to get people to believe in a false religion, then why aren't exorcisms always successful? Two reasons for this come to mind. One is that an unsuccessful exorcism of a false religion sometimes has the desired demonic effect by making those who witnessed the tragic death become more devout, especially since the witnesses will likely share the story. Thus, the demon's plan is successful in that respect. The other reason could be that it is a good Jinn that was explicitly commanded by God to harm a disbeliever for some sin they did, an example being a disbelieving tyrant who kills Muslims. Allah may instruct a Muslim Jinn to possess the disbeliever and refuse to leave until that person repents and embraces Islam, or is tormented for the rest of their disbelieving life. This would have the effect of punishing a disbeliever causing justice and preventing the disbeliever from doing more injustice, while also exposing the false religions' complete inability to cast out demons against their will. Perhaps a priest would begin to realize Christianity is false when a strictly practicing Christian who fights Muslims is possessed and the priest can't help; unfortunately he might think the person was possessed because they were good according to the crusader mentality. Personally, I doubt that Allah instructs Muslim jinn to possess disbelievers very often because there are much simpler ways to exact justice and guide people to Islam than having Jinn possess them. Also since there is no compulsion in Islam, Allah would never force it upon a person. Although legally if a Jinni or their family is harmed by a human, they have a right to extract revenge and that applies to all types of Jinn regardless of what religion they practice. If you accidentally kill their family a Jinni might just come for you. Thus, it's important to know how to live life correctly and how to prevent oneself from accidentally or unintentionally harming a Jinni. Anyways I'm just theorizing a possible explanation for why exorcisms of false religions do not always result in the possessed being relieved. One difference between the Islamic exorcism and all others is that there is no elite class of exorcists. Of course, some study and train to become specialists, but any Muslim could theoretically do an exorcism, even the person who is possessed. The Arabic Quran being the literal word of God verbatim has a visible effect which is very powerful and every Muslim knows some of the Arabic Quran to recite it while praying, unless they're new Muslims. Truly God is the only one who can protect us from anything and everything, including himself. In comparison if you read a bible on someone who is possessed, or even someone who's not possessed it has absolutely no effect at all. Whereas even if you don't understand the Arabic Quran or even know that what you are hearing is the Quran it has an effect on everyone who hears it which is unlike anything else. You might be interested to see an Islamic exorcism and videos of them abound on the internet demonstrating how different and genuine Islamic exorcism is from other religions. Although personally I don't think they should be filmed because of the honor of the person afflicted. For instance, if you were possessed and having unpleasant reactions/experiences you wouldn't want someone to put a video of you up on the internet so everyone can see you in such an embarrassing condition. Some other religions don't even allow exorcisms to be videotaped. When I studied to be a Catholic exorcist one of the first rules I learned was that it was forbidden to videotape an exorcism, which is why it is so ironic that Catholic exorcist Hollywood movies are so popular. This is another reason why it's bad for people to base their religion on what they see in a Hollywood production that has absolutely no responsibility to be factual. It is simply an entertainment business, movies are made for money and not many people will pay money to see the truth, it is much easier to sell a lie. People have become so foolish that now demons don't even need to do an actual possession to get a person to follow a false religion, all they have to do is make a movie about an exorcism and the masses flock to falsehood in fear from what they saw in the film. Not to scare you, but using the internet some jinn actually create websites/videos and comment on things pretending to be people in order to mischievously mislead. Although some Jinn don't take the horror approach to convert people, they take the healing approach. Jinn are capable of fixing health ailments, many of which they are capable of causing just so they can later fix them under religious auspices. There are 3 ways they can to do this. 1. They cause a disease or symptoms and then stop causing the disease/symptoms. 2. They use Jinn developed medicine to heal ailments humans have, which they may or may not have caused to begin with. 3. The Jinn use magic to heal people. Personally, whenever someone tells me that people get miraculously healed at their place of worship, I immediately think their religion is false because it's due to such tangible healings that false religions get promoted and prosper. If not for the "healings" typically they'd have no good logical reason to give for you to believe in their religion at all. Hence that's why Jinn employ the above 3 methods to "heal" people. Hindus, Buddhists, Jews, Muslims, Christians, Sikhs, Polytheists, every one of every traditional faith has miraculous healing stories that are genuine where people were ill or disabled and came to X place or person and after some religious activities were "miraculously healed". So obviously we can't use such "miracle healings" as evidence to determine a true religion when every religion has genuine "miracle healings" occurring in both the past and the present. Jinn can simply pinch a nerve to cause paralysis or blindness and then leave when evil religious rituals take place in order to make people believe in any false religion. This is actually one type of magic, many magicians in the ancient as well as the modern eras heal people from medical problems explicitly by doing something for the Jinn so they in exchange medically heal the person on behalf of the magician. Just because a devil is evil doesn't mean they don't know medicine and aren't willing to heal people for evil purposes. Satan can act as a doctor too, he doesn't always want to hurt you, if physically healing you can help him achieve his goals, then he will heal for the sake of evil. Yet surprisingly Christians tend to rely on such "healings" as proof of them being upon the truth more than any religious group. This is despite the bible explicitly saying there will be false preachers teaching false religions who will perform miraculous feats like healing. Most Christians tend to say those bible verses are about other Christians, not them and the other Christians say the same. Comically neither imagine they could both be wrong. Christians tend to rely on healings because Jesus was known as a healer, so they think if they can heal it means they are right just as Jesus' healings were a proof of his truth. Yet Jesus himself according to the bible admitted that devilish people with devils can perform "miracle cures". Biblically the Jews during the time of Jesus accused him of being one such person who heals people via magic or devils and do you know what Jesus said in reply? He just said how he wasn't like that. But more importantly he never said "that's not possible because only good people upon true religions can perform miraculous healing". Jesus knew that devils can cooperate with people to cure the ill or injured "miraculously", he never refuted the concept or possibility, he just clarified that was not how he operated. However biblically Jesus did confirm that "miraculous healings" can indeed occur as a result of people who are upon a false religion doing religious activities which God hates and will punish them for. Even the anti-christ will "miraculously heal" many people. That's what makes it funny when Christian's claim, genuinely or fraudulently, that "healings" take place at their religious activities because the same exact thing is done at the anti-christ's religious gatherings. So, healing or exorcising doesn't mean the religious teacher isn't lying when they say they are upon truth. They truthfully may believe what they say but neither healing nor exorcism is a valid proof that any particular religion is true. Thus, healings cannot be used as a proof and anyone who understands religion and has solid proof for their faith will not rely on "healings". Magicians can perform "miraculous healings" and they use the evil jinn (devils) to do so, thus when I hear of a "miracle healer" I don't take it as a "proof" but a caution sign to stay away just in case they aren't a fraud and are actually using magic or devils to heal. Rather than be skeptical of "healings" or exorcists it's smarter to be cautious for safety reasons because they could be very dangerous people working with devils, knowingly or unknowingly. Of which the one ignorantly working with devils can be even more dangerous than the intentional accomplice. However, don't get too paranoid, the point is that just because a Jinn leaves after a Christian exorcism or a Christian gets healed doesn't make Christianity true in the slightest, nor does it make Jesus divine in any way. In fact, the exorcisms done by Jesus as depicted in the bible are actually a proof against Christianity, because when Jesus cast demons out they would eagerly tell people he was the "son of God" as they left and Jesus would angrily tell the demons to shut up because they were lying. Yes, biblical Jesus said demons were lying when they claimed he was the son of God. The disbelieving demons were also the first to claim Jesus was a son of God.

People may say that because Jesus was born of a virgin and didn't have a father then God must be his father. Adam did not have a father or a mother, Jesus had a mother. If by not having a father it makes Jesus divine or the son of God then what does that make Adam and his descendants, you and me? Especially when Luke 3:38 says that Adam was the "son of God", but everyone knows that it's not meant to be literal because if it was then you and I would be the grandchildren of God and Eve would be the daughter in-law of God, and we both know that's not the case. Eve may God be pleased with her had no mother and she was made from the rib of Adam, but no one would claim that God is the mother of Eve. If your entire case for Jesus being the son of God is because he had no father then that is no justification whatsoever. According to that line of thinking Adam and Eve would have an even higher rank than Jesus. God is capable of miraculous things that defy our understanding of nature. Even the birth of Isaac the son of Abraham from his wife Sarah was miraculous, they were in their 90s. Sarah had gone through menopause and there were probably not even eggs left for fertilization yet she gave birth. Even the birth of the prophet John son of Zachariah was miraculous in the same way. Because Zachariah and his wife were both of old age, having children at such an age was considered to be impossible, but no one claims John was the son of God because he had a miraculous birth. There is no rule that says every human must have 2 parents. It is because Christians already believe Jesus to be God's son that they make up this rule that if you don't have a human father then God must be the father. This is not a proof to believe in something, it's an excuse to cling to an unscriptural belief they can't prove or justify.

It is of the utmost importance to stress that God does not beget or have children in any biological or literal sense whatsoever. All that is needed for God to do something is for him to say "Be" and it is done. Christians will use the verse that Jesus is the word made flesh misunderstanding what that means. "The word" is Be and that is how Jesus was conceived, via the utterance of a word by God which caused the flesh of Jesus to be created inside of Mary. Jesus was kept alive via a placenta in a woman's womb, God is not kept alive by a placenta nor confined to a womb. Jesus was born out of a vagina; God is not born out of a vagina. Jesus had a birthday; God doesn't have a birthday. Jesus was breastfed, God is not breastfed. Jesus was circumcised, God is not circumcised. Christendom actually use to possess what was believed to be the circumcised foreskin of Jesus; they called it the *"Holy Prepuce"*. It originally appeared on December 25th, 800 CE as a gift from Charlemagne to Pope Leo III. Charlemagne claimed an Angel brought the foreskin of Jesus to him while he was praying. In exchange Pope Leo III's Christmas gift was that he crowned Charlemagne Emperor of all Christendom. Foreskin for a Crown, that's Christmas. This foreskin allegedly played a role in many "miracles" and was a famous venerated relic. In 1527 CE it was stolen from Rome by a German soldier when Charles V sacked Rome. Although the looter was caught, he was imprisoned without the whereabouts of the foreskin being revealed, it was rediscovered in his cell in 1557 CE. An alleged vision from "Saint" Bridget confirmed that this hunk of flesh was indeed the foreskin of Jesus despite the unlikeliness of the skin being preserved for so long and the unlikeliness of somebody keeping the foreskin of Jesus after it was removed. Of course, some may say Jesus was known to be special since birth so that's why people kept his foreskin, but so was the prophet John and nobody kept his. From 1557 CE the rediscovered foreskin was venerated in Calcata and the Vatican offered any pilgrim who went to see it a 10-year indulgence. Which meant anyone who made the expensive trip to see it would be forgiven for 10 years' worth of sins. As a result, priests, nuns and monks swarmed the site and it became a popular tourist destination generating large revenue for the churches there and the city. Which is ironic since one would think priests, nuns and monks would have the fewest sins and smallest desire for indulgences. But maybe they just really liked to see foreskin and couldn't resist seeing what they thought was the skin of Jesus' penis and on top of that they thought Jesus was God. So, they actually believed they were seeing the foreskin that was removed from God's penis, God doesn't have a penis but this is why so many went to see it. However, there were as many as 18 different foreskins, all of which different Churches claimed to belong to Jesus. So, either Jesus had 18 penises, got circumcised 18 times, or many imposter foreskins were mislabeled as Jesus'. But how then does one explain all the "miraculous healings" that were caused by all 18 foreskins? Could real medically surprising healings possibly not be the result of Jesus healing someone? Most of these foreskins were destroyed during the French Revolution. However, in 1856 CE one foreskin was rediscovered and it caused a problem because then there were only two, the one from Calcata and the one that was rediscovered in a secret reliquary inside a wall of an Abbey. This was a major issue because every January 1st the Catholic Church would celebrate the *"Feast of the Circumcision of Our Lord"*. This annual celebration of God/Jesus getting circumcised continued until 1960 CE, when Pope John XXIII changed the Roman Calendar and eliminated this "Holy Day". Although it is important to remember that for a very long time January 1st was the day Christians celebrated God (whom they thought was Jesus) getting circumcised. Anyways the 2 foreskins problem was resolved by a papal decree in 1900 CE stating that anyone who wrote or spoke about the foreskin of Jesus would be excommunicated. Meaning if you mentioned it then you were declared a disbeliever. In 1954 CE since some people kept talking about those pieces of penis, the punishment was increased to include shunning as well. In 1983 CE the officially sanctioned Calcata foreskin was allegedly "stolen" by a priest and has been lost to history ever since. I've politely inquired as to whether the Abbey the 2nd foreskin was found in still has the foreskin available for visitors to see, and they never responded as though it never existed, but they don't even say that lest they get excommunicated. So officially if anyone asks about the foreskin now, they don't even acknowledge you asking about it. Obviously, God would not have his foreskin being treated in such a fashion, or even have foreskin at all. It is quite a coincidence that the foreskin was "stolen" and lost to history because if we had it we could test it to see what DNA code it had and if it really was Jesus' and if Jesus was God then we could learn the genetic code of God. That is why I think it has gone missing along with the other foreskin, because God doesn't have foreskin and a DNA test would prove that the skins were 100% human, not divine and likely not Jesus'. How crazy is it for people to spend big money to go see foreskin which they think is God's/the son of God's/Jesus'? Do you think Jesus would want people looking at skin from his penis? At least they didn't eat the foreskins in their Eucharistic ritual, or maybe that's what the priest in Calcata did and he reported it stolen out of embarrassment. Such a possibility raises other questions about the belief that the communion bread turns into the flesh of Jesus. If all those communion wafers around the world are being turned into a part of the body of Jesus, then somebody must be eating transfigured Jesus' penis in church as well as Jesus' butt and testicles. Therein lies a problem with communion in that since some claim they are literally eating the body of Jesus, then they have to pick a part. So whenever discussing Communion with Christians who believe the host is literally the body of Jesus, ask them which part of the body it is that they are eating and what do the different parts taste like, or do they always get the same part of the body when they claim to feast on the flesh of God's prophet? Also ask them if it's possible to overeat or undereat when eating a prophet of God? Lastly ask them why it is that the body and blood are always cited as being given and eaten, but who gets to eat the bones? Or did Jesus not give his bones to atone for the sins of the world? If he gave his bones then why are the communion hosts always boneless? Ask them who is eating the bones of Jesus? Do the priests keep the bones for themselves to eat? Or do they give the bones of Jesus to the dogs to suck on? If still the Christian insists that they are eating the body of Jesus in church then ask them if you can order out some boneless ribs of his for dinner. Then if they or any Christian ever brings you a host to the house, call the police and say the person is/are trying to feed you human body parts that they've told you belongs to someone who you heard went missing years ago, so as a concerned civilian you are calling to let them know X person has some body parts which they are serving to others as food. Seriously though, Christians claim they are waiting for Jesus to come back to earth while at the same time eating him every time they go to church. Why do they want him to return? Wouldn't they just eat him, bones and all? Imagine if/when Jesus does come back and sees such Christians claiming that they are eating his body and blood. What would he say and do to them? Do you think he'd give them a better recipe or ask for a plate? Or would he suggest they use some spices and cook his body or add some mixtures to his blood and boil it? Or would Jesus suggest they freeze the blood into ice cubes so it melts in their mouth? Honestly, I don't think he'd do either and don't think he taught people to eat bread and drink wine claiming it was his body and blood, neither literally nor figuratively. Jesus went through puberty; God does not go through puberty. God does not need someone to change his diaper. God does not lose baby teeth. God does not have reproductive organs or sexual desires. Jesus got hungry, thirsty, ate, drank and put on weight. God does not get hungry, thirsty, eat, drink, put on weight or lose weight. God does not urinate. God does not defecate. God does not fart. Jesus slept; God does not sleep. God does not dream. God does not get wrinkles nor have changing hairstyles. God does not bleed or get bumps and bruises. God cannot feel pain. One day Jesus will die, God does not die. Jesus is a prophet; God is not a prophet. Mary the mother of Jesus never claimed he was God, or that she gave birth to the very God she prayed to who was the same God all the prophets told mankind to worship. Mary who devoutly worshiped God would be the first to know if her deity came out of her uterus, but she never said such rubbish. Neither did Mary ever say she gave birth to a "son of God" and

Mary certainly didn't think her child was divine or that he could/should be consumed by her in the form of bread and wine. She didn't eat her kid or say he was God's kid either. Mary was a pious virgin who miraculously gave birth to a noble Messenger who was 100% human, 0% food and 0% drink. Jesus was a Messenger of God, not a divinely designed meal.

Some may say "*but God can do anything*", that is false, there are things God simply cannot do. God can only do things that are possible he cannot do nonsensical impossible things that are unimaginable theoretical figments of fantasy. For example, can God make a rock so heavy that God cannot lift it? No because this would be a contradiction. God cannot commit suicide (sacrifice himself) or die. Likewise, God cannot just quit his job and decide he's done being God and decides to hire someone else to take over. Also, God can't get sick, injured, senile or depressed. These are things contradictory to being immortal and all powerful. God does not lie or contradict. God cannot learn anything new because he is all knowing and already knows it all, past, present, future, you name it. Jesus admitted that he did not know when the hour of the Day of Judgment would be and learned things throughout his life. God cannot make another God because there is only 1 God, if there were others then God wouldn't be one or the only, so again this would be a contradictory negation. God cannot change because to do so would mean God is not eternal or everlasting. Therefore, when people claim that the God of Moses was God but then God changed and had a son and became a trinity this is blasphemy and means they disbelieve in God being eternal and everlasting. Even the most extreme Christians I met admit that Jesus was created by God, therefore Jesus cannot be God or the son of God because it would negate this eternal constant quality. God cannot be childless one millisecond and a father the next because that would be a God those changes. Christians will agree that there was a time when Jesus did not exist and/or Mary was not his mother, therefore thinking Jesus is a biological son of God or God incarnate makes them disbelievers in an eternal God. Please be warned because anyone who dies with such a belief about Jesus and God would be considered a disbeliever. May God protect us from all disbelief and grant us the death of a believer. The reason believing God had a son is so offensive and those who die believing such will be liable for eternal punishment is because of how severely insulting it is. If you had a pet rodent, lizard, fish, bird or dung beetle and I said that it was your son, how would that make you feel? You would probably ask me why in the world I would consider your pet animal to be your son and how I thought you reproduced with a different species than yourself. There could be many ways to reason this way: you named it, you care for it, you feed it, you talk to it, you love it and you shelter it so therefore it must be your son. Obviously, this is a crazy theory because a human is a different species than a rodent, lizard, fish, bird or dung beetle and it is impossible for one to be related to the other. Nonetheless many reasons can be made to try to justify it, but if I went about telling the world that you had a rodent, lizard, fish, bird or dung beetle for a son that was born out of wedlock then you would be pretty darn mad at me. Even though it would be impossible you would be insulted nonetheless for having people think you had sexual relations with a different species, and begot animal offspring. You would consider me to be someone who didn't believe the truth about you and you would hate me for believing such an incorrect idea, even if I just kept my belief to myself. To say God can do anything is to say God can go around having sex with animals and get them pregnant, or not even just sex but one would have to say that God could go raping angels, devils, humans, animals and eat poop for breakfast, lunch and dinner before hibernating through winter in his garbage can house built on the sun. If God can do anything then you might as well say he lives in a pineapple under the sea. Yet as ridiculous as that sounds some people claim "God is everywhere and everything". However, if everything is God and those who say otherwise are wrong then who is the one that is wrong? God? If God is everywhere and everything then the person saying God is not, must be God and thus God would be wrong about what God is. So, you see God can't be everything or everywhere because for that to be true then everything everywhere would know that and could not deny it, since if one part of God knew it was everything and everywhere all parts would know it. Since not everyone believes that everything everywhere is God then it simply cannot be true. But if God can really do anything then those perverted angels, devils, animals and humans could rape God too. Now some may say how that can't happen because it's God but if God can do anything then anything means just that. Afterall if anything is possible then who is to say God can't be the receiver of sexual pleasure? Couldn't God order creatures to have sex with him? Couldn't God let you or me or the devil rape him if God wanted? Couldn't you and me and everyone get married to God and have kids with him? Couldn't we get God pregnant if we tried? Couldn't God turn into an idol of stone so we could worship it? Couldn't God turn into a golden cow so we could worship it? Couldn't God turn into a human or have a human son? Couldn't God get injured and go into a coma and forget he was God? Couldn't God catch the flu? Couldn't God decide to stop being God? Couldn't God make you and him switch places so you are God and he is human? Couldn't God make a mistake? Or could it be that the people who say "God can do anything" are wrong? If God can do anything then there is no limit to crazy ideas about God. Do you know how I can prove that God can't do just anything? Because no prophet of God ever said this, the prophets actually explicitly said there were things God can't do. So, to postulate that God can do anything is to disbelieve in God and all the prophets which he has sent to mankind. While if you admit that God can't do anything/everything you must specify the cans and the can't and have proofs for all the cans and all the cant's. This doctrine of God being able to do anything developed as a desperate excuse to justify the claim of Christians when they say God has a son. Many use this as their argument ender when they get uncomfortable trying to justify crazy religious beliefs. If someone believes or tells you that God can do anything, then tell them that if they think that, then they are someone who is willing to believe anything and must believe in everything. That the Creator of everything would be biologically related to a mortal human with all the flaws and disgusting aspects that humans are known for is akin to atheism and insults God.

Now that is why calling Jesus a "son of God" is offensive to God, but it is also offensive to Jesus and his mother Mary, more so than it is to other prophets or believers. This is because to say Jesus is a "son of God" is to say that God is his father. Some Christians will maintain that this is true and not offensive to anyone. Since that is the case, they make we will take it and prove why it is offensive to Jesus and Mary, whom Christians claim to love, to say such a thing. Most people will agree that Mary was a virgin when she gave birth to Jesus. If Christians then say that God is the Father it would imply that Jesus is a bastard. The dictionaries define *"bastard"* as *"a person born of parents not married to each other"*. Since no Christian claims that the Creator married the human mother of Jesus then by claiming God is the father, or that God begot Jesus, and Mary is the Mother it means that Jesus must be a bastard according to Christianity. Of course, this is extremely offensive to anyone who has any iota of respect for Jesus, but Christians don't think about what it fully entails to believe and say that Jesus is the "son of God". What do you think Mary would think about someone who calls her son a bastard, but just in different words? What do you think Jesus would do to those people who proudly proclaimed this slander against him? To believe Jesus is the son of God means to believe that Jesus is a bastard. Now do you think that Jesus went around preaching that he was a bastard and that if people believe he is a bastard, then they would go to heaven? Obviously not. Yet this is what Christians profess and promote, thinking they are showing respect to Jesus or God in some way by slandering such a righteous Messenger of God who was miraculously born to the best woman of all time. If such Christians also believe that Jesus is God then to believe that means to believe that God is a bastard. Is that what the prophets taught? Officially according to the English language Christianity teaches that Jesus was a bastard.

Do you remember the verse earlier in Deuteronomy 23:2 that said: "No one <u>born of a forbidden marriage</u> nor any of their descendants may enter the assembly of the LORD, not even in the tenth generation." That is how the New International Version of the bible words it. The King James Bible, Jubilee 2000 Bible, American King James Bible, Darby Bible Translation, English Revised Version, American Standard Version, Webster's Bible Translation, World English Bible, Young's Literal Translation of the bible and many others all use the word "*bastard*" instead of "*born of a forbidden marriage*". Considering the bible to be a religious text, it seems unlikely that many bibles would use the word "*bastard*" if they didn't think it was the right word to use. The word "bastard" is largely considered a curse word, so that bible publishers include it indicates that "*bastard*" is the more reliable translation since people wouldn't put curse words in the bible if they could help it. Whereas any Christian who realized that Christianity teaches that Jesus is a bastard would be highly motivated not to translate this verse as "bastard". But this deception has worked against them because that it uses the word "forbidden marriage" leads us to ask whether Mary and God had a legal marriage? If not and Jesus was the son of God then either Jesus was a bastard since his parents weren't married or he was born of a forbidden marriage. Therefore, anyway you translate it, if Jesus was a literal son of God, then according to the bible Jesus would not be allowed to enter "*the assembly of the LORD*" meaning the Temple. However, Luke 2:41-50 say:   41 <u>Every year Jesus' parents went to Jerusalem</u> *for the Festival of the Passover.* 42 *When he was twelve years old, they went up to the festival, according to the custom.* 43 *After the festival was over, while his parents were returning home, the boy Jesus stayed behind in Jerusalem, but they were unaware of it.* 44 *Thinking he was in their company, they traveled on for a day. Then they began looking for him among their relatives and friends.* 45 *When they did not find him, they went back to Jerusalem to look for him.* 46 <u>After three days they found him in the temple courts, sitting among the teachers, listening to them and asking them questions.</u> 47 *Everyone who heard him was amazed at his understanding and his answers.* 48 <u>When his parents saw him, they were astonished. His mother said to him, "Son, why have you treated us like this? Your father and I have been anxiously searching for you."</u> 49 *"Why were you searching for me?" he asked.* **<u>"Didn't you know I had to be in my Father's house?"</u>** 50 *But* <u>they did not understand</u> *what he was saying to them."*

    This famous story is used by Christians to say that Jesus claimed God was his father. But clearly the verses say Jesus' parents would take him to Jerusalem and that his parents went looking for him, with Mary being attributed as telling Jesus "*Your father and I have been anxiously searching for you."* Thus, if you really think about it these bible verses actually say that Mary considered Jesus to have a human Father. But if that's the case then Mary could not have had a virgin birth and Jesus can't be God's son. To which the Christian will reply that Jesus said he was in his Father's house thus proving the son of God theory. However, in context since *"they did not understand what he was saying to them"* with the "they" including Mary, we can deduce that when Jesus is written to have said "Father" he meant it figuratively. This is also how the author of Luke must have understood it as well, because otherwise he wouldn't write that Jesus had two human parents if he thought God was Jesus' father and he was born of a virgin. But let us imagine the Christian was right and that God was the Father of Jesus. In that case since Jesus would have been a bastard, or not born via a legal marriage between God and Mary, then that would mean Jesus wouldn't be allowed to enter the Temple of God because of the prohibition in Deuteronomy. That the bible says Jesus was in the temple means either the verse in Deuteronomy is not from God, the verses in Luke are not from God, or Jesus is not God's son, or else God legally married Mary and took her as his wife. Those are the only 4 possibilities that involve Jesus being born of a virgin birth. The only other alternative is that Mary didn't have a virgin birth and that Jesus had a human father and mother, but that notion is blasphemy in both Islam and Christianity; even though Luke says Mary told Jesus he had a human father and John 1:45 says Phillip told Nathan that Jesus of Nazareth () was the "son of Joseph". I tend to think that Luke's account is not factual. While John 1:45 is clearly wrong because it says Phillip found and read about Jesus of Nazareth the son of Joseph in the law of Moses, whereas such a verse doesn't exist in the Old Testament at all. So, if the Phillip John tells us about was reading the Law of Moses, then that means the Old Testament is not the Torah. Although no Jew or Christian leader says it is, this is a layman misconception because only the first 5 books of the Old Testament are alleged to have been around since the time of Moses because the later books like Ezra, Psalms and so on were all clearly not around during the time of Moses and thus couldn't be part of the Torah. At the very least we can agree that something in the bible or Christian doctrine is false. Whether it's the Deuteronomy verse, Luke's verses or just the Christian doctrine that Jesus is God's son, something has to go. The bible itself is telling us that this is an impossible scenario, but if anyone of these things goes that means Christianity has been corrupted with falsehood. Thus, in order to get to the truth, one would have to disbelieve in Christianity and/or the bible. In response most Christians will reject the Old Testament and say it doesn't apply after Jesus left. Yet they still maintain the Old Testament is divine revelation and the excuse that the rules changed after Jesus left cannot be used in this instance, because this involves a 12-year-old Jesus who also taught that the laws were supposed to be followed and obeyed. According to Jesus, especially at this time, the law of Moses applied. Therefore, the best solution a Christian can hope for is to say that Deuteronomy 23:2 must not have existed during the time of Jesus and is not divine revelation. But what is the proof for this claim? Because they do not want to imagine that the New Testament could be false or that Jesus isn't the son of God. Yet the end result and the least damaging to their pride would be to admit that the bible is not 100% divine revelation, but that in itself is an impossibility according to Christian dogma. Thus, we discover that it is impossible for Christianity to be true no matter how one looks at it. The problem is that most Christians will never look at it but will blindly follow emotions, customs, popular opinions and traditions into hell.

The main reason Christians today are reluctant to say the Old Testament is inaccurate is because they rely on the theory that the Old Testament predicts their idea of Jesus. Therefore, if a divine revelation predicts their religious ideas, then they think it makes their religion true. So, they claim the Old Testament must be true divine revelation because they believe their religion to be true and they use this theory to justify that belief which they held before they even read those alleged predictions. It's a backward cycle of believing Christianity is true then scrambling for something to back up that claim and as a result saying that something else supports it and that the something else must be true because it's used to support what one already believes is true, with the effect being that a buffer is put up to prevent any attack on the idea of Christianity as possibly being false. Basically, Christians say "*My religion is true because of X proof, and X proof is true because it says my religion is true.*" Yet X proof isn't true at all nor is it a valid proof, and usually it doesn't support their religious beliefs even if it were a valid proof that could be used. The trouble is that their thesis is so wrong one almost doesn't know where to start explaining how wrong it is and why. Therefore, by the time a person destroys that buffer the Christian will feel so mentally exhausted as a result of their short attention span and emotionally infuriated that they will end the conversation before their core beliefs can be exposed as false. The Christian faith is thereby defended by delay tactics in the hopes that a non-Christian will get exhausted breaking down the barriers, while the Christian is pre-programmed to have an emotional reaction at the breaking down of such barriers and impatience so that they withdraw before their devilish doctrine can be eradicated. The Christian is programmed to be like someone who walks away from a chess match after losing a few pawns and by the time they come back to play they just start a new match from the beginning because they can't remember how those pawns in front of the king were destroyed in the last religious conversation. So they have a mental reset button preventing them from ever having a full religious discussion which would result in their Christian Faith, aka the King, being destroyed. The King of a Christian's doctrine is completely defenseless but many weak barriers are put up by Satan just as pawns are in chess as a delaying tactic, which are intended to cause the person to die upon a false faith before they can be saved from the ocean of error they are currently drowning in. Whereas if those weak pawns survive long enough through multiple generations, they can even become strong castles which are more of a barrier in preventing the message of truth from getting through to destroy the King. Therefore, some might think that the way I write or speak is like I'm "*beating a dead horse*". I don't call Christianity a dead horse, but that's what Christians tell me when I talk to them about the falsehood of various aspects of their faith. Yet even if I were "beating a dead horse" as Christians tell me, why would you still ride it when you know it's dead? Just imagine if you saw someone literally trying to ride a dead horse down the street. How stupid and crazy would that person be if they themselves referred to it as a dead horse? That's the same exact principle with a Christian who is still a Christian by the time they've read this far in the book. But maybe the person riding the dead horse just wants to be certain the horse is actually 100% dead before they dismount. Yet by doing so they risk contracting a spiritual disease from the unhygienic infectious falsehood they are upon. I'm actually trying to cripple a living beast taking someone to hellfire so it can't take anyone else any farther down the road to hellfire and as a result hope those currently riding it will get off when they see it can't take them to paradise even if it was on the road to paradise, which it's not. I just hope they dismount before they die while riding a crippled beast to the hellfire. As in chess despite the King being the weakest piece, if you try going straight to the King you'll rarely get through, especially when you have to announce checkmate to let the person know you're about to destroy their Satanic religion in one move which is leading them astray. Many will then move a barrier in front of such a threat to delay the confrontation since they fear the game ending which will cause them to return to their real life. I think with most people you have to destroy nearly all those barriers protecting their King of falsehood. I think of it as demolition dawah, in that I destroy the bad infrastructure before building a good one. Many people often forget that demolition is the first thing humans do to replace dangerous buildings with safe ones. The problem with humans is that this demolition involves destroying the poisonous ideas implanted by Satan in the heart and mind. Which means calling people to the true religion is like heart and brain surgery without anesthesia, this is because the true religion cannot be spread through deception or emotional and mental drugs. Although such an approach is not appropriate for every person nor every setting, one must teach to the person's level of intellect and use opportunities for learning moments as they present themself, just as how in chess you take down the pieces you can when you have the opportunity and ability. While just as in chess sometimes one has to hold back because if you take their most valued pieces too soon, they are likely to get enraged and quit before the game can be finished. You must build and guide while you demolish and refute. Thereby presenting the alternative life raft without neglecting to destroy the satanic sea monster they are attached to. Because without the demolition Satan will lure the person back to their own hellhole and without them being able to choose the liferaft they will cling to their satanic sea monster for dear life thinking it's their only option, and will even start defending the monster when you attack it. Yet it's not possible to use every weapon to fight every battle with every person, especially not in one conversation. Trust me I've tried it and that war strategy ends with Satan winning the war. Thus, as long as it doesn't involve sin, it's best to inform others of their errors and try to guide them in the manner you'd want to be corrected and guided. Refuting false beliefs is done in order to help them, not for the sake of argument, or to make them feel bad or stupid. It's hard enough to learn one is wrong, it's even harder if one learns it without compassion, and there is a big difference between passion and compassion. For example, saying *"that belief is wrong"* is a lot different than saying *"your belief is wrong"*. There is also a difference between knowing something and knowing how to teach what you know to others. Keep in mind it's not about the results you get, it's about doing what God wants you to do the way God wants you to. Every one of us has different skills, so I advise you to do good deeds with whatever you are good at doing, because that's how you end up doing great deeds. At the end of the day this chess match is between entire religious groups except only one religious group has the color of truth and all the others are just different shades of falsehood. Thus, if those weak barriers or pawns aren't destroyed as soon as possible they may end up becoming a much bigger barrier to the truth in the future. Anyways that's the way I used to play chess before I realized how it's a waste of precious time, distracts from remembering God, teaches a warfare which violates the rules of jihad and leads to enmity between people and manipulative aggressive personalities in which skill has nothing to do with victory but is just about capitalizing on the opponent's errors. I tended to try to eliminate every piece the opponent had on the board before eliminating their king after cornering him against a wall. I tend to try to eliminate every Satanic doctrine a false religion employs so a person can see how truly not one thing from their false religion is going to protect them from hell. Thus they'll choose the truth wholeheartedly. But unlike chess, the Islamic team never loses one of its tenets or doctrines because the truth can never be defeated by falsehood. So it's like a chess match where the false religions can attack Islam but they can't destroy one aspect of it unless the Muslims take it off the board themselves. Thus, enemies of Islam label other things as Islam and attack that trying to confuse people, just as a chess player might put a checker on the board and call checkmate before destroying the checker and then telling the audience to disburse before their opponent explains that the checker is not a part of their team at all, much less the King. Unfortunately, as in chess, sometimes people of the Christian faith will quit interacting with me when I destroy a major barrier or soldier of the Satanic army such as a WatchTower, Knight, Bishop, Queen or Pope because they weren't prepared to have such a strong barrier destroyed, so their brainwashed mind goes into shock and they react how they were pre-programmed to react. I hope you don't lose your temper and toss this book away as an angry chess player throws the pieces away when they feel they are going to be defeated. The thing is that unlike in chess, when one is a member of a Satanic religion it's good for that Satanic army to be destroyed in totality, because going down to every single piece makes the person feel confident that the other team truly is better when 100% of the Satanic faith is destroyed without any damage being done to the true faith. Also, this way a person won't introduce any Satanic doctrines or pieces from their previous faith to the Muslims should they choose to accept Islam. It's easier to travel the road to paradise if you destroy the bridges leading to the roads to hell and don't carry the extra satanic baggage picked up while traveling on those devilish roadways. But at the same time don't let Satan trick you into being exclusively a pawn hunter or excessively celebrating (by which excessive means at all) before, during or after taking an opponent's pawn off the board. It's hard enough to lose a piece of one's false faith, rubbing its falsehood and foolishness in just makes it harder for them to let it go and it really is only them who can take it off the board. Unlike in chess, with religion the individual will only remove their piece from the board if they agree to. Which makes it extremely frustrating sometimes when proof after proof is provided and they act like an immature child would by saying how you didn't really prove their doctrine false. For bigots their faith is in you being wrong and them being right, so to them they believe there can only be one outcome and if you say or prove how the outcome is not what they believed it would be, then they say you are unjustly attacking their faith. What they mean is you can't attack their beliefs about their false faith, "*unless of course you have proof*". However, what they don't say is that any proof is only proof if they believe it proves what they believe. To bigots only they can say they are wrong and it doesn't matter what proof you bring or what you or even their own scholars say the proof means. For bigoted Christians the bible means what they believe it means and it doesn't matter what it actually says or is, unless it is what they believe. Thus, with bigots one must try to communicate the invalidity of their excuses politely and calmly with compassion. More of in a personal way of why their opinion/excuse seems wrong or how it doesn't make sense to you, rather than saying directly how that's wrong, pathetic and stupid. Refuting bigots is like scoring a goal in a game and then they say no no no that's not a goal and doesn't count. What do you do? You got to be polite and try to kindly make a short small rebuttal of why it actually is a goal and then when they say they don't believe that and disagree, then just politely start all over again on the next issue or topic, or else they penalize you and count it as a point for themselves.  With bigots you can only score points in their opinion if they allow you to score points.  Although God records the points for us and that's why we play.  Obviously, this is not a scholarly, logical, fair or reasonable game, but they wouldn't be bigots believing in a false religion if they were scholarly, logical, fair or reasonable.  Fortunately not everyone is a complete bigot, but many have qualities of bigotry and resort to bigotry as a defense system, or they run to a bigot to bail them out when they see their satanic sea monster is sinking.  Never ever tell a bigot they're a bigot to their face.  You can define what bigotry is and say <u>we</u> shouldn't do that or be like that, but never label or expose them if you are in private or have a personal relationship, because then they quit playing and think they won via disqualification.  This is why conveying the message of Islam is truly Jihad, and as such it must be done according to how the prophets taught and not how the disbelievers would like us to do it.  Disbelievers don't spread their message the way Muslims do because Muslims have the truth and they don't.  So, Muslims refute all falsehood because one who has the real truth is able to tell why all falsehood is false, and not just because it isn't what we believe, falsehood is false regardless of what the truth is.  The hard part is doing this the prophetic way.  You might think this is just my opinionated or even bigoted thinking, that my religion is perfect and unassailable, but that's actually the definition of the true religion that was preached by Abraham, Moses, Jesus and Muhammad.  The true religion has been perfected and is flawless by definition.  So religion isn't even comparable to chess, it's more like dominoes, if one domino falls they all do.  Unfortunately, so many people have been fooled by falsehood they illogically think a true religion doesn't have to be 100% true.  Whereas if even one tiny part of a religion is false then that is a false religion.  Falsehood is like poison; one drop ruins the whole drink.

The other reason the Old Testament holds so much importance to Christians is because in the Roman Empire in order to be a valid religion it had to be old, since the idea of a new religion would mean social change and damage the endearment to long held beliefs and customs. If early Pauline Christians told Romans that Jesus came with a new religion it would never be accepted. Thus, Paul's doctrine had to be antiquated. Although even if a religion was old the Roman Empire decreed all religions had to tolerate the other religions and couldn't claim the others were wrong. Judaism was the exception because it was so ancient the Roman government didn't dare risk requiring it to change its old tradition of intolerance, since doing so would inspire ideas of changes to Roman politics and arrogance being possible too. Thus, Pauline Christians had to Judaize their religion in order to have it be accepted and proclaim exclusivity to the truth. Therefore, an Old tradition or Old Testament was needed. The Old Testament itself took thousands of years to write down completely as new prophets were consistently being sent and history was being recorded and then distorted as Jews became corrupt and racist. To this day there is actually no solid evidence to identify when exactly the Old Testament came about because the Jews were consistently changing their religious texts throughout history. It's not just about finding out a date for when a collection of books was finished, it's about finding out the date AND the contents of what was in the books at that date, because the titles remained the same but the contents within those titles frequently changed. It's truly sad because Jews believe that it's part of their religion to change their religious texts as time goes by. The rabbis actually call this "midrash" which is a type of "re-interpretation". Rabbis believed that since Scripture was the word of God then it was infinite. Therefore, any new meaning that they thought of a text as possibly having would automatically be deemed as a meaning that was desired by God so long as the new meaning would benefit the Jewish community. Rabbis actually believed and preached that Moses knew the Torah least of all because each generation gained new interpretations and therefore knew the Torah better and better. Jews thought there could be no definite interpretation of Scripture. Meaning that during the time of Moses, the same verses meant different things than it meant to them and what it means today is different than what it will mean tomorrow. Jewish exegetes thought revelation was upgraded every time a Jew read the text and applied it to his own situation with a fresh meaning. Essentially it was impossible for a Jew to misinterpret the Torah, because any new interpretation was deemed as divine revelation evolving. They actually believed and taught that the Torah could go through stages of evolution. Jews believed the Torah was what today is called "open-source", in that any Jew can improve it. Thus the rabbis considered their new interpretations to be equivalent to divine revelation and they called their added words the Torah as well. They said that this was because they were "God's chosen people" and that if God didn't approve of them then he wouldn't have let them alter what was sent to Moses. They thought if God let them do it then he must like it and agree. Of course, this is all atrocious and an epic literary disaster of a book. Yet this is the "ancient Torah" Jews tell everyone to revere and respect. Oh, and keep in mind that their "improvements" weren't just limited to adding words to the text but also deleting words too. Essentially if we imagine the Torah as a bound book given to Moses, the Jews edited it, added pages to it, took pages out and did this for centuries, all the while keeping it all in the same cover calling their book by the same name Moses called the book given to him by God. The Jews still do this today with their "Torah". Thus, one can imagine the hostility the prophets Jesus and John had for the rabbinical authorities. What is certain is that in 70 CE the Jewish "Scriptures" that were kept in the temple were destroyed when the Romans destroyed the temple. From that moment on there was no officially sanctioned Jewish text. Not that the officially sanctioned text was authentic anyways, since Jesus was sent specifically because the text had been tampered with. Although after 70 CE it was essentially an open market and this is where the Jews went one way with their opinion of what the pre-Jesus text was and the Christians went another. The Jewish Rabbis then created the "Mishnah" which was an anthology of traditions collected around 200 CE and this became the Jewish "New Testament" so to say, it is not to be confused with the Christian New Testament. They are both very different collections of post-Jesus texts. From the Jewish perspective the Mishnah is new because it was made after the destruction of the 2nd temple in 70 CE. Whilst within Christianity itself the many denominations differed drastically, to the point where today Jews have 24 books in their Hebrew Bible, Protestants have 39 books in their Old Testament, Catholics have 46 books in their Old Testament and Eastern Orthodox Christians have 51 books in theirs. Yet each maintains that their pre-Jesus texts are divine revelation and exactly the same as what existed during and before the time of Jesus. Unfortunately, most Christians assume that all Christians have the same Old Testament and that it's the same as what the Jews used during the time of Jesus. Regardless of what the actual year was when the Old Testament we have today was compiled in written form, it was certainly post 70 CE; which was after Jesus left earth. Meaning neither Jesus nor any of his companions read what the Christians today call the Old Testament and they certainly didn't believe in it because it simply didn't exist. Chronologically it should've existed, but the books of the Old Testament were written long after the events they purport to describe and those books were repeatedly destroyed whenever Jews were conquered or Jews choose to "improve" and "upgrade" the Torah. With the various Jewish versions of their Torahs having been lost multiple times before Jesus was born until finally whatever distorted text the Jews had left was destroyed in 70 CE. After which what is known as the Old Testament went through a creation process similar to the New Testament with different Christian groups taking different books thinking their books were right, but it's even more complicated than it was with the New Testament because there were different versions of these books. For instance, there are 4 different sources for the modern book of Genesis with each saying different things having been written at different times. The Yahvist version uses the word "YHVH" for God while the Elohist version uses the word "Elohim" for God and the Priestly version only has sacrifices done by Aaronites and all non-Aaronites who sacrifice get killed by God. However instead of eliminating all but one version, the compilers simply mashed them together trying to combine all the different versions into one narrative, thereby resulting in many biblical contradictions sometimes even as regards what is supposed to be one event. Thus, for those who read the texts they read contradicting stories similar as to how we read a contradictory Easter story because verse by verse the Old Testament is telling multiple tales. For more information on the contradicting Easter Story refer to my book "Contradicting Biblical Conjecture about the Crucifixion". Many don't realize it but there are 2 different conflicting Creation stories and 3 different conflicting Flood stories in the book of Genesis. Frequently people debate problems the stories in Genesis have with Science but the biggest opponent of the book of Genesis is the book of Genesis itself. Since Christians love to claim they are visual learners and need to see statues and pictures in order to learn religion, I've included a very useful chart of the books of Genesis, Exodus, Leviticus and Numbers which show the composition of the different sources used when compiling just the first 4 books of the Old Testament.

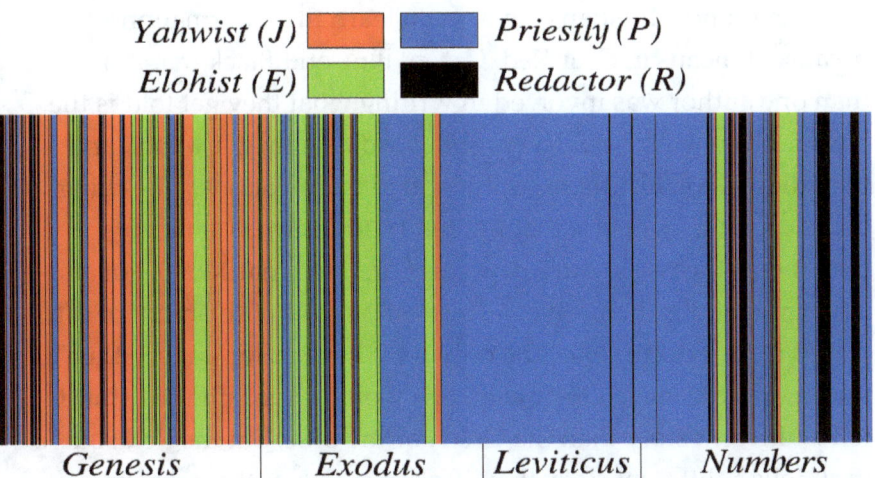

Now each color represents what is basically a different bible. Think of it as though Jews and Christians have a Red bible, a Blue bible, a Green bible and a Black bible for the first 4 books of the Old Testament. The problem is all these bibles tell different stories and as you can see if you took out a single color then you'd have a very different picture, the same applies to these books of the Old Testament. If you remove the Priestly source of information (the blue) you'd be missing a big part of the story and the rules and regulations. Likewise for any other source if it were to be removed. The problem is that these sources weren't chosen because of authenticity, it's just because they are old and it's all that there was available to choose from. No scholar thinks that the Red, Green, Blue and Black are equally authentic to each other or that they were written by Moses. Biblical scholars admit that Moses did not write any of these sources that are used to make the books that get attributed to him, but the texts are old so that's why they got used and then mixed all together in order to make the story seem chronological. However, when they print the bibles, they only use one color of ink and don't let bible readers see this beautiful plethora of contrasting colors or contrasting Scriptures. Most Jews and Christians never even learn this information because it means in clear Red, Green, Blue and Black that more than one author was involved in writing what they get told is the Taurat given to Moses. The prophet Moses only got 1 book and they didn't look like these sophisticated compilations. The thing that makes this worse is that in literary terms these source documents themselves are new compared to what Moses got and are compilations themselves. The first 4 books of the modern OT comes from 4 documents, the only 4 we have so far, maybe they'll find more someday. Obviously, one would expect the red stuff to tell a different story than the Green or the Blue, but the Red source itself tells a different story than itself. So each of these 4 sources themselves also contradict. What this means is that the source documents used and mixed together were also made via a similar mixing process with ingredients we don't know the quantity or quality of. If for instance we say this Red, Green, Blue and Black text is published as being all Brown then that's one thing. We would know this Brown is a rather crappy mash-up and not a good historical document nor a reliable trustworthy narrative. However, since nobody can tell whether any of the Red, Green, Blue or Black is true we get stuck with Brown and cannot just pick to read Red because Red could be all false and Green might be true instead. Or Blue could be true? Or maybe Blue and Red are true and Green and Black are false? Or maybe only Black is true and all of Red, Blue and Green are false? All we can say is that none of them are the originals and if you only take one source by itself you would end up with a very different religion than if you took a different source all of which are very different than if you took the Brown modern source. If you pick one then you must

reject the other 3 but nobody wants to pick one and scholastically nobody can even if they wanted to.  This is because each source (color) contradicts itself just as the color Brown contradicts itself letting us know that it is really made of Red, Green, Blue and Black.  Although unlike with Brown we have not found the ingredients that were used to make Red, nor those used to make Green, nor those used to make Blue, nor those used to make Black.  So, our 4 combo colors that gave us the first 4 books of the Brown Old Testament are also combination colors except we have no clue what colors were combined to make those sources and we don't even know how many colors/sources were used.  All we know is that our "ancient manuscripts" of the Old Testament's oldest sources are not natural original sources but mystery combinations.  Whereas the combinations that made each of the 4 isolated and identified OT sources are combination sources too.
Unfortunately, it is unknown exactly how many sources created the 4 main sources for the first 4 books of the Old Testament because the documents we need to find to learn this information have not been found, or if they have been they haven't been made publicly known as to what they are or what they say or how old they are.  Although Biblical Scholars have determined a minimum number regarding the sources of the existing sources:  The Yahvist version (Red) had at least 3 different sources.  The Elohist version (Green) had at least 4 different sources.  The Priestly version (Blue) had at least 9 different sources.  Hence the Red, Green and Blue of the first 4 books of the Old Testament came from a minimum of 16 different books.  The number of sources each of those 16 books had is unknown and the number of 16 is possibly even higher, that's just the current minimum possibility; which is actually too few because it's not counting the Black Redactor sources.  As you can see that's quite a literary mess and as time passes it's not likely to get any cleaner but dirtier as the oldest

colors/sources closer to the original sources decompose and biodegrade; that is if they even still exist, which nobody knows if they do. One thing that can be concluded from this literary disaster is very important and gives us the main point anyways. That point is that the modern Brown text people call the Pentateuch/Torah certainly was not written by 1 author. Thus, it couldn't have been Moses, nor can it be considered as the Taurat given to Moses by God. Oh, but the worst part of it all is that these 4 books of the Old Testament are not the messiest. The charts and graphs showing the sources of the rest of the Old Testament or New Testament cannot be made because the color spectrum doesn't have as many colors as there are different sources. The sad part is the bible publishers know this but they just print their books in black and white and don't explain how they made their bible. The point is that all the different versions of the "Old" Testaments available today would be considered new to Jesus, which is why most early Christians didn't distinguish between the rules in the New and the "Old" Testaments. This means that when the New Testament says somebody read about something in the "Law of Moses", that does not refer to the Old Testament as many Christians assume and this is evident by the fact that many times in the New Testament a verse will be quoted, sometimes even by Jesus himself, which does not appear in the Old Testament anywhere in any bible version of any denomination. So, either the New Testament is lying about what Jesus quoted, or else he misquoted something or lied, or else we don't have access to the "Law of Moses" or "Torah" which he was quoting. From an American perspective if we take the "American Law" today and call it such there is no problem, yet if we say that during the 1700s CE when George Washington was president he ruled by the "American Law" none would think we meant George Washington's American Law was the same as the law in America today. Nobody would dare to claim that the American law book used today was all written by George Washington and has never been added to or changed and refer to modern US law as "the law of Washington" despite him actually creating some of it many years ago. We'd all say that despite some laws that are part of the system today being laws set by Washington the overall law is not. Therefore, whenever the "Law of Moses" is mentioned, one must understand the Jewish meaning of the "Law of Moses" is not equivalent to the laws that Moses taught people to live by. Jewish Rabbis thought and taught the teachings of Moses were obsolete and that if he were to appear in their time, they would teach him the Torah because they knew it better than him since he only had an early version of it and they had the later version. Jews thought of their Scriptures similar to how we think of software. Jewish Rabbis explicitly believed in "amending" the law of Moses for every era but they would continue to call it the "Law of Moses" even though Moses had nothing to do with their changes. Another point of importance is that since the Old Testament was compiled after Jesus left earth, then obviously it would be easy to insert prophecies alluding to him in there. This is why Christianity teaches the Old Testament came before Jesus so they can claim that their idea of Jesus fulfilled prophecies. Yet I've examined these alleged prophecies and learned 2 things, firstly they aren't about Jesus and secondly, they couldn't be predicting Jesus because they were written after him. What Christians did when making their Old Testament was essentially tell people that last week's newspaper was written last year in order to make their publication seem prophetic and since nobody was around when the paper was published most don't know it was published last week and didn't predict the future at all. Calling the Old Testament "old" was done to make it seem old and because Paul's new religious doctrine claimed Jesus abolished the "Law of

Moses" (all versions of it) with a "New Covenant", which basically means "New Religion", based upon the "New Testament" with new/no rules.  Until then most Christians considered their texts to all be one long volume with Jesus being just the latest chapter, instead of an altogether different act.  Paul said Jesus was a new act and Pauline Christendom later made a split between the pre-Jesus narrative and the post-Jesus narrative calling the pre-Jesus material the Old Testament thereby being able to eliminate all those strict rules from the "New Covenant" which they wanted to follow.  Although the rejection of the Old Testament's rules didn't become the majority opinion until the Middle Ages.  Essentially, they made something new and called it old in order to have the Roman Empire allow them to exist.  Then as the new Pauline doctrines like the Trinity, Original Sin, Atonement and Baptism developed, which contradicted all the pre-Jesus material, it was decided to throw out the bath water and keep the baby so it could be re-clothed with new garments as needed.  Thus, they theologically threw out the "Old" and kept the "New" even though in the eyes of Jesus and his companions both the "Old" and "New" Testaments were new and not a part of their religion.  Then as time went by priests kept on changing the bibles so it said what they wanted.  Except unlike the Jewish Rabbis, they just made the changes and didn't think they needed to tell anybody because they figure people knew Scriptures were evolutionary.  However, the pagan Europeans didn't know that because they didn't know the Jewish tradition.  So eventually as Europeans became Christians, they just presumed that the books were always the same, because they didn't know what had happened while they were banned from reading the bibles.  The reason why as a Christian I couldn't go back to what Jesus taught by following the bible was because Jesus didn't teach either the Old or New Testament because he never read nor believed in the bible, since both the Old and New Testament were written down after he departed, long after he departed. Plus, I couldn't use the modern bible to practice earlier forms of Christianity because they had different bibles back then. The "Old Testament" is probably newer than the New Testament because the oldest Hebrew manuscript that contains the Hebrew bible (which is what the Jews use) is the Leningrad Codex which dates from 1009 CE. So, you have the Jews saying their Scripture can only be traced back to 1009 CE. The Jews actually have no proof to say what their Scriptures said prior to 1009 CE. Yet the Christians think and claim their Old Testament is what Jews used since the time of Moses! Now there are other manuscripts that are older however they aren't in Hebrew. Whereas the biblical books of Exodus, Leviticus, Numbers and Deuteronomy can only be traced back to as early as 538 BCE. The majority of scholars agree with this dating of those 4 biblical books, yet Christians claim Moses wrote them. However, it is a 100% undisputed fact that Moses was dead long before 538 BCE. So, the Christians are actually saying the Jews are lying and that their Scriptures are really thousands of years older than they claim them to be. What is their proof for this? Because their Christian leaders tell them so and tiny bits of ancient scraps exist which have some of the same letters on them as their modern Old Testament pages. Basically they see the letter "A" written on an ancient papyrus scroll and say that must mean the modern English alphabet must have been the very same alphabet used in ancient antiquity because we found a letter "A"! Yet it is a fact that the 26 letter English alphabet has only existed since the 16th century and even then we are using the 19th century variation of it today with 52 total uppercase and lowercase letters, since in the 16th century the English alphabet had different lowercase letters than we do today. So technically our English alphabet is only 200 years old. Finding an old document with the letter "A" doesn't mean our English alphabet is that old, it's just a letter "A". Likewise tiny scraps of biblical verses don't make the entire text that old either. When scholars say a bible is based on "ancient manuscripts" what they mean is they found thousands of different individual scraps and out of those, all of which were written at different times by different people as part of different books, they took some scraps translated them and published their translation as one book. One of their biggest tricks is their use of the word "manuscripts", in reality they are "scraps of ancient manuscripts". It would be akin to going into a museum and ripping up every document there is and then taking some scraps from some documents and some from others all of which were written at different times as different documents and then stringing the words and verses together like a puzzle and then translating that self-made puzzle that didn't exist before the scraps were pieced together, finally proclaiming "*this translation comes from ancient manuscripts*". Which can only be said due to legalistic technicalities. Except unlike with the weak museum analogy, these scraps were ripped up thousands of years ago and it is unknown who ripped them up or why and what was ripped up that wasn't recovered nor what the other parts of the original documents the scraps came from said. Seriously if the bibles had their verses color coded according to the different scraps each verse was translated from the bible would have more colors than the rainbow and the digital color palettes used for graphic design. There are actually thousands of ity bity scraps from different documents pasted together into the modern biblical translations. Yet what's even worse is that they don't translate from the oldest scraps available. This is because the oldest scraps don't support ancient or modern Christian doctrines, that's why they say "ancient manuscripts" and not "the most ancient manuscripts" even though the "manuscripts" themselves are fragments. The other scraps they don't include in their translation contradict the scraps they translated, so while they can say their bible is translated from "ancient manuscripts" they are intentionally not using all the "ancient scraps" and there is no complete ancient copy of their texts. Plus, they include modern scraps too, if they believe and like what the newer scraps of text say then it goes into their "bible translation of ancient manuscripts". In short Bible publishers have a picture of what they believe the bible says or rather what they believe it should say, so then they go looking for puzzle pieces they can use to force them to fit together but they don't really fit together and still don't fit the picture they wanted to make, therefore they mistranslate. To get away with making this pathetic biblical puzzle they say it was translated from "ancient manuscripts". Because some of the scraps are considered to be ancient to them. To show you a clear example of just how devious the bible translations work I've decided to use the New World bible translation as an example. The following charts show the various "ancient manuscripts" that were translated into their modern English bible. Since the Old Testament is believed to be Hebrew and the New Testament is believed to be in Greek there are different sources used for each.

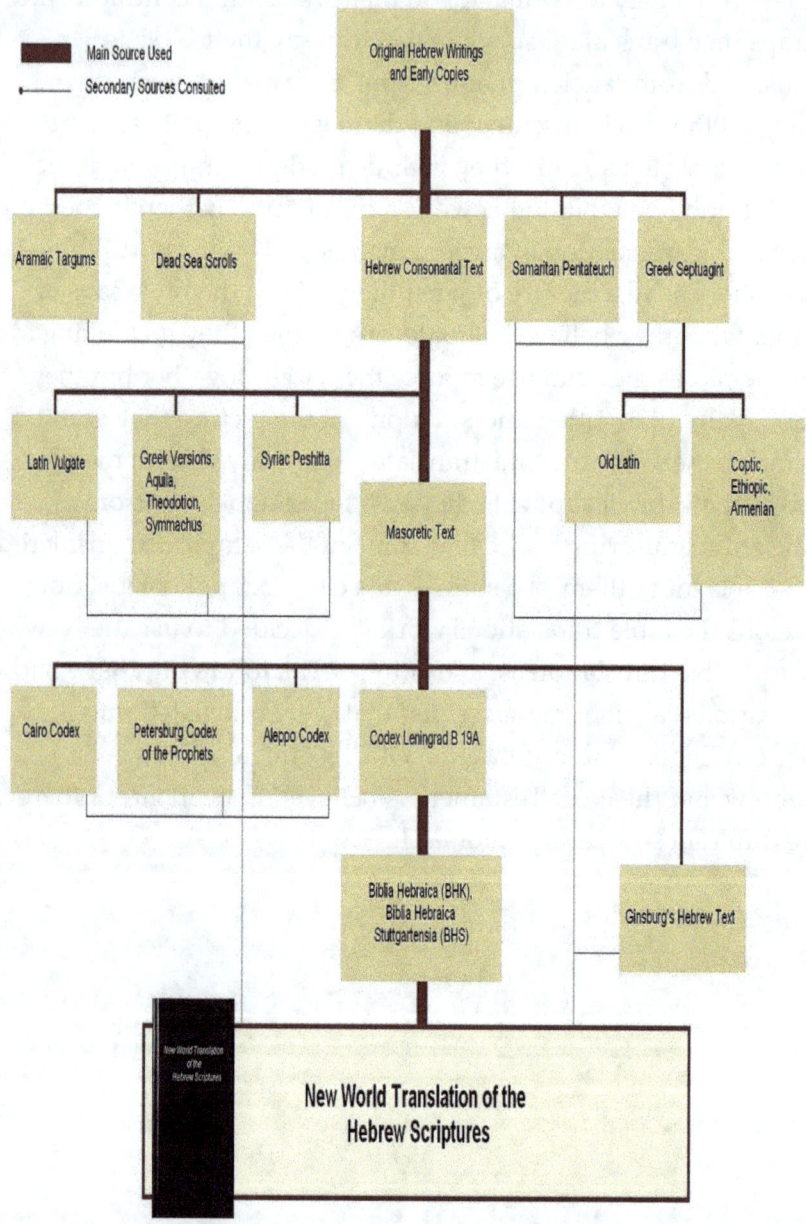

Now keep in mind each yellow box is just a category of texts. They used about 18 different categories from which to take scraps from, when translating the first half of their bible. Note this is just 18 different categories used when translating half of the bible known as the Old Testament. The total number of different texts which were used to make this compilation is information that is unknown to the public. Likewise, the translators' names are also unknown secrets of bible publishing. Also, they call them "Scriptures" saying that the word "Testament" is a mistranslation. Although considering the number of texts they used saying they translated "Testaments" would raise some questions and possibly give the game away which need not happen if they use the word "Scriptures". Since Scriptures is plural then by saying Scriptures instead of Testament, they can legally defend themselves should any accuse them of trying to pass off a compilation text as having been translated by a single source. So, Christians and bible publishes are deeply inclined to use the word "Scriptures" to cover their tracks and legally get away with sly misrepresentations of what their translation process is really like.

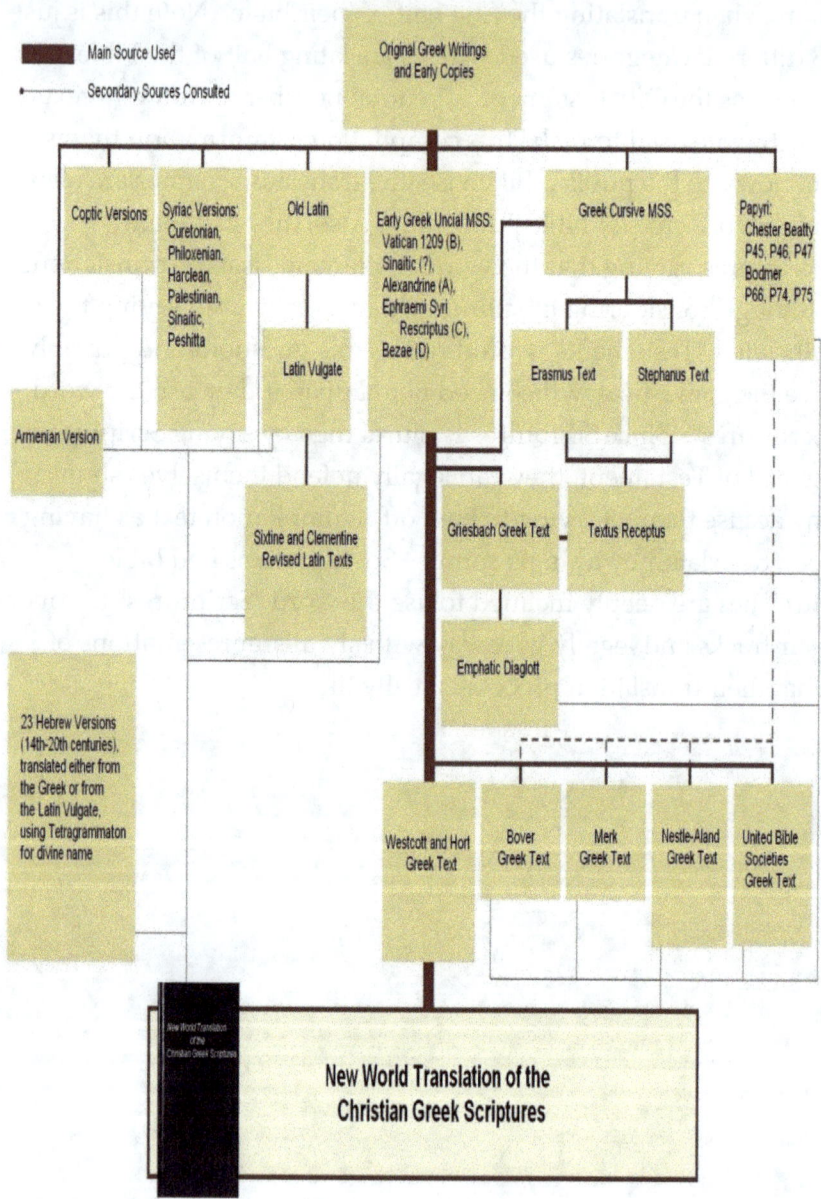

While for the Greek there are 21 yellow boxes, you will notice these boxes are condensed boxes themselves and full of multiple categories of texts which are not very old or "ancient". As you can see, they are actually translating copies of copies of translations of translations and this is a very messy book. Yet to be fair it's actually a lot cleaner than how many other bible publishers get their stuff. Although as with the Old the total number of different texts used in their New Testament is unknown just like the number of translators and their names. Unfortunately, bible publishers never put these types of charts in their bibles, so the bible reader never knows what exactly the bible publishers mean when they say translated from "ancient manuscripts". Although once the process is finished all the yellow boxes from both the old and the new are combined into one book and all the pages are the same colors written in the same ink making for a smooth seamless reading experience. Recently with the internet bible publishers get even more deceptive and then they type up their puzzle in digital text so that if anyone wants to see what they translated then they see a pretty crisp digital text and get misled into thinking it is all one big manuscript when in reality it's a freaky unnatural self-made puzzle with thousands of different pieces forced together. It's sad and shocking but that's exactly how many bibles get made today. Other publishers will just use older translations and alter the language so it says what they want, such as the King James bibles around today are nothing at all like the original Olde English King James bible. Someone who reads and writes English today can't even read the original King James bible because it's alphabet and dialect is different than modern English. Regardless in order to follow Jesus you would have to either follow what he taught or follow what he followed and today we don't have access to either. Now most Christians think that the Old Testament is what the Jews followed then and now and that they just reject the New Testament, but in actuality the Jewish Hebrew bible is different from the Old Testament and they don't consider the Christian Old

Testament to be divine revelation at all. The trouble is Christians think non-Christians believe what their Christian leaders tell them non-Christians believe and they never bother to research for themselves. Then on top of that some Christian evangelists lie to their people saying the Injeel given to Jesus is the New Testament or Gospel and Christians then think that Muslims are supposed to believe in the bible thinking that when the Quran says the Injeel is divine revelation that it means bible or gospel. Thus, the Christian is deluded into thinking that the Jewish and Muslim religious books tell them to believe in the Christian books when they don't. Unfortunately, some Muslims fall for this and even incorrectly translate the word Injeel into Gospel or Zabur into Psalms, but the Christians know there is no gospel of Jesus and the New Testament has never been called the Injeel nor have the Psalms ever been called the Zabur, yet the Christian missionaries make this claim to Muslims to trick them into becoming Christians. Then they give them the gospel of John leading the Muslim to think it was written by the prophet John the Baptist. However, the Christian missionaries are careful not to tell their born and raised Christian flock about how they lie to Muslims about Christianity to get them in the door and that those alleged "ex-Muslim" converts don't really understand Christianity and weren't actually Muslims, let alone devout, but part of deviant heretical sects like the Shia, Ahmadiyya, Murjiah etc. An important distinction is that from the Christian view such posterboard non-Muslims were once Muslims, but from the Islamic view they never were even though they may claim or think they were. It's similar to how from the Islamic view Mormons are Christians and claim to be Christians, yet according to Christianity they aren't. The Christian missionaries simply plan to brainwash that ignorant convert's kids to solve the theological misunderstandings and misconceptions, just as they did with pagan convert's kids in the past.  Then they put such converts up as mascots to preach exclusively to Christians about Islam spreading misconceptions, so as to prevent Christians from researching Islam themselves because they think these "ex-Muslim converts" are experts who wouldn't lie about Islam, especially now that they're Christians.  Those alleged "ex-Muslim" converts never preach to Muslims, unless they can find an ignorant one who's young, poor, dumb and sinful.  Such evangelists will claim they are fundraising to preach to Muslims, but in reality, they're just fundraising to publish lies about Islam directed towards Christians.  What Christians don't realize is that the vast majority of evangelization is directed at them to prevent them from being exposed to other religions in order to keep them Christians, and that the bulk of converts to Christianity who aren't forced into it through violence, economics, prison, politics, emotions or marriage were not known as intelligent religious people when they weren't Christians.  Deceitfully they'll usually claim they used to be devout non-Christians and Christians believe them because they don't know much about other religions and they want to believe that the best and brightest of other faiths are joining their own, but in reality, it's the opposite.  Thus, the Christian is trapped in an intellectual cocoon confidently thinking they will be resurrected in gardens of paradise not knowing they are on a conveyor belt leading to the fire.  Yet what's even worse is that most politicians and members of the media and financial elite are in on the deception pretending to believe in Christianity for the sake of the economy.  For instance, lets imagine Christianity was proven false and all its rituals were abandoned, meaning Christmas, Easter, Valentines, New Years, St. Patrick's Day, and many other holidays were abolished.  Do you know how many industries and jobs that would destroy?  The whole western economy would need to be nearly completely redesigned immediately or else it would suffer greatly in the short term, just as the western economy would drastically suffer in the short term if the Santa Claus myth were abolished. Therefore, those who worship their desires via money are keen on preventing such a drastic economic shock and encourage people to be Christians of the secular variety that are helpful to an exploitive economy of consumerism. Freedom + the Christian "ticket to heaven" allows for mass exploitation of tax slaves and the spread of evil due to each Christian's lack of responsibility since they feel they don't have to "earn salvation", but just accept it from somebody else who did all the hard work for them. There is no "war on Christianity" by Western materialism, Christianity is the Western economy's biggest market. They just want Christians to act less like the prophet Jesus, so they can make more profits to compete with the organized Christian denominations' income streams. Currently Big Business Religions and Big Business Businesses are fine tuning the balance so both can maximize profits. Yet some Christian groups just want all the profits to themselves so they can get power and prestige for more propaganda, in order to put their mind at rest thinking that if the masses believe what they believe then it must be right. This is because their soul within knows they are astray, so their bodies require mass conformity to remain in denial. Just like how kids need others to believe in Santa Claus with them for reassurance.

  Most Christians won't admit that Christianity teaches Jesus was a bastard yet they still maintain him to be a son of God, born of a virgin who wasn't married to God, who was crucified for mankind's salvation. If that is the case it would mean God is an abusive parent. To send one's innocent only son to death in the most painful and humiliating manner in order to forgive someone you're not related to is criminal, unjust, abusive and insane. If someone wrongs me and subsequently apologizes, I'd never ever say: "*I can't forgive you until I crucify my only beloved son.*" Muslims believe that God is the most Merciful. Humans can forgive one another without having to kill their children as a prerequisite, to say that God had to send his son to death for our salvation means that humans are more merciful to humans than God is. Christianity teaches humans are more merciful than God and that God is an abusive parent.

    Do you know the genealogy of Jesus? The gospel of Matthew lists 28 people in between the lineage of David and Jesus. While the gospel of Luke lists 42 people in between the lineage of David and Jesus. Now if both Matthew and Luke knew Jesus and were inspired by God, how come they have completely different family histories? The only names in the two contradicting genealogical biblical lists that are the same in both are David at the beginning and Jesus in the end. Accounting for an average lifespan of 40 years for the 16 extras listed in Luke we have a difference of 640 years between when Matthew and Luke say Jesus was born. On top of that both list a Joseph as the father of Jesus, whereas Jesus didn't have a father so the lineage should be traced through his mother Mary and not a Joseph. The gospels not only disagree on the number and names of people whom they trace Jesus' lineage to David, but they also disagree on who this Joseph was. Muslims believe Mary never married, remained a virgin her whole life and that her uncle Zachariah was her guardian. However, Muslims aren't alone in this belief, ancient Christians believed this as well. For the first few hundred years many Christian denominations including Catholicism taught that Mary was raised in the temple from the ages of 3-14 and was a special "Israelite virgin" who had vowed to be a virgin until she died. Even today the bibles mention such Temple virgins yet

Christians by and large tend to be unaware that Mary was raised in the temple of Jerusalem. Ancient legend has it that the High Priest of the temple tried to get Mary married at the standard female Jewish age for marriage at that time (12 years and 6 months) but she embarrassed him by reminding him she vowed to be a virgin forever so she wasn't going to be getting married. Yet then Christians claim that the High Priest after being publicly embarrassed "consulted the Lord" and decided she should get married determining the guy by a chance gambling game of throwing lots. According to Christians in spite of her vow to be a virgin Mary agreed because since she was inspired by God to make the vow Christians say that she believed the High Priest was also "inspired by God" when getting her married so she figured the will of the High Priest must be the will of God. The lesson Christians gleamed from this story in the past, before the bible was written, was that even if the clergy tells you to do something that you think is sinful then you should do it because the priests are inspired by God. So, Christians adopted this story about Mary the virgin getting married because it promoted taqlid or "blind following" of religious leaders and then the bible was written to say she got married to a guy named Joseph. Muslims believe this is a slander made by the Jews who denied the virgin birth of Mary by saying she committed illegal fornication with her cousin Joseph bin Jacob An-Narraj, who prayed at the same masjid/temple as her that was called "*Bait-ul-Maqdis*". Narraj means developed. This "developed" man was likely a temptation for women and would be easy for Jews to use in slandering the chastity of Mary since he was her cousin and they frequented the same place. Many Christians have perpetuated this Jewish slander by turning Mary's cousin Joseph into her husband, although there is no historical evidence to suggest Mary ever married especially when you consider that historical evidence from Christian sources say she vowed to be a virgin. Christians today say despite her vow to be a virgin she still got married because of the High Priest telling her to but never intended to have sex. Such a foolish notion can easily be refuted by asking why then couldn't Catholic priests and nuns who took vows of celibacy also get married and "just not have sex". If the early Christians had actually believed Mary could get married without ever having sex, then celibacy without marriage wouldn't have been preached nor practiced by the founding scholars of Christianity, nor would it have become institutionalized in the Middle Ages nor would it exist today. The reason for this idea of marriage without sex developed in Christianity because Paul wrote the end of the world was coming so soon that people shouldn't get married and if they were they shouldn't have sex because having kids was pointless and animalistic since Jesus was expected to return in his lifetime. Yet Jesus didn't come back so Christians had a problem because they had preached celibacy and non-marriage for apocalyptic reasons but realized the benefits of marriage and procreation. To get people marrying each other again they then claimed that Joseph and Mary both agreed to never have sex but still got married because even though sex was sinful, in early Christian thought, marriage was not. So, Christians said you could be married and still be virgins forever, knowing that people would marry and then the Church needn't worry about having to teach them how to reproduce or change their teachings on celibacy being virtuous. Yet the story of Mary getting married to Joseph continued to evolve and the Catholic Church as well as others today teach that both of them pledged to be perpetual virgins because they knew Jesus would be born via a virgin Mary so Joseph pledged virginity to fulfill prophecy, or so the story goes even though it's not shared in full with the masses. The Churches today unofficially teach that both Mary and Joseph promised to be virgins purposely so

Jesus could be born of a virgin Mary according to "biblical prophecy". The reason the Catholic Church added this part is because the male clergy had been forbidden to get married and the old story of Mary getting married but remaining a virgin was being used to justify clerical marriage by priests who wanted to get married citing this fictional marriage of perpetual virginity as an example. Nuns and Priests told the Catholic Church that if Mary and Joseph could get married without sex then so could they, but the Church not wanting priests or nuns to marry said the only reason they did that was to fulfill prophecy and since their marriages weren't due to prophecy and might lead to them breaking vows of celibacy then they couldn't do it even though Mary and Joseph did according to Church teaching. However realistically if Mary and Joseph know that a Messiah is going to be born of a virgin and that such a thing is hard to believe as it is, then why would 2 deeply religious people get married with the intention of not having sex and raising a kid whom it is obligatory for people to believe was born of a virgin or they go to hell forever? Common sense dictates that if Mary and Joseph want people to believe Jesus is born miraculously then they wouldn't get married to each other because if they were married then people would be less likely to believe in the miracle. Truly for Mary to get married gives people a reason to disbelieve in a miracle, so it's actually harder to believe in the truth about Jesus if his mother is married. That's why the Churches teach this mutual virginity pledge unofficially, because in reality it's a ridiculous story just added to a ridiculous story to justify evolving Christian teachings on marriage and celibacy. In reality Mary never married and the earliest pre-biblical Christians didn't believe she did and that's why it was such a miracle which was a proof that Jesus was a prophet. God never gives people an even half-logical excuse to reject a miracle, whereas Mary being married would be a good excuse for people not to believe in a virgin birth.  Thus, the very concept contradicts the purpose and conditions of miracles.  If it's easily refutable then it's not a miracle and the virgin birth is debatable only if Mary were married.  So that's why this marriage story is such a slander because the Jews said she Mary was a fornicator, while the Christians said she got married yet in effect both groups have cheapened the miracle and give people reason to disbelieve in it.  Of course, the Jews did it intentionally but sadly the Christians perpetuate this myth thinking it is true not realizing it is a Satanic myth designed to discredit the miracle.  That's one trademark of a false corrupted religion in that the doctrines they invent concerning true prophets become difficult to believe.  The Christmas story and "Holy Family" in reality cause more people to disbelieve in Jesus than believe in him and that's why Satan helps the Christians promote Christmas.  If you do believe Mary married Joseph bin Jacob An-Narraj then you believe she married her cousin.  However, the gospel of Luke doesn't even list Joseph bin Jacob An-Narraj as the father of Jesus, but lists Joseph bin Heli.  The gospel of Matthew lists Joseph bin Jacob, but it is not known if it is Joseph bin Jacob An-Narraj or not.  The gospel of Luke and Matthew both say Mary married a different man.  Historically Joseph bin Jacob An-Narraj was the closest to Mary and he was her cousin who never married her, yet that Joseph isn't mentioned in either of these gospels.  At the very least either the gospel of Matthew has false information or the gospel of Luke, it is impossible for both to be true and/or inspired by God, unless they are writing about two different people named Jesus.  Which they actually might've been because according to Luke 3:31 Jesus descended from David's son Nathan whereas Matthew 1:6 says Jesus descended from David's son Solomon.  So maybe Matthew wrote about one Jesus and Luke wrote about a different guy named Jesus and people just got confused and combined 2 different Jesus' into 1? If both Matthew and Luke are truthful then they must be writing about 2 different guys both named Jesus. I mean what other explanation could a Christian come up with? The slyest will try to say Luke was writing Mary's genealogy and Matthew wrote Joseph's and that's why they differ and that Luke wrote Joseph's name even though he meant Mary because society was hostile to females. Christian apologists use this excuse, however it's invalid because Luke says "Joseph's father" was Heli whereas Mary's father's name was Imran. So, it can't be Mary's genealogy and a new excuse must be invented or else the contradiction must be admitted. Whereas the biblical account is not Mary's genealogy for the simple fact that her genealogy is known and it's not the ones listed for Jesus in the bible. Mary's mother was Hannah who was the daughter of Faqud bin Qabil. Now some Christians ignorantly think Mary's mother's name was Ann. I even know of one named JoAnn who debated this with me and said she knows for a fact that Mary's mother was Ann and not a Hannah because her parents were going to name her Joseph because of his alleged relationship with Mary but because she was born a girl, she got called JoAnn because she was a girl and Mary's mother was Ann. That argument sounds pretty confident, no? Afterall to counter it you'd have to say her parents were wrong. Well, they and other Christians like them are wrong because Ann is not a Hebrew or Aramaic name, the Hebrew word for the name of Mary's mother is חַנָּה which is Hannāh. This Hannāh the mother of "Mary" was likely named after the mother of the prophet Samuel who had the same Hebrew name of Hannāh. The whole Ann identity comes from the "St." Ann whom early Christians built many temples to, and then forgot who this lady was or why they venerated her, therefore in the 4th century they said she was the mother of Mary and that she miraculously was a virgin who gave birth to a virgin

Mary. Yes, early Christians were so crazy about promoting perpetual virginity that they said Mary's mother was a virgin and that she had no father. However if Mary was born of a virgin and didn't have a father then Christians couldn't claim Jesus was the son of God solely due to his miraculous birth because people told Christians *"Well if Jesus is the son of God because of his virgin birth, then his mother is the daughter of God for the same reason and so God would have to be the Grandfather and the Father of Jesus but that's totally messed up and everybody knows Mary never claimed to be the daughter of God, nor did anybody ever claim Jesus was the grandson of God via Mary and the son of God via God. Either Mary had a father or she is a daughter of God and Jesus is of incestual lineage where God made his daughter into his own mother (if Jesus were God) or consort (if not). Or a virgin giving birth does not denote godhood or divine lineage."* Therefore, the myth of Mary being born without a father and her mother being Ann dissipated so the claim of virgin birth denoting godhood or divine lineage could continue to be used. Other evidence proves that Ann was not the name of Mary's mother. John Damascene said Mary's mother had married once, while other Christians claimed Mary's mother had married 3 times, first to Joachim, then to Clopas and then to Solomas, with each marriage resulting in 1 child with all of them being girls named Mary. Christians claim that Mary's mother named all of her children Mary, thus there was a Mary triumvirate with Mary allegedly according to Christian's having 2 sisters with the same name as her. Thus, when Christians say Mary was married to Joseph, you really have to ask which Mary are they talking about since in ancient antiquity Christianity taught there were 3 different Marys. But who was this Ann character whom Christians claimed was the mother of 3 Mary's or 1 according to John Damascene? Well, there used to be a fertility goddess the pagan people worshipped called Anu. This Anu was a Mother-

Goddess, the wife of the Sun God, and she was believed to be an ancestor of all the gods; or the "Mother of every god/goddess". Therefore with the trinitarian Christians saying Mary was the mother of Jesus who was a son of God and God then the pagans naturally said that Mary's mother must be Anu or Ann. Hence all the pagan temples devoted to Anu were converted to Churches dedicated to "St. Anne" and all the wells today called "St. Anne's wells" in Britain actually used to be the wells of the goddess Anu. So, the Christians in the past allowed the pagans to turn their goddess Anu into Mary's mother in order to facilitate conversions and then today modern Christians stick to the story of Ann being the mother of Mary, thinking it's true because it's such an old story it must be legit. On top of that in Africa the Coptic and Ethiopian Christians turned the idols of black goddesses such as Ceres, and Isis with her son Horus into "black Mary's". Yet the European Christians weren't too keen on a black skinned statue, because if Mary was black as the Africans claimed in their statues, then how could they have their white Jesus statues? I mean it's already a matter of faith to believe in a virgin birth, but for a black virgin to give birth to a white kid is stretching it a little. Thus, the pagans came up with a solution and claimed that all the black Mary statues or Black Madonna's were sent from heaven, some of them were alleged to have been carved by angels and even "Luke" the attributed author of Luke. By doing this the pagans played a real trick with the Christian racists of Europe in saying that miracles gave them their black female statues, so Christians could either benefit from the miraculous claims and use them as "proof for Christianity" or say the miracles were false and the idols had to go. In the end they went along and used the pagan ploys as "proofs" and the Jinn might've helped as well. But why are there black Madonna statues in places where the population isn't? Well, that is because the most fertile soil was/is the darkest, so the versions of the pagan "Mother Earth" fertility goddesses were usually black or brown. For instance, Artemis, Cybele, Demeter, Diana, Persephone, Kali, Nuit, Nyx and many other pagan female deities all had brown or black skin because of that agricultural symbolism. The problem with Christians letting pagans Christianize their idols was that the descendants of the pagans were so thoroughly brainwashed that the temporary allowance and Christianization of pagan deities to ease pagan transitions became official Christian doctrine. But that's just the story with Mary's mother. Thankfully the Christians don't really care much about Mary's father, even though now most of them admit she did indeed have a human father. Part of the reason they claimed Mary didn't have a human father was due to the original sin allegedly being passed along via sex and genetically inherited. But inventing the claim that Mary had no father because she had no original sin backfired because then people asked why she wasn't famous for being born miraculously so the Christians scrambled to concoct a story of Mary's father as well after having neglected that part of Jesus having a real human maternal grandfather. Yet such neglect wasn't mere neglect, these fantastical fictions peddled by early Christians were done both for theological and conversion purposes but also to cover up facts they didn't like or facts that contradicted the evolving faith. Mary's real human father was Imran, the son of Bashim, the son of Amun, the son of Misha, the son of Hosqia, the son of Ahriq, the son of Mutham, the son of Azazia, the son of Amisa, the son of Yamish, the son of Ahrihu, the son of Yazem, the son of Yahfashat, the son of Eisha, the son of Iyam, the son of Rahba'am, the son of the prophet Dawud (David). Yet Christian's tend not to know that Mary was a descendant of David and as a result they insist Joseph must be in the picture because they insist the Messiah must be a descendant of David via a Joseph. However

Jewish lineage is traced through the mother and not the father, so for Jesus to be a descendant of David his mother has to be one and he doesn't need any adopted father or anything. It was because non-Jews traced the lineage through fathers that a need for an adopted father's Davidic lineage was needed for them to believe in the prophecy of the Messiah being a descendant of David. Basically, Christians added Joseph to the picture with Mary because non-Jews figured if there was no husband for Mary then Jesus couldn't be the Messiah due to lack of a paternal lineage. Unfortunately, Mary's father, Imran, died before she was born, as a result Mary was raised as an orphan in the care of Zakariyyah, her closest male relative and God's prophet. Although Mary's name isn't really Mary because that's not a name, she could've ever used in the languages she knew. In Aramaic her name was

ܡܪܝܡ (Mariam); in Hebrew מִרְיָם (Miriam), and in Arabic it was مريم (Maryām). This name was likely given to her because of the Hebrew Miriam which is also said to have been the name of the sister of Moses and Aaron, the very sister who followed Moses while he was in a basket floating down the river. Thus "Mary" was likely named after the sister of 2 prophets, while her mother Hannah was named after the mother of another prophet Samuel, while her father Imran was also the same name as the father of Moses and Aaron. So, at the time she had a very religiously significant female name from a family with very religious names. Then when "Mary" turns up with a baby via a virgin birth, by the Jews calling her "Sister of Aaron" when denouncing her they were referring to her name being the same as the sister who followed the blessed baby Moses and then informed Pharaoh's family that his true mother could breastfeed her. So, their label "Sister of Aaron" for Mary when slandering her was like saying *"With the name you have, how can you dare falsely claim to have a virgin birth?*

*Either you are a whore covering up your promiscuity or covering for a whore falsely taking the baby from its true mother, thus putting shame to your name doing the opposite of what the original Miriam did for the sake of God!"* However, Jews also hated Aaron because of the long-held privileges of the Aaronite lineage of priests, thus they inserted a falsehood into the bible about Aaron being the one who made the golden calf. So "Sister of Aaron" also had a double meaning for Jews as a comparison to one they falsely claimed was an inventor of perhaps the most infamous idol in the history of global idolatry. Thus, those ancient Jews really knew how to pick good names and they also were highly talented at taking a good name and verbally transforming it into a bad name, depending on how they felt about you or your actions. They tended to have 2 sides to every name, for instance if you were David and they liked you they'd say your name fits since you are great like David slaying Goliath, and if they didn't like you, they'd say your name fit because you were filthy like David the adulterer. Or they'd call you a son of Adam if you had honorable ancestry while if they thought you were a big sinner unlike any others, they'd call you a son of Adam saying "like father like son". Names were very important then to shape one's social identity and should be given similar importance now as well. And with such a religious name from a family who loved to choose religiously significant names the only way to have an even more religious name for her kid would be to have an angel tell her what the name of her kid should be. That the name of Jesus and John were both announced by angels, as was the names of other prophets throughout history shows how important names can be. If names weren't that important then angels wouldn't specifically tell people what to name their kids. The point is that the name of the mother of Jesus was not "Mary". The English "Mary" comes from a translation of the New Testament's Greek word for Jesus' mother "Μαρία" and the Latin word of Maria. Now there may be pagan relations to the pagan virgin goddess Minerva influencing the Greek and Latin translations, but the error primarily comes from Christians believing that the Greek New Testament is the original instead of the Greek texts being translations. Everyone knows Mary was not a Greek yet they translate her name as Mary because the biblical New Testament is Greek and they insist those are originals written in the language of the characters the documents describe. So instead of Christians admitting their biblical documents are translations of something other than Greek, most choose to say "*no her name was Mary*" even though her name isn't even Mary in the Greek. English Christians just like to pretend sometimes that all of world history is in English. But world history is not in English, so they use the wrong name of Mary even though her real name is easily pronounced as Maryam or Miriam. Whereas it really gets stupid in this regard because people named Mary think and claim they are named after the mother of Jesus while many named Maryam or Miriam think their name which really is the same as Jesus' mother isn't. To put this absurdity in perspective this name change would be like saying the name of the first man was Alex, hence Alexander of Macedon was named after him. Anyone would know that's simply not true, but when it comes to the name of Mary people make this common linguistic error. But alas despite Mary not being her real name I will still refer to Jesus' mother as Mary to avoid confusion. Now when faced with their own ignorance and lack of genealogical knowledge regarding Jesus and the biblical contradictions between the Jesus genealogies given in Matthew and Luke, the go-to emergency Christian excuse is "*I'll have to research that*". When they say that then you know it's time to discuss another issue and move on, and most likely they will never ever research that because religiously it's easier for them to just assume you are wrong since if they research it and you are right then their very faith is proven false. Whereas how many Christians do you know want to learn or believe Christianity is false? On the contrary they want everyone else to think, believe and tell the world it's true. Just as I didn't want to research whether Santa Claus was truly giving me presents every year, most Christians don't really want to find out if Christianity is true or false based on factual unbiased information. Research is scary when you might find out you are wrong thus people tend to avoid it or distort their research so they get the results they want. The point is when Luke says his genealogy is the genealogy of Joseph it means Joseph, not Mary or Maryam. We can't let people play games with the bible and say, "*well since both gospels can't be about Joseph because the genealogies contradict then one of the genealogies of Jesus given must be Mary even though the bible authors said it was Joseph, because the bible can't be wrong and doesn't contradict*". This type of excuse to avoid admitting biblical gospels contradict each other is the most common one Christians use when it comes to the bible. It's like showing a kid who wrote 1+1+1=3 and 1+1+1=1 on their test that they are wrong and failed the test of life because their beliefs are contradictory, and rather than the kid admit that they have contradictory mathematical beliefs and something they wrote down is wrong and not inspired by God they insist there must either be something wrong with your vision or your understanding because it's impossible for them to be wrong or not have information that's inspired by God. Christians are constantly told "*It's a fact the bible is inspired by God and doesn't contradict.*" and they never check this "fact" but just believe it as a matter of faith without proving it, they ignore the real facts when the text itself is proven to be contradictory because they are biblically brainwashed and blinded to see falsehood as falsehood. The fact is that the "facts" they were told about the bible are not facts but fictional faith-based doctrines that are simply labeled as facts by people who believe in them and such facts are felt to be facts as a result of mob mentality, cultural tradition and brainwashing plus Satan. It's easy for Christians to believe Christians when Christians tell each other it's a fact the Christian bible is true or it's a fact their Christian religion is correct. The core fundamental reason for most Christian excuses is that deep down they cannot mentally imagine a scenario where any part of the bible is simply wrong, they think and believe a mistake is impossible. They will say the texts don't mean what they say and that 1 actually means 3 or that ABCD actually means FFFF or that, "*Well everyone has a different perspective so that's why the gospel authors all wrote different things but they all meant the same thing and wrote about the same thing. You can't expect the details of their stories to match up and be the same, because they are different people. If you combine them all together, you'll get the gist of it and that's all that matters is that you get the gist of it. Details aren't important.*" Basically, they tell me to just believe the gist even though the ingredients being used don't combine to create the gist they're promoting. They tell me it does but it just doesn't look that way because words in the bible don't mean what they say, although they actually mean what they believe them to mean and if there were contradictions then their leaders would know and they themselves wouldn't believe there aren't. For instance, with a Christian, I once examined the biblical contradictions of Matthew 27:28, Mark 15:17 and John 19:2 where Matthew says Jesus wore a scarlet robe while John and Mark say it was purple. They even saw the verses in their own bible. Initially they agreed with me and said I was right it looks like there is a contradiction BUT it's just a mistranslation and in the Greek they're both the same colors and don't contradict. So, I told him I think otherwise and asked him to look up the Greek for me so I can find out what the color really was because it can't be both, and he agreed. Yet he repeatedly neglected to look it up and I had to ask several times, until finally I looked it up myself and found that it was worse than I thought, because John's Greek word for "purple" is a different color than Mark's "purple" but in English they translated both as purple. So, in English there are 2 colors to choose from but in Greek there are 3, thus it was indeed mistranslated in English but it was mistranslated to eliminate a contradiction in the bible from 3 to 2. When I met the Christian to say how I looked up the Greek myself and showed him the Greek text itself, he surprised me by saying he looked it up too. But in reality, he didn't, instead he just read to me off of his cellphone his religious hierarchy's official explanation that, "*Matthew and Mark/John all saw the same color but it just looked scarlet to Matthew so he wrote down scarlet and looked purple to Mark and John so they wrote purple. They just had a different perspective on what color it looked like to them so they wrote down different colors but they actually all agree it was the same color.*" In response I plainly and directly told him, "*No they don't, they all disagree.*" Then he was dumbfounded and stunned that I said no, and rejected that explanation. He was literally speechless that I said no, after he read me what his religious leaders had said, he almost didn't think it was possible for me to disagree because personally his religion said he can't disagree with his leaders since he believes they are divinely guided to be correct. So, for me to tell him no, he must've felt like I was saying no to God or something. First of all, it was clear that the guy didn't even look up the bible verses in Greek, but just looked up an explanation because if he looked up the Greek, he would've known it was 3 different colors and not 2, and wouldn't even have came with the answer he came with. Whereas his organization knew he wouldn't look it up himself and would fall for their coy 2 color deception that says "*Don't worry everything's okay, the bible doesn't contradict, trust us and say X.*" So, when Christians tell you

"I'll research that" or that they'll find out the answer, what they really mean is that they are going to ask their religious superiors for an answer to give you in response. Most of them will never really look into something for themselves to see if they or their beliefs or their faith is wrong, instead they will just research something to say to you to get you to convert or shut up. Whereas realistically the whole idea of "the same color looking like a different color to different people" is impossible. It sounds good, it does sound like a really good explanation, but scientifically it's impossible. To illustrate, everyone knows most grass is the color green and urine is the color yellow and poop is the color brown. Visually we all have different eyes and visually scientists have said that we might even see the same colors in different ways, however we can never ever tell that we see the same thing in different colors because we use the same names for the colors we see. As an example, how would you define/explain what a particular color looks like without using any colors in your definition? Colors are truly what is called "visual learning" in that you really have to see it to know what it looks like to you, but even when you see it you can't confirm whether other people are seeing exactly the same color that you are seeing. You might use a wrong name but when using the same name, you truly don't know whether you are talking about the same color or not. Basically, when I see yellow urine, I've learned that color is yellow, just as you have, but we might actually be seeing a different color than each other, although since we both learned that specific color is called yellow, we call it yellow and agree it is yellow despite not knowing if we see the same color. So, whether we see the same object in different colors we still agree on what color to call it, and linguistically there is never ever a difference in name. Honestly, we might all have the same favorite color but because our eyes see it in different colors than others do, we all call it by a different name. Meaning when I see something I call green, I might actually be seeing the color you think is red and when I see red, I might be seeing what you call green, yet since we both agree on the names for the colors, we would never discover that our reds are visually interpreted by each of us as different colors. I'm not saying they are but if we were seeing colors differently, we would still agree on the name of every color. Essentially, we refer to X color as X and it doesn't matter whether you see X as black and I see X as white because we both agree on it being X and call it X. Another example are flags, have you ever met 1 person who had a different opinion on what color a national flag was? This unanimity of color names even applies to people who are color blind. I used to play on a tennis team with someone who was color blind and I didn't even know he was color blind until he told me, and I didn't believe him because he had been identifying all the colors correctly the whole time, I knew him. I honestly thought he was joking until he explained that being color blind doesn't mean he can't tell colors apart, but that he sees things in a different shade of color, which he says I would call grayish. He could correctly identify each color for what it is because he learned the different names for the different shades. The only trouble he sometimes could mess up on was confusing blue with purple. That's crucial to this biblical dilemma because even if we pretend that the biblical authors were color blind even a color-blind person can tell the difference between scarlet and purple, and I've met such a person. Thus, this is an instance where the bible clearly contradicts and the authors simply cannot have been writing about what they actually saw or what actually happened because if they did then such a 3-way color contradiction would not exist. Yet the Christian guy insisted that it doesn't really contradict they just saw the same colors in different ways and wrote different things, which is what his

Christian leaders told him. He didn't even believe me when I showed him the Greek text that shows there are 3 different colors written in the bible and not just 2 as the English says, he insisted there were 2 colors in the bible and it doesn't even matter because since it can only be one color in reality then they all really saw the same color even if they wrote down different colors. So, he said it's really just one color. At the time I dropped the issue out of disgust, but if you are ever in this situation and face such an explanation just tell them, "*Ok tell me then what 1 color was it? The bible gives us 3 colors, pick one and tell me which one it really was and which 2 wrote down the wrong color. Who knows maybe it was polka dotted? Was it a rainbow color? Maybe it was all black and had a picture of my face on it, but they just called it purple instead? Or was it some special Jesus color never used before or since but only in existence in that one time in history? If they can't even write down the right color then how can you trust anything they wrote down? Just try this game with a police officer and have one person say it was a red light, another say it was a yellow light and you say it was a green light and then say you all agree it was the same color when you drove through it and smashed up your car but it just looked different to each so that's why you all say different colors.*" Essentially, we're just supposed to trust Christian leaders truly understand the unwritten meanings and that it just seems to contradict to us because we're stupid and their leaders who believe in the bible know better. This excuse is the very definition of blind faith in the bible, meaning when they see a contradiction they pretend it doesn't exist and make excuses for the bible giving it the benefit of the doubt automatically before they've even read it and give it the benefit of the doubt even after they've read it too. Some Christians even use this excuse with other biblical contradictions confidently saying, "*Just because the stuff in this gospel isn't mentioned in that gospel or the others doesn't mean it didn't happen and that all the authors didn't believe in it happening. They just didn't write it down. You got to look at all the gospels to get the full story. But each one of them knew the full story, they just all decided to write different parts of the same story in different ways saying different things because they wrote for different people. Yet they all believed the same exact thing; they just didn't write down the same story even though they all agreed because they had "different perspectives". It's like 4 people recording a video of the same event from different angles, obviously all 4 are going to show different things or in this case say that different things happened. You can't expect 4 different people to tell us the same exact details."* (Sadly, the Christian usually doesn't know that these different gospels were actually used by different types of Christians and that's why they say different things, because they were combat writings originally used to support different religions within Christianity and that each Church had its own gospels and belief systems. That is until the church of Rome took over the empire and unified the rest under its own doctrine via force. Hence, they combined the 4 gospels they liked most into one book because by having more than 1 gospel it meant those who already believed in those other gospels would be more willing to accept the Roman Catholic faith, so they could be absorbed rather than violently converted.) To which I say well then if you only had 3 gospels you wouldn't have this "full story" so how do you know with 4 you got the "full story" when thousands of gospels were destroyed and lost? What else happened that they didn't write down that you don't know about? How do you know that X gospel author agreed with Y gospel author's extra details if he didn't write them down and never read Y gospel? The video camera excuse isn't even valid because the gospels conflict with each other on details such as, colors, phrases, times, numbers, persons involved and many more details that can only have one version regardless of the "camera angle". As an example, when watching a sporting event have you ever seen a camera angle make the colors appear to be different colors, or the score to change based on the camera angle, or maybe the time and date as well? Does the camera angle ever make it seem like the teams were changed into different teams or the game was being played in a different city or that the camera angle can make you think a completely different sport is being played? I mean haven't you ever been watching a hockey game on TV and then the camera angle changes and it looks like a football game? Apparently, that's how camera angles work when discussing biblical camera angles. In reality we'd say somebody must've changed the channel and regarding the bible the channels of information cannot be from the same source (God). Yet then again, the authors of the bible we are told were "eye witnesses", not just watching on TV. So, have you met 4 people who said they attended a live sports game and when they returned each of them told you individually that they saw different teams playing and they were wearing different colors, the final score was different, the time they played was different and the rules they played by were different? No? That's never happened? Well, if it did what would you think? Would you think that maybe they were lying, crazy or on drugs? Or that none of them actually went to the event in question and they never knew what the other was going to say before they said it? Well, if you then told someone else who thought these 4 sporty people were "inspired by God" that you find them suspect and don't believe their story and then they said in defense of the 4 witnesses that, *"Well it's like with different camera angles each person will have a different perspective and interpret the same thing different ways, but all their stories are the same and true."* Anyone would rationally say that the person who believes all 4 of those "witnesses" are telling 1 true story is even crazier than the 4 liars. But then again it is called Christianity and not Rationality. The funniest part about the Christian who repeatedly gave the "camera angle excuse" is that he also repeatedly insisted that he doesn't watch movies. Although maybe that explains why he didn't understand how his camera angle excuse was utterly unacceptable. The biblical accounts aren't different perspectives, they're different conflicting stories. It's just a blind assumption that they all agree because the Christian wants them to agree because religiously they agree with all of them and if the gospels disagree with each other then the Christian has to disagree as well, which would mean disagreeing with part of the bible which they religiously can't do. Thus, they desperately come up with any excuse they can to avoid and escape this reality that believing in one part of the bible means disbelieving in another part. When they use such an excuse it tells me that they just aren't ready to accept the truth that the bible isn't what they were told, contradicts itself and doesn't say or teach what they believe. In any other aspect of life this excuse would never be accepted by them, but because it's the bible for some reason they think it makes sense that 4 people have 4 different contradicting stories and that they all meant the same thing and were inspired by the same God to write different things. So many use this same excuse spontaneously I actually think it's whispered into each one's ears by Satan. Sometimes I want to tell a Christian who uses this excuse that they should just write their own version of the bible so that it says what you believe it means. But because they are physically, mentally and emotionally hurt by the truth I try to restrain myself, because the truth seriously hurts people and can make them sick. Many people actually can't handle a heavy dosage of truth and if they get too much truth at once or too soon then it literally blows their mind and destroys them as a person. I've experienced difficulty coming to terms with the truth myself and seen others lose their humanity when I passionately shared more truth with people than they can handle. So, I apologize if when discussing the genealogy contradiction or anything else in this book it is too much or too soon, I'm just explaining the situation fully. There is a famous theory that good books are written by those whom nobody can stand talking to. My problem is I can be too honest, impatient, insensitive and tend to talk how I write. Whereas while people might be able to read the truth, most can't handle hearing it; at least not the way I tell it. Anyways regarding the bible's genealogies of Jesus, the only way both Matthew and Luke could be correct is if Mary married two men named Joseph and had two sons named Jesus, either that or the Joseph she married had two fathers, but both of these scenarios are impossible. Given the circumstances I'd say either the gospel of Matthew, Luke, or both are wrong. But let's say the Christian is adamant in that both genealogies tracing Jesus to David are accurate, what do you say then? Well Matthew 1:1-6 lists David as the 9th generation descendant of Pharez bin Judah. Who was Pharez bin Judah? Genesis 38:24-38 alleges Pharez was an incestuous bastard child of Judah and his daughter Thamar. So, if Jesus was a descendant of David, then he has a bastard's lineage according to the bible. Also remember Deuteronomy 23:2 says a bastard can't enter the temple of the Lord, not even until the tenth generation. Biblically David was the 9th descendant of a bastard, meaning David's kids couldn't enter the temple according to the bible. Yet David's kid Solomon is famous for having built the temple and going inside it frequently. So, this is where biblically several things are messed up and false, especially with genealogy. Other biblical genealogies of Jesus trace his lineage to Abraham or Adam and also conflict with each other. God would never give multiple conflicting genealogies, or have discrepancies such as these in divine scripture. Nor would God have a genealogy of himself, especially one with God as the son of human beings, thus Jesus can't be God. In fact, this whole theory of God having a genealogy led the French Merovingian dynasty to forge their own genealogical records trying to make themselves appear to be descended from Jesus, allegedly through a fictional sexual relationship with Mary Magdalene. This is what some people think is the "Holy Grail", or secret of the Templars who were supported by this same Merovingian dynasty. In reality the Merovingians saw the Catholic Church saying Jesus was God and decided that if they could make it seem that they were the descendants of Jesus then they would basically be considered God-men and have a divine mandate to rule the whole world. The problem today is conspiracy theorists fell for this scam, thinking it was true because of the secrecy, not knowing the big secret is that the genealogies of Jesus both in the bible and the alleged "Holy Grail" are false. Then some go to the complete opposite extreme saying there are so many lies about Jesus he must not have even existed at all. It is this extreme that too much of a dose of truth can push people to and they then abandon religion or embrace paganism and in doing so reject the one true religion giving Satan victory. That is why Satan gives disbelievers such crazy excuses because he hopes we will give them a shocking dose of truth that will overload them and lead them to greater disbelief. So even though information can get you fired up don't let your attitude or tone be inflammatory or people will burn instead of learn. I apologize if my book is inflammatory instead of informative, there is a very fine line between the two and those two attitudes are contradictory as well. Be informative not inflammatory.

    The Roman State wanted Jesus to be portrayed as a hard-working taxpaying citizen, whereas in reality Jesus didn't work and would be considered a vagrant by most social standards today. Historically Jesus was not a carpenter but was a poor wanderer who went around preaching, surviving off of gifts and whatever provisions he could find. Jesus lived a similar lifestyle as that of his cousin and contemporary the prophet John. Obviously, the Roman State wouldn't want this type of lifestyle to be adopted, or to have a homeless man portrayed positively, especially since they turned Jesus into God/son of God. Pagans would never accept a poor homeless wandering deity and it wouldn't be good for the economy if they did. Thus, the Romans drew from the Jewish slander of Mary and her cousin, they turned Joseph and Jesus into carpenters in order to make the fictional crucifixion story have irony and foreshadowing. This is another reason why Jesus is not divine. If as many Christians claim that Jesus was a hardworking carpenter then it is inconceivable to imagine God being a carpenter working for people getting bossed around by employers or customers. The bible mentions nothing about Jesus interacting with customers, making carpentry mistakes, or what his best wood work ever was. It is blasphemy to think God could be a carpenter or that he would suffer a son of his to work for humans, or that he could even have a literal son. Had Jesus ever been a carpenter then some specific story or reference would have been recorded in the bible. Only once is he associated with carpentry in the bible, when teaching in the synagogue by those who were offended by his teaching. Whereas he is called "Rabbi" about 13 times and "Teacher" about 47 times. Since Jesus was teaching in the temple it shows the religious authorities knew he was qualified and not a carpenter. This instance is from Mark's gospel 6:1-6 (written first and copied by other gospels) in an English translation of the New International Version of the bible: *"Jesus left there and went to his hometown, accompanied by his disciples. 2 When the Sabbath came, he began to teach in the synagogue, and many who heard him were amazed. "Where did this man get these things?" they asked. "What's this wisdom that has* *been given him? What are these remarkable miracles he is performing? ³ Isn't this the carpenter? Isn't this Mary's son and the brother of James, Joseph, Judas and Simon? Aren't his sisters here with us?" And they took offense at him.⁴ Jesus said to them, "<u>A prophet is not without honor except in his own town, among his relatives and in his own home</u>." ⁵ <u>He could not do any miracles there</u>, except lay his hands on a few sick people and heal them. ⁶ <u>He was amazed at their lack of faith.</u>"*

    Most likely if the bible verses about offended people calling him a carpenter and the son of Joseph are authentic then the people were merely just repeating the old Jewish slander they had heard about Mary. Since the label of carpenter is in the form of a question, as are his having brothers and sisters, it proves the accusers themselves aren't sure of what they are saying and are asking for confirmation of the rumors they've heard. They don't know for certain; they're just repeating Jewish gossip. The bible says that's what those who were offended by Jesus said, the bible never says that what they said was true. Also, the verses say his disciples accompanied him, if the charge of being a carpenter were true when it was made then that would mean the disciples would've known Jesus was a carpenter and would have seen his business since they were in his hometown. Yet no letters or other gospels from the New Testament mention Jesus being a carpenter, thus the disciples dismissed this spurious slander as we should. Jesus said to his slanderers, "A prophet is not without honor except in his own town, among his relatives and in his own home." This verse is very revealing because it shows Jesus considers himself a prophet, not God, or a son of God. God is honored everywhere and doesn't have relatives. Just imagine how if Jesus were God, then it means all his grandparents, uncles, aunts, cousins etc. are all the grandparents, uncles, aunts and cousins of God. It's disgusting! It is unclear whether Jesus is speaking about prophets generally in the verse or about himself, but either way the relatives he speaks of are not those the slanderers accused him of having. Regardless Jesus would be related to Joseph bin Jacob An-Narraj since Mary was, so the kids of Joseph would be his relatives no matter what, even though Mary never married. Yet it is important to know that there is no separate word in Hebrew to distinguish between siblings and other family members, so the English text translated as brothers and sisters doesn't mean Jesus had brothers or sisters it just means he had family. The gospel also states how Jesus could not do any miracles in his hometown except healing a few sick people. This contradicts the slanderers' question, *"What are these remarkable miracles he is performing?"* which indicates Jesus was performing miracles in his hometown that they witnessed, or else they were being sarcastic using his lack of miracles against him. Next the bible says Jesus was *"amazed at their lack of faith"*, God is not amazed at people's lack of faith, God is angry, humans get amazed at humans; thus, Jesus was 100% human and not God or a son of God. It is important to note that Jesus was teaching on the Sabbath, because this was the most religious day of the week and you needed credentials to teach religion in the synagogue; of which no women would be allowed in to hear Jesus. This reveals that the Jewish religious leaders felt Jesus had religious credentials. Muslims believe Jesus spoke from infancy, was a prophet on the first day he was born and began his ministry then. This would be his credentials for those who accepted his prophethood. Many Christians don't believe Jesus was speaking to people on day one, therefore in order to have credentials Jesus would have needed to study in a religious school. If Jesus was raised by a carpenter, he wouldn't have been able to study in a religious institute. On the other hand, if Mary wasn't married and was supported by the Prophet Zachariah, her uncle, then Jesus would have been given religious instruction throughout his life under the best religious teachers. The bible says Jesus was teaching at the temple in Jerusalem at the age of 12. From a Catholic perspective this would be like a 12-year-old teaching the Pope and Cardinals in the Vatican, they would never let it happen. Jesus would not be permitted to teach rabbis, or there, at such an age unless the religious leaders recognized his qualifications and knew he was a religious student, or prophet. Now I don't know whether Jesus learned at a religious school, although Ibn Kathir stated that Jesus went to a religious school at age 7 and ended up teaching the teacher instead of being taught. If Jesus did it would mean Christianity is a false religion and Christians would have destroyed any records and evidence showing Jesus studied in the religious institutes of his day. Keep in mind the bible is silent and blank for over 27 years of Jesus' life except for him teaching in the temple at 12. The bible tells us Jesus taught at the temple for days, but we aren't given many lessons from his extensive alleged childhood teachings. If Jesus were teaching at 12 then it means his ministry had begun and he was already doing his job giving lessons that we can learn from. Therefore, for the bible to be blank it means we have missed out on years of Jesus teaching people, performing miracles and expanding his ministry. If he was teaching in the temple then he was teaching outside of the temple as well. Had Jesus been a religious student, when being instructed he would have been obligated to share his concept of God both at the school as well as the temple. If as Christians claim Jesus were God, or the son of God, then he would be obligated to tell his religious teachers and classmates that he was God or the son of God, but because he wasn't he didn't. It is because Jesus agreed with the Mosaic monotheistic concept of God and the laws that any scholastic record of Jesus has been destroyed. Had Jesus been a religious student he would have learned about the deviant Jews who say

Ezra is the literal "son of God". Then Jesus would have been taught how to refute such a false belief because God can't have literal sons. Realistically one can imagine Jesus doing his thesis on this and saying how God does not beget nor is he begotten and that there is only one God who is not comparable to his creation. Also, it is ridiculous to imagine that God would go to school as a student. So, if Jesus went to school, then he can't be God and Trinitarian Christianity is false. Thus, you can see why if Jesus went to a religious school throughout his childhood and young adult years, Christian authorities would delete this information and prefer people know nothing about young Jesus rather than the truth. Repeatedly throughout the gospels people come up to Jesus asking him to heal them, cast out demons, advise them, settle disputes and talk about religion. This reveals that Jesus must have been known as a learned religious man and dressed like it, because carpenters don't get asked those things. When the Pharisees interacted with Jesus, they never attempted to discredit him by saying he was a carpenter or from a carpenter's household. Instead, they invite him to dinners for religious discussions and always treat him as though he carried some type of religious certification. Not once did the Pharisees or anyone else say that Jesus was unqualified or unlearned in religious teachings. Even though they disagreed with him the Pharisees treated Jesus as a colleague, not a carpenter. They even called him a Rabbi! So, if his Rabbinical enemies were calling him a Rabbi, it was probably because he went to school like a normal human and became a Rabbi. If Jesus were a carpenter, then how did his fellow workers, customers and rival carpenters respond to his religious message? Did he ever use miracles in carpentry? How much money did he earn? What happened to the business after he started preaching? Did he gain customers or lose customers? Who were his customers? How many customers did he have? Did he only work for Jews or work for Pagans too? At what age did he start working, as a child, teen or adult? What happened to the business after he ascended to heaven? Why get fishermen as apostles and not ask carpenters first? Because the developers constructing the Christian mythology took into account that Jesus was born near the beginning of the new pagan zodiac millennia during the age of Pisces. With Pisces being the star constellation resembling a fish, the bible story of Jesus telling fishermen that he will make them "fishers of men" became cliche and the pagan symbol of Pisces the fish, which is a graven image, became a popular Christian emblem as Christians swallowed the story "hook, line and sinker". If Jesus' disciples really were fishermen, then they would've been extremely strict regarding religion since Judaism and the Old Testament prohibits many types of seafood. To be a Jewish fisherman you had to be strictly religious in order to keep kosher. As a carpenter was Jesus ever contracted to construct weapons of war for Rome, or crosses for executing innocent or guilty people? Did he ever make any wooden religious objects like a pulpit or place of worship for Jews or Pagans? Did any customer ever refuse to pay and how did Jesus react? Was he organized or disorganized? What wood did he use and where did he get it from? Where did he get the tools and which types did, he use? Was it a one-man operation or did he have employees? Who were the employees, were they male or female and how long did they work? If Jesus was a carpenter, then why didn't he give his cousin and fellow prophet John a job? Did Jesus ever fire any employees and how? Did he pay taxes and how much? What about rival carpenters? Was he ever extorted, robbed or scammed? These are all things that would be mentioned in the bible if Jesus were really a carpenter or had a stepfather carpenter figure. Realistically if Jesus were a carpenter, he would not have had time to travel and preach. Also, there would have been conflict with creating wooden idols or graven images. Even if Jesus weren't a carpenter, had Joseph been a carpenter step-father of Jesus the bible would have mentioned either why wooden statues and images were allowed or that he didn't make them because of the 2nd commandment thereby being different from pagan carpenters. Although if this stepfather carpenter called Joseph was a Roman insertion, then being ignorant of the 2nd commandment the Romans would have neglected mentioning its conflict with carpentry as well as any details. Conveniently most Christians assume Joseph simply died before Jesus began his public ministry and that is the reason why he is never mentioned in the bible once Jesus reaches adulthood. Yet the more likely reason Joseph isn't mentioned during Jesus' public ministry is because the Joseph lie served its purpose already and it was easier to leave him out than insert more lies that would jeopardize the deception's success. Never in the gospels do people ask Jesus about carpentry, neither do any of the many parables attributed to Jesus have anything to do with carpentry. If Jesus was a carpenter or his mother's fictitious husband a carpenter then at least one parable would have been about carpentry if not many. Jesus has nothing to do with carpentry in the bible because he was not a carpenter and his mother never married a carpenter. Yet the real kicker is that the word used as carpenter can also mean "craftsman", as in "stone mason". So, then the freemasons and alien conspiracy theorists come along and falsely accuse Jesus of being a freemason. Yet all these claims are false because Mary never married or had sex with her cousin Joseph!

    Some Christians may mention the nativity story and that Jesus was born in Bethlehem in a manger with shepherds, animals and wise men because Joseph and Mary had to go to Bethlehem (allegedly Joseph's hometown) in order to participate in a census done by the Roman Empire and all the inns were full. The problem is that the nativity story told and portrayed every December contradicts the gospels of the bible, and the famous "manger scene" made its first appearance in 1223 CE thousands of years after Jesus was born. First of all, the gospels of Mark and John never say Jesus was born in Bethlehem. While the gospels of Matthew and Luke mention 2 different Bethlehemian versions of Jesus' birth. When saying "the bible tells us about the birth of Jesus" Christians never say that only 2 out of the alleged 11 authors of the New Testament mention it. Meaning 82% of the people who are alleged to have written the New Testament do NOT tell us about the birth of Jesus. Obviously, that's rather odd if the birth of Jesus was so important and miraculous, the only way for it not to be suspicious is if they didn't know anything about the birth of Jesus and that's why they didn't write about it, but if that's the case then it lays suspicion on the 2 who did, Matthew and Luke. Of which Luke starts his gospel by saying he is not an eye-witness and is just writing down what he thinks is true based on what others have written or said. Also keep in mind out of all the 27 books in the New Testament, Matthew's book was the 16th to be written and Luke's was the 18th. Yet for some reason despite 15 books being written before Matthew's gospel, the first book presented in the New Testament is Matthew's gospel. Why is that? Because the first 15 books of the New Testament that were written don't talk about the birth of Jesus! So, in order to give people, the illusion that the doctrine of the birth of Jesus didn't develop after the doctrine of Christianity they rearranged the order of the texts in the New Testament claiming to put them in chronological order according to the events as they happened. Which sounds good but they don't do that either, since the events are out of order and the Luke's birth story comes 2 books after Matthew's instead of saying all that

Luke and Matthew say about the birth at the same time. There is a reason for that as well, because Luke and Matthew disagree on a few things regarding the birth of Jesus so if their stories were read together or if their gospels were side by side such differences would be noticed and confuse Christians as to which version is accurate. Nonetheless Christians say "*the bible tells us about the birth of Jesus*", even though 25 out of 27 books of the New Testament (92.5%) don't. There are actually more verses in the Quran regarding the birth of the prophet John than there are verses in the bible about the birth of Jesus, and the Quran also mentions the birth of Jesus more than the bible does, as well as the birth of Mary which the bible doesn't mention. Regardless Christians believe the nativity and birth of Jesus is accurately depicted in the bible, so for that reason rather than object or just hear the claim and then let them tell us whatever the hell they want about the birth of Jesus claiming "it's from the bible", we shall examine what the bible does and doesn't tell us about the birth of Jesus. "Matthew" thinks Mary and Joseph lived in Bethlehem and that Jesus was born in their house while "Luke" thinks Mary and Joseph lived in Nazareth and had to go to Bethlehem with Jesus born in a manger. "Matthew" says the birth took place during the reign of King Herod "the Great" who died in 4 BCE. "Luke" also says it took place during the reign of King Herod "the Great" but also during the time Quirinius was governor of Syria. However, Quirinius didn't become governor of Syria until 6 CE, 10 years after Herod died; which means "Luke" is discussing a period in time which never existed. Also, Rome didn't control Bethlehem until 6 CE, 10 years after King Herod died. Thus, if any census ever took place in Bethlehem the earliest it could have ever been was in 6 CE, 10 years after Herod had died. Historically the Roman Empire never took a census at that time period, and they never did a census in the manner described in the bible, no one ever has. Biblically this census wasn't a normal census where people go around checking how many people live in each city, instead the people were supposed to go to the hometown of their ancestors in order to be counted and taxed. This would be akin to the next American census having everyone go back to their ancestral land in order to be counted. Since most all Americans are immigrants and have families originally from other nations, almost everyone in America would leave the country except for Native American Indians. Obviously, this is crazy and it's not how you do a census at all because then the government would have lost all its citizens and lost the ability to enforce and tax which the census is supposed to be for. This meant people would have been going outside of the taxation jurisdiction of Rome in order to pay Roman taxes even though there wouldn't be tax collectors in their ancestors' foreign country. If implemented this would've destroyed the Roman Empire's prestige, respectability, authority, population, treasury, military and civilization. Yet on top of that very few people in the Roman Empire knew how to read. How illiterate peasants tracked their genealogy and felt about taking a dangerous journey to their ancestors' homeland, which would have bankrupted them, just so that they could pay Roman taxes is something the bible neglects to mention. Furthermore, it would be impossible for the census to occur in winter because the population at that time would not be able to travel, it would be genocide to have such a census in winter. However, winter was the only time during the year labor didn't take place. So, either everyone had to quit their jobs, move a great distance and then pay taxes or the census didn't happen. Whereas even if one believes that the Roman government told everyone they had to quit their jobs, freezing the economy, spend lots of money in order to travel so they could pay taxes this disqualifies the shepherds from being present at the birth of Jesus because they couldn't leave their flocks exposed in the fields at night during the non-winter rainy season. This is the reason "Luke" and "Luke" alone gives for why Mary had to go to Bethlehem to give birth to Jesus, because Joseph her alleged husband was allegedly a distant descendant of people from Bethlehem, even though that has nothing to do with her and she would have had to go elsewhere to the land where her family was from. Which also shows that Luke's genealogy of Joseph couldn't have "really been Mary's" because Luke says Mary's ancestors weren't from Bethlehem and she went there because of Joseph's ancestry. Also, on top of all that only Roman citizens had to participate in the census. Meaning that according to the gospel of "Luke" Mary and Joseph were Roman citizens. Historically they were not and typically only the Jewish traitors who collaborated with Rome were. If they were Roman citizens as "Luke" implies then that means the son of Mary, Jesus, would have been a Roman citizen. The problem is that one of the special privileges Roman citizens had was that they could not be executed. Which means if there was a census and Mary was married to Joseph and they participated because they were Roman citizens which resulted in Jesus being a Roman citizen, then Jesus could never ever be executed by the Roman government. Roman citizenship could not be stripped or lost, so the gospel of "Luke" implies that it would have been illegal for Jesus to have been crucified. However biblically Mary was actually not married to Joseph at the time of the birth but merely engaged, this is an important detail because it means Jesus wouldn't have been a Roman citizen and could be crucified if he was born when Joseph and Mary weren't married but there is a problem. Since if Mary wasn't married to Joseph at the time of the birth of Jesus, then if there were a census, which there wasn't, but if there were then she would not be traveling with Joseph to his hometown of Bethlehem because legally she would not be "filing jointly" but would still be a dependent of her parents and be "filing taxes" at her own ancestral hometown which scholars have said was Jerusalem. Also, since biblically Mary was only engaged to Joseph at the time of the birth, then she according to the religious laws she practiced would not be allowed to have Joseph look at her, have him touch her or even be with her alone. It seems as though the people who wrote the story of this escapade in the bible were clueless about the religious laws that were in effect at the time of the birth of Jesus, plus as Jews Mary and Joseph couldn't travel on the sabbath but that little detail is never mentioned. Yet Mary still wouldn't be "filing taxes" at all because she wasn't a citizen since if she was Jesus couldn't get crucified. Plus, the Jews at that time didn't pay taxes because the emperor's claimed to be gods. No practicing Jews in the whole empire paid taxes to Rome, so whether there was a census or not neither Mary nor Joseph would've participated in it because they didn't pay taxes because Jews didn't pay taxes to the Roman empire. That's why the Romans hated the Jews so much and killed them. Yet on top of that do you think the Roman empire would say "*Everybody pay money to travel to location X to pay us the correct amount of taxes.*" or would they say "*Instead of paying money to travel to pay us the just amount of taxes in your ancestor's hometown, how about you just pay us what we want you to pay us on demand?*" Honestly if Rome implemented this census to tax people, they would lose money, they'd actually make more money by taxing less people where they currently lived since then people wouldn't die in transit nor have to quit their jobs. So, Rome never really had this crazy international census taxation event and the bible is wrong when it says it did. Now if you were a Roman of the 4th century trying to insert Joseph as a carpenter stepfather of Jesus in order to make Christians obedient patriotic taxpaying civilians who loved the Roman Empire, such a person may not realize how historically inaccurate their fictional census was because of the poor literacy rate and lack of access to historical records hundreds of years old. Afterall if the "mother of God" migrated while pregnant and the birth of Jesus took place in the prophesied spot due to compliant citizens paying taxes then what do you think the Christian attitude towards taxation will be? The lesson the Roman government saw in such a fictional census being inserted in the bible was that people who believe in that story will think taxation is good and a religious obligation since it was part of the miraculous birth of Jesus. That's why governments today promote Christmas, because politically the Christmas story says everyone should pay taxes no matter what the price is, even if paying taxes means you can't go to a hospital and have to give birth in a barn. The biblical Christmas story subliminally tells people to pay taxes no matter what and that's why the bible says a census took place even though it never did. Of course, with the writer who inserted this fictional census information knowing that the Christian population and the Roman population to be approximately 80-90% illiterate they might not really worry if their writing was historically impossible, since the masses wouldn't have access to the records and likely wouldn't read their insertion anyways. Also, if it could just get passed off as true for a generation or two then it would become widely believed and the masses would drown out anyone trying to poke holes in a religious belief held for generations. I mention the nativity story because it is often used as an argument for Mary being married and Jesus being a carpenter because of his relation to Joseph. I don't mean to belittle or insult anyone's religious beliefs or customs, I used to believe these very things myself. It is because I love Jesus and Mary that I'm attempting to clear her of the Jewish slander and clarify who Jesus was. It is because I personally was deceived in the past about the event of Jesus' birth that I will examine the nativity story more closely so that we can better understand what the bible tells us about Jesus and his miraculous virgin birth. It doesn't matter how many people believe something to be true or how long such a belief has been held. It doesn't matter if a million, or a billion, or even a trillion people believe something for a gazillion years and entire economies arise out of that belief about a person, place or event, that doesn't mean it is right or true. It hurts to learn that one has been deceived, especially if it's been for a long time and everyone you know has also been deceived. But so does having a dislocated joint put back into place hurt, or having a lifesaving surgery without anesthesia. Yes, things hurt in life, but we shouldn't let any of that pain or hurt prevent us from doing what is right or be afraid of experiencing the hurt and pain of enlightenment. Concerning religion if someone has been lied to and they believe something that is false, they will get hurt one way or the other. Either they'll suffer in the hellfire for eternity forever in the next life, or they'll suffer earlier the sting of having learned that they've been fooled. Satan felt the sting of being told by God he was wrong for disobeying God and that he wasn't better than Adam. Satan reacted by refusing to accept his own self-deception as wrong, rejected the truth, voluntarily believed what was false even though he knew better and became an enemy of God, the prophets and us; thereby choosing to get hurt in the hellfire as well. Don't make the same emotional mistake.

    A famous part of the nativity story is about how the "wise men" came to see Herod "the Great" (who was historically long dead at the time this allegedly took place) before going to see the "star" over Bethlehem prior to gifting Jesus. The nativity depicts them at the actual site, however biblically there is no proof to say they met Jesus, it only says Jesus received their gifts. Then when the "wise men" don't return to Herod and tell him where Jesus was, so Herod orders all infants under the age of 2 to be killed. Joseph was allegedly told by an angel in a dream to flee to Egypt to safety. This sounds exactly like the infanticide myths of the polytheistic savior religions. Historically Herod never ordered such a thing and there was no mass slaughter of babies. The famous historian Josephus lived during this time, he personally hated Herod and wrote extensively about many bad things Herod had done, yet Josephus never says anything about this alleged mass infanticide. But maybe you reject history, ok let's use the bible, the gospel of Luke has no mention of Herod slaughtering any babies and actually depicts Jesus being brought to the temple in Herod's capital city Jerusalem to be publicly circumcised. So according to "Luke" and history, King Herod didn't slaughter babies en masse. It is irrational as well for Herod to kill all babies under the age of 2 because it implies Herod waited 2 years before realizing nobody was telling him where the baby had been born. Also, it makes absolutely zero sense for Herod to not personally accompany the wise men, send someone else with them, or follow them. Someone may have inserted this bit about Herod to correlate with the pagan religions which had similar stories about infanticide, or to dehumanize Jews since Herod was a Jewish ruler thereby such a story would make any Christian hesitant of allowing any Jew into an authority position. The nativity makes the Jewish ruler Herod who built a grand temple for God alone to be worshiped, despite being surrounded by powerful pagan enemies who detested monotheism, comparable to the Pharaoh who demanded to be deified. Herod did lots of bad stuff, but he didn't order mass infanticide. Herod would have been dead at the time of the nativity story regardless but the gospel of Luke has no "wise men" or "star of Bethlehem" in the story at all! Instead, Luke has angels appear to shepherds whereas Matthew has "wise men" following a star. Modern storytellers and Christian preachers just combine the two stories together as well as the other two gospels hoping nobody reads the bible noticing what they did and the contradicting information they left out and forgot to leave out of the nativity story. Biblically the gospel of Matthew says Jesus went to Egypt but the gospel of Luke says Jesus never went to Egypt and was raised in Galilee never leaving it. At least one of them is wrong on that point because Jesus and his mother couldn't possibly have been in two places at the same time. Allegedly the "wise men" were Magians from Persia who practiced astrology, which would make them disbelievers, yet they apparently traveled all the way from Persia to Palestine following a star. Somewhere somebody telling the nativity changed the "wise men" into "kings" even though the gospel explicitly never says they were kings. Since they are depicted as coming alone, what countries would let their leaders travel alone all the way to Palestine into a foreign country unprotected carrying expensive treasures? That would be extremely dangerous since they would have been the most attractive targets for robbery, kidnapping, assassination, rape, ransom, assault, etc. It's just unbelievable and the gospel which includes them never hints that Herod treated them like kings. If they were kings and failed to return to him then that would have been means for declaring war. Also, how can 3 kings possibly leave a foreign country without getting noticed? But it wasn't just any "foreign country", it was the Roman Empire and the king of the region wanted to see them, oh and on top of that they were all alone without any translators to be able to speak to people, including Herod for which they'd need a translator to speak with. So most assuredly there were no 3 kings. If they were plain Magians from Persia, they wouldn't have been able to afford lugging expensive gifts all the way to Palestine especially without protection. If they were following a star then they would have been only traveling at night, which is completely ridiculous to expect 3 people with riches only traveling at night on foot or camel from Persia to Palestine. Also, for them to follow a specific star because it was so especially bright, I feel confident in saying that more than 3 people from Persia to Palestine would have seen this star had it ever existed. The closest star to earth is the sun. The sun is approximately 93,000 miles away from earth. Biblically and according to the nativity the "star of Bethlehem" was over a specific building, it was that close. Clearly earth would not exist if that were the case. Also if you look up at the sun or any other star it is impossible to say which house, city, state, country or even which continent that star is over. It is impossible to follow a star to a specific square foot. Generally, people only look at stars to find their direction or which latitude they are at. Realistically have your neighbor come outside at night and ask them whether they think a certain star in the sky is over your house or their house and see how they respond. Really if you could tell which building a star was over then why is it the nativity scene never includes the neighbors or any locals who obviously would've seen a star hovering above a nearby building and investigated. Yet biblically not even the shepherds saw this "star" and angels had to tell them to visit baby Jesus. Which again apparently nobody but the shepherds heard or saw the angels. So, was the birth of Jesus an "invite-only" private event which everybody could see due to the star but they weren't allowed to visit? Or was this narrative a sloppy work of unrealistic fiction? Also keep in mind that every hour the earth rotates hundreds of miles, so for a star to stand still above a spot on earth it would have to match the exact speed as earth and spin on the same exact orbit at the same exact angle, for a very very long time. Yet for that to happen the very solar system would be thrown out of whack due to the extra star in the system, of which the solar system is a "1-star system". If a star were that close to earth that it could pinpointedly be above a select location the size of a building and earth didn't cease to exist everybody on earth would see that star and there would be no darkness. It would be brighter than the brightest day, so bright that people and animals would go blind. There would be no nighttime because there would be two stars, and it would constantly be daytime in Palestine. It would be so hot that all the vegetation and living organisms would be vaporized, the mountains and sands would be melted to nothing and the water would have boiled the planet. But this star isn't said to have only been above a certain location for one night. Some would have us believe this star was over a specific building for years. Wouldn't people get a little suspicious that a star is over a manger for years on end? Surely some contemporary writer who lived during that time would've wrote about such a crazy phenomenon had it actually happened. After such a wonderous journey these Persian "wise men" or "kings" return according to the bible. You would think they'd tell somebody about Jesus and the amazing journey they had, right? Afterall people would be bound to ask them about their adventure. However, when Muslims went to Persia and later conquered Persia ending the polytheistic oppression the Persia government was guilty of, the Persian people knew absolutely nothing about Jesus and never heard of him. Historical records show they have no stories of a virgin birth or a star in Palestine or anything in their folklore, religious beliefs, culture, books, or history about anything remotely resembling the Christian nativity story which 3 Persian kings were allegedly present for. Also, no astronomical data has been found to support the theories concerning the alleged star of Bethlehem. Some Christians claim there is, but there isn't. They will claim they used modern data to find out what the sky looked like on the night Jesus was born, but this is a fraud. It is impossible for us to know with any certainty what the sky looked like during the time of the roman empire regardless of what calculations are made. Secondly nobody knows what day, month or year Jesus was born. So even if it were possible to know what the sky looked like in the past, which it isn't, we still wouldn't know which night sky we are supposed to examine. Anyone today who says they have proven the alleged star of Bethlehem existed is a liar and then again even if they could, which they can't, they still wouldn't be able to prove that a certain star was over a specific building of a specific city. The Christian nativity story and the Santa Claus story are told on the same day for the same reason. I don't mean to go on and on about it but this is what the gospel of "Matthew" says took place on the night of Jesus' birth. Since I love Jesus, as all Muslims do, I wanted to think about the event in question and imagine what it must have been like to experience it in the flesh. But it's just too hard for me to believe in the version "Matthew" tells, what does "Luke" say about the event?

    Regarding the account in "Luke" which lacks the "wise men" and "star" from Matthew, "Luke" substitutes them for shepherds being told about Jesus by angels. Apparently, these angels were only seen and heard by the shepherds and nobody else. Why were these shepherds so special? Who were they? What happened to them afterwards? Did they tell others? Did any follow Jesus later on? All these questions are ignored. Now the nativity pictures usually just display a few shepherds with a sheep or goat. Although to be a professional shepherd at that time you needed to have hundreds if not thousands of lambs and goats. Obviously, no nativity depiction includes all these thousands or hundreds of livestock because it's so comedic. Everybody in the whole city would have known if "the shepherds" came to town just by the smell, let alone the sound of the hooves and the braying. If they all converged on one central location it would have surely attracted extra uninvited guests who followed along. The smell of hundreds or thousands of livestock might even have killed a newborn baby suffocating it as it struggled to take its first breaths of air after having breathed water in the womb; it'd likely suffocate the adults in the manger as well. Surely nobody in that environment or any environment would've sung to the infant baby Jesus "Happy Birthday to God" because by definition anyone or anything with a birthday cannot be God; much less an eternal unchanging being.

    Now that's just the 2 different versions the gospels of Matthew and Luke give about the birth of Jesus. The other two gospels say Jesus wasn't born in Bethlehem at all! Fortunately, we don't have to go over the differences between the birth or lack of birth stories in the gospels of Mark and John because the gospels of Mark and John don't include any information or version about the birth of Jesus at all. Thank God for that because with so many contradictions between the 2 stories of Matthew and Luke if Mark and John had said something we'd likely be looking at dozens of extra pages full of contradictions. This is precisely why Christendom has selectively chosen a "nativity story" rather than tell people the conflicting biblical accounts. If you read the biblical accounts, you would never believe the "nativity story" because it goes against what the bible says and, on this instance, the biblical versions go against history, science, logistics and common sense. The most important detail is that none of the authors of the gospels nor the people whom the gospels have been attributed to were present as eyewitnesses to the event in question. If the gospels disagree on the birth and alleged death of Jesus and the nature of as well as the religion and teachings of

Jesus, then it's hard to think these gospels are the "word of God" or "inspired by God".

If I don't believe in the Christian nativity then why do I believe Mary gave birth as a virgin, especially when many pagan religions taught that their "sons of God" had virgin births? The short answer is because the Quran says she was a virgin and there is proof that the Quran is trustworthy divine revelation and there are many examples of supernatural births done by the will of God as well as many lessons in the virgin birth God would want us to learn. Such as how God doesn't need men to make people and that men are not irreplaceable, also showing the importance of virginity and that sex is not how babies are created but rather God creates them with or without sex taking place. Whereas the pagan claim of virgin births comes from the pagan practice to determine whether a child was legitimate or not. When a pregnant woman was suspected of having an illegitimate child pagans would toss the child in the river and if it floated to safety, they thought it was legitimate, if it died, they thought it wasn't. Of course this was nonsensical murder for the most part, but whenever a pagan woman claiming to have been a virgin gave birth and the child passed the floating test then the mother could claim the child was the son of a pagan deity in order to maintain her reputation and acquire fame for herself and her bastard child. But Mary's case was different, she was a believer and 3 prophets of her time supported her claim to a virgin birth as did Allah and Muhammad. So, while the nativity story is false the virginity of Mary is true. The specific details of the story still matter though, because the devil creates false details that lead to disbelief.

Even if after reading all you have thus far, if you still believe the bible to the inerrant divine revelation and in Christianity, one part of the bible contains blasphemy even according to Christian doctrines. While I have included it below as found in the English translation of the New International Version of the bible, it is blasphemous in all versions and in all languages. The verses are found in the New Testament book of Hebrews 7:1-4, "This <u>Melchizedek was king of Salem and priest of God Most High. He met Abraham returning from the defeat of the kings and blessed him,</u>[2] *and Abraham gave him a tenth of everything. First, the name Melchizedek means "king of righteousness"; then also, "king of Salem" means "king of peace."*[3] *<u>Without father or mother, without genealogy, without beginning of days or end of life</u>, resembling the Son of God, he remains a priest forever."*

    According to this biblical passage Melchizedek has a more miraculous genealogy than Jesus, without father or mother and has the immortality of God. This is a completely blasphemous statement to say that a person is immortal "*without beginning of days or end of life*" this is beyond most pagan beliefs even, yet it is in the bible in that anonymously written book of Hebrews. What's even worse is that some Christians will maintain that God inspired these blasphemous words. Fortunately, this verse is verifiable. If this biblical verse were true then this Melchizedek who allegedly met Abraham who gave him 10% of the spoils of war, how the author of Hebrews knows this is unknown just like their name, would still exist today and we should be able to meet him. Melchizedek could come forth and prove his existence and the truth of the bible so all would believe. He wouldn't have to worry about getting assassinated because as the bible says he has no "*end of life*". He cannot be worried about fame because the bible says "*he remains a priest forever*" so it would be his duty to come forth and guide mankind under his ministry. Obviously, this hasn't happened nor will it, because this portion of the bible is false information and whoever believes in this verse or it having come from a divine source is mistaken. Believing in the 3rd verse would constitute blasphemy and again make one a disbeliever liable to eternal punishment in the hellfire. Seriously when people say they believe the bible is the word of God, or inspired by God, it's terrifying to me because they have no idea what that means when they say it and the blasphemous statements that are contained within it. Even according to their own doctrines believing in some biblical verses makes them disbelievers in their own religion. For instance, let's say someone still believes in this Melchizedek without a mother or father, in that case they have to disbelieve in Genesis 3:20 " *Adam named his wife Eve, because she would become the mother of all the living*." So thus, Eve must be Melchizedek's mother but Hebrews says he has no mother, but technically speaking Genesis says of "all the living" which of course doesn't really mean "all the living" such as animals and plants but just means humans. Thus, Melchizedek must not be human but since he resembles the "Son of God" then that would mean Jesus is 0% human, yet Melchizedek was a king of Salem and a priest. Therefore, at one time there was a non-human king and God has a non-human priest, or else it's a human without father or mother and isn't of "the living". So, what is it then? A zombie or monster? The bible just gets crazier and crazier until you want to puke due to disgust and the more you learn about the bible the worse it gets; it still shocks me how it still gets worse the more I learn about it. It's heartbreaking to think about the billions who have fallen into disbelief in this manner not even realizing the torment that awaits them. If God doesn't guide us, we could be just like them. All thanks and praises be to God that he let us know this stuff before we died.

    The question remains, which edition of the bible is the word of God or from God? It is not an easy or short answer. I would say all editions I know of are not 100% the word of God, or 100% inspired by God. Although there are elements of the original revelations that remain from the Taurat given to Moses, Zabur given to David and the Injeel given to Jesus. Unfortunately, so much has been corrupted and lost through time and translations that much of these originals are not accessible to us today. The bibles that I've come across and know of while still containing some traces of divine instruction also contain blasphemous statements, contradictions and unverified information. My answer is that of all the bibles I know of, none are 100% divinely inspired. They contain both good and bad, true and false with contradictions making the bibles impossible to follow. That gospels are called "*The gospel according to___*" also reveals that these are just attributions and that the gospels weren't actually written by Matthew, Mark, Luke or John; if they were they'd be called "The gospel written by ___" just as you would say "this is the book written by Gregory" and not "this is the book according to Gregory". Also, whenever people say "*The bible says___*" they know internally that it's not really God's word and that's why Christians will never ever replace the words "*The bible says___*" with "*God says___*" *the* way Muslims do interchangeably when they say "*The Quran says ___*" and "*Allah says___*". The bible was written by humans who had human intentions and abilities, they tried the best they could, but mistakes were made. The gospel writers were spokesmen who wrote down the oral traditions they had heard describing events that allegedly took place 30-40 years (at the earliest) before they were written about. It is probable that many changes were already made to the oral traditions by the storytellers through the years prior to the gospel writers recording them. To claim their writings to be the word of God is to deify the gospel authors. To claim they were divinely inspired by God is to say that they were prophets, since only prophets are capable of receiving divine revelation firsthand. It is impossible for God to have sent so many prophets at the same time, instructing them all to write about one other prophet yet have all these prophets contradict each other and write down different stories. This would be like God giving 10 commandments to Moses and 10 commandments to Aaron yet each being given different contradictory conflicting rules to follow. Divine revelation has always had one person to convey it to the people and 1 version. If it's not from a Messenger of God, it's not divine revelation. But wait, do you remember those 10 commandments? Well, there are 10 found in Exodus 20, but there are also 10 found in Deuteronomy 5:6-21 and Exodus 34:12-26. According to the bible there are 3 different lists of the 10 commandments. So before one can even attempt to follow them one has to find out which 10 are the true 10 and which 20 were written by men. In reality all 30 were written by men, yet Biblicists tell us they were all inspired by God to write different things, except they never tell people that different conflicting things were written because they either don't know or they don't want you to know. The plot thickens when you learn that Catholics, Jews and Protestants all propagate a different version of the 10 as well and that different bibles translate them differently making them mean different things. Such as one biblical version saying "*Do not kill*" and another saying "*Do not murder*" makes a big difference. But I have good news for you, so you can relax and calm down. There technically is no contradiction at all between the different biblical versions of the "10 commandments", the bad news is the reason why I say there is no real contradiction between the different biblical "10 commandments". This is because if you ask Jews what the "10 commandments" are they say that there are 613 commandments and the 10 are just categories which the 613 were organized under. Yes, take a deep breath.

The Jews actually teach that God gave Moses 613 commandments and not 10 as the Christians falsely claim. So that's good news, right? We don't have to argue over which 10 rules the bible wants us to follow because there are actually 613. But wait, it gets better and I'm not being sarcastic this time. Research from paleo linguists indicates that the Hebrew language didn't exist at the time Moses received these commandments but came into being approximately 1,000 years after Moses, and the oldest fragment of paleo-Hebrew writing that exists is over 250 years before the earliest possible date Moses is believed to have died. So, nobody really knows what language Moses spoke or what language his revelation was in, and we don't have the Ark of the covenant or any original documents to read in order to find out. Jewish Kabbalists even say that the Torah was flawed, incomplete and presented relative truth instead of an absolute truth. The Jewish Kabbalists even though 2 whole books were missing from the Torah and that the Hebrew alphabet lacked one of the letters that the Torah was in. Thus, the Hebrew language dislocated the Torah and the Hebrew version was missing a good chunk of information due to Hebrew missing letters of the alphabet of the language of the Torah. Likewise, Abraham didn't speak Hebrew either but is believed to have spoken "proto-Canaanite", which is why we don't have access to the Suhuf given to Abraham. However, Abraham's son Ishmael is known to have learned Arabic and married into Arab tribes who spoke Arabic. Also, since Abraham is known to have spoken to Ishmael in adulthood as well as his wives, it is most probable that Abraham knew and spoke Arabic. However, keep in mind that does not necessarily mean the Suhuf given to Abraham was in Arabic, it could've been but we cannot say for certainty because Abraham could've known other languages besides Arabic; such as "proto-Canaanite" whatever that is. Could "proto-Canaanite" be Arabic? It's possible but obviously if non-Muslim scholars were to say such a thing Jews and Christians would get quite upset because of the serious implications such a discovery would entail. Some Muslim scholars have claimed Arabic was spoken by Noah and some even say it was the original language of Adam, but I do not yet know where those particular scholars got such information from and have not examined its authenticity or reliability. Although historically the language of Arabic is said to have been spoken by Sam bin Noah. History books relate that Noah partitioned the land of earth and gave his son Sam the land from Syria to Yemen and Sam spoke "natural Arabic" as did his descendants. Whereas biblically all 3 of Noah's sons spoke a different language. (Most Christians don't know this because they believe in the tower of babel language origin story of Genesis 11 and ignore Genesis 10:1, Genesis 10:4-5, Genesis 10:20 and Genesis 10:31-32 which all contradict the tower of babel languages origin story of Genesis 11:1-9.) So historically Arabic is an ancient language spoken by Sam the son of Noah. Now this is very important because it relates directly to Jesus. You see Jesus is known to have raised people from the dead. However, Jews still refused to believe in his prophethood despite such miracles and they said it was too easy for Jesus to raise the recently deceased and that they might not even have been truly dead. So, the Jews challenged Jesus to raise somebody who had been dead for a very long time, specifically they asked him to resurrect Sam the son of Noah from the dead so they could talk to him. Jesus did this and Sam talked to Jesus and the Jews confirming that Jesus was a prophet of God before going back to being dead. Now Sam did not speak Hebrew because Hebrew did not exist and he didn't speak Aramaic either. My research indicates he spoke Arabic, but you need not accept that opinion. The point is Sam did not speak Hebrew or Aramaic yet was raised from the dead and spoke to Jesus and Jews. Now it could have been a language other than Arabic or it could have been Arabic and even if Sam did speak Arabic that does not necessarily mean Jesus would have, even though they spoke. Because maybe Jesus raised Sam from the dead and he had another guy to translate Sam's language so Sam could be understood, that's possible but then that would risk the point of the miracle if a translator need be relied upon. Also, a translator seems unlikely because the Jews specifically asked Jesus to raise Sam from the dead, so it doesn't make sense for them to ask Jesus to raise one they couldn't communicate with. Thus, it is most probable they could speak the language Sam spoke and it is a fact that Sam did not speak Hebrew. It could be possible for Sam's reported "natural Arabic" to have been similar enough to ancient Aramaic for them to understand each other but the point is that Hebrew was not as prominent during the time of Jesus or other prophets as modern Jews and Christians believe. Whereas leading up to the Babylonian exile the Jews used Aramaic which is a derivative language of Arabic. To compare them Arabic would be like ancient olyde English vs. modern American, they are very similar but clearly distinct enough to be quite different. So again, it is possible that Sam's Arabic need not be translated for Jesus and the Jews who knew Aramaic. Although in the holy land itself Arabic was spoken during the time of Jesus. It wasn't the same as the type of Arabic Muhammad spoke, it was an earlier form called Nabataean Arabic. The language of Nabataean Arabic was an offshoot of the Aramaic of the Achaemaenic Empire. The Achaemaenic Empire ruled from China to Greece across the middle east to about where Libya is today, from the years 550 BCE to 330 BCE until Alexander invaded and crippled their kingdom annexing vast portions of it. This Achaemaenic empire is the same as was ruled by Darius I and Cyrus I both of whom are mentioned in the bible during the Jewish exile in Babylon. The

Achaemaenic empire was the empire which conquered the empire that conquered the Jews. Their imperial language was Aramaic. Ezra allegedly rewrote the Torah, that had been lost, by memory in Aramaic after Jews returned to Jerusalem from Babylon during the reign of Cyrus I, while the Samaritans used proto-Hebrew which eventually became the official language used for the Jewish text as it was translated from Aramaic to Hebrew. Now some might be thinking I'm going too deep into this language change and the development of Hebrew within Jewish religion. However, when things got changed into Hebrew that's an entire religion getting translated. Things get lost in translation as well as distorted. When you translate a religion, it doesn't quite come out the same, especially when this is done in ancient times where record-keeping itself within one language was dubious due to technology and human errors from handwriting and copying handwriting multiple times over and over throughout generations. So, the Jews translated the religion of the prophets into Hebrew even though originally it was not preached or practiced in the Hebrew language. That is an undisputed fact. You need not accept that Sam spoke Arabic or even that Jesus raised him from the dead, but every ancient historian, anthropologist, paleo linguist and archaeologist knows with 100% certainty that the old biblical prophets did not teach in Hebrew and Hebrew was only invented long after the Jews had corrupted the religion their prophets had taught them. While on top of that it is known that Jesus spoke Aramaic and it's assumed he spoke Hebrew for practical religious reasons to accommodate the circumstances of his time due to the Jewish translation of religion into Hebrew. While after Alexander and the fall of the Achaemaenic empire, their imperial Aramaic turned into Nabataean Arabic and was spoken and written in a very special region. The region Nabataean Arabic was used in consists of the area of Negev between the eastern bank of the Jordan River and the Sinai Peninsula. However, from 85 BCE on when the Romans came to power in the middle east the Nabataean Arabic started getting replaced with Greek and Latin. Yet before 85 BCE Nabataean Arabic was the main language in the region and archaeological evidence proves it was still used until 356 CE. Whereas Jesus is predicted to have been born somewhere around/between 4 BCE and 6 CE. So, it is a real possibility that Jesus spoke Nabataean Arabic as well as Aramaic, or his Aramaic may have been Nabataean Arabic since Nabataean Arabic was a derivative of Imperial Aramaic. However, keep in mind Nabataean Arabic is different than the "classical Arabic" which Muhammad spoke in the 600s CE, because Nabataean Arabic is a forerunner of classical Arabic. They are similar though. Yet as the Latin and Greek speaking churches conquered the holy land, the ancient Nabataean Arabic went extinct in the region. Hence it was said that Jesus spoke Hebrew and only recently has it been made known that Jesus spoke Aramaic of a particular dialect. Whereas for obvious religious reasons it's unlikely the Christian or Jewish world would let any facts that could prove Jesus spoke Arabic (Nabataean Arabic) surface. Since that would lead people to wonder if maybe those Muslims speaking Arabic may actually have some information about Jesus or God or even a connection with the prophetic religion. Thus, such findings of which I'm speculating will likely never be made known, at least as long as the state of Israel exists, and the world will be told that Jesus was a just a Jew who spoke Hebrew; with the more astute Christians thinking they're smart for knowing Jesus spoke Aramaic too. However, the dialect of the Aramaic of Jesus has been declared to be "Western Aramaic". That is a big step closer to the truth being known because it limits the possibilities bringing the language of Jesus into more focus. This is because there are only 5 different types of "Western Aramaic" known. The 5 types are, "Western Neo-Aramaic" (which is modern and disqualified because it didn't exist at the time of Jesus), Samaritan Aramaic, Jewish-Palestinian Aramaic, Christian-Palestinian Aramaic, and Nabatean Arabic. Whereas Samaritan Aramaic can be discounted because the Samaritans were their own sect and Jesus would not have grown up with them to pick up their language since he was not a Samaritan. The same applies to Christian-Palestinian Aramaic as well as Jewish-Palestinian Aramaic. Why is that? Because Jesus grew up in Egypt. What type of "Western Aramaic" did Egyptians speak? Nabataean Arabic as did Southern Palestine. So historically speaking there is a very high probability that Jesus may have spoken Nabataean Arabic. I say high probability because Muslims believe Jesus spoke from birth so God was the one who made him speak and taught him his first language, but we can't say with 100% certainty what that was or whether that was his language throughout his life, or if his first language was his only language. However, we must remember that baby Jesus did not go to Egypt alone or via spaceship. By all accounts it was a journey over land, meaning those making the journey would've had to speak the language of the places they were traveling through and to in order to blend in as they were trying to do. So, Mary the mother of Jesus likely spoke Nabataean Arabic, at least during the journey. Also, her uncle Zachariah would've likely spoken Nabataean Arabic because he was a prophet and he had to communicate with the people living in Southern Palestine, the same applies to his son John. Also, for what its worth Nabataean Arabic writings have been found at Qumran, which is the same place those famous "Dead Sea Scrolls" were recovered; so that proves people in various diverse parts of the holy land spoke Nabataean Arabic. Therefore, since Mary, Zachariah and John all had a dire religious need to speak Nabataean Arabic then I'm inclined to think they spoke it and by extension Jesus also would've had a similar need, grown up in the region where it was spoken, had relatives who spoke it and would've found it useful to be able to speak it throughout his time on earth.  Also, <u>when Jesus comes back to earth he is going to speak and some people will understand what he is saying</u>.  Whereas ancient Hebrew is a dead language and Aramaic is a dead language.  Yet Nabataean Arabic is similar enough to classical Arabic in which the Quran is in and modern Arabic, both of which millions of Muslims speak today.  Thus, if we are going to pick a language that Jesus will be speaking when he returns to earth Arabic is the most likely choice, especially from a Muslim perspective if say in theory they were right about Jesus being one of them.  I mean nobody really thinks he's going to come down speaking Chinese or English, do they?  (Don't feel bad if you did, it's best to find out now than when he comes.)  Why then is the high probability of Jesus speaking Nabataean Arabic not published in newspapers and broadcast on TV?  Well, that's because nothing from the bible comes from a Nabataean Arabic source.  So, if global headlines said Jesus spoke or possibly spoke an early form of Arabic, then Allah's and Muslims' claims about Jesus and Islam would have to be seriously examined by everyone on the planet who was interested in Jesus.  While to accept such a thing like Jesus  speaking Nabataean Arabic as true would force Christians to reject the whole New Testament as unreliable, since it's an incomplete copy of copies of copies of copies of compiled Greek translations of an oral Hebrew tradition, which if translated from an original Nabataean Arabic speaking Jesus  would be too much translation and thus impossible for ancients to have correctly translated to any degree of accuracy required to justify religious beliefs or practices.  Although it's still too much translation anyways, but to add Nabataean Arabic would completely sink the Christian's ship because they have never claimed any source of information, they have came from a Nabatean Arabic source, thus it's too late for them to make something up. Thus, they can only say *"Shut up! It's not possible!"*. It would also completely discredit Paul because Paul taught people in Greek and if Jesus was speaking Nabataean Arabic, or even if we just stick to Aramaic which we know he was speaking a version of Western Aramaic, then for Paul or any companion of Jesus to teach about Jesus in Greek is foolish and crazy. This is because it's easier to teach what a prophet taught without translating it, while we do know for certain that Jesus didn't speak Greek and that many in the holy land spoke the language he did speak. Why then would Paul and the companions of Jesus teach Greeks in Greek and write in Greek, instead of in the original language of Jesus to people who would understand that language? It only makes sense if Paul and the authors of the bible were not translating Jesus, but making up their own Jesus. I repeat, and this may be the most important point about the New Testament in this book, <u>it makes no sense for Paul or the companions of Jesus to teach and write in Greek when they could've taught in the language Jesus actually spoke in the holy land to people in the holy land, unless the authors of the New Testament were making up stuff about Jesus.</u> Since <u>if they made stuff up then it'd be harder for people who knew Jesus' true teachings to refute them if they had to learn a foreign language to do so. The easiest way to change a religion is to change the language it's taught in to something different than the language it was originally taught in</u>. Also consider Greek was the language of the enemies of Jesus and his followers. So, for those who wanted to safely transmit Jesus' teachings without being harmed if discovered with them, to use Greek would be the absolute worst thing they could do. To use Greek would mean they wanted to be persecuted and have their literature get destroyed. However, that literature wasn't destroyed, the Hebrew and Aramaic literature was though, which also happens to be the language(s) it's known Jesus spoke. So, you have the New Testament written in the language other than Jesus spoke that could not be read by the people whom Jesus preached to but could only be read by the enemies of Jesus and his followers. This is because those who wrote the New Testament were the enemies of Jesus, their chief being a guy named Saul who changed his name to Paul. Therefore, due to religious beliefs and prejudices, it's unlikely the Christian world would allow such information or proof about the language of Jesus to become a widely accepted truth. Thus is the problem with religious people, because if the truth means your religious beliefs have no trustworthy connection to God or a prophet then what does one do? Quit their religion? Many cannot bring themselves to do that no matter what, those types would rather lie or kill than let the truth be told to or accepted by others. Also, it's very curious that the latest known inscription of Nabatean Arabic dates from 356 BCE and it was found in the Hejaz region, which is the region Mecca is located in. So, it does seem that it could be entirely possible that the prophetic language was Arabic or proto-Arabic in various forms throughout history. Personally, I have no problem with Hebrew, it's just a language, but unfortunately it is not the language of the ancient prophets of God. So that's good and bad news. The bad news is that we don't have the ancient Aramaic texts and don't know what language the original Taurat was in or the Zabur given to David for that matter. However, in regards to the Zabur given to David we know for certain 3 important details that could indicate a potential candidate for the language it was in. 1. Solomon kept the Zabur in the same language as it was in during the time of David (his father). 2. Solomon wrote to and spoke to the Queen of Sheba who subsequently believed in his prophetic religion. 3. This

Queen of Sheba by all accounts lived in and came to Solomon from Yemen which is the southwestern portion of the Arabian Peninsula. Those are 3 facts everyone agrees upon. The exact time of Solomon's reign is unknown. However, it's projected that David reigned from 1010 BCE to 970 BCE and that Solomon reigned from 970 BCE to 931 BCE, again such numbers are just the scholastic projections given today. This projection however falls within Aramaic's extensive existence as a commonly used universal language throughout the middle east region and we have written examples of Aramaic being used at that time, which we don't have for Hebrew. Aramaic was used by the ancient Assyrians who also used Akkadian and Sumerian and are widely believed to have fought against the believers in the Holy land after Moses left Egypt. Aramaic was also used by the Neo-Babylonian Empire which conquered Israel after the reign of Solomon, except they only spoke Akkadian and Aramaic. So, we can confidently eliminate Sumerian as a candidate for the prophetic language in the post Moses era. We can eliminate Akkadian as a candidate too because the Achaemaenic Empire which conquered the Neo-Babylonian empire used Aramaic as their imperial language. Whereas since Daniel and Ezra are known to have favored using the Aramaic language instead of the Akkadian and since Yemen is known to have spoken a form of Aramaic, then circumstances would dictate that because Ezra is said to have rewritten the Taurat in Aramaic, and the Yemeni people from whom the Queen of Sheba came when she visited Solomon spoke a version of Aramaic, and Jesus spoke a version of Aramaic which may or may not have been Nabataean Arabic, the odds are that Aramaic is the best candidate for the language of the divine revelation of the Zabur given to David as well as the Taurat given to Moses . I say both because a major indicator is Ezra rewriting the Taurat, allegedly from memory, in Aramaic.

Now if he is rewriting a lost book of divine revelation from memory then he's probably going to write it in its original language and not translate it, particularly since Ezra was a prophet of God he'd stick to the original script. Thus, if the Taurat were in Aramaic, which we can reasonably presume it was because of Ezra, then it's most likely the revelation given to David would be the same language since they had the Taurat at the same time and the Zabur is thought to be a supplement to the Taurat rather than an entire abrogation. Although that's just my guess, it is possible the Taurat was gone by the time of David and God sent revelation to David in a different language, but that seems less likely. If the Taurat and Zabur were Aramaic texts then Jews and Christians have a big problem, because their texts which they claim to be from Moses and David are not in Aramaic nor are they translated from Aramaic. They are Hebrew. Yet Ezra is widely reported to have rewritten the Taurat in Aramaic. Anyways that's just my analysis and theory of the language of the post-Moses prophets and their texts of divine revelation. Don't consider it a 100% fact or anything like that, that's just my personal theory that Aramaic is the best candidate language. Yet <u>it's a fact that the Taurat was not in Hebrew</u> when it was given to Moses and that Hebrew was not used by Jews until long after they returned from exile in Babylon, and even then, Aramaic was the language commonly used before Hebrew was made and during the time of Jesus. Whereas since Jews changed the book of God, it makes complete sense they'd make up the Hebrew language to do it. Since they changed the book why wouldn't they change the language too? I mean that's what the Christians did just decades after Jesus, so are we to think the Jews had more integrity for thousands of years? Changing the language of the book would make it much easier to cover up their changes to the original. It'd actually be stupid for them to change the book without changing its language as well. In conclusion we can with certainty say that the Taurat was not a Hebrew text and neither was the Zabur, because the Hebrew language simply didn't exist when those books were revealed. Jews and Christians can say what they want, but facts are facts and Hebrew did not exist during the time of Moses and there is no evidence to suggest it existed at the time of Solomon and Ezra is reported to have rewritten the lost Taurat in Aramaic not Hebrew. We can't just pretend they were Hebrew books because the Jews use Hebrew. Sorry, the holocaust does not give them a free pass to say and do whatever they want and get believed or praised. We can't blindly trust the Jews at face value when it comes to religion, especially when both Jesus and Muhammad condemned them as liars concerning religion. The good news means that technically speaking one could say that you and I don't have to follow any of the rules in the Old Testament or modern Hebrew "Torahs" because they aren't the actual letter for letter words/rules revealed by God. Although the gist might be the same, so it's probably a bad idea to just reject everything in the biblical rulebook because Jesus knew this and he didn't say not to follow any rules just because they've been translated. This is why the smarter Christians say the whole bible and not just the New Testament is "inspired" by God because deep down even though they claim the Old Testament or part of it is the Torah, they know (or they should know, but probably don't) that the best it could be is a translation of a Hebrew translation. Although that's just the theoretical best it could be IF the Jews had 100% trustworthy Hebrew texts, but Jesus was a proof that they didn't. Whereas the Samaritans say the alleged Torah used by the Rabbinical Jews is false because their post-Moses material in the Tanakh says the Torah was lost for 50 years, according to the biblical books of 2 Kings and Chronicles. The Samaritans say it's impossible for the Torah to have been lost then they say the

Tanakh as well as the Christian Old Testament is false. The Rabbinical Jews and Karaites say the Torah was lost because the Tanakh says so. Thus, Rabbinical Jews and Karaites both say each other's understanding of the "Torah" is false while the Samaritans say their Masoretic "Torah" isn't even the Torah but that the Samaritan Torah is the "real Torah". Meanwhile the Christians are completely oblivious to these Jewish disputes and they think the Torah was never lost and that the books they get based on the Jewish Tanakh are divine revelation too. Some unlearned Christians even comically think the Tanakh is the Torah. Yet all of the Samaritans, Karaites and Rabbinical Jews despite their differences unanimously agree that the Christians are wrong to have such beliefs about their books that are crudely based on some parts of the Rabbinical Tanakh and Masoretic "Torah". Basically, Christians are unwittingly saying that the Samaritans are right to say the Tanakh is wrong when it says the Torah was lost, however at the same time Christians also say the Tanakh is divine revelation when it says the Torah was lost. Whereas those Jews believe the Tanakh is right, say that the Masoretic "Torah" they have is not the original text nor a copy of the original but a "recovered version" of the Torah. Yet Christians say the Masoretic Torah is the original even though not one Jew in the entire world believes that. That's an example of thinking Jews are lying when there is no reason for them to lie and actually many reasons for them to accept the Christian position because it would make them look better, but they don't because they know they can't because facts are known. So, Christians claim their Old Testament text, of which the first 5 books are loosely based on the Masoretic "Torah", is the original but the Jews say that their Masoretic "Torah" is NOT the original. Whereas those Samaritans, who agree with the Christians claim the Torah was never lost, have their version of the Torah get labeled as false by Christians because most

Christians don't even know about it. Therefore, when it comes to Jewish books and pre-Jesus text, the Christians have nearly no clue what they are talking about and their beliefs about their own texts of Jew influenced material have absolutely no basis or validity at all. Yet on top of that the Jews say the Christians miscopied and mistranslated their Jewish books! They prove this too. Thus, the Jews say and prove that the Christians 1. Don't know what they are talking about when talking about the Jewish texts. 2. Can't even translate or copy the Jewish texts accurately. So, Christians invented their own form of Judaism, then put their own spin on corrupted Jewish books and proclaim to the world that Jews believe what they say Jews believe, and most Christians live life having such a completely false understanding of Judaism and Jewish texts all the way until they die. It's almost funny to think of how not only did Christians invent their own form of Christianity but they also invented their own form of Judaism too, of which nobody in the world actually follows either. Essentially Christians invented their own form of disbelief in Christianity, which they called Judaism while being ignorant of actual Judaism, and none of the disbelievers joined the Christian form of disbelief in Christianity.   Meaning nobody has ever believed in what Christians say that the Jews have always believed in, but Christians tend not to listen or even hear the truth of it. Instead, Christians think that the Jews all have and always have believed in the Christian fantasy of Judaism. Now that's what you call ignorance. Currently Christians are trying to invent their own forms of Islam too which they say Muslims follow or are supposed to follow, the violent extremist type and the peaceful interfaith Americanism-esque extremist type. In summary the bible has translated writings from many different people, some of whom we don't know, some of whom lied about who they were and they all tell a different version of what is supposed to be the same events. While not one letter in any version or edition of the Old or New Testament is in the original language, but they are all translations of translations that have been copied by hand by copies written by hand by people who we do not know anything about. Seriously not one bible in the world today is a translation, they are all translations of translations, except for Paul's Greek letters but then again few can read ancient Greek. While Paul used to be known as Jesus' biggest enemy Saul. To unequivocally state the Bible is 100% the word of God is to lie about God and to call people prophets who dishonestly wrote in the names of others. The Taurat is one whole book, it is not a collection of 5 books in the Old Testament as Christians allege, nor is it 5 books of the Tanakh as Rabbinical and Karaite Jews allege, nor is the Samaritan version authentic. Regarding the original Taurat given to Moses, we don't have it and don't even know what language it was in. The reason different gospels exist in the New Testament is because the different gospel authors thought the other gospels contained incorrect information that disagreed with what they personally believed, so they wrote their own gospel. Yet their gospel was suspected of containing incorrect information as well, so they only added to the confusion and amount of incorrect information. Likewise, Christians have different editions and versions of the bible for the same reason, because the other bibles don't say what they believe in so they make a bible that does. The existence of multiple gospels shows that none of the gospel authors considered the other authors to be divinely inspired. Nor did they claim or think they were writing down divine revelation themselves. The gospels were written by Christians to support their own beliefs, none of the gospels in the bible say they are written by or inspired by God. The problem is later generations got lazy and said *"well we got all these books so they must all have been inspired by God because we have them and we are God's special people so they must be authentic"* not realizing the only reason they have those books is because if they eliminated all the false books, it would destroy their whole religion. Jews and Christians said, "*We're special so therefore our books must be special. And why are we special? Because our books say we are. And how do we know our books are true when they say we are special? Because we are special and those are the books us special people have.*" Sorry if this offends Jews or Christians, but they just aren't as special as they think and say they are. The reason Jews and Christians think their books are special is not because the books were ever proven to be special, but it's because Jews and Christians consider themselves spiritually special by default thus when their book says they are special they automatically label the book as special to make them feel even more special. Whereas the Jews feel so special they consider themselves an elite race and Christians feel so special they want you to join their club so you can feel special too and make them feel even more special for having you as a member. Judaism and Christianity are 2 types of egotistical extremism. The various Jewish Torahs and Tanakhs were political books made via continuous addition to make Israelites feel special, racially superior and to justify their actions. While the Christian bible was made through a process of elimination that has been stopped short before all the faulty texts were eliminated because Christians realized searching for the truth through process of elimination would eliminate the bible and their religion. Or at least that's what my studies have indicated. The thing is when people feel so special like that and learn their "special books" which say they are special aren't really special books, they find it difficult to accept such an idea because their self-esteem and ego pressures them to reject such a notion because they like feeling super-special. So, if I say they aren't super special and their special books aren't special they believe I'm a satanic liar because they believe they are special, they feel special and have been told they are special for a very long time. Satan wants them to feel special and react like that so they join him in a very special fire for eternity. Thus, I will still entertain such a desire for specialness because while a book might not be special and the reader might not be special, the book may still possibly contain special teachings that may or may not be from a special source.

    Most who believe the bible is the word of God have never read any version or edition of the bible completely, the few who have either don't understand it correctly or are exploiting religion misleading people for deplorable reasons. The prefaces and commentaries included in the bible which contain false information, even according to devout Christian scholars, also contribute to the widespread misunderstanding on what exactly the bible is and what it isn't. The religious environment today is similar to how it was during the time of Jesus in Palestine when the world was ruled by disbelievers and hypocritical puppet leaders thought to be believers while the Pharisees with religious knowledge didn't apply it correctly and incidentally misled the masses of people who weren't learned in regards to religion, while extremist zealots committed acts of terrorism against the disbelieving Romans which gave the Romans excuses to kill the believers. The most common misconception today amongst people is that what you believe is most important and actions aren't as important. While having the correct belief is of great importance, belief motivates one to act in accordance to it, just as someone who believes they are afflicted with a disease that will cause their imminent death will act different than when they didn't think death was imminent. Someone who believes wholeheartedly will act upon that belief and it will have an impact on their life and deeds, thereby having an effect on their afterlife.

Basically, if you believe in the rules then you will try to follow the rules and eventually have success in following them. The flaw among people today is that many think as long as you believe in a form of God and that God made rules then you're okay and don't have to follow the rules themselves or even have the correct belief about God. This is a Satanic deception particularly plaguing Christianity with the notion that the rules of the Old Testament don't have to be followed. This may be true it may be false, but the only one qualified to make such a ruling is God who would have communicated this to us through either divine revelation or a prophet. Thus, let us look at the bible to see what it says the prophet Jesus said regarding such a concept. Nowhere in the New Testament is Jesus directly or indirectly quoted as saying the laws of the Old Testament are not to be followed. Paul says stuff like that but Jesus never does. In fact, throughout the bible Jesus is depicted as teaching that the Pharisees aren't strict enough in upholding the laws of God and that they hypocritically pick and choose which laws they want to follow despite knowing that they should follow them all. As in the English translation of the New International Version of the bible in Matthew 23:1-29, *"Then Jesus said to the crowds and to his disciples:* 2 *"The teachers of the law and the Pharisees sit in Moses' seat.* 3 *So* **<u>you must be careful to do everything they tell you. But do not do what they do, for they do not practice what they preach.</u>** 4 *They tie up heavy, cumbersome loads and put them on other people's shoulders, but they themselves are not willing to lift a finger to move them.* 5 *"****<u>Everything they do is done for people to see: They make their phylacteries wide and the tassels on their garments long;</u>*** 6 ***<u>they love the place of honor at banquets and the most important seats in the synagogues;</u>*** 7 ***<u>they love to be greeted with respect in the marketplaces and to be called 'Rabbi' by others.</u>*** 8 *"But you are not to be called 'Rabbi,' for you have one Teacher, and <u>you are all brothers.</u>* 9 *<u>And do not call anyone on earth 'father,' for you have one Father, and he is in heaven.</u>*

¹⁰ Nor are you to be called instructors, for you have one Instructor, the Messiah. ¹¹ <u>The greatest among you will be your servant.</u> ¹² For those who exalt themselves will be humbled, and those who humble themselves will be exalted. ¹³ "Woe to you, teachers of the law and Pharisees, you hypocrites! You shut the door of the kingdom of heaven in people's faces. You yourselves do not enter, nor will you let those enter who are trying to. [14] [b]

¹⁵ "Woe to you, teachers of the law and Pharisees, you hypocrites! <u>You travel over land and sea to win a single convert</u>, and when you have succeeded, you make them twice as much a child of hell as you are. ¹⁶ "Woe to you, blind guides! You say, 'If anyone swears by the temple, it means nothing; but anyone who swears by the gold of the temple is bound by that oath.' ¹⁷ You blind fools! Which is greater: the gold, or the temple that makes the gold sacred? ¹⁸ You also say, 'If anyone swears by the altar, it means nothing; but anyone who swears by the gift on the altar is bound by that oath.' ¹⁹ You blind men! Which is greater: the gift, or the altar that makes the gift sacred? ²⁰ Therefore, anyone who swears by the altar swears by it and by everything on it. ²¹ And anyone who swears by the temple swears by it and by the one who dwells in it. ²² And <u>anyone who swears by heaven swears by God's throne and by the one who sits on it.</u> ²³ "Woe to you, teachers of the law and Pharisees, you hypocrites! You give a tenth of your spices – mint, dill and cumin. But <u>you have neglected the more important matters of the law – justice, mercy and faithfulness.</u> **You should have practiced the latter, without neglecting the former.** ²⁴ <u>You blind guides! You strain out a gnat but swallow a camel.</u> ²⁵ "Woe to you, teachers of the law and Pharisees, you hypocrites! You clean the outside of the cup and dish, but inside they are full of greed and self-indulgence. ²⁶ <u>Blind Pharisee!</u> **<u>First clean the inside</u> of the cup and dish, and <u>then the outside also will be clean.</u>** ²⁷ "Woe to you, teachers of the law and Pharisees, you hypocrites! You are like whitewashed tombs, which look beautiful on the outside but on the inside are full of the bones of the dead and everything

unclean. ²⁸ *In the same way, <u>on the outside you appear to people as righteous but on the inside, you are full of hypocrisy and wickedness.</u>²⁹ "Woe to you, teachers of the law and Pharisees, you hypocrites!* **You build tombs for the prophets and decorate the graves of the righteous."**

Jesus starts his speech by telling his audience "You *must be careful to do everything they (the pharisees) tell you.*" The problem wasn't with what the pharisees were teaching, the problem was they weren't practicing what they were preaching. Next, he describes the pharisees' extravagant clothing with tassels and long garments as well as their arrogant habit of having places of honor in social settings and being treated with respect in public. Reading this as a former Catholic Seminarian it sounds like Jesus is describing Catholic priests, bishops, cardinals and popes even down to details such as the tassels. In Verse 8 Jesus gets metaphorical and tells his audience they *"are all brothers"* obviously Jesus meant this figuratively as brothers in faith and not biological kindred. While in verse 9 Jesus distinctly says, "do not call anyone on earth 'father,'" yet in violation of what the bible says celibate childless men ordained as Catholic priests call themselves "Father" and instruct everyone else to do so. However, this is explicitly prohibited in the bible by Jesus himself! Ironically the Catholic priest calling himself "Father" believes this verse to be the very word of God spoken by whom he considers the "son of God" concerning people who hypocritically don't practice what they preach. Not to be too harsh but regarding that verse it would seem that such "Fathers" are bigger hypocrites than the Pharisees were whom Jesus was speaking about. Also, this bible verse means that it is a sin for Christians to call their dad the word "Father". So, this is a simple test to use to prove to a Christian they don't follow the bible nor Jesus. Ask if they have a

Father or if they were born of a virgin birth like Jesus, then casually ask what his name is out of curiosity and then ask if they are sure he is their father and stress that you want to make sure they aren't just making it up or lying to you. Then calm their suspicions by saying you just wanted to be sure they were a human and not some alien or monster. Then verify one more time their father's name is ____ (whatever name they gave). Finally, you can tell them that since you told me your Father is ___ then they just sinned according to the bible and proved beyond a doubt that they don't follow Jesus or the bible according to Matthew 23:9. The reason Jesus gives for forbidding anyone to call themselves "Father" is because they "only have one Father and he is in heaven". This demonstrates that in Jesus' view God wasn't his exclusive Father but was everybody's. Just as how when the bible says Jesus was telling them they were all brothers, this is another figurative metaphor not meant literally, because Jesus knew that those who he was speaking to had living human male parents as paternal fathers. Someone who thinks Jesus never spoke metaphorically would have to interpret this to mean that everyone whom Jesus was speaking to was a literal son of God without a human father and must have been born miraculously through a virgin birth as he was and since Jesus said they were all brothers, then Jesus and they must have all been the offspring of Mary the virgin. Thus, taking a literal interpretation of the bible amounts to believing that Jesus is not the only "son of God", that there are many "sons of God" and that they were all alive at the same time in history gathered together, all coincidentally born of the same women Mary who just so happened to be a virgin all her life despite repeatedly giving birth to so many children; according to a literal interpretation of the bible. This is why it is so dangerous to take things in the bible literally when they are figurative. But if people take snippets of the bible out of context, then they will invariably fall into misinterpretations and misunderstanding. Although one thing in verse 23:9 that can be understood literally is what Jesus says regarding the divinity as "being in heaven". This confirms that heaven is a real place. This also means that according to Jesus, God is not everywhere, he is in a specific location. Thereby refuting the misconception of people who think God is everywhere. Obviously, God is not in the hellfire, or in the toilet, or the garbage, or in the sewer so the notion of God being everywhere is ridiculous at face value, unfortunately many Christians think God is everywhere despite the bible saying that Jesus said otherwise. Also, by Jesus saying that God is in heaven it reveals that Jesus did not consider himself divine or part of the godhead because he was clearly not in heaven when he said this statement, so if there were a trinity he would have been required to explain it at that time. Again, in verse 22 Jesus confirms that God has a specific location and mentions his throne which relates to what the Quran says about God and what Muhammad taught and what Muslims are obligated to believe. If you ask a Muslim who has the correct Aqeedah where God is, they will tell you "Above the heavens above his throne". Ask a Christian and they won't tell you anything at all like what the bible says Jesus taught people, most likely you will find they have a very different idea of where God is than what the bible says Jesus said. Matthew 23:11 links greatness with servitude which when we reflect on popes with butlers, presidents with assistants, priests with altar servers, queens who have maids, parents who let machines raise their kids and such people who we consider leaders and dignified with some measure of superiority or greatness, according to the bible they are the least great of all mankind. Then the following verse reveals that due to such person's exaltation in this worldly life they will be humbled in the next life, signifying an undesirable location in the afterlife.  Whereas those believers who humbled themselves in this worldly life will be exalted in the afterlife.  In a nutshell biblical Jesus taught that we should save our pride for paradise and shun all exaltation from the creatures of this planet as well as follow all the rules of God.

      Then comes the famous verse of Matthew 23:14 which is nothing.  I'm serious, it is literally a blank verse in the bible typically covered up by a footnote reference redirecting the reader to another gospel.  I'm not taking the verse out of the quote in order to take the bible out of context.  In context this chapter in the gospel of Matthew has a big blank hole in the middle of it with no data for verse 14.  Have you ever heard of such silliness?  Yet repeatedly Christians will tell me with the utmost sincerity that the bible is the word of God or inspired by God, even the gospel of Matthew not realizing that there is an empty void for verse 23:14.  Now honestly do you think God would send divine revelation down with a big blank left in it?  Or if you think the author of "Matthew" was inspired by God to write what he wrote do you think God was telling him "After verse 13 put verse 14 but then skip straight to verse 15 without writing anything down for verse 14"?  This is blatant evidence that most Christians by and large don't read the bible.  Most all don't even know this empty spot exists.  Simply ask a Christian if they believe in the Gospel of Matthew, then ask them about chapter 23 then ask them about verse 14.  At that point they will likely ask what verse 14 says since you are so specific regarding a book they hardly read, but they will likely try to mask their own ignorance.  Imagine their reaction when you reveal that Matthew 23:14 is literally nothing, a blank verse in the bible.  Such a person literally believes that nothing is divine revelation.  Either that or it's written with invisible ink but then why would God send a book which has one verse written in invisible ink that cannot be decoded by anybody? In reality it's not invisible ink, it's just plain old invisible because it's nothing. It is a verse that has nothing yet millions believe it is sacred scripture. If the bible is a guide for us to live our life, then how are supposed to apply a nonexistent verse to our lives? Someone who still maintains blind faith in the bible after knowing such information or lack thereof in the verse would literally believe God revealed nothing to the author of the gospel of Matthew. It's funny but it's sad because humans devoutly believe that such an incomplete text is from the almighty Creator. Many are sincerely mistaken as I was because we've been brainwashed to believe in the bible before we actually read it and find the blank spot. Shamefully many bible publishers knowing that the verse is blank will copy a verse from another gospel and paste it into the gospel of Matthew despite it not being present in the manuscripts they use as a source. However, the New International Version, the New Living Version, the English Standard Version, the NET bible, the God's Word Translation, the Darby Bible Translation, the English Revised Version and the Weymouth New Testament bibles all leave this verse in the gospel of "Matthew" blank and empty. That's 8 different bibles which have no verse for Matthew 23:14! If we admit that not all bible publishers are honest and we face the reality that 8 bibles intentionally leave Matthew 23:14 blank, sometimes referencing a footnote but still neglecting to put any words for the verse, then what can we conclude? Either those 8 bible publishers are malicious and intentionally deleting verses from a text they publicly pronounce and market as divine revelation, or the other publishers lacking the integrity to admit the bible has a blank verse are inserting a verse that doesn't belong hoping that people don't notice their insertion. Which do you think is more likely? Also note that it's not just 8 who leave this blank but many, I only mentioned 8 to show it's not an isolated example. There are many more than 8 who leave it blank. If Christians are going to lie about and distort the bible, it seems far more likely they would make stuff up and insert something that doesn't belong to save face than to delete something authentic and risk embarrassment, humiliation and ridicule. It hurts to learn this stuff, but Jesus was harsh with the hypocritical pharisees because they were learned and knew that what they were doing and calling people to was wrong. Jesus was mad that people gave pharisees the benefit of the doubt trusting that they were honest guides and pious people just as people trust Christian preachers and missionaries today. Such Christian evangelists seem to imitate those described in Matthew 23:15 who "travel over land and sea to win a single convert". Today there are no Jewish or Muslim missionary organizations that I'm aware of, but Christians are famous for traveling to different continents and countries to preach and convert others, that is the very definition of Christian Evangelism. Verse 16 describes such zealous proselytizers as "blind guides" which is another instance of Jesus speaking figuratively. Obviously the immediate pharisees he was referencing were not optically impaired. Once again Jesus continues figurative metaphors in verse 24 saying the pharisees "strain out a gnat but swallow a camel" which most definitely is not literal in meaning. History would have surely preserved records of Pharisees accomplishing such bizarre feats had Jesus said this because they literally did such things. Instead, Jesus was characteristically figurative and meant that they focused on the minute details of the law of God and ignored the major laws and manners which they were required to act in accordance with. Never did Jesus say they were extremists who were making religion more difficult than it needed to be. Jesus was chastising them because they weren't strict enough and their priorities of strictness were backwards because they let the major sins slide but condemned the small sins people did. The pharisees were basically guilty of major sins but free from small sins yet they paraded themselves as holy men and condemned those free from major sins but guilty of small sins. Eerily suggestive of priests guilty of sodomous pedophilia condemning people for not giving charity. Throughout this entire speech exposing the hypocrisy of the religious leaders of his day Jesus is never interrupted by someone interpreting him literally and saying how he is wrong in what he was saying because people understood Jesus was frequently figurative. Just look at Matthew 12:46-50,

> "While <u>Jesus</u> was still talking to the crowd, his mother and brothers stood outside, wanting to speak to him. 47 Someone told him, "Your mother and brothers are standing outside, wanting to speak to you." 48 He <u>replied</u> to him, "Who is my mother, and who are my brothers?" 49 Pointing to his disciples, he said, "Here are my mother and my brothers. 50 For <u>**whoever does the will of my Father in heaven is my brother and sister and mother.**</u>"

Biblically Jesus taught that you, me and anybody and everybody who does the "will of Jesus' "Father in heaven" thereby is the brother, sister and mother of Jesus all at the same time. So how would you like to join me and many others in being the mother of Jesus, and also being his sister and brother? Oh, and if Jesus is God that means we would become the mother of God and the brother of God and the sister of God. Don't worry if it's a transgender incestual and logically impossible relationship, the bible says Jesus said it are you saying Jesus is lying or the bible is lying? I tend to think these bible verses are lies because surely Jesus would never dishonor his mother in such a way and he didn't have biological brothers. Regardless this isn't literal but figurative and neither is biblical Jesus ever literal when referring to his "Father in heaven" but Christians vastly misunderstand the bible. Jesus was known for metaphors yet today many Christians fail to grasp this concept and tend to only interpret Jesus figuratively when it suits them. They may even try to say that the empty Matthew 23:14 is just a metaphor, but never has nothing been a metaphor in all of history. Unfortunately, I know all too well that as ridiculous as it sounds some Christians will try to use apologetics to justify believing Matthew 23:14 is divine by using the Santa Claus belief methodology or what could be called placebo prophesy. This is because the very foundation of belief in baptism, communion and being confirmed or inspired by the "Holy Spirit" requires blind faith, believing something is true because you are told even though all proof and evidence says the opposite of what you are told. So, they don't have to see the bible to believe it. They don't have to see what verse 14 says, they just believe it through circular logic, because they already believe the bible is scripture then everything in it must be revelation or inspired even if it's a big blank of nothing. But this is not what is meant by believing in the unseen, God doesn't reveal invisible and inaudible verses we're required to believe in. This isn't the only blank in the bible either, just look at Acts 8:37 "____" which is another verse where more than 12 different bible publishers publish as a blank in their bibles. Where again there are more than 12 which leave it blank, I just got tired of counting a bunch of invisible verses in different bibles. Or look at the bible verse of Mark 11:26 "___". Some people say you got to read between the lines but with the bible you can't do that because in between the lines of text you have holes of invisible verses, and these blanks are in the ancient manuscripts. Biblicists believe such big blanks of nothing are holy divine revelation, or maybe the "e" in "holy" is invisible too. To admit any part of such invisible bible verses are not revelation means they are wrong and have a false religious belief. To admit such a thing is the hardest thing in the world to do. But the reward for admitting Satan misled you and then accepting true guidance and changing one's life is the most rewarding thing one can do and can earn them eternal bliss in paradise. However, refusing to change admitting that you were wrong for so long and choosing to believe in falsehood and blind faith can cause one to be in hell for eternity. This is what Jesus taught, now you can understand why the majority of people didn't like him. This is because Governments don't like this, Schools don't like this, Employers don't like this, Cultures don't like this, Nations don't like this, Parents don't like this, False religions don't like this, Humans don't like this. But God does like it and the prophets taught it. If we want to be with the prophets in paradise then we have to teach the same and live accordingly.

After a lengthy diatribe accusing the pharisees of committing major sins and being negligent when teaching people what is right and wrong, the bible says Jesus openly blasts them for one of the major sins they are publicly guilty of saying: "You build tombs for the prophets and decorate the graves of the righteous." Now this is in complete agreement with Islam and the prophet Muhammad's teachings concerning not making the graves of prophets a place of worship or decorating graves of people whether righteous, loved, or famous. Islamically graves aren't labeled and only have a small generic marker so people know it's a grave so they don't step on it disrespectfully. This is because idolatry came into the world when Satan inspired people to honor dead righteous humans and gradually increased their enthusiasm until they ended up worshipping dead relatives and made statues and worshiped the statues. Many don't know this but the very reason idols and idolatry entered the world was because of people being devoted to the dead and wanting to honor their grave. The scholar Ibn Abi Hatim explained how the people of Noah began to worship idols and related the event of the creation of the very first idol on earth. He relates: "*Waddan was a righteous man who was loved by his people. When he died, they withdrew to his grave in the land of Babylonia and were overwhelmed by sadness. When Satan saw their sorrow caused by his death, he disguised himself in the form of a man saying: 'I have seen your sorrow because of this man's death; can I make a statue like him which could be put in your meeting place to make you remember him?' They said: 'Yes.' So, he made the statue like him. They put it in their meeting place in order to be reminded of him. When Satan saw their interest in remembering him, he said: 'Can I build a statue of him in the home of each one of you so that he would be in everyone's house and you could remember him?' They agreed. Their children learned about and saw what they were doing. They also learned about their remembrance of him instead of God. So the first to be worshipped instead of God was Waddan, the idol which they named thus.*" So being excessively devoted to people, especially dead people, is what lead to grave worshipping which led to idols and idolatry. It took many generations but affection for righteous people who died, is what eventually led people to burn in hell. Thus, we can understand why Jesus would be so fierce when condemning the pharisees for decorating the graves of the righteous and building tombs for prophets. Grave worship continues today when people of many faiths go to graves of people and pray despite God prohibiting people to pray at graveyards. When God orders people not to pray at a graveyard and then people go to a grave and pray at it, even if they were praying to God alone, they aren't worshipping God because it is impossible to worship God by doing something God has forbidden. The Vatican is an example of a place of worship built on graves, and I have been in a church and seen a dead body underneath the altar. The prayers made in such places will not be accepted. Unfortunately, the situation today is even worse than that because people go to graves and pray to the dead people again violating God's commands to pray only to him alone and no others. When God tells us to worship him alone, that means we can only pray to God, nothing else. Number 1 you don't know if a recently dead person is going to heaven or hell. Number 2 the prophets whom we know are going to heaven told us to never pray to them as intercessors. Nobody prays to Moses for him to pray to God on their behalf. Yet the prophet Moses spoke to God and heard God with his own ears on earth which makes him much greater than the random dead family member or apparently pious person in the grave that people pray to. Logically people praying to dead people doesn't even make sense for numerous reasons. Aside from the fact that they're dead and you don't know what God thinks of them, such people choose to bypass prophets and pray to lesser humans. Yet those who do go to extremes and pray to prophets are also illogical because those same prophets specifically said not to pray to them whether they were alive or dead. So, you are not going to get points with God by praying in a place God told you not to pray in, praying to something God told you not to pray to, praying to someone whom you don't know what God thinks of them, or by praying to a prophet who said "Don't pray to me!" This means all those prayers said to "saints" or prophets of any faith are actually bad deeds and considered to be worshipping other than God, which is the worst deed. This has happened because Satan manipulates people's ignorance and emotions making us fools to pray to rotting corpses or to prophets who instructed us to worship God alone. However, in the bible Jesus doesn't just condemn prayers at graveyards or towards deceased people. He condemns decorating the graves of the righteous. Jesus wasn't saying don't decorate the graves of bad guys. These were good people in the eyes of Jesus who died as believers. According to Jesus it was damnable to decorate the graves of good people. Today the graves of dead people are more expensive than many people's homes. A typical bland generic tombstone can easily cost over 6,000 dollars! That is, if it's cheap. Society would be better off if that money was just thrown on the ground to blow away in the wind. Such labeled tombstones are unislamic and against the bible and the teachings of Jesus, they are actually sinful for those who put them up and for those who order them and everyone involved in the process. Meaning these tombstones, you see today that people purchase out of love for dead relatives can actually cause torment for the dead person in the grave and the living relative who put it there, if they don't repent before they too are in the grave. A tombstone, flowers, candles and prayers at the grave are not going to help a dead person. If anything, it will cause more misery to those in the grave as well as those who tenderly adorn the grave with such things. This is what the bible says Jesus taught. Of course, one could easily point to most Christians and say they don't follow the bible on this ruling too, but unfortunately many Muslims also fall into error in this regard as well and don't follow what Muhammad taught concerning the etiquettes of the grave; even concerning his own grave. The bible says that Jesus condemned the pharisees for building tombs for the prophets, who were the best of people and for decorating the graves of those whom Jesus considered righteous. That means there is absolutely zero justification for building tombs for anybody. It also means we shouldn't be decorating the graves, especially for people who die nowadays. If it was wrong to decorate graves of a righteous person in the time of Jesus then in comparison those considered righteous by today's standard should have very undecorative graves. Afterall we aren't that special. This special treatment syndrome for dead people stems from tribalism in which the family rituals of cultures and ancestors are given more respect than they deserve, which get followed even when they conflict with the religion the prophets taught us.  It is hard to tell your family that what they are doing is wrong and sinful, but it's better for us to tell them now than for them to find out the hard way later in hell.  They may not like that we don't join them in sinful cultural practices and may say we are disrespectful or extreme.  But if we advise tenderly the way the prophets did then Godwilling we will have done the right thing.  Doing the right thing doesn't always mean it will be easy.  As an example, the father of the prophet Abraham used to make idols.  For many years Abraham calmly confrontationally advised his father and politely told him why what he was doing was wrong and he should stop, then he broke the idols his father had made for the community to worship.  This led Abraham's father to threaten he would stone Abraham to death so he'd better leave if he wanted to live.  That is just one test Abraham endured.  Which also must have been on Abraham's mind when God commanded him to kill his own son.  Just imagine your father threatened to kill you on behalf of his false gods and then in old age you get a dream you believe is from the true God telling you to kill your only son for the sake of the true God.  It was a double standard that from Abraham's perspective was very "anti-family", first as a youth God makes him get in trouble with his father and then God wants him to slay his son?  The message is clear.  God tested Abraham with his family to see which was more important to him, doing what God wanted or "being nice to his family".  And Abraham still went through with it and did what God commanded.  We want to be with him in paradise so we have to abandon those sinful practices that our families may practice as well.  If we worship God then we will base our actions on what God wants before what our family, friends, communities, bosses or countries want.  When they conflict, we do what God wants, in the way that God wants because we worship God. If we choose family customs when they conflict with God's instructions then we would technically be worshipping our family. Which is what Confucianism and culturalism teaches people to do. Confucius even taught people to mourn dead relatives for 3 years, deeming it impious and disrespectful to mourn any relative even a day less. If we worship our family when they are alive then we will likely worship them when they are dead as well and that is why people fall into grave worshipping yet don't consider themselves grave worshippers. Just as those who worship their family don't consider themselves family worshippers despite giving their family precedence over God. Shintos literally pray to dead relatives and bring food and flowers to graves, yet they don't consider themselves grave worshippers. Don't think the flower shop is going to tell you that putting flowers at a grave is grave worshipping, they just want to sell their product and don't care if you use flowers to worship dead people. If people weren't worshipping graves, then the flower industry would crash, especially if the pagan holidays like Valentines, Easter and Mother's Day were abolished too. Also do understand that putting flowers at someone's grave is grave worshipping. This pagan tradition has existed for thousands of years. The ancient Greeks and Romans are recorded to have put funeral wreaths near graves to represent the ouroboros' "circle of life" along with flowers in exactly the same manner which funeral wreaths and flowers today are put near graves. Why do they do it? To be "nice", but who are they being "nice" to? The dead person. Well does the dead person smell the flower? No. Do they see, hear or feel the flower? No. So then how in the world does putting a flower at a grave benefit that dead person in any way at all? It doesn't, it's a foolish form of worshipping dead people. It's not "being nice" it's being stupid and following satanic culture. Then the people are dumb enough to replace the flowers when they wither and die. Now the dead person doesn't know the flowers were even there to begin with and wouldn't know that they died. So then why do the living replace them with new ones? Because they subconsciously think the dead person is going to be upset or disrespected if they don't, or some superstitious curse will come upon them as the pagans used to believe. Thus, some put fake plastic flowers at graves, just to be safe and fool the ghost into thinking people care enough to maintain their grave with live ones. People do this because they subconsciously fear the being they worship and are grave worshippers even though they don't think they are. The most stupid thing about it is that the dead person didn't even tell anybody to put flowers at their grave. So even if the grave worshippers false ideas about the dead were semi-true it's still stupid because the dead person might not even like flowers. You'll even have people who are allergic to flowers die and then some fool goes and puts flowers at their grave to "show respect". What's next, will people be putting money or animals at the grave? Pagans actually used to do such things with their wealthy and rulers having servants buried alive with them to "serve them". This is what the pyramids are. They are the Pharaoh's tombs full of a bunch of rooms filled with junk that the Pharaoh wanted to eat, drink and play with in the next life. Today we say that was stupid, but people still do this when they visit graves and leave stuff there "out of respect". At least the pagans were more logical in that they thought the stuff could actually be utilized by the dead. So, today's grave worshippers are actually further astray than the ancient pagans were. This is also one of the reasons Pharaoh was so opposed to Moses. The Death Industry was a major part of the Egyptian economy, the Egyptian priest got paid to "open the mouth" and try to blow the life/soul back in when someone died, then they would sacrifice a calf afterwards. Then Egyptians would remove the organs and embalm the bodies, that is if you could afford it. If not, then the dead would not enjoy their afterlife without a body. The organs could only go in specific expensive canopic jars, there was one for nearly every organ, there was 1 for the liver, 1 for the lungs, 1 for the intestines, 1 for the stomach and for as many more parts you wanted your dead relative to have in the afterlife. Then the dead would be laid on a table with Natron powder for 70 days, if you could pay for that, then amulets were attached with a copy of the "Book of the Dead" because your dead relative will need reading material you know and then they were wrapped up and then the funeral might begin. I say might because your relative expected a very grievous affair and you would've had to hire professional grievers to publicly express great grief throughout the funeral procession, the more you could afford the more grief they would display at your relative's death. Yet because they were paid to cry, some or all of their tears might've been for joy at a paycheck rather than true grief for a death. But if that's the case, then it meant you were cheap and you would've shamed your relative if people suspected you paid people to display grief, even though everybody did it, they just didn't want to get caught. Also, since the embalmers knew their practice was a huge scam, they would play jokes and mismatch body parts in different jugs, not letting the family know, sometimes even using body parts from multiple bodies and then getting paid for their "work" by the family for assuring "all their organs are in the right jugs". The worst part is that those poor bodies that weren't mummified were actually preserved better by the dry Egyptian sand than those who were mummified. Then there were Egyptians who got paid to guard the graveyards, because you didn't want a grave robber to ruin your ancestor's afterlife by taking their parts away since without the body, they thought the spirit would die. Basically, Egyptians thought if their family didn't pay enough to get properly buried or guarded when they died then their afterlife would be ruined. Thus, each generation taught the next to have the utmost respect and duty for their dead ancestors. Yet conveniently the grave-robbers worked together with the grave guards to rob the grave together while letting the family stay unaware of the scam. Some grave-robbers even got paid to guard the very graves they would rob, thinking it was the perfect crime that was a legal full-time job. Suddenly Moses comes saying that all the Egyptians have been wrong for centuries, the holidays have to stop, the government must change and the lucrative death industry must be shut down. Imagine how the death industry reacted then, as compared to how it would react now to my suggestion that it be shut down. Once, after writing this paragraph, at a party a distant Catholic relative even asked me if I wanted to visit a grave of our dead Catholic relatives and pay the typical respects as one does. I didn't really know quite how to gently say no and how evil that is. So, I said I don't go to non-Muslim graveyards because Islamically most of the stuff Christians do at graves is grave worshipping, while in Islam Muslims don't even use tombstones but just bury the body without them and then the soil can be used for something in the future rather than having the land be permanently wasted by expensive extravagant tombstones for dead people. I figured that was a good answer that won't seem extreme or too detailed, without stressing how much I hate disbelievers and believe all our non-Muslim relatives are going to hell and are being currently punished in their graves for their evilness. Yet do you know what they said back? They laughed at the notion that I would think they were grave worshipping and sternly confidently said, "Well the Catholic Church says the graveyards are sacred lands. So that's sacred ground." I was speechless, and thought to myself, "Oh my! Not only are you a disbelieving Christian grave worshipper. But you also think that because some dead Catholic gets buried in a certain area that it somehow gets transformed into a holy land because the Catholic Church says so? And you tell me this confidently as if I'm stupid?" I didn't even know what to say in response but just thought I better put this in my book because it's even worse than I wrote. Not even the Pharisees or the Pharaohs claimed that their extravagant graveyards were "Sacred Ground". They literally think that because a Catholic is buried there that means it becomes holy land which can never be used for anything else because their precious loved ones are buried there. Catholics aren't the only ones who think this, many Christians consider graveyards as sacred grounds. It's identical to the policy the US military has. Although Muslims have more respect for the dead because we don't step on graves even though we don't consider the graveyards eternally sacred, whereas Christians walk all over graves but think it's sinful to walk or sit on a tombstone. Yet somehow Christians still think they aren't grave worshippers? There are billions of people on the planet right now, they will all die. Earth does not have enough land for everyone to get buried in "sacred ground" with a tombstone so the land they are buried in never gets used for anything else again. We will run out of land to live on, plant on, hunt on and build on if people keep making tombstone graves on "sacred ground". If the nonislamic graveyards don't start recycling instead of scamming people with exclusive graves and tombstones we will have a planet of graveyards and have to live in the oceans or another planet. Zombies won't take over the world, the tombstones will. I mean really, we got people with no shelter whatsoever while others buy thousands of dollars' worth of fancy rock to put on a dead person's grave? Why aren't the rocks for the tombstone industry used to build houses for the homeless instead? You can actually build a house for a poor person in another country for the price a tombstone costs. Whereas consider all the people taking time to put flowers at a tombstone for a dead enemy of God yet they ignore the sick people starving and don't give them anything. Do you think God likes them doing that or curses them for it? In retrospect in the future, I plan to reply to relatives' questions about visiting graves by saying "I don't even go to disbeliever's funerals or "wakes". If I go to their grave, I'd be obligated to give them the glad tidings of hellfire as Muhammad taught Muslims to do if they visit a grave of someone who dies as a non-Muslim. Do you really want me to go there and tell them to enjoy hell?" Now that may seem rude to say to a relative asking you to visit a dead relatives grave, but it will get us talking about religion and quickly make my position regarding their religion and the path they are on clear so that we can discuss it. Maybe you think I'm making a big deal out of this; well, the bible says Jesus made a big deal out of this. When saying that the pharisees were exposed as evildoers by Jesus for focusing on small things and not big things people may misunderstand what that means. The big things are what God says are big things and small things are what God says are small things. To you or me something might be considered insignificant but in the sight of Allah they are major. Something that may seem major to us may seem insignificant to Allah. This is the trap the pharisees fell into. They used their definition of what is big and small sins instead of what the prophets defined as big and small. The root problem in the world today comes from a lack of people looking at life the way the prophets did. What was important to the prophets should be important to us, what was trivial to the prophets should be trivial to us as well. In concluding this stream of thought the lesson is that Jesus rebuked the pharisees for not keeping the law of God 100% and hypocritically focusing on the less important aspects of the law. They still would have been blameworthy had they done the minor sins and avoided major sins, but they would have been even more blameworthy had they committed the smaller sins as well as the major sins. Whereas had they not taught any aspect of the law of God nor followed any of it they would have been even more reprehensible and foul. Unfortunately, today we have become more sinful than the pharisees and we teach others to do even less good than they did. The solution is through knowledge and sincere application of the knowledge. The pharisees had the knowledge but they weren't sincere. But a sincere person without knowledge can easily fall into error and start grave worshipping thinking it's a good deed or blow themselves up thinking they will be a martyr. The way to obtain sincerity and knowledge is to ask the Creator of everything to grant you sincerity and knowledge and the ability to act correctly. Then to sincerely seek the correct knowledge the correct way from the correct sources and to apply it as you learn it consistently until you die. The way to do that is by sincerely striving to learn from the prophets with the proper etiquettes. Since the prophets are not amongst us, we can only use what is available. Meaning we are limited to the divine revelation given to the prophets and the teachings of the prophets. Unfortunately, not all the divine revelations are available to us and not all of the prophets' teachings have survived intact. Thus, God sent new prophets whenever they were necessary to guide us back to the road to paradise. Since the divine revelations God had sent had not been preserved there was a need for another prophet to be sent. Even the English translation of the New International Version of the bible says besides the Messiah another prophet was expected in John 1:19-26, *"Now this was John's testimony when the Jewish leaders in Jerusalem sent priests and Levites to ask him who he was.* [20] *He did not fail to confess, but confessed freely, "I am not the Messiah."* [21] *They asked him, "Then who are you? Are you Elijah?" He said, "I am not." "Are you the Prophet?" He answered, "No."* [22] *Finally* they said, *"Who are you? Give us an answer to take back to those who sent us. What do you say about yourself?"* ²³ <u>*John replied in the words of Isaiah the prophet*</u>, *"I am the voice of one calling in the wilderness, 'Make straight the way for the Lord.'"* ²⁴ *Now the Pharisees who had been sent*²⁵ *questioned him,* <u>*"Why then do you baptize if you are not the Messiah, nor Elijah, nor the Prophet?".*</u>

  In these verses John the Baptist is asked by the pharisees who he is. First, they ask him if he is the Messiah and he says he is not. Later they ask if he is "*the Prophet*", which means there is another prophet after the Messiah. Meaning that the Messiah, Jesus, is not the last prophet. At the end of this excerpt the pharisees again reveal they distinctly differentiate between the Messiah and "*the Prophet*". John is not "*the Prophet*" they are talking about because the bible says they asked "*Are you the Prophet? He answered, "No."* John was indeed a prophet, but the question was about "*the Prophet*" not "a prophet". That John didn't object when the Pharisees repeatedly separated "*the Messiah*" and "*the Prophet*" means according to the bible during the time of the prophet John, 2 different people were expected "*the Messiah*" and "*the Prophet*". John publicly proclaimed he wasn't "*the Prophet*" and he didn't say the Messiah is "*the Prophet*". If John was "*the Prophet*", lying and saying he wasn't would've been a sin and rejection of prophethood, whereas Jesus can't be both. Biblically speaking there is another prophet who is not John, or the Messiah Jesus. Who is "*the Prophet*"?

  The stories in the bible about the baptism of Jesus by John are contradictory with each gospel describing a different event taking place. One gospel says John didn't know Jesus before, during, or after the alleged baptism and only learned Jesus was the Messiah while he received letters in prison describing his miracles. Another gospel says John recognized Jesus on sight before the alleged baptism. Another gospel says that John didn't know Jesus while baptizing, but then the skies opened up and a dove came down and God informed John of who he was. These gospels each tell a different story and not all of them can be true. Fortunately, all the gospels agree in that never did the prophet John ever label Jesus as God or a son of God. Contradictions concerning the alleged baptism of Jesus aside there is something that must be pointed out regarding baptism. Christians allege that Jesus is the son of God and some say God himself, they also claim that everyone must be baptized because of the Original Sin Adam committed which they believe is inherited by all his descendants and if we aren't baptized we will go to hell. If this were the case then that means all the people who lived in between Adam and John the Baptist such as Noah, Abraham, Jonah, Joseph, Salih, Moses, David, Job, Solomon are all in hell because they were never baptized. Many Christians (not all) believe they were all in hell but then somehow when Jesus was allegedly killed, they finally got sent to heaven because of Jesus, despite the bible saying in 2 Kings 2:11,

*"As they were walking along and talking together, suddenly a chariot of fire and horses of fire appeared and separated the two of them, and Elijah went up to heaven in a whirlwind."*

In Hebrews 11:5, *"By faith Enoch was taken from this life, so that he did not experience death: "He could not be found, because God had taken him away." For before he was taken, he was commended as one who pleased God."*

Paul says in 2 Corinthians 12:2-4, *"I know a man in Christ who fourteen years ago was caught up to the third heaven. Whether it was in the body or out of the body I do not know – God knows. ³ And I know that this man – whether in the body or apart from the body I do not* know, but God knows ⁴ *was caught up to paradise* and heard inexpressible things, things that no one is permitted to tell."

And finally, the gospel of John 3:13 says, " **No one has ever gone into heaven except** the one who came from heaven – **the Son of Man**."

Now we have a big problem as you can see. In the Old Testament Elijah is said to have went up into heaven. In the New Testament Enoch is said to have never have died because God "took him away" (which means he went to heaven, and the Islamic belief is that his soul was extracted from his body by the angel of death while in the 4th heaven). While Paul says that he personally knows someone who went up to the 3rd heaven and then came back to earth. So, all this evidence from the bible says people went to heaven, some of which got in without Jesus being killed beforehand thereby meaning original sin doesn't exist or prevent entry to heaven nor is Jesus being killed or baptism a prerequisite for going to heaven. However, then the gospel of John, verse 3:13 to be precise, says "NO ONE" has ever gone into heaven except the "Son of Man" who came from heaven, by which he means Jesus. So, we have 3 biblical books vs. the gospel of John, and we have Paul vs. the gospel of John. Also keep in mind Paul's letter was written before the gospel of John. Thus, we can only conclude that whoever wrote the gospel of John didn't know what the bible said, in either the Old Testament or the New Testament. Or the author of John did know what the bible said but he didn't believe in it, thought it was wrong and thought he knew better than the bible. But wait a second, if John 3:13 is wrong, as it clearly is then what about the words written in it just 3 verses later in John 3:16? You know the famous one about God loving the world so much he gave his only begotten son? That verse Christians base their religion upon is literally 3 verses away from John 3:13 which contradicts the Old Testament, the New

Testament and Paul! It really is the gospel of John vs. the bible. One must be rejected because they cannot reconcile. Or did God inspire John to say the rest of the bible is wrong? Whereas if the Christians believe Paul, then even Paul himself is saying the author of the gospel of John is wrong. Thus, if John 3:13 is wrong then John 3:16 cannot be accepted. Also as a side point the Catholic idea of Mary ascending to heaven body and soul without dying is also wrong according to John 3:13. I advise that you remember these 4 verses of 2 Kings 2:11, Hebrews 11:5, 2 Corinthians 12:2-4 and John 3:13 so that you can discuss and share them when Christians tell you about John 3:16. Sadly it's even worse than I described, because the reason Christians like to quote John 3:16 so much is because the bible portrays Jesus as the speaker. Well, the bible also says Jesus is the one who said what John 3:13 says. So, all that stuff I said about John being wrong, that's not quite the full story. Because it's not just John but the Jesus whom John writes about. So, you have the Old Testament, New Testament and Paul all against John's Jesus. Thus, we must really have an answer to the question of who is wrong? The Old Testament, New Testament and Paul or John's version of Jesus? If John's version of Jesus is the real version, then it would mean Jesus is wrong. While if John's gospel account is wrong then that means the Jesus written about in John is not the true Jesus. Also, Jesus is famous for having taught in parables but the gospel of John has zero parables attributed to Jesus. According to the gospel of John, Jesus didn't use parables. It seems to me that whoever wrote John's gospel didn't know Jesus.

  Anyways if Original Sin means you can't go to heaven without baptism, then how did Elijah and Enoch get in as the bible says they did? But most importantly regarding Christianity, is that zero of the disciples of Jesus were baptized. Peter and the rest were never baptized, so according to Christian doctrine they would have Original Sin, aren't really Christians, couldn't receive the Holy Spirit and are doomed to hell. So, if Christians need to be baptized to go to heaven, then Peter, the founder of the Church and alleged keyholder of heaven, is going to be in hell forever because of the Original Sin doctrine. Although it's hypocritical for God to hold people accountable for the sins of Adam yet when the Israelites who followed Moses out of Egypt disobeyed God, and were thus prevented from entering the promised land, that their children would not also be prevented. Biblically the next generations of Israelites were not left to wander because of the sins of their parents, which means sin is not inheritable no matter what it is. For example, the father of Abraham created idols for people to worship, Abraham was not punished as a result of what his father did. Also keep in mind Adam and Eve simply ate something forbidden, they didn't worship idols. The reason Christians in the 4th century CE began to believe that every human is guilty because of Adam's original sin stems from the idea we were all literally "in him" as sperm. However, this contradicts the idea that Mary and Jesus were without original sin because if we have it since we were "in Adam" as sperm then Mary and Jesus would be in the same sinful sack as us. Original Sin is basically thought of as a venereal disease obtained by parents copulating yet even by this logic Mary would have it since her parents copulated when conceiving her. Regarding baptism if as Christians claim man is contaminated with sin and Jesus is God, or the son of God, then that would mean Jesus would not have had original sin and would not have needed baptism in the first place. Some might say, *"but he was also the son of Mary who was human"*, however Christians also say that Mary was specially chosen to be the mother of Jesus specifically because she didn't have original sin. Thus, Jesus couldn't have caught it from his mother. Also, if God could forgive "Original Sin" in the case of Mary then he can forgive it for all humans. Therefore, if the baptism of Jesus did take place the baptism must have been different than the baptism we know of today. In fact, it was because those who get baptized today get a "Godfather" and "Godmother" proxy who testify to their belief in Christianity and promise to raise the person as Christian if the parents don't. Whereas in the bible the baptism candidates had no sponsors or proxies. A "Godparent" title itself is blasphemous because it violates the 1st, 3rd, 5th, 9th, and 10th commandments; technically the 8th too. Becoming a "Godparent" for someone at baptism actually breaks 50-60% of the 10 categories of the 613 commandments! Biblically baptisms were done in a "mikevah" by Jews as a means of purification after repentance and people would get baptized many times during their lifetime, never with a "Godparent". Every festival day prior to going to the synagogue Jewish men would also take a ritual bath, in Judaism women weren't allowed in the synagogue so they only took ritual bathes for repentance or after menstruation, sex or giving birth. Plus, since Christians say Jesus was baptized then if "Godparents" were ok to have then Jesus must have had them, but he didn't. Also, in the bible John the Baptist is alleged to have said, *"after me will come one who will baptize not with water but by fire"* some think this refers to Jesus, but he never baptized one person the entire time he was on earth. Some may cite John 3:22 as saying Jesus baptized, but John 4:2 explicitly says Jesus didn't baptize anyone. Others think the Holy spirit of the trinity is referred to, but if that is the case since according to Christians the Holy spirit has come then all baptisms done by water are no longer valid or necessary, because they are to be done by fire. On top of that those John baptized didn't even know of a "Holy Spirit" as the bible says in Acts 19:1-3, *"While Apollos was at Corinth, Paul took the road through the interior* *and arrived at Ephesus. There he found some <u>disciples</u> ² and asked them, "Did you receive the Holy Spirit when you believed?" They answered, <u>"No, we have not even heard that there is a Holy Spirit."</u>³ So Paul asked, "Then what baptism did you receive?" "John's baptism," they replied."*

So biblically these "disciples" who "believed", before they met Paul, were baptized by John and yet never even heard about a "Holy Spirit". Thus, John must never have taught anyone about a "Holy Spirit", even though he is quoted to have said one will come after who baptizes with fire, thus it can't be the "Holy Spirit" whom John said would come after him and we already know it wasn't Jesus. Also, today Christians still baptize by water and not by fire, which implies they are still waiting for the one to come whom John is alleged to have spoken of. Therefore, anyway you look at it someone is to come after Jesus. Yet the best refutation of baptism is that <u>John the Baptist never got baptized himself</u> nor did he baptize his father or mother. Just ask a Christian "*Who baptized John the Baptist?*" the answer is nobody. So, baptism must not really be that important and is definitely not a requirement for belief or paradise. Elsewhere Luke 1:13-15 says of John: "*He will be a joy and delight to you, and many will rejoice because of his birth, ¹⁵ for he will be great in the sight of the Lord. <u>He is never to take wine or other fermented drink, and he will be filled with the Holy Spirit even before he is born.</u>*"

Which "grape juice" is mistranslated as "wine" and yes it was grape juice because since John was a Nazirite, he had special restrictions in that he was forbidden to consume grapes or grape juice. Yet the point is the bible says John was filled with the "Holy Spirit" since before birth yet the "disciples" who were baptized by John had never even heard that there is a "Holy Spirit". So, either John didn't have the "Holy Spirit" and Luke's gospel is false or Paul's version of the "Holy Spirit" is very different than the "Holy

Spirit" John was filled with. Now the Greek word used in both sections is πνεῦμα but unfortunately this word has 18 very different meanings, ranging from wind, air blown from your nose, to an angel, to the human soul, to a demon, to the 3rd part of God, and even is defined as "evil spirits" who possess people in other parts of the bible. The same exact word is used in Matthew 8:16, 10:1, 12:45, Mark 1:26-27, 3:11, 3:30, 5:8, 5:13, 6:7, 7:25, 9:17, 9:25, Luke 7:21, 8:2, 11:26 and many other verses when describing demons. Now of course the prefix of "holy" isn't present in such instances but then again "Holy" is a matter of perspective, since what is "Holy" to someone of one religion may well be demonic to one of another religion. Thus, it may well be that Saul/Paul's "Holy Spirit" could be a demon or evil spirit different than that which filled John. Also, if *"the Prophet"* were the *"Holy Spirit"* then John would've clarified when questioned and why would the rabbi's ask John if he were the "Holy Spirit" or the "Holy ghost"? John was clearly human thus *"the prophet"* is clearly a human and not a ghost. Are there any clues to help us identify *"the Prophet"*? There are many prophecies in Isaiah that concern Arabia as well as other books, but all the different prophecies about *"the Prophet"* could fill books. Rather than list all the clues I will keep it brief. In the English translation of the New International Version of the bible Deuteronomy 18:18-22 says God said: *"[18] I will raise up for them <u>a prophet like you</u> from among their fellow Israelites, and I will put my words in his mouth. <u>He will tell them everything I command him</u>.[19] <u>I myself will call to account anyone who does not listen to my words that the prophet speaks in my name</u>.[20] But a prophet who presumes to speak in my name anything I have not commanded, or a prophet who speaks in the name of other gods, is to be put to death."* [21] *You may say to yourselves, "How can we know when a message has not been spoken by the LORD?"*[22] *<u>If what a prophet proclaims in the name of the LORD does not take place or come true, that is a message the LORD has not spoken.</u>*

*That prophet has spoken presumptuously, so do not be alarmed."* The 18th verse is believed to have been revealed to Moses. telling him that God will send a prophet "like him". Now let's examine what that means. Christians claim this refers to Jesus and Muslims claim this refers to Muhammad. The following table compares Moses, Muhammad and Jesus.

| Moses | Muhammad | Jesus |
|---|---|---|
| Natural birth he had both a Mother and Father | Natural birth, he had both a Mother and Father | Miraculous unnatural birth, only had a Mother |
| Had Wives + kids | Had Wives + kids. | No Wives, no kids. |
| Became prophet when he was age 40 | Became prophet when he was age 40 | Became prophet at age 30 according to Christians, at birth according to Muslims |
| Led in emigration | Led in emigration | Never emigrated |
| Accepted by his nation | Accepted by his nation | Rejected by his nation |
| Victorious against enemies in battle | Victorious against enemies in battle | Never won a military battle |
| Ruler who could inflict Capital Punishment | Ruler who could inflict Capital Punishment | Not a ruler, Christians believe he suffered Capital Punishment |
| Came with New Law in Torah | Came with New Law in Quran | Followed and taught Law of the Torah, abrogating some of it |
| Natural Death | Natural Death | Christians say crucified, Muslims say lifted alive to heaven. Either way, not a natural death |
| Buried in ground | Buried in ground | In heaven, will return. |

No one can deny that Muhammad is more like Moses than Jesus is. Also, many Christians say that Jesus is God, or the son of God, therefore such a claim would immediately disqualify Jesus from being like Moses for many reasons. On top of that, God is not like Moses and the verses are allegedly God talking to Moses. Thus Deuteronomy 18:18 cannot be about Jesus if Jesus were God or a son of God. Even though Jesus isn't divine the verses still cannot be about him. In other translations Deuteronomy 18:18 says, "*I will raise them up a prophet <u>from among their brethren</u>, like unto thee, and I will put my words in his mouth.*" Although I have used the New International Version of the bible as my source throughout and it would be hypocritical to pick another translation at this stage in the book, just because a different translation further proves the point. I cannot reject the entire translation just because I disagree with it on this one verse, likewise Christians should not reject it solely because of its translation of John 3:16, which does not have the word begotten in it. It may be our ideas of what the verses should be are wrong and that the earlier translations which support our beliefs are wrong. Also, it is against intellectual integrity to only use translations that agree with us just because they agree with us. Nevertheless, I feel it is interesting that other older translations say, "*from among their brethren*" because this means the prophet will not be of Jewish ethnicity. Who could be considered brethren to Jews? Israelites are descended from Israel also known as Jacob who was the son of Isaac who was the son of Abraham. The prophet Abraham also had another son Ishmael who was his firstborn son, whose descendants are known as Ishmaelites. The formerly Jewish mathematician and son of a Rabbi, Samual al-Maghribi stated in his book " Ifḥām Al-Yahūd" that based on the biblical descriptions of Esau and his children as being brethren of Jacob and his children, then Ishmael's children can also be described in the same manner as brethren to Israelites. He was a 12th century Jew who became a Muslim and hid his Islam for years until he later wrote a book exposing Judaism denouncing the Jews. So, in the past the bibles used to say that this prophet promised in Deuteronomy 18:18 would be from the Ishmaelites, yet in modern bibles they say from "fellow Israelites". It seems that doctrines and racism distorted modern bible translations.

    The bible states Abraham took his "only son" to be sacrificed, but then the angel stopped him as he passed the test God had given him. Both Ishmael and Isaac were alive at the time Abraham died and were present to bury him together according to Genesis 25:8-9, so Ishmael is the only one who could ever have been the "only son" of Abraham. Yet many Christians and Jews will say Ishmael wasn't legitimate because his mother Hagar was a slave and Sarah was Abraham's wife. Now Muslims believe Hagar was a slave and still see Ishmael as a legitimate son, but Christians tend to insist legitimate sons can only be born from married spouses. However, in the bible Genesis 16:3 says "*So after Abram had been living in Canaan ten years, Sarai his wife took her Egyptian slave Hagar and gave her to her husband to be his wife.*" So biblically speaking Hagar was the wife of Abraham too. The bible says Abraham had 2 wives at the same time, and it was his wife's idea for him to marry her slave Hagar. Genesis 16:15-16 continues "*So Hagar bore Abram a son, and Abram gave the name Ishmael to the son she had borne. ¹⁶Abram was eighty-six years old when Hagar bore him Ishmael.*" While Genesis 21:13 confirms that Ishmael was indeed the legitimate son of Abraham when it says God said "*I will make the son of the slave into a nation also, because he is your offspring.*" Of course, the New International Version of the bible translates it as offspring instead of " seed" but the earlier verse provides clarification that the son of the slave is indeed Abraham's son in Genesis 21:11 "*The matter distressed Abraham greatly because it concerned his son.*" This shows the biblical text considers and states that Ishmael is a legitimate son of Abraham. So since biblically Ishmael is indeed Abraham's son and his firstborn son, who then could possibly be Abraham's "only son" who was almost sacrificed? According to the bible it can only be Ishmael. Then in Genesis 17 the bible says:

<u>When Abram was ninety-nine years old, the **LORD** appeared to him and said</u>, "I am God Almighty; walk before me faithfully and be blameless. ² Then I will make my covenant between me and you and will greatly increase your numbers." ³ Abram fell facedown, and <u>God said to him</u>, ⁴ "<u>As for me, this is my covenant with you: You will be the father of many nations.</u> ⁵ <u>No longer will you be called Abram; your name will be Abraham</u>, for I have made you a father of many nations. ⁶ I will make you very fruitful; I will make nations of you, and kings will come from you. ⁷ <u>I will establish my covenant as an everlasting covenant between me and you and your descendants after you for the generations to come, to be your God and the God of your descendants after you.</u> ⁸ The whole land of Canaan, where you now reside as a foreigner, I will give as an everlasting possession to you and your descendants after you; and I will be their God." ⁹ <u>Then God said to Abraham, "As for you, you must keep my covenant, you and your descendants after you for the generations to come. ¹⁰ This is my covenant with you and your descendants after you, the covenant you are to keep: Every male among you shall be circumcised. ¹¹ You are to undergo circumcision, and it will be the sign of the covenant between me and you.</u> ¹² For the generations to come <u>every male among you who is eight days old must be circumcised</u>, including those born in your household or bought with money from a foreigner – those who are not your offspring. ¹³ Whether born in your household or bought with your money, they must be circumcised. <u>My covenant in your flesh is to be an everlasting covenant.</u> ¹⁴ Any uncircumcised male,

<u>who has not been circumcised in the flesh, will be cut off from his people; he has broken my covenant."</u>

¹⁵ God also said to Abraham, "As for Sarai your wife, you are no longer to call her Sarai; her name will be Sarah. ¹⁶ I will bless her and will surely give you a son by her. I will bless her so that she will be the mother of nations; kings of peoples will come from her."¹⁷ <u>Abraham fell facedown; he laughed and said to himself, "Will a son be born to a man a hundred years old?</u> Will Sarah bear a child at the age of ninety?" ¹⁸ And Abraham said to God, "If only Ishmael might live under your blessing!"¹⁹ Then God said, "<u>Yes, but your wife Sarah will bear you a son, and you will call him Isaac. I will establish my covenant with him as an everlasting covenant for his descendants after him.</u> ²⁰ <u>And as for Ishmael, I have heard you: I will surely bless him; I will make him fruitful and will greatly increase his numbers. He will be the father of twelve rulers, and I will make him into a great nation.</u> ²¹ <u>But my covenant I will establish with Isaac, whom Sarah will bear to you by this time next year."</u> ²² When he had finished speaking with Abraham, God went up from him.

²³ <u>On that very day</u> Abraham took his son Ishmael and all those born in his household or bought with his money, every male in his household, and circumcised them, as God told him. ²⁴ <u>Abraham was ninety-nine years old</u> when he was circumcised, ²⁵ and his son Ishmael was thirteen; ²⁶ Abraham and his son Ishmael were both circumcised on that very day. ²⁷ And every male in Abraham's household, including those born in his household or bought from a foreigner, was circumcised with him."

Now if you examine this chapter critically you will notice an aberration between verses 15-22. The chapter starts by saying Abram was 99 years old and God told him to change his name to Abraham and circumcise himself and his descendants. The circumcision was to be the sign of an everlasting covenant with Abraham and his descendants. This is the bible story from Genesis 17 verses 1-14. Then from verses 23-27 we are told "*On that very day"* Abraham circumcised Ishmael, thereby establishing the covenant with him when he was 13 years old and Abraham was 99. Together those sections make complete sense and flow smoothly. However in between there is another paragraph of verses 15-22 where we are told God renamed Abram, Abraham's wife and informed him she will bear a son. In response Abraham uncharacteristically laughs at God and asks how he can have a son when he is "*a hundred years old*". God says it will happen and that his covenant will only be with that son named Isaac who will be born the next year when Abraham is 101 years old. But then in verse 23 we get told "*On that very day*" "*Abraham was 99 years old*". So, we have a problem in that biblically Abraham went from being 99 to being 100 back to being 99 years old all in one day. Or else someone has corrupted the text and put things out of order. But why would they or God do that, if this is indeed divine revelation? Well let's imagine the bible was in chronological order and a person read that the covenant is made with Abraham and his descendants at age 99 and he only has 1 kid at that time. The sign of the covenant is circumcision and he circumcises his only son Ishmael "*on that very day*" he is told of the covenant. Everyone would understand biblically the covenant is made with Ishmael, it doesn't mean it's only with Ishmael, but it was undeniably made with Ishmael when he was 13 years old. Likewise, when God makes a covenant, according to the bible, it's never an exclusively genetic covenant. This is evident by the biblical covenants God made with Noah and David of which their descendants were listed as being part of the covenant. Yet then the bible curses those very same descendants of Noah and David because of their disobedience. Although some of these biblical curses again seem due to racist Jews, such as Canaan (Noah's grandson) being cursed by Noah before he is born because his father Ham allegedly walked in on Noah when he was passed out drunk and naked. Whereas I don't think that post-flood Noah would've drunk himself into such a stupor that he passed out naked and then when he wakes up he curses his unborn grandson whom God made a covenant with. It's more likely that Israelites just wanted to wage war with Canaanites so they put this curse of Canaanites in the bible to justify their war policies. Anyway, just because God makes a covenant doesn't mean it's a free pass or irrevocable, it's more of a contract that can be broken if humans don't fulfill their part. Although if we go into covenants being legitimately broken and we say God made a covenant with Abraham and his descendants, it's clear that not all of the descendants kept their part of the covenant. If we get genetic and say Ishmaelites and Israelites both had the covenant then it's easy to see examples of Israelites breaking the covenant but when did the Ishmaelites? Also, just because individuals or a collective people may break God's covenant that doesn't mean that covenant isn't still available to their race. A covenant with God is more like a special contract only offered to certain people, that is different from the offer God gives to the whole world. So, when a covenant is made with people that means an offer is on the table, if the people accept that offer there are conditions to be fulfilled and if they don't fulfill those conditions, there are consequences. Covenants are high risk/high reward contracts with God but then again nobody ever refuses a covenant because it's truly a gift, similar to a prestigious job offer. Few will turn down a job offer even though they know it will require work and could cause big trouble for them if they mess up on the job. The point is that biblically the covenant was made with Ishmael too and not just Israel. The bible's next chapter Genesis 18 relates a version of what happened when angels appeared to Abraham in the form of men to announce the destruction of Sodom and the birth of Isaac. The points relevant to us are Genesis 18:9-15, ""*Where is your wife,*

Sarah?" they asked him. "There, in the tent," he said. ¹⁰ Then <u>one of them said, "I will surely return to you about this time next year, and Sarah your wife will have a son."</u> Now Sarah was listening at the entrance to the tent, which was behind him. ¹¹ Abraham and Sarah were already very old, and Sarah was past the age of childbearing. ¹² So Sarah laughed to herself as she thought, "After I am worn out and my lord is old, will I now have this pleasure?" ¹³ <u>Then the LORD said to Abraham, "Why did Sarah laugh and say, 'Will I really have a child, now that I am old?' ¹⁴ Is anything too hard for the LORD? I will return to you at the appointed time next year, and Sarah will have a son."</u> ¹⁵ Sarah was afraid, so she lied and said, "I did not laugh." But he said, "Yes, you did laugh."

Lots can be learned from this. Firstly, we should note that Sarah was clearly surprised at the news of her having a child and she laughed as a result. Yet pages ago in Genesis 17 we were told that God already informed Abraham that his wife Sarah would have a child. In that version Abraham laughed at the news. Why then would God tell him again and why didn't Sarah already know? Did Abraham just keep the news a secret and not tell Sarah that God blessed her and she would give birth? It's very unlikely Abraham would keep Genesis 17:15-22 a secret from his wife especially if as it says God would make a covenant with Sarah's son and not Ishmael. Although if we do pretend Abraham kept God's revelations and good news a secret from his beloved wife then why would God in Genesis 18 give Sarah such a hard time for laughing when Genesis 17 says Abraham laughed and it was no problem? Genesis 18 chastises Sarah for laughing but when Abraham laughs in Genesis 17 it's ok? I do say something is very funny about this biblical narrative and it is not the funny kind of funny. It actually seems that whoever wrote Genesis 18 didn't know about the verses in Genesis 17:15-22 which coincidentally happen to list Abraham as 100 even though verses 1-14 and 23-27 have him at age 99. Yet these suspicious verses also happen to be the ones which say the covenant is only with Isaac/Israelites and they specifically say it's not with Ishmael despite other parts of the bible saying that it is with Ishmael. Sadly, it seems somebody made up some racist verses and put them into the bible and it has been passed off as revelation for many generations and modern Christians and Jews have been fooled. Furthermore Genesis 18 says that Sarah lied about laughing whereas the bible says God hates liars. So biblically God hates Sarah for lying but then blesses those he hates? And if Sarah could lie to the prophet Abraham and/or God then isn't it possible the author(s) of Genesis was lying when they wrote? The majority of Jews and Christians would be appalled at such a question but just look at the bible verses of Genesis 19:30-38,

> "*Lot and his two daughters left Zoar and settled in the mountains, for he was afraid to stay in Zoar. He and his two daughters lived in a cave.* <sup>31</sup> *One day the older daughter said to the younger, "Our father is old, and there is no man around here to give us children – as is the custom all over the earth.* <sup>32</sup> *Let's get our father to drink wine and then sleep with him and preserve our family line through our father."* <sup>33</sup> *That night they got their father to drink wine, and the older daughter went in and slept with him. He was not aware of it when she lay down or when she got up.* <sup>34</sup> *The next day the older daughter said to the younger, "Last night I slept with my father. Let's get him to drink wine again tonight, and you go in and sleep with him so we can preserve our family line through our father."* <sup>35</sup> *So they got their father to drink wine that night also, and the younger daughter went in and slept with him. Again, he was not aware of it when she lay down or when she got up. So, both of Lot's daughters became pregnant by their father.* <sup>37</sup> *The older daughter had a son, and she named him Moab; he is the father of the Moabites of today.* <sup>38</sup> *The younger daughter also had a son, and she named him Ben-Ammi; he is the father of the Ammonites of today.*"

These bible verses say that the prophet Lot, the same who condemned homosexuality in Sodom who fled it with his 2 daughters, later on impregnated those same daughters via drunken sex. As bad and slanderous as this is Christians and Jews say that Moses wrote this about Lot. Of course, it is written in narrative fashion and is not an eye witness account, as evidenced by the phrases "of today". Biblically one of Lot's incestuous sons was the father of the Moabites and the other was the father of the Ammonites. Both these nations were enemies of the nation of Israel so it wouldn't be surprising if Israel lied about them being of incestuous lineage simply due to war propaganda. Both Moabites and Ammonites did indeed exist during the time Moses is said to have existed so there is no issue there, he could've written about them. However, Moabites arose in the late 14th century while Ammonites arose in the 13th century. So, the problem with these bible verses is that Moabites existed about 100-200 years before the Ammonites existed. It'd be a reasonable mistake for someone in the nation of Israel to make if they were to say Moabites and Ammonites came to prominence at the same time because ancient historical records were spotty and inaccessible, especially the records of the enemies. Yet the bible says the father of the Moabites was conceived only one day before the father of the Ammonites. So, God could not have gotten this wrong and Moses couldn't have gotten it wrong either. Thus, Moses could not possibly have written that Lot got drunk and had sex with both of his daughters who gave birth to the Moabites and Ammonites. Furthermore, it is impossible that the Moabites and Ammonites could have been brother nations because the Moabites preceded the Ammonites by 100-200 years. Unless of course one of Lot's daughters was pregnant for 100-200 years longer than her sister was, but we know that isn't the case. Afterall if she was, they would've put that detail in the bible, right? Or are important details needed for a story to be true just not included in the bible for some special reason?  Could people writing religious fiction be that "special reason"?  These are some of my most disliked bible verses because they not only accuse Lot of being a drunkard and incestuous but they also blame this slander on Moses and or God.  To put this in perspective it'd be liking saying that Jesus called Moses a drug dealing sodomite rapist.  Anyone would say that's extremely disrespectful to both Jesus and Moses, but Christians and Jews still maintain this double slander concerning Moses and Lot because it's in the bible.  Even if a Jew or Christian tries to put polish on the story and say Lot didn't really know what was going on because he was drunk (which is sinful to say in itself) then they are still saying that Lot's daughters raped him on 2 consecutive nights.  So, their way of trying to say the bible doesn't say Lot was incestuous but was just drunk also requires them to say that the bible says the believing daughters of Lot raped their prophet!  As you've seen the bible says that a prophet of God who condemned sodomy, later got drunk and was raped by his daughters.  The bible says it's good for girls to rape their father and that it's good for girls to rape their prophet.  Not quite a child friendly book, unless you want your kids to rape you.  But let's go back to the biblical narrative concerning Abraham's kids who were actually related to Lot and his daughters because Lot and Abraham were cousins.  Fortunately, the bible does not say they were "kissing cousins", as far as I know.  Maybe that plot twist will be revealed in next year's edition.  Although biblically according to Genesis 11:27, Abraham was the uncle of Lot.  Meaning biblically 2 of the 2nd nieces of Abraham incestually raped the nephew of Abraham.  However, the biblical story gets even worse as Matthew 1:5 lists Ruth as the grandmother of David and the ancestor of Jesus.  Why do I say that makes the story worse?  Because this Ruth was a Moabite (Ruth 2:2) slave who married her master/relative Boaz, according to the book of Ruth in the bible. So, this biblical incestual rape of Lot led to the direct progeny of David's Moabite grandmother and by extension every prophet who descended from David, such as Solomon and Jesus. Thus, the bible says that David, Solomon and Jesus descended from a rapist who raped her father/prophet Lot despite both being relatives of the friend of God, known as Abraham. All this filthy slander against such persons exists in the bible despite God praising the family of Abraham and singling them out for a special covenant with him.

In the Bible Genesis 21:14-22 describes Ishmael and where he lived:" *Now the LORD was gracious to Sarah as he had said, and the LORD did for Sarah what he had promised. 2 Sarah became pregnant and bore a son to Abraham in his old age, at the very time God had promised him. 3 Abraham gave the name Isaac to the son Sarah bore him. 4 When his son Isaac was eight days old, Abraham circumcised him, as God commanded him. 5 <u>Abraham was a hundred years old when his son Isaac was born to him.</u> 6 Sarah said, "God has brought me laughter, and everyone who hears about this will laugh with me." 7 And she added, "Who would have said to Abraham that Sarah would nurse children? Yet I have borne him a son in his old age." 8 The child grew and was weaned, and on the day, Isaac was weaned Abraham held a great feast. 9 But Sarah saw that the son whom Hagar the Egyptian had borne to Abraham was mocking, 10 and she said to Abraham, "Get rid of that slave woman and her son, for that woman's son will never share in the inheritance with my son Isaac." 11 The matter distressed Abraham greatly because it concerned his son. 12 But God said to him, "Do not be so distressed about the boy and your slave woman. Listen to whatever Sarah tells you, because it is through Isaac that your offspring will be reckoned. 13 I will make the son of the slave into a nation also, because he is your offspring." Early the next morning Abraham took some food and a skin of water and gave them to Hagar. He set them on her shoulders and then sent her off with the boy. She went on her way and wandered in* *the Desert of Beersheba. <sup>15</sup> When the water in the skin was gone, she put the boy under one of the bushes.<sup>16</sup> Then she went off and sat down about a bowshot away, for she thought, "I cannot watch the boy die." And as she sat there, she began to sob. <sup>17</sup> <u>God heard the boy crying, and the angel of God called to Hagar from heaven and said to her</u>, "What is the matter, Hagar? Do not be afraid; God has heard the boy crying as he lies there.<sup>18</sup> Lift the boy up and take him by the hand, for I will make him into a great nation." <sup>19</sup> <u>Then God opened her eyes and she saw a well of water</u>. So, she went and filled the skin with water and gave the boy a drink. <sup>20</sup> <u>God was with the boy as he grew up. He lived in the desert and became an archer.<sup>21</sup> While he was living in the Desert of Paran</u>, his mother got a wife for him from Egypt."* This narration differs in certain aspects from the version in the Quran regarding Hagar and Ishmael but we will look at it for what it says regardless of its authenticity. The bible says Abraham sent Hagar and Ishmael away because of his wife Sarah being jealous Ishmael was getting attention over Isaac. The bible literally says it was all Sarah's plan to just "get rid of them" and God agreed with her. Yet that seems very uncharacteristic since Sarah was the one who got Abraham married to Hagar to begin with, but conveniently this part of the bible just refers to Hagar as a "slave woman" instead of Abraham's wife like Genesis 16:3 says. While Genesis 21:11 says Hagar wasn't even a concern for Abraham, despite being his wife, and he was only distressed because it concerned Ishmael. So again, it's like whoever wrote Genesis 21 didn't read Genesis 16, or Genesis 17 or Genesis 18. This is because Genesis 21 refers to Sarah laughing and asking " *Who would have said to Abraham that Sarah would nurse children? Yet I have borne him a son in his old age.*" Whereas biblically speaking all kinds of beings said this to Abraham and her well before the birth took place, you had God say it several times, the angels, Abraham but the Sarah in Genesis 21 seems to have forgotten all these beings who said the very thing she thinks none would have said. The bible even says she got in trouble and interrogated for laughing when she heard Abraham get told. So, first of all it's unlikely she'd laugh after getting in trouble for laughing before AND it's insane for her to say what Genesis 21 says she said after giving birth. It almost makes you wonder if this is the same Sarah. Did she have Alzheimer's or a split personality? If so, I don't think Abraham would've obeyed the inhumane demands of such a senile wife who is so prone to forget things. Honestly if they made a movie about this, we would be all confused and say what kind of movie is this where the actors don't remember the plot that they were a part of. But of course, those movies don't use the bible as a script, so the movies flow smoothly and seem to make coherent sense. Now in regards to the alleged laughs of Sarah in the bible, some of which are labeled as sinful some of which are not, Muslims don't believe in these laughs, however the Quran does mention a laugh which Sarah did laugh. In 11:69-72 of the Quran it relates that when Angels came to visit Abraham, he roasted a calf for them to eat, thinking they were human visitors. They didn't eat it and they told Abraham they were angels who came to tell him they were going to destroy the Sodomites. Abraham then became afraid. At this point Sarah who was overhearing the conversation laughed. The reason was because Abraham went through all this trouble of killing and cooking a calf for his visitors to eat and after all that it turns out they are angels and don't eat, but Abraham was so polite he never bothered to ask if they ate or if they wanted to eat, he just made a meal and did not expect to be serving angels. Obviously, especially when you consider Abraham probably didn't get many visitors, that's kind of funny because on the one hand you'd be mad at the wasted effort but at the same time you can't really get mad because you got real angels coming to visit you. So, Abraham can't get mad at the angels or be mad that they visited but can only get mad that he didn't ask if they were angels beforehand. But who in the world ever asks their guests if they are angels before they bring food out to eat? It's funny because that's what he should've done but that's just something people don't do. The other reason why Sarah is thought to have laughed is because Abraham got afraid of the angels after they told him they were sent to destroy the sodomites. So, his wife, knowing that Abraham was no sodomite would also likely find it funny he was afraid of angels sent to destroy the sodomites. Those are the 2 reasons why Sarah could have laughed, then she was informed of Isaac being born to her, after the laugh and the laugh is not related to her news but she was actually worried by it because she was so old and childbirth ain't easy. Afterall if you tell a 90+ year old women that it's a 100% fact that she's pregnant there is no way she's going to find that funny, because of the pain of childbirth and stress over who will take care of the child when the parents are so elderly. Now in comparison to the biblical events the Quranic are more realistic and depict real believable human emotions. Anyways in biblical context Sarah has a baby and basically says to her husband *"Get rid of your other wife who gave birth to your first son, and get your firstborn son out of here too because I don't want him to get any inheritance from you which would make my baby boy possibly get less."* It sounds unrealistic to me but since Christians and Jews believe, let's examine it. Chronologically this story is impossible because at the time Ishmael and Hagar went into the desert Ishmael was a baby and Isaac wasn't born until long after Ishmael, so Sarah didn't have kids at the time. Now I know that's not what Genesis 21 says, but I'm taking the full context of the story. The bible repeatedly refers to Ishmael being a helpless boy when the incident in the desert took place. If Abraham sent away his firstborn and at that time only son, as well as the boy's mother, into the desolate desert because of his wife that would have been sinful and tantamount to murder. Sarah was rewarded with Isaac by God for being pious, for her to advocate murdering Ishmael in the desert out of envy for her miraculous child is uncharacteristically hypocritical. Sarah and Abraham are role models not murderous racist child abusers. Rather God had specially commanded Abraham to do this, possibly to prevent any issue of jealousy from arising between Sarah and Hagar which would cause Abraham difficulty. Now what reason could I give for insisting Ishmael was the only son of Abraham when the desert fiasco took place? Well, I use the reason that the Genesis 21 version of events is impossible according to the bible itself. According to the Bible in Genesis 16:16, Abraham was 86 years old when Ishmael was born. While according to Gensis 21:5 Abraham was 100 years old when Isaac was born. This means biblically Ishmael was 14 years older than Isaac. In Genesis 21:8 the expulsion of Ishmael and Hagar is alleged to have occurred after Isaac was weaned. Now Muslims wean their children for two years. However biblically the babies were not weaned until the age of 3. So biblically Ishmael would've been 17 when Sarah tells Abraham to get rid of his wife (Hagar) and her "boy" (Ishmael). He's clearly described as if he were a baby who's too weak to carry anything, or help his mother and just lays down crying his eyes out because he's thirsty and there's no water, which saddens his mother so much she goes away from him not being able to bear to watch him die. Now for a baby that's appropriate behavior, but for a 17-year-old in the time of Abraham who was the son of the prophet Abraham? I don't think so, and if he acted like that, I don't think God would treat him the way the bible says God treated him. Also do you think a 17-year-old son of Abraham is going to mock his 3-year-old brother who was miraculously born to a woman well past child-bearing age, whose birth was foretold by God and angels? And then after doing so Sarah tells Abraham to expel his wife and her/his 17-year-old son abandoning them to the desert? Don't you think the son will just walk right back to his home? Also, Genesis 21:15 says "*When the water in the skin was gone, she put the boy under one of the bushes.*" Biblically Ishmael was 17 years old when "*she put the boy (Ishmael) under one of the bushes*". Now call me skeptical, or heretical, but I simply do not believe that Hagar put her 17-year-old son under a bush! Even a 2-year-old can't fit under a bush! This is just a biblical impossibility. I challenge every Jew and Christian in the world to go to the desert of Paran and demonstrate how a woman can put her 17-year-old son, who is dying of thirst, under a single bush. In fact, this would be a miracle if it happened. So, either the bible has some seriously false information or else Hagar and Ishmael performed a miracle, simply because Hagar didn't want to see Ishmael die of thirst. Which also if true would point to the noble character of Ishmael. Because if you are a 17-year-old boy stranded in the desert to die with your elderly mother, what 17-year-old is going to let his mother drink the water and choose to die of thirst first? You'd have to say Ishmael was quite a great 17-year-old if he did that. Yet that doesn't mesh with the biblical narrative of a 17-year-old Ishmael mocking his 3-year-old brother who is the son of his prophet. Furthermore Genesis 21:18 says God told Hagar "*Lift the boy up*". Now explain to me how this old woman was able to lift up her 17-year-old son, despite being on the brink of death via malnutrition and dehydration? That would be another miracle God helped biblical Hagar do with Ishmael. And again, I challenge every Jew and Christian to replicate this event in the desert of Paran today. If I'm supposed to believe it's possible and they, did it then show me how they did it yourself, otherwise one must credit Hagar and Ishmael with many miracles. But Christians and Jews say God hated Hagar and Ishmael so much

Ishmael was excluded from the covenant despite being the firstborn son of Abraham. Thus, this biblical tale is unrealistic for many reasons and nobody really believes in it, as evident by bible believers holding antagonistic views towards both Hagar and Ishmael with some even claiming they were cursed for all eternity along with their offspring. Also note that biblically Abraham was 103 years old at the time. Do you think a 103-year-old man is just going to be able to abandon a strong 17-year-old man in the desert with his elderly mother, no questions asked? Realistically you'd expect the 17-year-old to physically take over and leave the 103-year-old and the 93-year-old Sarah and the 3-year-old Isaac in the desert to die. That's more probable, but that didn't happen either. Also, how many 103-year-old guys do you know who are pushovers when their 93-year-old wife tells them to basically kill their other wife and son? But what's even more shocking is that then Christians and Jews will say that when Isaac was a teenager, Abraham took him out to sacrifice him because of a dream he had. Yet the bible doesn't mention the age of Abraham at the time, nor the age of Isaac nor does it mention anything at all of what Abraham thought of allegedly going to kill Isaac. Whereas obviously those are very important details that would be included if this incident took place since the bible says Isaac was weaned and specifies many other ages and dates. Anyways do you think Sarah would be ok with Abraham trying to kill Isaac? Biblically Sarah was the type who ordered murder out of love for her son, so I don't think she would tolerate a biblical Abraham going out to kill her teenage son. According to Genesis 23:1 Sarah was 127 years old when she died. Whereas the alleged near sacrifice of Isaac is related in Genesis 22, so Sarah was biblically alive at the time the biblical Abraham was alleged to be going to slaughter Isaac, at least chronologically. But we could make the case that Sarah's opinions are not mentioned regarding the attempted alleged slaughter of Isaac because perhaps she was dead and the bible is out of chronological order. However, in Genesis 17:17 the bible says Isaac will be born when Abraham is 100 and Sarah is 90. Now Genesis 21:5 confirms Isaac was born when Abraham was 100. Therefore, in order for the bible to get away with not mentioning Sarah's views on Abraham allegedly attempting to kill her son, which she was willing to order the death of 2 others to ensure a larger share of inheritance for, then she would've had to be dead when the near sacrifice took place. Biblically this would mean that Isaac was 37 years old when Abraham allegedly tried to sacrifice him. It goes without saying that is completely unrealistic and as such the Jewish and Christian notion that Isaac was almost sacrificed is also unrealistic and doesn't fit the biblical narrative even though Genesis 22 says explicitly that Isaac was the one Abraham attempted to slaughter. Which again may offend Jews and Christians, but Genesis 22 also says Isaac was Abraham's "only son" and we know that is just not true. However, the person who wrote Genesis 22 might not have known that or wanted his readers to know that, which is why they wrote what they wrote. Also, regarding all these promises the biblical God is said to have made with Isaac then during the attempted sacrifice it is interesting to note that Abraham never once bothers to ask God *"What about all those promises you made about Isaac and his offspring? How will they come true if I sacrifice Isaac?"* Also from a logical biblical perspective, if Abraham boots Ishmael out of his life and then God tells him to kill Isaac, logically Abraham would wonder if he was being punished by God for expelling Ishmael and that maybe he'd be better off had he expelled Isaac instead of Ishmael. On top of that when biblical God tells Abraham that Isaac is his "only son", Abraham goes along with it and doesn't object or ask what is meant by that or anything, almost as if the Abraham in Genesis 22 really thought he only had one biological son. The only other explanations to justify this odd Abraham in Genesis 22 is to say he knew he had another son and was trying to fool God by playing along thinking that if he told God he had 2 then he might get told to kill both or the sacrifice might not get him as many points with God. Either that or Ishmael was a disbeliever in God and the prophethood of Abraham and that is why neither God nor Abraham in Genesis 22 remember that Ishmael is a son too. But the apostate theory doesn't hold up when we consider the time biblical Ishmael spent with Abraham, and the miracles God facilitated with Ishmael in the desert and that Abraham kept in contact with Ishmael throughout his life and was on good terms with him, as was Isaac when the bible says both Ishmael and Isaac buried Abraham when he died. So, it's really a big slip up in the biblical narrative that makes it seem like a fictional story because it's so unrealistic without suspense or stress. Romantic Science Fiction Horror Comedies are more realistic than this biblical narrative. No realistic logical rationale is ever expressed in this biblical narrative. Thus, either the Abraham who Christians and Jews say nearly killed Isaac must have not known about the biblical Abraham whom God apparently made all these promises to in regards to Isaac and his offspring, or the author of the biblical narrative didn't know what the other parts of the bible said. So again, we have the problem of biblical characters not knowing their own life story which the bible narrates. The bible characters have practically no character development at all and don't even seem human because they just act so fake and unrealistic. These prophets were sent to be real live human role models, but their biblical portrayals make them seem more mythical than man, especially in regards to Jesus. Some refer to the biblical plot as *"the greatest story ever told"* but it seems more like the biblical story is, *"the greatest story ever sold which is false but thought of as true"*. In reality at the time of the attempted sacrifice

Ishmael was Abraham's only son, which made this sacrifice more difficult for Abraham since he had prayed to have offspring for years. To say that Ishmael was hated by Abraham is a lie because Abraham kept in contact with Ishmael and even advised him to divorce his first wife when he met her and later advised Ishmael to keep his second wife when Abraham met her. Likewise, Hagar couldn't have been hated by God, especially if the bible is true in saying that "God opened her eyes" and sent an angel to speak to her. There aren't many ladies who can claim such honors like the honors the bible gives to Hagar, yet Christians and Jews slander her saying awful things despite what the bible says. The birth of Abraham's son Isaac by Sarah wasn't announced to Abraham until the angels came to inform him, they were going to destroy the sodomites where his cousin Lot lived, which was after Ishmael and Hagar had already settled in Mecca. The angels announced the birth of Isaac to Abraham specifically as a reward for having nearly sacrificed his "only son", thus it's impossible the birth of Isaac could be the reward for nearly sacrificing Isaac. This is an instance where the biblical verses contradict the biblical timeline and alerts us to an interpolated textual addition by Israelites. I know it might've been confusing to go through and analyze the biblical narrative, because corrupted texts are confusing. That's why Christians make movies and put on plays because otherwise nobody can follow the biblical plot, which is why they don't read the bible and if they do they read it very very slowly so they forget the plot as they read along. Many Jews and Christians will say Ishmael was an illegitimate son of Abraham and only Isaac was a prophet. But if we are to talk about possible illegitimacy Genesis 20:11-12 depicts what Abraham thought of Sarah according to the English translation of the New International Version of the Bible: "*Abraham replied, "I said to myself, 'There is surely no fear of God in this place, and they will kill me because of my* wife.' ¹² Besides, <u>she really is my sister, the daughter of my father though not of my mother; and she became my wife</u>." Biblically Sarah was the half-sister of Abraham, Muslims don't believe this, but this is what the bible says. So biblically Isaac was the son of an incestual relationship, married his first cousin, and Isaac's son Jacob (aka Israel) married 2 of his first cousins. Muslims don't have an issue with first cousin marriages, they aren't promoted but they aren't prohibited, Christians tend to prohibit them as incestual. But according to both Muslim and non-Muslim standards the biblical depiction of Abraham and Sarah is incest, thus Isaac is biblically a product of a sinful sexual act that involved a miracle from God. Whereas according to Christian standards Isaac committed incest by marrying his first cousin Rebekah. So honestly tell me does God say incest is good? Because the bible says Abraham did it and his favorite/best/blessed child came out of that incestual sexual relationship. On the other hand, Ishmael was not born of incest, didn't marry his cousins and as far as I know only had 1 wife at a time his whole life. If anyone between Ishmael and Isaac were to be disqualified from the covenant one would think it'd be Isaac and not Ishmael. Afterall Ishmael was the firstborn son of an elderly friend of God and no sins of his are known to us. Biblically in Genesis 17:25 Abraham even circumcised Ishmael when he was 13 years old. Whereas since circumcision is the very sign of the covenant that means Ishmael is part of the covenant. It is evident from Genesis 21 that God had a special relationship with Ishmael and provided a miraculous well for him to drink from in the middle of the desert. The specific desert of Paran is named as the place of the well and where Ishmael lived. Paran is another name for Mecca and that well, known as Zamzam, is flowing there to this day, everyday thousands of gallons come forth every hour. The miraculous water is known as Zamzam water and has miraculous curative effects for those who drink it, for both believers and disbelievers alike. The water itself is free, but the bottles the water comes in can be very expensive if you don't get the water from the well yourself. All the historians of that region agree the Zamzam well today is the same one God created for Hagar and Ishmael. The historians of Arabia also unanimously agree Abraham and Ishmael built the Kaaba in Mecca. It is rare for historians to unanimously agree on anything, usually there is one or two different opinions, but all the records of all historians in the region say there is no dispute that Abraham and Ishmael built the Kaaba and the Zamzam well is the well God made for Hagar and Ishmael. The surprising thing is that Jews and Christians don't care in the slightest to see, visit or drink from this well. This well is a literal miracle people can witness today. It's on par with the miracle of Moses striking a rock and having water gush forth, which we don't know where that took place or if those streams of water even exist today. Yet this is a past and present miraculous well with miraculous water which the bible itself mentions yet Jews and Christians don't care and most don't even know about it. Why is that? Because it's Ishmael and Hagar and subconsciously they hate them. They might try to avoid admitting this but eventually they'll say God himself hates them so that's why they hate or don't like them. But there is no such thing as God "doesn't like someone", either God loves you a little or a lot or hates you a little or a lot. So, God either loved Hagar and Ishmael or he hated them, but the fact is he performed a miracle on their behalf which still exists today for all to see, feel and drink from so that action alone is quite a strong indication of love. This is a serious matter because to love who God hates is disbelief and makes God hate you, while to hate who God loves is also disbelief and makes God hate you.

Since Ishmael was biblically 14 years older than Isaac (Genesis 16:16 and Genesis 21:5) there was a significant time frame when Ishmael would be considered the "only son" of Abraham, peace be upon them all. Now some may say the whole age issue can be explained away by saying copiers and translators wrote down the wrong numbers when saying the age of Abraham when each kid was born. This argument is invalid because in the text the numbers are written in letter format in word form. If it were a valid argument then it means the words written in the bible are the wrong words and thus cannot be the word of God or inspired by God. Also, if this argument were valid then one could say well maybe they also made a mistake in saying there is only 1 God, and they might've meant a different number and all kinds of crazy things which basically would mean any mention of a number in the bible can be claimed to be the wrong number. Such as God creating things in 6 days, creating 1 man and 1 woman, the 3-day theory, 40 years or 40 days or with all the 40s it might not really be 40 but just 4 or maybe 0 or 250 trillion; one can literally make up any number they want with this argument. Instead, Christians and Jews should just accept the truth that Ishmael was the son nearly sacrificed by Abraham, there is no doubt about it. That the bible says Isaac was Abraham's "only son" and was almost sacrificed is an impossibility, either it was Isaac or Abraham's only son, Isaac was never the "only son" of Abraham. Thus, the biblical version of what happened isn't correct and something has been tampered with. Plus, Genesis 17:23 and Genesis 25:8-9 say Ishmael was Abraham's son AND in the same exact capacity as Isaac was Abraham's son, they are equal in their sonship. And if "only son" doesn't really mean only literal son but just favorite or blessed or chosen then you tell Christians that if so then John 3:16 must not really mean that Jesus is the "only son" or "only begotten son" of God and that maybe God had lots of literal sons born of virgin women throughout history, but they all turned evil. Or maybe they were good guys that God liked but they just didn't make the cut. Or maybe Jesus went and killed them all so he was the last one left, or maybe they mocked Jesus the way the bible says Ishmael mocked Isaac so that's why they weren't considered sons of God anymore. You know maybe the virgin Mary had more than one miraculously born son but the earlier ones mocked Jesus and got sent to go die in the desert? So, this whole "only son" doesn't really mean "only son" excuse doesn't work either. Also, since they will agree Ishmael and Isaac were both sons then the real difference is just with the word "only", and if "only" doesn't really mean "only 1" but means "only good 1" then I guess the bible really means there are many gods which exist but God is the "only good 1". So, the more they try to argue their way out of it, they just dig themselves a deeper grave. They should just let their protests lie down and die already. But sadly, some will as a last resort out of desperate loyalty to the bible and their faith say, *"it doesn't really matter who it was but the important thing is that it happened"*, but it does; imagine being an elderly Abraham and you are told by God to kill your son. Now if you only have one child that will be much harder to do than if you have two so it really does make a difference. Even if one were to go with the lie that Abraham didn't like Ishmael and God didn't like him, having 2 sons whoever they are and wherever they are makes a huge difference if God tells you to kill one of your sons, because you will know that you have a backup to continue your lineage and hang out with or get some help from someday if you need it; and Abraham was an old guy at the time too in a land where old people didn't survive. Also, we don't want to be lying about who Abraham almost slaughtered either. Keep in mind that when God commanded Abraham to give a human sacrifice there was a specific way to do it and it wasn't crucifixion. Also, if you know it happened then you got to know who it happened to and this "who" really does matter for political, ethnic and religious reasons around the world today. The bible says it was Isaac, the Quran says Ishmael. So, one of those 2 books is wrong and thus cannot be from God. This question of who is literally a Bible vs. Quran battle, then the Christian and Jew will brush it off and say *"it doesn't really matter who"*. No Muslims say that, but the Christians and Jews do. Why? Because they religiously can't let the bible be proven wrong because that would mean their religious beliefs are wrong. Thus, when they give this argument of "it doesn't really matter" they don't even believe that, they just don't want to argue or debate it because they don't want to face the fact that the bible is wrong on something, and they know if they try to prove who it was or argue over it then it will damage their religious convictions. So, in order to keep believing in their bible and religion they flee from the battlefield saying *"it doesn't really matter, let's not argue "*. Whereas this is the catchphrase of theological retreat upon fear of expected defeat. On the other hand, there will still be some staunch firm devoutly committed Christians who say, *"If the bible says it then it's true. It was Isaac! I don't care what you say!"* I used to be one of those people, and I do hope that you currently aren't one but if you are then hear me out before cursing me out. I appeal to the bible itself in Deuteronomy 21:15-17, "*If a man has two wives, and he loves one but not the other, and both bear him sons but the firstborn is the son of the wife he does not love,* <sup>16</sup> *when he wills his property to his sons, he must not give the rights of the firstborn to the son of the wife he loves in preference to his actual firstborn, the son of the wife he does not love.* <sup>17</sup> *He must acknowledge the son of his unloved wife as the firstborn by giving him a double share of all he has. That son is the first sign of his father's strength. The right of the firstborn belongs to him.*"

Therefore, since Genesis 16:3 says "*So after Abram had been living in Canaan ten years, Sarai his wife took her Egyptian slave Hagar and gave her to her husband to be his wife.*" Then biblically Ishmael cannot and never can be deprived of his biblical God-given rights as a firstborn son regardless of who his mother is. Likewise, the children of Isaac, Jacob cannot and never can usurp the rights of the firstborn son Esau. Whereas the whole thing with Esau and Jacob doesn't even come close to comparison to the Ishmael and Isaac case because both Esau and Jacob had the same mother. Whereas the bible says Hagar was Abraham's wife. Now Muslims say she was a slave and not a wife and still legitimate, but the Christians and Jews say she was a slave and not a wife thus he is illegitimate. So anyway, you look at it either the bible is wrong to say Hagar was the wife of Abraham so that would mean Jews and Christians are wrong to say their book is right, or the bible is right to say Hagar was Abraham's wife and Ishmael cannot be disinherited or considered illegitimate. However, let's say that Hagar wasn't Abraham's wife but just a slave. Maybe the "inspired word of God" in the bible just made Hagar a wife because of a typo? Then if she was a slave according to the bible, Jewish and Christian religions Ishmael would be illegitimate and deprived of inheritance and the covenant, right? Wrong! Do you know why that's wrong? Because biblically Jacob (also known as Israel who is the son of Isaac) had 2 wives, Leah and Rachel and he had 12 sons. Hence the 12 tribes of Israel. But guess what? Only 8 of those sons were born to Leah and Rachel. You see biblically Jacob had sex with Leah's slave Zilpah who gave birth to Gad and then Asher, and Jacob also had sex with Rachel's slave Bilhah who gave birth to Dan and Naphtali. So, 4 of Jacob's 12 sons were born via sex with slaves. This is all related in Genesis 30. However, a Jew or Christian will quickly point out how "well the English bible says the slaves became his wives", yet the dialogue doesn't say this. Genesis 30:3 says Rachel told Jacob *"Here is Bilhah, my servant. Sleep with her so that she can bear children for me and I too can build a family through her."* It's only after that in commentary which alleges Jacob took the slaves as wives. Yet Genesis 35:22 also mentions this very same Bilhah saying *"While Israel was living in that region, <u>Reuben went in and slept with his father's concubine Bilhah</u>, and Israel heard of it. Jacob had twelve sons:"* Now don't be tricked by the mentioning of Israel and Jacob in the same verse, Israel is Jacob. Who was Reuben? Well, the next verse in Genesis 35:23 answers that, *"The sons of Leah: <u>Reuben the firstborn of Jacob</u>, Simeon, Levi, Judah, Issachar and Zebulun."* What a story! Jacob/Israel had his firstborn son Reuben (son of Leah) have sex with his concubine Bilhah (slave of Rachel (Leah's sister/Reuben's aunt))! Actually, if she's just a concubine, that's not really that bad, is it? It's kind of disrespectful but it's not that bad, it's just biblical. Always remember the difference between bad and biblical. Generally, the Jewish and Christian rule is that if it's bad outside of the bible then when it's in the bible it's not because it's biblical. Or as the Christian may say *"Well that's the Old Testament, that's all pre-Jesus"*() as if that makes bad things good things if they happened before Jesus came to earth. That despite Christians doctrine saying that bad things are worse during the pre-Jesus period because that's before the alleged atonement where you had to strictly follow all God's laws or go to hell. Apparently, Christians think Jesus *"saved us from that super strict impossibly hard to follow moral standard"*. However, remember Genesis 30 and how Christians insist that the bible says Bilhah was Jacob's wife? Well Genesis 35 says she was Jacob's concubine. If she was his wife then Reuben would've been guilty of Adultery with his father's and a prophet's wife. This same Reuben was the firstborn of Israel, essentially the head of the first tribe of Israel. And people think soap operas are full of sex drama? The bible's steamier than any soap opera on tv, they wouldn't even be able to put the bible's sex tales on tv because they're so scandalous. Now the truth of the matter is either Bilhah was Jacob's wife, or she was his concubine, or she was his wife and she got demoted to being a concubine by the time his son had his turn with her. Like father like son isn't that how it goes, or is that just in the pre-Jesus period? Who knows maybe the Christian will say Jacob the prophet divorced his wife so his son could have sex with her? If so when did that happen? Biblically there was no divorce, the only clue we have is in Genesis 33:1-2 which says, "*Jacob looked up and there was Esau, coming with his four hundred men; so, he divided the children among <u>Leah, Rachel and the two female servants</u>. ² He put <u>the female servants and their children in front</u>, Leah and her children next, and Rachel and Joseph in the rear.*" What happened to Jacob's 4 wives? I guess the modern bible only counts them as wives when they were having sex. Or did I use the baby's bible? Nope I used the adult version, it says "wives" in Genesis 30, "servants" in Genesis 33 and "concubine" in Genesis 35. Could it be that the adult bible is deliberately censored? What other explanation could there be for the same women having such different status' in those 3 biblical chapters? The sad thing is that bible believers will read these chapters and not even notice these contradictions because they have such a firm faith that it's all from God. Yet they insist it's not "blind faith", which it's probably best not to say "blind faith" lest we offend blind people, so we'll just call it "biblical faith". Realistically Bilhah was just a concubine and biblically legitimate children can be born from concubine slaves. Jews and Christians who insist this can't be only do so because they say Ishmael was the son of a slave women and is illegitimate, thus they changed the bible; a lot. Yet the bible also says Abraham took Hagar as a wife. The reason the bibles say this is because in modern times if the bibles were printed saying that some guy had sex with his slaves who gave birth to his kids it would be scandalous. So, the bible publishers add in the wife bits to make it more "decent". In the past the bible said different stuff, and American slave owners quoted the bible to justify everything they did to their slaves from beatings, to whippings, to raping their slave girls. Some black slaves who escaped American plantations even wrote on how the reason they didn't become Christian was because their masters would bring them to Church every Sunday and they would get told all the bible verses that said all their masters did to them was the same as God commanded them to do to them. So, if there were some biblical rule that prohibited men from having sex with their slaves, (rape is rape and that's different, I'm just talking about consensual sex) and if it were prohibited between a man and his female slaves then why did the devout Christian bible thumpers a few hundred years ago not know about it? They weren't ignorant folk; they knew everything the bible said about slaves and not once did they think of marrying their slaves prior to having sex with them. Now the Jew or Christian may say, no it's not like that they really were wives. Okay then if so that means Jacob had 4 wives at the same time AND they were all okay with it. Islam also allows men a maximum of 4 wives if they can afford it and be perfectly just between them all, but the Christians find this outrageous. Yet when it comes to Jacob, the progenitor of all the tribes of Israel, he can have 4 wives and it's okay? They'll say that was then and this is now. Well, when did God ever say a change was made? Did God ever say it's one man for one woman? Or was it a government and pop culture? Christians will say how in Genesis God made 1 man Adam and 1 woman Eve, therefore 1 for 1. But then again, the book of Genesis also says 4 for 1 according to bible verses in Genesis 30. So, who knew better, Jacob or you? Also remember that Cain killed Abel because he wanted to marry the girl Abel was going to marry, so that means there was an extra woman in the 2nd generation of humanity. Meaning ever since the time of Adam and Eve, before they died there was an imbalance to the 1:1 male/female ratio so that it was no longer 1:1. Plus Adam and Eve got married in paradise, so one can't use marital examples of people in paradise when declaring marital rulings for people on earth. Was Adam's extra daughter just supposed to spend life single forever because 1 guy got killed so some woman had to be the odd one left single? Keep in mind prophets are never wrong about religious rulings, such as the number of wives a man can have. Some people, if you say a prophet had multiple wives, will actually say that *"Well maybe the prophet was wrong to do that."* If you hear this reply, tell them *"Who do you think you are? Where does this attitude come from where you think your opinion matters when compared to a prophet's opinions, teachings and actions? The prophets said and proved a man can have more than one wife under certain conditions if they all agree. God has promised all the prophets eternal paradise. Has God told mankind that you are going to paradise? The prophets aren't wrong. YOU are wrong. You don't have to have multiple wives if you don't want, but you can't condemn the prophetic teachings regarding this. If you dislike it or denounce it then you could spend eternity in hell. You don't have to practice it and you don't have to preach it, but it is permissible and nobody can ever say it's wrong or generally forbid it."* If every male today gets one wife, there will be about 2 billion extra women left single. Are those 2 billion women just forced to be celibate and never have a husband or kids because of God making a mathematical imbalance when creating people? The whole notion that God made 1 man for 1 woman just doesn't add up. Do the math! Hypocritically some Christians who believe in the 1 man for 1 woman doctrine also believe in clerical celibacy where the male priests don't get married to any women. So where does that doctrine of 1 million men for zero women come from and fit in? The Catholic will say God wants both 1 for 1 and 1 million for 0. But it can work both ways. It's either 1 for 1 or 1 for 1+. Never ever can it be 1 for 0. God proved that by making Eve for Adam. The 1 for 0 ratio doesn't work for men even in paradise. Monastic celibacy was unfit for Adam in paradise so it is generally unfit for every man on earth. (I say generally because some guys like Pharaoh, Goliath or the Anti-Christ probably shouldn't be married since they truly are unfit for marriage. But then again, I'd also say monastic Christian men are unfit for marriage too, so I don't pity them for not having kids to raise. The fate of celibate Christians results in the very same which Zachariah feared happening to his religious propagation.) God made more woman than men, so why make extra ladies? Surely God doesn't want guys to commit adultery. Furthermore, God does not make marital rules for us to follow and then mathematical mistakes when making the human population. What if one wife is sterile, is the husband doomed to be childless? What if a wife becomes braindead on the wedding night and goes into a permanent coma, is the guy forced to just be married forever to a braindead unconscious person? What if the one wife gets disabled and wants her husband to have a more active marital life than he can experience with just her? What if a woman cannot survive on her own but a married man wants to marry her and provide for her needs and his wife agrees to share? Should she just die in the streets, or live with him for free out of the kindness of his heart and fight any sexual attraction there may be, or should the man be forced to divorce? Honestly does love have a limit when it comes to men? Are men truly incapable of truly loving more than one woman at a time? Has it never happened that multiple girls who are friends loved the same guy and would prefer he marries more than 1 of them? Should all single women just be given a free house by the governments to live in like nuns until they kill themselves as a result of depression or start raping guys? What if all the women who don't get husbands want a husband but all the guys are married and she decides to go kill another woman so that way she might be able to get a husband of her own? Seriously if it's only 1 man for 1 woman then the women will start killing the women who are married to men so that they can get a husband. Cain killed for the sake of marrying a girl, so women may well commit genocide for the sake of a husband. Some of the guys might get stuck with an ultimatum from some of the women who tell them, "*Marry me or I'll kill any women you marry because I can't stand to live single and every other guy is already married. So, if you don't want someone to die, then marry me.*" Don't think that can happen? Then you don't know women. Or maybe just maybe some guys could be allowed to have more than one wife? Which do you prefer? Women World War or some guys with multiple wives? I'm not saying it's ideal, but religiously it's legal and a good thing in certain situations under certain conditions. It's not promoted but it is permissible. At the time Muhammad received revelation saying God only allowed a man to take up to 4 wives maximum many Arabs at that time had more than 4 wives, including Muhammad and it was shocking to the Arab world that the limit God set was 4. Regardless Muhammad told the Muslim men who had more than 4 they had to choose which they wanted to stay married to and divorce the others. (With Muhammad God said there was an exception and he didn't have to divorce his extra wives because he was the prophet, but he didn't marry anymore after that. I mention this because most those who hear Islam says 4 wives are allowed at most think in modern terms of expanding the number of wives legally allowed, but at that time it drastically limited the number of wives a man could have and caused people to get divorced who had more than 4 at once. Thus, Islam limited the number to 4 wives, it didn't expand it to 4. Recently some people have limited it to 1 without divine justification. The same nations who legislatively prohibit having multiple wives have no laws prohibiting 4 girlfriends though.) Anyways this bit about Jacob having 4 wives doesn't even really count because Genesis 30 says Jacob was given Rebekah's slave to be his wife because she couldn't have kids. Then it says Leah copied her sister and gave Jacob her slave to be his wife because she stopped having kids due to old age. Although then after Jacob's 2 allegedly sterile wives give him slaves to allegedly be his wives it turns out Leah starts having kids again and Rebekah gives birth to kids too. Interestingly both of these women giving birth to multiple kids after giving their slaves to be wives never make a big deal of this as though they were miraculous births. Sarah is recorded as making a big deal when she gave birth but Rebekah and Leah don't? Maybe that's because they never had an issue with childbirth and thus never had a reason to make their slaves co-wives and they were just slaves who had sex with their husband. The reason this is obvious is because in Genesis 30 both Leah and Rebekah name the children who their slaves give birth to. Now I'm not going to use Islamic principles here, I'm just using biblical principles. Biblically Hagar was Sarah's slave and Abraham's wife simultaneously, yet Sarah was not allowed to name the child Hagar gave birth to. Yet dozens of chapters later Leah and Rebekah get to name the children of their slaves/co-wives? Also, from the biblical text one gets the impression that Rebekah and Leah considered the sons of their slaves to be literally their own sons. Now this could only theoretically be justified if they were slaves only and not wives. Because if you recall Sarah did not consider Ishmael her son in any way and if she did then she wouldn't have been surprised to hear she would have a son because she would have already considered herself as having given Abraham a son via her slave's son. Therefore, the most reasonable thing we can conclude is that Jacob had sex with his slaves and they were not his wives and despite this those sons were legitimate in every way. On the other hand, if a man having sex with his slave means those kids aren't legitimate, we have to say there are only 8 tribes of Israel and that Jacob only had 8 sons. So, I guess somebody better tell God there are only 8 tribes of Israel and that he miscounted and that Moses was only supposed to take out 8 tribes away from Egypt and not 12 and that when he struck the rock causing water to gush forth only 8 streams were supposed to come out and not 12. Whoopsie! Also, the bible has to get changed in many places to say there are only 8 tribes instead of 12 and many prophets who are considered Israeli prophets can no longer be considered Israeli, because of their tribes coming from the 33% of Jacob's sons who were born via sex with slave girls instead of his wives. Also, even if one believes the modern translations which depict the slave girls as Jacob's wives then the bible also says Hagar was a wife, yet Christians and Jews maintain her son isn't legit because of slave status. Thus, it's a bigoted double standard, where slave-wife kids count if they're Israeli but not if they aren't. Especially concerning the tribe of Dan, many illustrious biblical characters are member of the tribe of Dan, including many Judges of Israel. The famous Samson is from the tribe of Dan and the interbreeding is so extensive that Jesus himself probably had a little bit of Dan in him, or if not Dan then definitely some Gad, Asher or Naphtali. So, if slave kids don't count in the covenant, then many biblical prophets get excommunicated as a result. There is one little loophole that could fix all these issues up. Jews and Christians could just admit that Ishmael is a valid legitimate son and God made a covenant with him, whether his mother was married to Abraham or not, regardless of what Sarah may or may not have said. Thus, the only reason a Christian or Jew can give to think that Ishmael was not part of the covenant is because of their own personal prejudice, racism or their doctrine because the bible destroys that favoritistic Jewish and Christian belief. In context the bible supports the legitimacy of Ishmael and a covenant being made with him, out of context and with extra textual insertions it doesn't, but the main issue is just Jewish and Christian personal opinions based upon ancient racist traditions. Theologically racism has shaped Jewish and Christian doctrines. Their anti-Ishmaeli beliefs have no support from biblical context.

Now what does all of this have to do with "*the Prophet*"? Considering that the older bible translations state "*the Prophet*" will be from among the brethren of Israel, since Ishmael and Isaac were brothers, it means the descendants of Isaac (Israelites/Jews) and the descendants of Ishmael (Meccans/Arabs) are like brethren to each other. Muhammad is a direct descendant of Ishmael and Abraham. A Jew or Christian who hated Muhammad would be motivated to cover up these facts and distort scripture in order to remove Ishmael as to diminish the closeness Muhammad has to Abraham. I suspect this has been done because other places of the bible explicitly state the covenant with Abraham and the descendants of Abraham does not apply to Ishmael despite the verse of the covenant clearly using all-inclusive language in the bible. A tale about Jacob usurping his older brother's birthright and deceptively getting blessed by their dying father by "*bearing false witness*" is also a likely insertion done by the racist Jews to try to eliminate non-Jew descendants of Ishmael from the covenant. It turns out that many pagans practice tying goat skin strips around their wrists and necks just as the bible said Jacob did to fool his allegedly poor sighted dad, Isaac. Coincidentally the pagan tribes throughout the world did/do this considering it a way to be "born again" in order to legally transfer the children to adopted parents and give the children inheritance rights and to ratify a contract or covenant. Some pagans reenacted the birthing process pretending to be goats, involving goat guts and skins, mimicking goat births with the child playing along until the ritual ended and the adopted child is *"born-again"* as the new mother's "kid", since the children of goats are called "kids". Seems a bit too coincidental that the bible says Jacob stole his brother's blessing by utilizing goat skins while pagans also use them in order to transfer inheritance rights. Let's face it, Judaism is another form of Racism. So, if a progenitor of the Arabs was also part of the covenant Jews had with God, then don't you think racist Jews would change the book of God to kick Arabs out of the picture as they had with so many other things they didn't like? It also seems unlikely a 100% divine scripture would say there is a covenant with all the descendants and then later on say that all doesn't really mean all but only means one of the two, it is a blatant contradiction and God isn't contradicting. The bible itself says in reference to Ishmael *"God heard the child crying"* and *"God was with the child as he grew up"* also when taking into account the fact that God created a well in the middle of the desert so this child and his mother could survive tells us that this Ishmael was indeed very special and had some important role to play if God cared about him so much. God saved Ishmael's life because he wanted him to live and reproduce bearing heirs, he wasn't a mistake, God created him. The name Ishmael itself means "God heard", which was the name given to Ishmael when God told Abraham that he answered his prayer for offspring. Ironically one meaning of the name "Israel" is *"struggled with God"* which is apt to describe this situation in which the nation of Israel struggled with the fact that Ishmael was part of the covenant and struggled to justify kicking the Arabs out of the picture until they made a story about Israel the prophet stealing a blessing and obtaining the older firstborn son's right.  When you think about it the story in the bible of Jacob disguising himself as Esau to steal Isaac's blessing would mean Israel had broken 3 of the 10 commandments the nation of Israel would later receive; by stealing, bearing false witness and coveting the blessing intended for his brother.  Plus, the story just seems stupid.  How can a prophet mistakenly bless the wrong son and then say, "*Whoops! I used up my blessing abilities on Jacob thinking it was you, sorry I can't bless you Esau, your brother pulled a fast one on me and now God will never ever bless you.*"  If Isaac wanted to bless Esau, then he could have done it whenever he wanted, yet the bible story says he needed to be served his favorite dish before he could give his blessing.  How else do Christians and Jews justify this stolen blessing?  By saying Genesis 25:29-34 relates: "*Once when Jacob was cooking some stew, Esau came in from the open country, famished. ³⁰ He said to Jacob, "Quick, let me have some of that red stew! I'm famished!" (That is why he was also called Edom.) ³¹ <u>Jacob replied, "First sell me your birthright."</u>*

*<u>³² "Look, I am about to die," Esau said</u>. "What good is the birthright to me?"³³ <u>But Jacob said, "Swear to me first." So, he swore an oath to him, selling his birthright to Jacob.</u> ³⁴ Then Jacob gave Esau some bread and some lentil stew. He ate and drank, and then got up and left. So, Esau despised his birthright.*"

        Today this is called extortion and it is illegal.  It was also illegal for believers to do and especially brothers.  First of all, Jacob was a prophet of God.  No prophet of God would treat their brother the way the bible says Jacob treated Esau.  If he did God would probably curse him rather than bless him.  The bible clearly even says Esau told Jacob that if he didn't feed him, he would literally die.  Thus, Esau was in a compulsive survival situation and any deal he made to survive is not legally binding, and most definitely not valid in the sight of God. Another issue I take with this is that it's clearly written by men as evidenced by the *"(That is why he was also called Edom.)"* and *"So Esau despised his birthright."* bits. God knows that Esau didn't and wouldn't have "despised his birthright". Realistically what would you do in that biblical situation? Your brother has food and if you don't get to eat it then you will die. He refuses to give it to you unless you promise him your entire share in the inheritance of your father. You could either beat up your brother and take his food by force, or you could say whatever he wanted you to say in order to keep on living, or you could just starve to death. Also keep in mind your father and grandfather are prophets of God who taught you to be a good big brother. Of course, in such a situation every decent person would do what the bible says Esau did and none would think the deal counted and that God would hate Esau because of making a deal to get food from his brother in order to stay alive. If anything, we'd say Jacob was a very bad guy to do what the bible falsely alleges, especially considering that his father was a prophet and his grandfather was a prophet and his grandfather Abraham even met him and taught him. So, the way the bible portrays Jacob here is entirely unrealistic and uncharacteristic. Yet today the world believes the prophet Jacob acted this way. Why? Because the Bible, Jews and Christians say so. Whereas to me this seems like exactly the type of nonsense a racist Jew would make up to justify their immoral business ethics by saying a prophet made immoral deals and also in order to get away with excluding Ishmael and the Arabs from the covenant promised to Abraham's descendants. Because this Jacob and Esau incident is what's commonly used to justify the raw deal the bible gives to Ishmael and Jews/Christians will say *"Well Esau was the firstborn son too, and look God didn't give him part of the covenant."* Yet the bible even says God said about Ishmael, *"I will make him into a great nation"*. Whereas when God refers to "nations" he refers to groups of believers who follow a certain prophet and uses the word "people" to describe disbelievers. For example, we have the people of Pharaoh vs. the nation of Moses. Or the nation of Israel, which doesn't mean every ethnic Jew but everyone who followed the religion of Israel. Another very popular error many Jews and Christians have is that they think all the prophets are Israeli, yet this is another anti-biblical belief. For instance, the prophet Job is accepted as a prophet by Jews and Christians alike. But Job was a descendant of Esau and not Jacob/Israel. Meaning that Job was not an Israeli, yet the bible says he was a prophet. So, you don't have to be a Jew to be a prophet and you don't have to be a descendant of Jacob to be a prophet either and if we believe the bible saying that all of Esau's birthright was given to Jacob, then I guess prophethood is NOT included in birthrights nor inheritance. God simply makes whoever he wants to be his prophet his prophet, whether people like it or not. God is the one who picks his prophets, we don't. Thus, in full biblical context when the biblical God promises to make a great nation of the Ishmaelites, this means with prophethood and belief. How else could a nation be considered "Great" by God if they had zero prophets? This promise of prophethood and belief to Ishmael also extends to his descendants. Therefore, when Ishmael's descendant Muhammad claims to be "*the Prophet*" it warrants us to examine the claim and study it to see if he meets the criteria of "*the Prophet*". Also, in the name of fairness if God makes such a promise to 2 brothers, like Ishmael and Isaac, they will naturally wonder whose nation will be better than the others because of competitive human and brotherly nature. Now God could either make one better and more numerous than the other, or give both nations equal numbers of prophets, books and believers, or God could give the bulk of prophets and books to the second born and give the firstborn son the last prophet and the last book to be sent. So that the firstborn son will get the last prophet who will lead the last nation of believers. The third option seems to be the most just and fair since having the last prophet and last book balances out, so that both brothers will feel equally as great as the other. Lastly the covenant God made with Abraham and his descendants must include Ishmael as well as Isaac or else the bible is false. This is because Genesis 17:7 says God told Abraham, "*I will establish my covenant as an <u>everlasting covenant between me and you and your descendants after you</u> for the generations to come, to be your God and the God of your descendants after you.*" The covenant is everlasting, meaning will not end or be broken. However, in regards to the covenant with Israel the bible says God said in Hosea 6:4-10,

> "*What can I do with you, Ephraim? What can I do with you, Judah? Your love is like the morning mist, like the early dew that disappears.⁵ <u>Therefore I cut you in pieces with my prophets</u>, I killed you with the words of my mouth – then my judgments go forth like the sun. ⁶ For I desire mercy, not sacrifice, and acknowledgment of God rather than burnt offerings. ⁷ As at Adam, <u>they have broken the covenant</u>; they were unfaithful to me there. ⁸ Gilead is a city of evildoers, stained with footprints of blood. ⁹ As marauders lie in ambush for a victim, so do bands of priests; they murder on the road to Shechem, carrying out their wicked schemes. ¹⁰ I have seen a horrible thing in Israel: There Ephraim is given to prostitution, <u>Israel is defiled</u>.*"

These bible verses inform the world that the covenant God had with Israel in the past was broken. Broken means "not everlasting". Thus, if the covenant God made with Abraham was only through Isaac and the Israelites alone then God lied when calling it everlasting. However, if the covenant God made with Abraham also included Ishmael, then the covenant would still be considered everlasting and we would have one less biblical contradiction. So, either Genesis 17:7 is false or the covenant is with Ishmael too. Another important lesson

from the covenant being broken with Israel is that this means their so-called "right to possession of the Holy Land" is null and void since they broke the covenant. This is why some Jews will publicly say they have no right to have a state, Palestine or the holy land the biblical God once promised to Israel because the covenant God had with Israel was broken according to the bible. Also, by me claiming the covenant was broken and God rejected the Israelites don't think this is out of context either. The bible actually paints a vivid and ugly picture of how God displayed his disgust with Israel and their rejection in Hosea 1: 2-10 ,"<u>When the LORD began to speak through Hosea, the LORD said to him, "Go, marry a promiscuous woman and have children with her, for like an adulterous wife this land is guilty of unfaithfulness to the LORD."</u> ³ So he married Gomer daughter of Diblaim, and she conceived and bore him a son.⁴ Then the LORD said to Hosea, "<u>Call him Jezreel, because I will soon punish the house of Jehu for the massacre at Jezreel, and I will put an end to the kingdom of Israel.</u> ⁵ In that day I will break Israel's bow in the Valley of Jezreel." ⁶ Gomer conceived again and gave birth to a daughter. Then <u>the LORD said to Hosea, "Call her Lo-Ruhamah (which means "not loved"), for I will no longer show love to Israel, that I should at all forgive them.</u>
⁷ Yet I will show love to Judah; and I will save them – not by bow, sword or battle, or by horses and horsemen, but I, the LORD their God, will save them."
⁸ After she had weaned Lo-Ruhamah, <u>Gomer had another son. ⁹ Then the LORD said, "Call him Lo-Ammi (which means "not my people"), for you are not my people, and I am not your God.</u> ¹⁰ "Yet the Israelites will be like the sand on the seashore, which cannot be measured or counted. In the place where it was said to them, 'You are not my people,' they will be called 'children of the living God.'

These bible verses are very very stern, it says God told Hosea who Jews and Christians consider to be a prophet to go marry a promiscuous woman who commits adultery to symbolize the infidelity of Israel and their betrayal of the covenant. Then the biblical God even tells Hosea to give the kids bad names like "not loved" and "not my people" with the reason being that God wants to make it clear to Israel that they are not loved, not God's people and he is no longer their God despite them being called the children of God in the holy land where he declares that they are not his people. While Hosea 13:4-16 reiterates:

> "<u>But I have been the LORD your God ever since you came out of Egypt. You shall acknowledge no God but me, no Savior except me.</u>
> <sup>5</sup> I cared for you in the wilderness, in the land of burning heat.
> <sup>6</sup> <u>When I fed them, they were satisfied</u>; when they were satisfied, they became proud; then they forgot me. <sup>7</sup> So I will be like a lion to them, like a leopard I will lurk by the path. <sup>8</sup> Like a bear robbed of her cubs, <u>I will attack them and rip them open</u>; like a lion I will devour them – a wild animal will tear them apart. <sup>9</sup> "<u>You are destroyed, Israel, because you are against me</u>, against your helper. <sup>10</sup> Where is your king, that he may save you? Where are your rulers in all your towns, of whom you said, Give me a king and princes'?

<sup>11</sup> So in my anger I gave you a king, and in my wrath I took him away. <sup>12</sup> The guilt of Ephraim is stored up, his sins are kept on record. <sup>13</sup> Pains as of a woman in childbirth come to him, but he is a child without wisdom; when the time arrives, he doesn't have the sense to come out of the womb.

<sup>14</sup> "I will deliver this people from the power of the grave;
I will redeem them from death. Where, O death, are your plagues?
Where, O grave, is your destruction?

"I will have no compassion, <sup>15</sup>even though he thrives among his brothers. An east wind from the LORD will come, blowing in from the desert; his spring will fail and his well dry up.
His storehouse will be plundered of all its treasures.
<sup>16</sup> The people of Samaria must bear their guilt,

> *because they have rebelled against their God.*
> *They will fall by the sword; their little ones will be dashed to the ground, their pregnant women ripped open."*

The reason given for God's extreme hatred towards Israel is because they did not acknowledge God as their exclusive deity and their exclusive savior. This puts Christians in the same boat, because they say Jesus is their savior and then some say he's God too while others say God is God but Jesus is their savior. Yet the bible is clear that the only God and the only savior is the very same being who was God since the Jews came out of Egypt and the very same who cared for them in the wilderness and fed them there, with manna and quail. Now Jesus didn't do any of that stuff so he cannot be a savior or God. The bible says God destroys them in brutal fashion, so much so that he will bring them back to life and the grave isn't going to save them from the punishment and death isn't going to save them from punishment either. The bible says God says "*I will have no compassion*" towards Israel and then the Christians say that God is all-loving and loves everybody for all time and Jesus saved everybody who came before him etc., etc., etc. So, it makes you wonder what bible are Christians reading? The bible portrays God as one who gets pissed off at people he allegedly made an exclusive covenant with who he will never have compassion on even after they die and God is going to bring them back from their grave and state of death just to hurt them some more. But that's not all. Ezekial, whom Jews and Christians believe is a prophet of God, also bore a severe load due to God's hatred of Israel as the bible says in Ezekial 3:22-27,

> "*The hand of the* LORD *was on me there, and he said to me, "Get up and go out to the plain, and there I will speak to you."* 23 *So I got up and went out to the plain. And the glory of the* LORD *was standing there, like the glory I had seen by the Kebar River, and I fell facedown.*

24 Then the Spirit came into me and raised me to my feet. He spoke to me and said: "Go, shut yourself inside your house. 25 And you, son of man, they will tie with ropes; you will be bound so that you cannot go out among the people. 26 I will make your tongue stick to the roof of your mouth so that you will be silent and unable to rebuke them, for they are a rebellious people. 27 But when I speak to you, I will open your mouth and you shall say to them, 'This is what the Sovereign LORD says.' Whoever will listen let them listen, and whoever will refuse let them refuse; for they are a rebellious people."

Although the biblical God didn't just make Ezekial, a biblical prophet, mute and put him under house arrest. In the next book Ezekial 4:1-14 continues with the biblical God's instructions to a biblical prophet of Israel,

"Now, son of man, take a block of clay, put it in front of you and draw the city of Jerusalem on it. 2 Then lay siege to it: Erect siege works against it, build a ramp up to it, set up camps against it and put battering rams around it. 3 Then take an iron pan, place it as an iron wall between you and the city and turn your face toward it. It will be under siege, and you shall besiege it. This will be a sign to the people of Israel.4 "Then lie on your left side and put the sin of the people of Israel upon yourself. You are to bear their sin for the number of days you lie on your side. 5 I have assigned you the same number of days as the years of their sin. So for 390 days you will bear the sin of the people of Israel.6 "After you have finished this, lie down again, this time on your right side, and bear the sin of the people of Judah. I have assigned you 40 days, a day for each year. 7 Turn your face toward the siege of Jerusalem and with bared arm prophesy against her. 8 I will tie you up with ropes so that you cannot turn from one side to the other until you have finished the days of your siege. 9 "Take wheat and barley, beans and lentils, millet and spelt; put them in a storage jar and use them to

<u>make bread for yourself. You are to eat it during the 390 days you lie on your side.</u>
<sup>10</sup> Weigh out twenty shekels of food to eat each day and eat it at set times. <sup>11</sup> Also measure out a sixth of a hin of water and drink it at set times. <sup>12</sup> Eat the food as you would a loaf of barley bread; <u>bake it in the sight of the people, using human excrement for fuel."</u> <sup>13</sup> The LORD said, "In this way the people of Israel will eat defiled food among the nations where I will drive them." <sup>14</sup> Then I said, "Not so, Sovereign LORD! I have never defiled myself. From my youth until now I have never eaten anything found dead or torn by wild animals. No impure meat has ever entered my mouth."<sup>15</sup> <u>"Very well," he said, "I will let you bake your bread over cow dung instead of human excrement."</u>"

    So biblically speaking God was so mad at Israel that he made their prophet lie on his left side for 390 days followed by 40 days of lying on his right side, during which he was supposed to eat bread baked with human excrement (aka poop). Although merciful as God is he allowed the biblical Israeli prophet to use cow poop as a substitute for human poop because the Israeli prophet was a good guy in God's view. This bible section is often misunderstood and taken out of context by people saying God made a prophet eat human poop. It wasn't actually human poop, it was cow poop and poop was only used as the cooking source instead of oil, but most importantly this was the biblical God and a biblical Israeli prophet; which are two important details to remember. Now just because the bible says this biblical prophet set the world record for lieing, on one's side, does not mean he was a liar or that the bible contains lies. The bit that makes me doubt the authenticity of this text is that it says Ezekial can bear the sins of Israel and Judah simply by lieing, on his side, for a certain number of days. Sorry if it's immature but I just think it's very ironic the bible says that centuries worth of sins can be forgiven via a person lieing. Since the bible strongly condemns lying. Yet I think that's just an English linguistic irony rather than an actual textual irony. Although if you do meet any English people who say that lieing is a sin you can always tell them the bible says God says lieing is how sins get forgiven. However, the thing about lieing on one's side for hundreds of days is that it is impossible to do without getting deadly bed sores and having one's organs get stuck together. This is why God makes us turn over when we sleep for extended periods, because we would get sores and die if we weren't turned over when sleeping for extremely long periods. Now someone who is familiar with the Quran may wonder what about the people of the Cave whom Allah says slept for hundreds of years? Well, the Quran says Allah turned them over while they slept, and it said this thousands of years ago before people even knew humans would die if they didn't turn over when they slept or layed on their sides for long periods of time. Scientifically Ezekiel would've died had he lied on his side for 390 days or 40 days, he had to have turned over but the bible says he didn't and wasn't allowed to. Perhaps the authors didn't know what would happen if someone actually did this when they wrote it, and it can't be called a miracle because no Jew or Christian ever claimed such a thing before, if they do it now it would just be an excuse they made up all by themselves to justify their personal beliefs in the bible being 100% true. Anyways this concept of lying sins away is unjust and impossible according to Islam but it also contradicts Christianity which teaches Jesus bore all sins via death on a cross, or stake, or whatever they are guessing nowadays. The bible says Ezekial bore a total of 430 years' worth of sins, so that means Jesus couldn't have since they were already taken care of by Ezekiel according to the bible. So, is Ezekial the savior of centuries worth of Israelis? No, he's just some guy the bible says had to lie on his sides for 430 consecutive days and eat bread he cooked with cow poop, oh and God made this biblical prophet's tongue get stuck to the top of his throat except when he was inspired to speak, which I actually don't find any problem with. If only Christians and Jews could have such a policy where they only say what the bible says and don't add any extra stuff from other people. Another reason I don't believe Ezekiel bore 430 years' worth of sins for Israel is because I've tried to transfer money from America to other countries and it almost can't be done. That's with money, consensually being digitally sent while paying people to do so. If that is so hard to do then there's no way sins can be transferred from Adam to us, or from us to Jesus, nor from Israel to Ezekial when that's unjust and nonconsensual. There would be too much paperwork and regulations. It can't be done. As regards Ezekial why does the bible say he was put through such a humiliating disgusting ordeal? Because God was mad at Israel for breaking the covenant. The bible says God was mad at them for hundreds of years. Yet then people say God made Israel his chosen people for all time and has always loved them ever since Isaac was born. Now regardless of what else the bible says it is crystal clear that after Israel had a covenant, that covenant was broken beyond repair. Perhaps God could've made a new covenant but the covenant with the Israelites was not everlasting. So, either God also included Ishmael in the covenant he made with Abraham or the Israelites made God break his promise to his friend Abraham. We know God is a great enemy but he is also a great friend who would never break a promise he made to Abraham and his descendants or an everlasting covenant. Unfortunately, pro-Israel people quoting God's biblical favor of Israel to justify Zionism never get past the first few chapters or bother to take the bible in context, otherwise they'd know God's covenant was made with Ishmael too and that *"the prophet"* will come after Jesus departs from earth to guide us into all truth which the bible says Jesus was unable to do while he was on earth.

    This is prophethood we are concerned with, so rather than play blame games and contemplate plausible conspiracies, let's return back to the Deuteronomy prophecy. Deuteronomy verse 18:18 continues to describe the prophet, "*and I will put my words in his mouth. He will tell them everything I command him.*" In numerous places the Quran says how Muhammad is not speaking from his own inclination or desires and that the words of the Quran he recites are not his words, but the words of God. The Quran even exposes and rebukes Muhammad several times criticizing something he had done, whether it was giving up honey in order to please his wives, or turning away from a blind believer to teach Islam to disbelievers instead. Had Muhammad wanted to maintain his reputation and was making up what he said then it would be very foolish to mention such verses that criticized him, however if they were the words of God then he would have to say them even if they were embarrassing or critical of himself; this fulfills the prophecy of "*He will tell them everything I command him.*" The Quran 69:40-51 actually threatens Muhammad if he attributes something to God without permission.

إِنَّهُ لَقَوْلُ رَسُولٍ كَرِيمٍ ۝ وَمَا هُوَ بِقَوْلِ شَاعِرٍ قَلِيلًا مَا تُؤْمِنُونَ ۝ وَلَا بِقَوْلِ كَاهِنٍ قَلِيلًا مَا تَذَكَّرُونَ ۝ تَنْزِيلٌ مِنْ رَبِّ الْعَالَمِينَ ۝ وَلَوْ تَقَوَّلَ عَلَيْنَا بَعْضَ الْأَقَاوِيلِ ۝ لَأَخَذْنَا مِنْهُ بِالْيَمِينِ ۝ ثُمَّ لَقَطَعْنَا مِنْهُ الْوَتِينَ ۝ فَمَا مِنْكُمْ مِنْ أَحَدٍ عَنْهُ حَاجِزِينَ ۝ وَإِنَّهُ لَتَذْكِرَةٌ لِلْمُتَّقِينَ ۝ وَإِنَّا لَنَعْلَمُ أَنَّ مِنْكُمْ مُكَذِّبِينَ ۝ وَإِنَّهُ لَحَسْرَةٌ عَلَى الْكَافِرِينَ ۝ وَإِنَّهُ لَحَقُّ الْيَقِينِ ۝

"That this is verily the word of an honored messenger; It is not the word of a poet: little it is ye believe! Nor is it the word of a soothsayer: little admonition it is ye receive. (This is) a Message sent down from the Lord of the Worlds. And if the messenger were to invent any sayings in Our name, We should certainly seize him by his right hand, And We should certainly then cut off the artery of his heart: Nor could any of you withhold him (from Our wrath). But verily this is a Message for the Allah-fearing. And We certainly know that there are amongst you those that reject (it). But truly (Revelation) is a cause of sorrow for the Unbelievers. But verily it is Truth of assured certainty."

Jesus does not fulfill the criteria of "*the Prophet*" as is evident in John 16:12-13 which says Jesus said: "*I have much more to say to you, more than you can now bear.* ¹³ *But when he, the Spirit of truth, comes, he will guide you into all the truth. He will not speak on his own; he will speak only what he hears, and he will tell you what is yet to come.*" This statement of Jesus has been very controversial for centuries and most translations are incorrect, for consistency I used the English New International Version. Right off the bat Jesus allegedly says,

"I have much more to say to you, more than you can now bear." This means Jesus is not someone who "will tell them everything" so he is not "the Prophet" told of in Deuteronomy. Interestingly Jesus goes on to say, "But when he, the Spirit of truth, comes, he will guide you into all the truth. He will not speak on his own; he will speak only what he hears, and he will tell you what is yet to come." This statement is nearly an exact description of "the Prophet" Moses is told about in Deuteronomy. The word "he" is used 6 times and this being is also called "the Spirit of truth" once. Many people will say that the "Spirit of truth" is the Holy Spirit but this is impossible according to Christian dogma. Because this "spirit of truth" is said to be forth coming, meaning is not yet existent when biblical Jesus spoke those words. God always exists so this actually contradicts the Christian trinity theory because it would mean parts are continuously being newly created and added to God which are not eternal. Likewise, the bible tells us the Holy Spirit was already present on earth before Jesus and while he was on earth, because Luke 1:41 says Elizabeth was filled with the Holy Spirit before John was born and Luke 1:67 says Zachariah was filled with the Holy Spirit and prophesied. So, the Holy Spirit was already out and about at the time Jesus promised a "Spirit of Truth" would come in the future. That "he will guide you into all truth" means the "he" will provide the solution for every social-economic-political-marital-communal problem. Meaning this person will guide people to the solution for everything. If as Christians maintain this being is the "Holy Spirit" then what has the "Holy Spirit" done for mankind? What economic-social-moral-political-domestic-military-religious problem was solved by the guidance we allegedly got from this alleged "Holy Spirit"? Okay maybe that's too broad of a subject, maybe "all truth" doesn't mean "all" according to Christians. I'll stay simple what does the "Holy Spirit" teach us about hitting our children? Can we hit them or not? How? When? For what reasons? Christians have absolutely no clue and nothing in the bible says anything about whether a Christian can hit their kids for disciplinary reasons or not. The "Holy Spirit" has not given an answer, but Muhammad did. Muhammad taught Muslims they can never hit anyone in the face, unless it's in warfare. While when it comes to kids Muhammad forbid Muslims from hitting their kids unless they are at least 10 lunar years old. But even then, no bruises, scratches or blood can result and there is only 1 reason to hit one's Muslim child if they are over 10 years old. At the age of 7 lunar years Muslim kids are instructed to pray 5 times a day, but if they are 10 years old and they don't do their obligatory prayers, which would mean disbelief and apostasy, then and only then can a parent hit their kid, lightly. Since intentionally not doing one's daily prayers is practically the worst thing a Muslim can do and the kid would've had a 3-year warning and had the chance to practice thousands of prayers beforehand. Muslims can never hit their kid for personal reasons. Nor can they hit their child more than 10 times at once because it was narrated from Abu Bardah al-Ansari that he heard Muhammad say: *"No one should be given more than ten lashes except in the case of one of the hadd punishments of Allaah."* narrated by Al Bukhaari (6456) and Muslim (3222). This 10-hit limit is another mercy of which non-Muslims have no religious standard when it comes to hitting their kids and frequently they go over the limit in quantity and quality of hits. Besides since the Muslim is forbidden to hit their kid for its first 10 years of life, then they will know how to discipline without violence. The light hit is only done for the psychological effect of being hit for the first time in their life because they didn't do their daily prayers. Thus, most likely a Muslim kid will never ever get hit, if their parents are practicing Muslims and they are Muslims too. So, Muhammad taught "Kids rights" as well. What if a kid doesn't respect their parents' rights, or even harms them? Well then they go to the Shariah court and it is determined how/if the kid violated their rights and justice is done, but if the parent(s) is guilty of violating any of the kids rights (and they have rights before they are born, and before the parents even get married, such as giving them a good name, picking a good parent(spouse) and teaching them Islam) then the kid is not punished because the parent would be guilty long before the child was and thus the child's oppression of his parents would be the just reward for the parent(s) having oppressed the child. Yet then the score is deemed settled after the oppression is stopped, forgiven and the damages repaired so that afterwards neither party can blame the other for any further oppression should it occur. Unfortunately, most non-Muslims don't know about the rights kids have and they oppress their kids which causes the kids to later on oppress their parents and evil sins destroy the family, or they keep in contact and continue to oppress each other or deny the other's rights. It's truly sad because I can see everyone in my non-Muslim family and every non-Muslim family oppressing each other and they don't even know it because they think they are normal or good people. Kids today don't know how they get oppressed by their parents and parents don't know how they are getting oppressed by their kids. Then if they do find out, they have absolutely no way to fix it and repair the damages. All these problems occur because people get their ideas of raising kids from other than "he" who "will guide you into all truth". Most just think those working for unislamic governments can tell us how to raise our kids, or announce what parents' rights and child rights are. Or they are dumb enough to make their own rules or copy the crappy childrearing job of their own parents continuing the cycle of oppression thinking their tribe is always right. Realistically only a prophet of God can tell us this stuff, so I ask the Christians again if the "he" Jesus promised who will "guide you into all truth" is not a prophet but a "Holy Spirit" then where has the "Holy Spirit" been all this time? Aren't Christians inspired? If so, as they claim, then why don't they have any concise clear code of conduct which they all agree upon for raising children and how each family member can and cannot act? Why didn't Christians announce "Kids rights" to the world until non-Christian governments forced some rights upon them? Muhammad was teaching not to hit one's kids in the 600s CE. Whereas Christians were brutally beating their kids saying "Jesus said turn the other cheek, when you get hit". Thus, for thousands of years Christians slapped their kids around and told them Jesus said they should turn the other cheek, whether it's the cheek on the face or the butt cheek both were getting hit again and again until red and sore. Whereas Muslims aren't even allowed to slap someone in the face no matter who it is. Allah made every person's face special and a Muslim can never slap a human face for any reason, unless it's a kafir face on the battlefield during war. Yet today with all of these fancy "human rights" the non-Muslims claim to spread to all, whether they want them or not, no unislamic or non-Muslim nation in the world says humans cannot slap or hit someone in the face. Islam says every human face has the right to not be slapped or hit, no matter what, unless it were in combat during a violent war. Even when stoning an adulteress Muhammad said to make sure her face does not get hit. Thus, if you never want to get harmed in the face, you want Islamic Shariah. Shariah protects people from getting slapped or hit in the face. While non-Muslims not only tolerate it, and encourage people who get hit in the face to "turn the other cheek, and get hit again" falsely claiming Jesus came to teach mankind how to take a punch, the non-Muslims also made hitting people in the face a sport called boxing. Islam says boxing is a sinful crime, a waste of time/money and medically it's dangerous. Truly consider if civilized people would have a sport where people just hit each other in the face, with special gloves on to make the punches hurt more than they would if it was a fist thus protecting the first when it hurts another's face, having the sole intention being to knock another human unconscious? No prophet supported barbaric pagan Greek sports, yet Paul preached to the Greeks so why didn't he ban boxing? Why were/are the Christians so far behind in "Kids rights" and "Face rights" if they have guidance that's better than Islamic guidance? If you want to know "all truth" about what one can and can't do when raising kids, the bible can't tell you and the Christian "Holy Spirit" has never told anybody. Or does God not care about how kids are disciplined? It seems more likely that the "Holy Spirit" does not fit the criteria of the one promised to come after Jesus departs. What about animal rights? One of Prophet Muhammad's companions narrates, *"We were on a journey and during the Prophet's absence, we saw a bird with its two chicks; we took them. The mother bird was circling above us in the air, beating its wings in grief. When Prophet Muhammad returned, he said, "Who has hurt the feelings of this bird by taking its chicks? Return them to her."* (Sahih Muslim) In another narration, a Companion of the Prophet came to him carrying baby chicks in his clothing and mentioned that the mother bird had hovered over them. He was directed to return the chicks back to the same bush. (Abu Dawood) Yet in Deuteronomy 22:6-7 the bible's animals have no such right *"If you come across a bird's nest beside the road, either in a tree or on the ground, and the mother is sitting on the young or on the eggs, do not take the mother with the young. ⁷ You may take the young, but be sure to let the mother go, so that it may go well with you and you may have a long life."* Clearly the biblical error in animal rights needed to be addressed but nothing in the Judeao-Christian world has given us the truth about bird rights. The bible says "he" will let us know the truth about everything, but I can't think of anything which the "Holy Spirit" has let the world know. So, does "all truth" mean silence? Even if one believes in the alleged Pentecost inspiration of the apostles, the inspiration they are said to have received has never been relayed. Most Christians believe the "Holy Spirit" inspired the apostles but not one of them will tell you what message this spirit gave them or what guidance they received from it which influences their daily lives today. The bible tells us Jesus had "much more to tell", so we should be getting quite a lot of information from this being prophesied by Jesus. Not only can Christians not point to one iota of guidance given through the "Holy Spirit" but this Pentecost event was not interpreted by the disciples of Jesus to be a fulfillment of what Jesus prophesied. Acts 2:16 describes that after the apostles were allegedly inspired by the "Holy Spirit" people accused them of being drunk. In response to the sinful charge Peter says they aren't drunk but that *"this is what was spoken by the prophet Joel"*. Meaning that according to the biblical book of Acts the alleged events of Pentecost were not a fulfillment of any prophecy of Jesus but they were a fulfillment of the prophecy of a prophet whom was called Joel. So according to those who knew Jesus, heard him promise this "Spirit of Truth" and who were allegedly inspired by the "Holy Spirit", the "Holy Spirit" is not the *"he who will guide you into all truth"* whom the bible says Jesus promised would come. The bible tells us that Jesus said "he will speak only what he hears", not only is "he" emphasized but this means the being has limited knowledge and that "he" doesn't know everything. Therefore, according to Trinitarian belief that the "Holy Spirit" is all knowing it cannot be the "Holy Spirit", or else the "Holy Spirit" cannot be divine. The fact that the word speak is used more than once is significant as well, because it means this will be an audible message, it is not going to be a silent inspiration as people claim the "Holy spirit" who possessed the apostles was, even though biblically these apostles apparently didn't even know the prophet John had received the "Holy spirit". The message will be spoken and "he" will tell what is yet to come, which is the very definition of prophesying. This also fits the criteria of Deuteronomy of how to tell whether a person is a true prophet or not, *"If what a prophet proclaims in the name of the LORD does not take place or come true, that is a message the LORD has not spoken."* If we take the English gospels of John at face value when they say Jesus predicted a "Spirit of Truth" would come, then we can see in the epistle of 1 John 4:1-3 exactly what a "Spirit" is according to "John". In the English New International Version of the bible 1 John 4:1-3 says,

*"Dear friends, do not believe every spirit, but <u>test the spirits to see whether they are from God, because many false prophets have gone out into the world</u>. ² This is how you can recognize the Spirit of God: <u>Every spirit that acknowledges that Jesus Christ has come in the flesh is from God</u>, ³ but every spirit that does not acknowledge Jesus is not from God. This is the spirit of the antichrist, which you have heard is coming and even now is already in the world."*

      This excerpt shows us that according to "John" a "Spirit of Truth" is a prophet of God because "John" uses the words spirit and prophet interchangeably. Thus, when the gospel of John refers to the "Spirit of Truth" it actually means the "Prophet of Truth". The second verse says the test to see whether a person is a prophet is whether they acknowledge that Jesus has come in the flesh. Meaning that any later prophet must acknowledge Jesus to have existed and been a prophet. Muhammad not only acknowledged Jesus as existing but proclaimed that he was born of a virgin Mary, and was a prophet who spoke from the time he was a baby and also said how and under what circumstances Jesus would return and that he would defeat the antichrist who was already in the world at the time of Muhammad, which John also says how the antichrist was already in the world when the gospel was written. So according to this biblical criteria of a prophet, Muhammad is a prophet of God. Not only did the prophet Muhammad acknowledge Jesus, but he prophesized about Jesus. Anyone who levels the charge that Muhammad is the antichrist or that Islam is antichrist-like is going against the very definition the epistle of "John" gives to the antichrist. Even if you completely hate Muhammad, to say he is the antichrist is utter nonsense because both Christians and Muslims agree that Jesus will kill the antichrist. Muhammad died a natural death, but most importantly he wasn't killed by Jesus! Interestingly the epistle of "John" found in the bible doesn't say anyone must believe Jesus is a son of God, or God or that he was crucified for the salvation of people, or that he was resurrected. According to the bible a prophet of God is not required to believe that or testify to such doctrines. Now if they were true beliefs requisite for salvation surely "John" would have mentioned that as part of the criteria for "Spirits of truth" or prophets. But these Christian beliefs aren't mentioned because not believing in them doesn't disqualify someone from being a prophet of God, according to the bible. Thus, it follows that if a prophet of God doesn't have to believe those things about Jesus yet still has to believe Jesus came in the flesh and was a prophet, we can interpret this to mean that it is not required for a believer to believe that Jesus was God, a son of God, was crucified, died or was resurrected. Also, that the epistle of "John" contains such a criteria for identifying true prophets from false prophets reveals that the author recognizes that there will be another true prophet of God to come after the time of this epistle being written. Clearly the "Holy Spirit" would have come by the time the author wrote this document so if the author knew of the alleged "Holy Spirit" or believed in it, the author still believed another prophet was forthcoming. That is why the author gave criteria by which we "*can recognize the Spirit of God*" or "*the Prophet of God*". He wouldn't tell us how to identify a true prophet if he thought there wouldn't be any more prophets after Jesus. This means that the authors of the bible believed that another prophet of God would be sent. Obviously, the beginning of the third verse refers to "spirits" or prophets after Jesus. We know this because many of the prophets before Jesus are well known for not having acknowledged Jesus simply because he hadn't existed yet during their time. This is why it's important to take things in context because taking the third verse out of context would mean labeling Moses, David and Abraham as false prophets because no sources available to us say they acknowledged that Jesus "*has come in the flesh*". Also, the bible says that Jesus said in Matthew 12:31-32, "*And so I tell you, **every kind of sin and slander <u>can be forgiven</u>, but <u>blasphemy against the Spirit will not</u> be forgiven.** ³² Anyone who speaks a word against the Son of Man will be forgiven, but <u>anyone who speaks against the Holy Spirit will not be forgiven,</u> either in this age or in the age to come.*" This is interesting for many reasons. First it says every sin and slander "can be forgiven" some mistranslate as "will" or "shall" but "can" is what is correct. The reason some bibles say "will" or "shall" is because the verse itself indicates that sin being forgiven is not guaranteed via an alleged crucifixion thus some Christians don't translate it correctly. Also, that it offers forgiveness for speaking against the "Son of Man" is interesting because some say that means Jesus and that speaking against him means damnation but it could simply mean humans. However, verse 31 says blasphemy against the "Spirit "will not be forgiven period and 32 says blasphemy against the "Holy Spirit" will not be forgiven. Thus, we know the spirit is different than the holy spirit and blasphemy against either equals disbelief that won't be forgiven. Notice both verses give different time outlooks. For blaspheming the "Holy Spirit" we're told no forgiveness in "this age or the next" although this means "in this life or the next. Although blasphemy against the "Spirit" is not given an all-encompassing time, meaning that there is a certain time that sin can be committed and contextually it refers to a future time frame not yet possible to commit during the time of Jesus because the "Spirit" is not yet come or known. Islamically the "Holy Spirit" is the angel Gabriel and anyone from all time could blaspheme him and such a thing is disbelief. Whereas this "Spirit" is a future prophet who must be accepted/followed when he comes and not blasphemed or else.

In addition to this many biblical scholars have come to the conclusion that the Aramaic manuscript of the verse in the gospel of John 16:13 had the Aramaic word for "Comforter", or "the praised one" and many modern bible translations today use the word "Comforter" instead of "Spirit of Truth". However, these are the descriptive nouns instead of personal nouns, whereas each descriptive noun also has an accompanying name corresponding to it. That is the reason why names have meanings. For instance, my name "Gregory" in Greek means "Watchful". Now if there were a prophesy about "Gregory" and someone didn't like me and wanted to disguise the prophecy so people didn't know it said my name, they could change the English translation of the Greek to say "Watchful" instead and nobody would be able to accuse them of incorrectly translating it because it technically means both things. But there is a big difference between saying "Gregory will guide you into all truth" and "The Watchful will guide you into all truth". This is the type of translation that has been done with these biblical verses of "Comforter". The root of the name "Muhammad" is "Ahmad" which means "the praised one", "one who constantly thanks God" or "Comforter". Biblical scholars have said that this means in Aramaic the gospel of John has Jesus mentioning Muhammad by name. Likewise, today the name Muhammad has the honor of being the most popular name in the world. Now if you were a 7th Century Christian priest, or scribe, witnessing the rapid rise of Islam and the spread of the teaching of Muhammad, then read in the gospel of "John" that Jesus foretold of a Muhammad who would guide all, such a Christian would be left with two options. Either he would embrace Islam, or he would remove the name of Muhammad from all translations and bibles that he could so that people wouldn't leave the lucrative church he was profiting from. Remember the bible was forbidden from the masses and only priests were allowed to read the gospel until very recently under penalty of death. This means nobody except for priests had knowledge of what the Aramaic or any other bible said. Many Christian leaders during that time did in fact become Muslims such as Adi bin Hatim. As did prestigious rabbis such as Al-Husayn ibn Salam who said Muhammad was foretold of in the Torah. Even in modern times many Christian priests and preachers have left Christianity and become Muslims saying the bible teaches Islam and announces *the Prophet* to be Muhammad. The Roman Catholic Archbishop of Uramiah, David Benjamin Keldani, wrote a book called *Muhammad in the bible* listing many prophecies he believes Muhammad fulfilled. The bishop also left Christianity and became a Muslim as a result of his study of the bible, changing his name to Abdul Ahad Dawud. When religious leaders are becoming Muslim after reading the bible it makes one wonder what are these learned Christians reading that makes them change their religion? One would expect a Christian priest and preacher would be more Christian after reading the bible, not become a Muslim as a result. Regardless of whether you believe Jesus said the name of Muhammad or not, Muhammad fits the criteria of the "he" whom Jesus said would come after him. Does Muhammad fit the criteria of the Deuteronomy 18:18-22 prophesy?

> "*18 I will raise up for them <u>a prophet like you</u> from among their brethren, and I will put my words in his mouth. <u>He will tell them everything I command him.</u>19 <u>I myself will call to account anyone who does not listen to my words that the prophet speaks in my name.</u>20 <u>But a prophet who presumes to speak in my name anything I have not commanded, or a prophet who speaks in the name of other gods, is to be put to death.</u>" 21 You may say to yourselves, "How can we know when a message has not been spoken by the LORD?"22 If what a prophet proclaims in the name of the LORD does not take place or come true, that is a message the LORD has not spoken. That prophet has spoken presumptuously, so do not be alarmed.*"

Verse 20 mentions how those "prophets" who speak something in the name of God that they were not commanded, or one who speaks in the name of other gods is to be put to death. In my interpretation this is not a simple legal ruling but is a threat from God, that God will put such people to death. The Quran continues this theme in the verses which threaten Muhammad if he were to make up his own verses claiming they were from God. In the end Muhammad like Moses died a natural peaceful death. Paul on the other hand who claimed to receive divine revelation from God and a vision of Jesus, was put to death by the roman emperor Nero, the same Nero who had married Paul's former girlfriend. Perhaps Nero wasn't motivated to kill Paul because of his religious message after all? Nero didn't need a special reason to kill people, he even gave orders for his own mother to be killed. Nero was known to be a jealous man who executed Poppaea's first husband Rufrius Crispinus long after they had divorced. At Poppaea's request Nero even ordered the murder of his first wife

Empress Octavia. Nero cared so deeply about Poppaea that when she died he embalmed her with spices and placed her corpse in the mausoleum of the roman emperor Augustus. It was also said that Nero burned one year's yield of Arabian incense at her funeral. Although the historian Pliny the elder said that Arabia doesn't produce as much incense in one year to be enough to account for all the incense Nero burned on the day of Poppaea's funeral. Nero wouldn't have had any moral qualms about killing Paul based solely on the fact that he previously proposed to his dearly beloved Poppaea; Paul's heretical teachings aside. Nero also would've had political reasons to kill Paul because he would realize Paul was unifying the pagan religions into one, usually politicians hate for their citizens to be united because united citizens can overthrow governments. Regardless if we look at Deuteronomy and my interpretation of verse 20 is correct, that it is a threat that false prophets will be put to death, then Muhammad is a true prophet and Paul was a false prophet. Fortunately, we don't have to rely on my interpretation. The next two verses clarify how to know when a message is not from the Lord. If what they proclaim to happen does not happen then they are frauds and that message is not from the Lord. According to an English translation of the New International version of the Bible in his first letter to the Thessalonians 4:14-17 Paul writes a startling prophesy:

> "" *For we believe that Jesus died and rose again, and so we believe that God will bring with Jesus those who have fallen asleep in him.*[15] *According to the Lord's word, we tell you that we who are still alive, who are left until the coming of the Lord, will certainly not precede those who have fallen asleep.*[16] *For the Lord himself will come down from heaven, with a loud command, with the voice of the archangel and with the trumpet call of God, and the dead in Christ will rise first.*[17] *After that, we who are still alive and are left will be*

*caught up together with them in the clouds to meet the Lord in the air. And so we will be with the Lord forever."-*

Initially the way that Paul uses the word "we" is not a reference to fellow Christians but is referring to himself because he says "we tell you" this implies that he is saying what he says is not just him but someone else as well. He would like them to believe that God is that someone else. Paul then says, "*According to the Lord's word,*" which means that Paul is saying what he is writing and telling people is from the word he received from the Lord. Pause for a second, because this is the exact test that Deuteronomy proposes regarding one who presumes to speak in the name of the Lord. If they do so without authority they shall be put to death, as Paul later was, if what they say doesn't come true then you will know that their message is not spoken to them by the Lord. Paul says "*the Lord himself will come down from heaven, with a loud command, with the voice of the archangel*" which completely contradicts the biblical canon's apocalyptic book of "Revelation". Paul also mentions the Lord having the voice of an archangel despite Moses, who actually heard the voice of God with his own two ears, never once describing the voice of God like that. Interestingly Paul taught that Satan was an archangel and came down from heaven, could that be his Lord that he is referring to? It is also interesting that Paul says the Lord will come down from heaven yet "we" will meet the Lord in the air, then he says "we" will be with the Lord forever, Paul never says that those who believe as he does will be in heaven forever but only with "*the Lord they meet in the air*". Paul doesn't even say they will be with Jesus forever. If Satan was an archangel as Paul claimed and Satan was Paul's lord then that would make perfect sense, especially since Paul says "*the dead in Christ will rise first*" yet he refers to himself as "*we who are still alive*". If you read between the lines Paul essentially says those who believe in Christ are dead and those who believe what he teaches about Christ are "*still alive*". When Paul says that all this will happen to "*we who are still alive*", this "we" is clearly different than the "we" used when referring to himself in my opinion, but I could be wrong. Paul could still be referring to himself, or I could have been wrong about him ever referring to himself. Either way this "*we who are still alive*" means people who are alive at the time he is writing that letter. This prophecy was supposed to happen during his lifetime according to his own words. Obviously, it didn't happen and according to Deuteronomy that means he is a false prophet and shall be put to death. Paul was put to death and this prophesy, like many others of his, failed to happen how or when he said they would. Therefore, according to the bible Paul is a false prophet. This is important to establish because you don't want to be following a false prophet and some people may think that if Jesus isn't "*the Prophet*" then maybe it was Paul, but it is not Paul. Also remember that Paul allegedly saw a vision of Jesus, no prophet ever claimed to see a vision of God. Therefore, Jesus cannot be God and if Jesus did actually appear in a vision to Paul, then it would mean he lied to Paul. Jesus was not a liar. Paul on the other hand, who was killing Christians prior to the alleged vision and was then rejected by the companions of Jesus after it, seems more likely to be a liar. This is also important to reflect on because people today claim they've seen Jesus, so did Paul. Biblically Paul is a false prophet therefore his vision must have been false and he made it up, or if it were true then it was not really Jesus that he saw. What many people forget is that Jesus left earth and Paul had never seen him, so Paul did not know what Jesus even looked like. It is easy for Satan to take the appearance of Jesus, but to fool Paul Satan wouldn't even have needed to look like Jesus because Paul wouldn't have known the difference. Likewise, no images of Jesus were made during his lifetime, or by those who saw him so any depiction we know of today is not really Jesus. Even the Catholic Encyclopedia states the St. Augustine said, "*in his time there was no authentic portrait of Christ, and... the type of features was still undetermined, so that we have absolutely no knowledge of His appearance.*" According to the Catholic Church it is unknown what Jesus looked like. Thus, beware of anyone claiming to see a vision of Jesus who looks like the popular statues we see today because that is not what Jesus looked like and the thing in that vision of the person is not Jesus, if they really had a vision at all. Paul is nevertheless important because by distorting the message of Jesus he set in motion events that lead to the message of Jesus being irrecoverable which meant "*the Prophet*" would be needed on earth. Despite the damage Paul did he set the stage for God to send further revelation. This is how the Creator uses Satan's plot against him, thus manipulating Satan's actions to end up doing the will of God.

There is another prophesy in the bible as well, even though this one is not attributed to Paul, it still concerns him. In the English translation of the New International Version of the bible Acts 21:10-12 states: "*After we had been there a number of days, a prophet named Agabus came down from Judea. 11 Coming over to us, he took Paul's belt, tied his own hands and feet with it and said, "The Holy Spirit says, 'In this way the Jewish leaders in Jerusalem will bind the owner of this belt and will hand him over to the Gentiles.'"*

Since very few Christians actually read the bible most of them have no idea the bible says this person called Agabus was a prophet who existed on earth after Jesus' exit. Most Christians actually believe that after Jesus there are no more prophets despite the verses previously mentioned alluding to "*the Prophet*" and this biblical passage which clearly says there is another prophet in existence after the departure of Jesus. If any Christian ever tells you that Jesus is the last prophet, you can tell them that idea contradicts the bible which says Agabus was a prophet on earth after Jesus. If you're a Christian you know that practically nobody knows about Agabus, I myself just learned about him recently and I had been Catholic for 19 years and studied to be a priest, so don't feel bad if you've never heard of him before. This demonstrates just how little people know of the bible despite professing to believe in and follow it. You can see the ignorance for yourself and ask the Christians you know or meet if they know about "the prophet Agabus" and see what response you receive. Unfortunately, most Christians are so ignorant of what the bible actually teaches that if you stood outside of a church on Sunday and asked everyone who left *"Have you heard the teachings of "the prophet Agabus" who taught after Jesus left earth?"* More than 99% would likely say no, get upset and say how they believe in Jesus () and don't follow Agabus who is a false prophet, then they would probably ask you to leave for calling people to Agabus on Christian property. The irony is that according to their bible, which they claim is the word of God, this mysterious Agabus is a prophet who allegedly existed during the time of Jesus and afterwards prophesied to Paul. If they called the police to remove you from the property for calling Christians to Agabus, the police would likely comply thinking that you were calling Christians to a different religion on Christian property inciting or soliciting them. Realistically it is not hard to imagine such a situation where a person is forcibly removed from Church property for calling people to believe in the teachings of someone whom the bible says is a prophet, the reason is because people by and large really have no idea what the bible actually contains. You could try the same thing with the book of Habakkuk in the Old Testament. Go to a Christian and say, *"I recently learned about this text called the "book of*

Habakkuk" and people are saying that it's divine revelation from God. What do you think about this thing? Do you think this book of Habakkuk is just some hoax or what?" In response the Christian will most likely say how they believe in the bible and that the book of Habakkuk must be some kind of fraud and falsehood because the bible is the word of God so that means the book of Habakkuk can't be. Then tell them: "*Well this book of Habakkuk is in the bible right after the book of Nahum.* (Note they likely won't know about the book of Nahum either.) *You just told me that the bible is divine revelation while at the same time telling me that an entire book of this very same bible is falsehood and not divine revelation. So, you believe that something is not the word of God while at the same time considering it to be the word of whom you worship. Thus, I can only conclude that you must worship a false god, believe in a false scripture, or simply believe in something that you are absolutely clueless about. You sure don't sound like someone who knows the true religion or is worshipping the true God.*" While the bible is immensely popular and widely owned, it remains one of the least read books in the world; of the few who do read it even fewer understand it correctly. Most people actually think the books in the bible have remained in it for thousands of years, but several books that used to be part of "Scripture" are no longer available today, and the bible itself says this. For example, the bible mentions several "books" that it says are authentic but these books don't exist. Some of them include: "*The Book of Jasher*" (mentioned in 2 Samuel 1:18 and Joshua 10:13), "*The Book of the Wars of the Lord*" (Numbers 21:14), "*The Book of Samuel the Seer*", "*The Book of Nathan the Prophet*", and "*The Book of Gad the Seer*" (1 Chronicles 29:29), "*The Acts of Rehoboam*", "*The Chronicles of the Kings of Judah*" (1 Kings 14:29). Although what is the point of all these "missing books" that used to be a part of what Jews/Christians today claim is divine revelation? Well, I think the point is that such "missing books" proves the

"Scriptures" are not preserved and have been tampered with throughout the centuries so that the material originally believed in no longer exists today and as such the material in the bible today can no longer be treated as if it is pure uncorrupted revelation that has never been altered. Though that's just my interpretation of the lesson to be learned from the "missing books". That is if these "missing books" ever existed, which we can't say for sure because it is possible these listed books may never have existed but were just named for other reasons to make the bible seem legitimate and confirmable when the biblical texts were written in a time when books were rare to come across. That way a reader of the bible would think *"Well they couldn't have written this in the bible and said X book confirms it, if the bible story never happened because then people would know the bible was wrong and untrue once they read X book. So, since the bible tells people to check other books that must mean the bible is 100% true."* and this is actually what readers of the bible today think when/if they learn about the "missing books". However, these other books the bible mentions don't exist and only the bible says they ever existed, so since the bible encourages readers to refer to non-existant books to corroborate itself then such faith in the bible must be withheld until such books are made public. So that the bible mentions X books confirm it and these books don't exist then clearly the bible doesn't know what it is talking about and is not meant to be read by people today. Likewise, for those who claim they follow the bible, they don't because the bible tells them to read books that do not exist. Thus, it is impossible to follow the bible. So, for anyone who tells you they "follow the bible" tell them they are a liar. Christians on the other hand have said the following when asked about books the bible mentions that are missing from the bible and do not exist today, *"The point is that the divine Author of the Bible used materials chosen from many different sources, fitting them into His grand design for the Scriptures."* Which contrary to the Christian's intentions to alleviate doubt in the bible, such "lessons" are a concession that the bible has been corrupted, consists of *"materials chosen from many different sources"* (meaning the biblical material is not original and is not all divine revelation) and that the "Author of the Bible" was not involved in the editing process which resulted in the bibles which are being published today. Fundamentally this proves that later generations removed stuff from the bible and the books marketed as bibles today are not what bibles used to be in the ancient past. In short, the biblical "Old Testament" isn't old. Coincidentally the bible contains a parable about the blind leading the blind, whereas today there are Christian preachers leading people down a path claiming to follow a book that neither the congregation nor the preacher has read, perfectly illustrating the biblical parable of the blind leading the blind being a metaphor for many modern Christians who believe things they haven't seen because they think they are mentioned in a book which they haven't read. Believing whatever you are told is called blind faith and this is the type of faith Christians who haven't read every verse of the bible have. What's sadly amazing is how firm their faith is considering that they haven't even read the book which they claim to base their faith upon. For those who claim to "read the bible daily" frequently they know even less about the bible because when they read it's an act of worship that makes them feel righteous/religious and they aren't actually reading critically to learn things but are reading to confirm their belief in the bible and their fake piety. The "daily bible readers" read it daily because they think they are supposed to do so and that reading it daily means following it even though they can barely remember what it says from page to page and when they do remember they don't correctly interpret it. Bible readers follow the footnotes more than the text itself. They believe in the commentaries more than the commandments and apply the appendix/preface more than actual teachings of the book. It's very similar to tunnel vision where drivers can't see much except a few objects directly in front of them as they visually appear. The majority of Christian bible readers have cross-eyes or "crucifixion vision" where they see Jesus as the answer to salvation and ignore most details in the biblical documents thinking that the goal of reading the bible is in the experience. Most of them read it out of love for the bible not out of a love for learning what to do in life according to the bible. Most biblical reading is done either for the sake of reading or for the sake of preaching. The tiny minority of the minority of those who read to practice end up rejecting the bible after seeing it is impossible to apply, contradictory and not holy. The other 2 types of bible readers are blind to the bible despite reading it. Just as they claim the writers of the bible are inspired, they claim the bible inspires its readers no what matter what it actually says. To bible readers the content of the book is mainly irrelevant. If any book in the world acts as a religious placebo for a reader, then surely it is the bible. I firmly believe that the bible is a book you can only respect or believe in if you never sincerely try to practice what it actually tells people to practice. Hence while in one sense not practicing what the bible preaches means one doesn't believe in it, one can't believe in it if they try to practice it. So, the believers in the bible have blind faith either because they don't read the book or because they read it with "bible vision" instead of with sincerity and knowledge. They either don't read it or they don't know the meaning of it. In short, the fundamental problem is that they don't truly know how to read correctly. Many are literate but unqualified readers, which sadly makes them become blind followers of blind leaders who have the same problems as them but can disguise their ignorance with passion and quotations to seem knowledgeable. Blind faith is dangerous so let us see what the bible says about this alleged prophet called Agabus. The verse in Acts says Agabus talks to Paul, but it is important to note that Church historians claim Agabus was one of the 70 or 72 disciples mentioned in the 10th chapter of Luke. How they came to this conclusion when none of those disciples are mentioned by name, I do not know and find it suspect. Since the Christian Churches say Agabus was a disciple of Jesus then that disqualifies him from being "*the Prophet*" who would come after Jesus, because he would have already existed during the time of Jesus and been amongst him. It is also suspicious that there would be another prophet who lived during the time of John and Jesus and knew them yet the only time Agabus is ever mentioned in the bible is in Acts, 2 times total. One of which has already been mentioned, the other is in Acts 11:27-29,"*During this time some prophets came down from Jerusalem to Antioch. 28 One of them, named Agabus, stood up and through the Spirit predicted that a severe famine would spread over the entire Roman world.*"

    Most prophets of the bible get entire books devoted to them, but this Agabus who is allegedly a contemporary of John and Jesus, only gets 3-4 verses. Despite biblically being the most recent prophet, allegedly, we have the least information on him. While Agabus isn't mentioned much, fortunately the only times he is mentioned it is in connection to future predictions both of which are allegedly "*through the Spirit*". Remember Deuteronomy was very specific "*the Prophet*" would speak in the "*name of God*" not on behalf of the Spirit, or the name of the "*Holy Spirit*". Therefore, this biblical case not only allows us to examine whether Agabus is a prophet according to Deuteronomy, but also allows us to determine if this Christian/biblical idea of the "Holy Spirit" offers truthful inspiration. It would be very easy for me to have ignored the mention of Agabus allegedly being a prophet in the bible and few Christian readers would have known, but that would not be honest. We want the truth whatever it is, I refuse to take things out of context to support my beliefs. If my beliefs are true then there is no reason to hide or ignore data. Remember we are talking about "*the Prophet*", so we really must be diligent in narrowing down the list of candidates. If the bible says Agabus is a prophet then he would be someone we should follow and therefore this biblical claim deserves to be scrutinized. The first prophesy is in Acts 21:10-12, "*After we had been there a number of days, a prophet named Agabus came down from Judea.* ¹¹ *Coming over to us, <u>he took Paul's belt, tied his own hands and feet</u> with it and <u>said, "The Holy Spirit says, 'In this way the Jewish leaders in Jerusalem will bind the owner of this belt and will hand him over to the Gentiles.'"</u>*

Some verses later in Acts 21 Paul is arrested in Jerusalem, but before the verses describing Paul's arrest, which are important to us in order to see if the prophesy of Agabus was fulfilled, there is a description of Paul's teachings as his followers described them which are very interesting. Acts 21:20-25 says: "*When they heard this, they praised God. Then they said to Paul: "You see, brother, how many thousands of Jews have believed, and all of them are zealous for the law.* ²¹ <u>*They have been informed that you teach all the Jews who live among the Gentiles to turn away from Moses, telling them not to circumcise their children or live according to our customs.*</u> ²² *What shall we do? They will certainly hear that you have come,* ²³ *so do what we tell you. There are four men with us who have made a vow.* ²⁴ *Take these men, join in their purification rites and pay their expenses, so that they can have their heads shaved. Then everyone will know there is no truth in these reports about you, but that you yourself are living in obedience to the law.* ²⁵ *As for the <u>Gentile believers</u>, we have written to them our decision that <u>they should abstain from food sacrificed to idols, from blood, from the meat of strangled animals and from sexual immorality.</u>*"

This clearly demonstrates that according to the bible Paul was known for teaching people not to follow the teachings of Moses. To Paul Christianity had nothing to do with the Jewish God or Jewish prophets. Paul was also against the practice of circumcision which God instituted with Abraham as a command. Despite Jesus being circumcised, Paul taught such a practice was un-Christian thereby contradicting Christ according to Galatians 5:2 " *Mark my words! I, Paul, tell you that if you let yourselves be circumcised, Christ will be of no value to you at all.*" which means that Paul taught if you got circumcised you were doomed because you disbelieved by getting circumcised. So, if any Christian male says they follow the bible or Paul then ask them if they're circumcised. If they follow the bible they have to be, because of the Old Testament and Jesus, yet because of Paul they're not allowed to be circumcised and if they are then they're going to hell because according to Paul Jesus only died for the uncircumcised. So, in order for a Christian man to follow the bible they have to both be circumcised AND never circumcised at the same time. Which is impossible unless such a man were to have 2 penises. Meaning for a guy to follow the bible it is required that he have more than one penis, if God only gave him one then he can never follow the bible. However, why is circumcision so important? Frequently today people will cite medical benefits but keep in mind Abraham did not know about the medical benefits and he also did it as an old man who was promised children by God. Now imagine that you are an elderly man living thousands of years ago and God says you are miraculously going to be a father. After hearing such news, you wouldn't naturally be inclined to start cutting off a piece of your penis. Logically that would be a very foolish thing to do, especially when nobody else is circumcised, meaning nobody knows how to safely do that operation including Abraham who learned by doing it on himself first. Whereas circumcising yourself isn't something you can afford to "mess up the first few times and try again until you get it right". Yet despite how crazy it may seem on the surface there really is a reason for God to have commanded it be done. You remember the Phallic idols? Where for thousands of years people worshipped penis idols? What do you think such penis worshippers would think about a religion that says men have to have their penis partially cut off? They would think that to be an "anti-penis" religion that goes against everything they hold sacred. As Christians commonly preach "Your body is a temple"(since they think they got the Holy Spirit or the Eucharist in them, or are made "in the image of God") the phallic pagans taught that a penis is a fleshly idol. To circumcise was a declaration of war against the phallic faiths. It would also prove to phallic worshippers that the penis doesn't produce life but God the Creator does regardless of one's penis. Plus, circumcision would act as a permanent sign of hatred for phallicism and a physical opposition to the belief in phallicism. It was simply impossible for a believing man to be accused of worshipping phallic idols since his own organ was physically altered, which would not have been done if he considered the penis to be sacred. Also, this ensured that when phallic worshippers converted to the true religion, it was genuine because you can't go from worshipping penis to getting circumcised unless you really don't worship penis anymore. And this is the reason why Paul says his Christian converts don't need to get circumcised and shouldn't. Paul wasn't really preaching the religion of Jesus but was preaching a syncretic combo faith in the name of Jesus. Basically, Paul was repackaging the penis idols turning the erected cock into Christ on the cross. The male reproductive system is essentially the trinity with 3 parts, one part (the cock) comes into "mother earth" to shed his bodily liquids so others can be reborn and saved from the "prince of darkness" (non-existence/womb). Then the cock/Christ leaves but comes back again "after death/de-erection" and just as the magicians believed eating semen was the divine nectar of immortal life the Christians were taught, they needed to eat the body/blood of Christ/cock-man in order to achieve eternal life/salvation. So that's where a phallic idolater really wouldn't have any objections to Christianity as Paul taught it, Paul's faith was actually a more socially proper version of penis worshipping that was less vulgar because of the symbolism. The "Mysteries" were rife with pagan symbolism. Paul preached dignified dick idolatry that was fit for the unperverted masses. Yet one snag was the whole Muslim/Jewish circumcision law which was irreconcilable to phallic worshippers and discouraged fake converts as well as mass conversions. This was because phallic worshippers were willing to go along with an official image change for phallicism, since it was a pornographic faith, but they couldn't convince phallicists that Christianity was phallicism rebranded if Christians had to get circumcised as Jesus and his followers had been. Actions always speak louder than words, symbols and professed creeds. Naturally phallic worshippers wondered how could Jesus have preached and been the incarnate cock in the flesh crucified for the sake of phallicism if he was circumcised and all his male followers were? They doubted whether Paul's phallic message was really the legitimate Jesus, so to allay their doubts and gain converts Paul changed the rules directly opposing what Jesus preached and practiced to say that post-crucifixion circumcision was not necessary and even forbidden just as it was in Phallicism and that Jesus abolished the laws via his alleged death. Which while it may sound ridiculous to us, this made sense to phallicists since the act of intercourse itself changed the laws/relationships between pagan phallic worshippers making what was once obligatory forbidden and what was once forbidden obligatory.

Since for phallicists them having sex, changed their legal responsibilities/obligations/allowances, they accepted that the "special moment" for Christ could have changed all the laws even though Jesus may have actually preached the opposite during his life before "giving his body and spilling his bodily fluids for us". So much of Christian doctrines originate from phallicism it's disgusting, with Christ as the cock incarnate the crown of thorns was added as a sadistic symbolic cock ring with the cross doubling as a metaphorical uterus or a downward representation of the phallus. The Tau cross symbol symbolized the penis prior to it symbolizing pagan saviors prior to it becoming the symbol of Christ's cross. While the Ouroboros and symbol for the uterus/womb were added on top of the Tau to make the popular ankh cross. The Egyptian ankh, which was one of the earliest crosses Christians used, is simply a symbol of the male and female reproductive organs coming together as one item that "gives life to mankind". Even the phrase "My god why have you forsaken me?" alleged to be the last words of Jesus on the cross is exactly what male phallic worshippers said after their erections ended during intercourse. Seriously Paul and the bible have literally put the words of cock worshippers into the mouth of Jesus. Talk about perverting religion, Paul turned perverted paganism into a religion attributed to the prophets. The communion of bread and wine was even an aphrodisiac to facilitate sex, since eating natural whole grain or whole wheat bread increases sexual stamina/libido and one glass of wine encourages sexual interactions. Early 1st century Pauline Christians were even accused of having orgies after their Eucharistic religious ceremonies. Fundamentally Paul's version of Christianity was a sex cult made socially fit that was so symbolic that eventually they forgot their sexual origins and promoted celibacy. Of which that was partially Paul's goal as he wrote how he wished no men ever married women, just as he didn't. Although preaching a less obscene sex cult with a semi-moral code could be what Paul meant when writing " *It has always been my ambition to preach the gospel where Christ was not known.*" Perhaps Paul wasn't entirely ill in his intentions to distort the message of Jesus, maybe he just felt and thought the phallic worshippers and cults of Greece and Rome would never accept the truth but needed to stop their pornographic idolatry, so he created a religion inculcating admiration for the true prophets despite his faith being a blend of polytheism perhaps in the hopes that eventually Christianity would make the pagan masses more likely to accept the truth when it reached them. It's possible that is why Paul preached what he did, it would still be wrong and blasphemous despite seemingly good intentions but I'm just trying to be semi-merciful to rationalize why Paul would preach what he most certainly knew was false paganism costumed in Jesus and Jewish traditions. Of course, Paul might have actually believed what he preached but I find that unlikely since he was not that stupid to be ignorant of all the pagan doctrines he symbolically rebranded. Anyways whether Paul's conversion of the pagans was for a good reason in his mind, or for 100% purely evil reasons, Paul vehemently hated those preaching the truth, particularly those preaching circumcision was obligatory for all male believers as all the prophets since Abraham taught. Paul even goes so far as to write about the Christians who tell Christians to get circumcised in Galatians 5:12 "*As for those agitators, I wish they would go the whole way and emasculate themselves!*" Paul wrote that he "wishes" other Christians who disagree with him regarding circumcision would cut their penises off. That was the ultimate penalty for phallic worshippers, for a male to lose his penis was to lose his idol and faith so implicitly Paul is implying those Christians who believe in circumcision are disbelievers in his Pauline religion and should be marked as such by castration. Hence Paul was semi-genocidal in that he felt either you follow his faith as he teaches without circumcision or you have no penis, which in effect means such people can't reproduce and at that time would likely die as a result of castration. To Paul circumcision was not allowed for anyone, and since self-castration is practically suicide, especially in Paul's time, this implies the prophetic religion is not allowed according to Paul; since he basically says those who believe in circumcision should kill themselves by cutting themselves off at the point of disagreement. To Paul there was no "talking it out" Paul felt you just "cut it out" when disagreeing with him, or cut their head off. (either their penis head or their physical head) Not exactly the kind of teachings you'd expect from someone who follows Jesus and "loves their neighbor as themselves" or "turns the other cheek". Yet Paul not only wished such disfiguration of Christian penises but he publicly wrote that he wished it. This wasn't just "locker room talk" this was Paul's public policy pertaining to penis and non-Paulinians. In response to this some may say Paul didn't really mean castrate but meant circumcise and it's just my misunderstanding based on a mistranslation or something. The word used by Paul in Galatians 5:12 is, ἀποκόψονται(apokopto) meaning "*to cut off, amputate, mutilate*". This very same word is also used in many other New Testament bible verses such as Mark 9:43 "*If your hand causes you to stumble, cut it off; it is better for you to enter life crippled, than, having your two hands, to go into hell, into the unquenchable fire,*" Mark 9:45 "*If your foot causes you to stumble, cut it off; it is better for you to enter life lame, than, having your two feet, to be cast into hell,*" John 18:10 " *Simon Peter then, having a sword, drew it and struck the high priest's slave, and cut off his right ear; and the slave's name was Malchus.*", John 18:26 "*One of the slaves of the high priest, being a relative of the one whose ear Peter cut off, said, "Did I not see you in the garden with*

*Him?""* and Acts 27:32 *"So the soldiers cut the ropes that held the lifeboat and let it drift away. "* So, if one says Paul didn't mean castrate in Galatians 5:12 but meant circumcise, as Christians have actually told me, then in Mark does Jesus say to circumcise your hand or to circumcise your foot? Did Simon Peter circumcise a guy's ear? Did the soldiers circumcise the ropes so the lifeboat drifted away? NO. The word means to cut completely off or castrate. Now you could say Paul meant something different than what he actually wrote, but then that would mean the biblical words are wrong in their original Greek form and that those who wrote them didn't write what God wanted them to write and made mistakes saying things that were the opposite of the "truth" they wanted/intended to teach. By extension that would mean Paul is not inspired by God and the bible is not inspired by God nor accurate in conveying the beliefs of the humans who wrote it. Which would mean we shouldn't trust or follow the bible and can't do so even if we tried, if that were the case. Or else one could accept that Paul wrote to others that he wishes certain people would castrate themselves. It's rather intolerant and I think Paul's view was/is wrong. But this is in the bible so that's "God's words" right? Is it God who wishes Christians cut their penises off? Or is it the "inspired word of God" in that God "inspired Paul" to write that he wishes people cut off their penis? Is that what the "Holy Spirit" told Paul to teach? It seems Satanic to me. Fortunately, the bible clarifies that it is not God's words nor inspiration because Galatians 5:2 says *"Mark my words! I, Paul, tell you..."* so it's clear that the biblical text is not quite God's words or inspired words, because Paul takes 100% credit and doesn't say he's inspired or anything but says they are all his words that he says based on his own opinion. In context Paul taught that if Christians are circumcised then they have to follow 100% of the law and if Christians have to be circumcised then the cross doesn't count for anything and nearly his whole religious doctrine is false. Paul taught that you don't need to get circumcised because the cross of Christ means all sins are forgiven and you don't have to follow even one law that Moses preached and Jesus practiced since "faith" is all you need according to Galatians 5:6 *"For in Christ Jesus neither circumcision nor uncircumcision has any value. The only thing that counts is faith expressing itself through love"*. Some Christians disagree but that's what Paul taught, other New Testament authors taught differently stressing works were needed too but Paul actually taught the law was nailed to the cross and is no longer applicable, and not only isn't applicable but is condemned and blameworthy/evil. Some Christians agree with that and think they can do anything because Jesus saved them and as long as they believe then they're going to paradise automatically. Despite this Pauline doctrine, Acts 21:25 reveals how early followers of Paul still had dietary restrictions. This verse of Paul's in Acts completely contradicts the common Christian claim that God has allowed people to eat any food they want because Jesus allegedly said nothing that enters the body defiles it. According to the teachings of the New Testament, Christians do have dietary restrictions on what they are allowed to eat and Paul said you can't eat certain stuff. So, if a Christian says they are following Jesus who they think said they can eat anything then they are simultaneously saying that Paul was wrong to forbid people from eating certain foods. So, Christians must either say Paul was wrong or Jesus was wrong or whoever is teaching them about what the bible means and what Jesus taught is wrong. Anyways at least one person whom Christian's think is a religious leader to follow is wrong. This is why blind faith can have disastrous consequences because even if Christianity is true, a Christian who goes to church and hears the priest say they can eat anything they want because nothing that enters the body can defile it will be sinful according to the bible. Thus, even if the Christian is upon the right religion, then they are still wrong because they aren't following that religion. Also of importance is the biblical prohibition from consuming blood. This applies to the blood commonly found in raw or rare or medium cooked meat which many Christians eat, biblically they can't eat such foods because Paul said it's sinful because he forbids Christians to consume blood. That's all types of blood including the blood of Jesus. So even if those priests really were doing magic and turning wine into blood, it's sinful to drink it according to the bible and Paul. Wine has already been discussed as being biblically prohibited, so regardless of what is in that cup they are passing around in church biblically it's a sin to drink that liquid whether it's what they say it is or not. Yet it might be that the "wine" isn't even "just wine". It wouldn't surprise me at all if they put drugs in the wine too. Stimulants, anti-depressants or hallucinogens may just be considered as extra ingredients. Even if it were water they had in communion cups it'd be a sin to drink it, because they use golden or silver chalices and God's religion teaches that gold and silver utensils are forbidden to use and whoever uses them is merely swallowing the hellfire. Also, Jesus certainly didn't drink out of any golden or silver jewel encrusted cups. Thus, when Catholics and other types of Christians give the " *Jesus said Do this in remembrance of me*" excuse for their communion ritual, ask them if Jesus also said to use golden cups and to ring bells during the process and did, he also says everyone is supposed to get in a big line to get served by one or two people and that all of you are supposed to drink out of the same cups? Also, at the "last supper", of which Paul was the first to say it ever took place because he said God told him so, no females participated in the eating. So, if Christians say they are doing it because Jesus said to then when did Jesus give them permission to do it with girls? The bible doesn't say he said "*Do this in remembrance of me, but next time get some girls in here to eat some. It ain't no fun if the girls don't get none.*" The bible says there were no girls at the party, so who invited them and when? Likewise, there were no kids or old people on the guest list either. If there were only 12 at the "Last Supper" maybe the "spiritual meal" can only accommodate 12 servings a day and there is a 12-person maximum occupancy for this alleged ritual. If you want to do it as Jesus allegedly, did it then you can't go inviting the whole world when he didn't. Maybe if it happened at all, which is highly doubtful, only those 12 were supposed to do it? Or maybe there is a time limit expiration date in that the meal can only be served for so many days before the "spiritual food" expires and the meal time is over. Meaning that maybe the "Last Supper" was the last, it's not a tradition to continue for 2,000+ plus years. Anyways whatever liquid they're serving at communion, it's sinful to drink it according to the bible. Although things are changing as a Communion industry has sprung up. Now you don't even have to go to a church to get communion because some companies sell communion juice and wafer sets. They use juice instead of wine because they know alcohol is illegal to give to kids and Jesus didn't drink it. So, I guess the infamous "*Do this in remembrance of me*" really is quite open-ended with all these different ways of doing it.

      Why don't Christians obey Paul's rules in Acts 21:25 "*As for the <u>Gentile believers</u>, we have written to them our decision that <u>they should abstain from food sacrificed to idols, from blood, from the meat of strangled animals and from sexual immorality.</u>*" It's well-known Christians have no issues about how their meat is killed and what it's sacrificed to/for, or eating blood from raw, rare or medium cooked meat, and sexual immorality needs no comment. What do they say about Paul forbidding certain meat? They say Jesus said it's ok. But when the bible says Jesus said something is forbidden, they turn around and say "But Paul said it was ok". So, in reality most Christians don't follow Jesus or Paul but just do whatever they like and maybe try to find a bible verse to support their current lifestyle. It comes down to Christianity vs. Churchianity vs. Paulianity vs. Selfianity. This is a continuation of the theme prevalent among Christian preachers in that most don't practice what they preach, and on top of that they don't even preach what they are supposed to. Not one Church that I know of teaches the religion of the bible, it's simply impossible because of all these contradictory conflicting teachings. Not even Jesus himself could teach people a religion based upon 100% of the bible! The other reason the dietary restrictions interested me was because Muslims are also prohibited from eating food sacrificed to idols, blood, the meat of animals who died from strangling and from committing sexual immorality. Ironically most Muslims actually follow the bible more than most Christians do, yet they don't claim to follow the bible, or view it as a source from which to base their religion upon. I've found that most Muslims who never read a bible actually follow it more, by accident, than the zealous Christians do who read it daily. Some might disagree but that's because they don't know the contradictions. Paul also writes this in 1 Corinthians 8:4-13,

> "*So then, <u>about eating food sacrificed to idols</u>: We know that "An idol is nothing at all in the world" and that "There is no God but one."*
> *⁵ For even if there are so-called gods, whether in heaven or on earth (as indeed there are many "gods" and many "lords"), ⁶ yet <u>for us there is but one God, the Father, from whom all things came and for whom we live</u>; and <u>there is but one Lord, Jesus Christ, through whom all things came and through whom we live.</u> ⁷ But not everyone possesses this knowledge. Some people are still so accustomed to idols that when they*

*eat sacrificial food they think of it as having been sacrificed to a god, and since their conscience is weak, it is defiled. ⁸ But <u>food does not bring us near to God; we are no worse if we do not eat, and no better if we do.</u> ⁹ Be careful, however, that the exercise of your rights does not become a stumbling block to the weak. ¹⁰ For if someone with a weak conscience sees you, with all your knowledge, eating in an idol's temple, won't that person be emboldened to eat what is sacrificed to idols? ¹¹ So this weak brother or sister, for whom Christ died, is destroyed by your knowledge. ¹² <u>When you sin against them in this way and wound their weak conscience, you sin against Christ.</u> ¹³ Therefore, if what I eat causes my brother or sister to fall into sin, I will never eat meat again, so that I will not cause them to fall."*

    This bible passage is very contradicting even within itself. Firstly, Paul says "There is no God but one". Ok I understand that 1=1 it's exclusive, only 1. Yet he defines God as "*from whom all things came and for whom we live*", I get that too, God created everything and he's the only one you should live for, although I disagree with the Father bit. Then Paul says Jesus Christ is the "*one Lord*" "*through whom all things came and through whom we live*". Which contradicts what Paul said about God. The only way the verses they could be almost reconciled is to say that Jesus is God too but then Paul said it is through the Father "through whom all things came and through whom we live" so Jesus would have to be the Father too, but if he's the Father then who is the son? If Jesus is the Father and the son then he might as well be the mother, brother, sister, auntie, uncle, cousin, wife, husband, grandparent and grandchild too. Furthermore, the fundamental issue exists in that Paul says to live for God and then to live for Jesus so that's where you can't live for but one being. Then Paul contradicts Acts by saying how it doesn't matter whether you eat food sacrificed to idols. Paul also says food doesn't bring one closer to God, which thereby means the communion ritual according to Paul is absolutely worthless. Although then Paul says if by person A eating food sacrificed to an idol it causes person B to eat it then both are sinning and that when someone does so they aren't sinning against God but against Christ. So then again, the question is raised is Christ God according to Paul or not? Trinitarians will say of course but then they say he's not the father, while non-Trinitarian Christians will say he's not God and Paul never taught he was. To which I'd like to say Jesus is not God, and Paul taught that he was but he was wrong. But the Trinitarians can't handle that and the non-Trinitarians say I couldn't possibly know what Paul taught better than them and will quote bible verses proving that God isn't a trinity. To which I agree with them that the bible teaches the trinity is false, but other parts of the bible and Paul taught it to be true. The problem is the bible teaches many different contradicting things, especially about God. Another interesting doctrine Paul teaches here is that sin is basically anything you do that causes someone dumber than you to sin. Such a teaching is nonsensical especially with the example he gave. He said if you do X it's not a sin, but if an idiot does X after seeing you do X then you get a sin because they did X, even though doing X isn't a sin. As you can see Paul was very philosophical and would say clever things that don't really make sense. Anyways I don't see how such "sins" amount to "sinning against Christ" either. Where does Paul get this stuff from? Did Jesus tell him "If *person A eats X it's fine but if person B eats X after seeing person A do it then they are both sinning against me*"? What does it mean to "sin against Christ"? Does it hurt him? Did it cause him pain on the alleged cross? Does it mean to go against the teachings of Jesus? Also, Paul writes eating food doesn't bring one closer to God. If true then food cannot take one further away from God or Jesus whether or not Jesus is God or not. This is because if eating X can ever under any circumstances be a sin, then not eating X and eating Y instead when given the option between the two it would by necessity bring one closer to God because it would be an act of obedience. Also, if people want to just say that Paul meant the sin in eating food sacrificed to idols is in one's intellect and idea of what they are doing then we must also apply that rule to the same stuff Paul prohibited in Acts 21:25 such as sexual immorality. In the same sentence Paul forbade food sacrificed to idols he also forbids sexual immorality, so does that mean Paul meant sexual immorality is only a sin if some idiot sees you doing it and then copies you thinking something incorrect about it? No, sexual immorality is forbidden across the board with no exceptions. Thus, one can only conclude that whoever wrote Acts must not have known about what 1 Corinthians said and whoever wrote 1 Corinthians must not have known what Acts said. Meanwhile most of the Christians today don't know what either of those 2 books say.

    Then Acts 21:30-36 portrays the arrest of Paul in Jerusalem. Let us see whether the arrest matches the prediction of the biblically alleged prophet Agabus, who said Paul would be bound by his hands and feet in the same fashion he had bound himself with Paul's belt, "*The whole city was aroused, and the people came running from all directions. Seizing Paul, they dragged him from the temple, and immediately the gates were shut.* ³¹ While <u>they were trying to kill him</u>, *news reached the commander of the Roman troops that the whole city of Jerusalem was in an uproar.* ³² *He at once took some officers and soldiers and ran down to the crowd.* <u>When the rioters saw the commander and his soldiers, they stopped beating Paul.</u>³³ <u>The commander came up and arrested him and ordered him to be bound with two chains.</u> *Then he asked who he was and what he had done.* ³⁴ *Some in the crowd shouted one thing and some another, and since the commander could not get at the truth because of the uproar, he ordered that Paul be taken into the barracks.* ³⁵ <u>When Paul reached the steps, the violence of</u>

*the mob was so great he had to be carried by the soldiers.* ³⁶ *The crowd that followed kept shouting, "Get rid of him!"*"

      Verse 33 says the roman commander came and arrested Paul, which doesn't match the prediction of Agabus who allegedly said "*The Holy Spirit says, 'In this way <u>the Jewish leaders in Jerusalem will bind</u> the owner of this belt and will hand him over to the Gentiles.*" The bible says it was the commander who bound Paul with 2 chains, which also doesn't resemble the one belt Agabus used as a prop. Not only is Paul not bound with a single belt and not handed over, but the Jewish leaders of Jerusalem are not even mentioned as being present! Instead it is a Jewish mob, who likely would have killed Paul had the roman commander not arrested him. The gentiles took Paul from the Jews, Jewish leaders didn't hand him over according to the bible. Yet we are supposed to believe the Romans killed Jesus at the behest of the Jews while the bible says the Romans stopped the Jews from killing Paul? This story also doesn't make sense if as verse 20 says "*thousands of Jews have believed*". Where were these thousands of Jews who converted to Paul's teachings when Paul was getting his butt kicked? Did they even exist at all? If thousands of Jews actually converted then Paul would have had more than 4 bodyguards and wouldn't have to pretend to be Jewish when he first arrived. Also the Jews likely would have accepted him and his message since the bible claims so many had already converted. These verses which are 13 verses apart are irreconcilable with each other. Biblically the prediction of the alleged prophet Agabus about Paul was far off the mark and false. Which means biblically Agabus is not a prophet and the "Holy Spirit" he claimed told him the prophesy was not God, as Deuteronomy says, "²² *If what a prophet proclaims in the name of the* LORD *does not take place or come true, that is a message the* LORD *has not spoken.*" If the bible is truthful in telling us that Agabus proclaimed the "*Holy Spirit said*" then because it didn't come true it means that biblically not only is Agabus not a prophet, but also the "*Holy Spirit*" is not God, or a part of God, or a messenger of God. The only other possibility is that the bible is false in its reporting about what Agabus had claimed, which would mean the bible is not inspired by God; at least in those parts.

While it's not directly relevant, what the bible says happened to Paul next is important because it establishes Saul/Paul's character, giving us a clear picture of who he was. Acts 21:37-39 says, "*As the soldiers were about to take Paul into the barracks, he asked the commander, "May I say something to you?" "Do you speak Greek?" he replied. [38] "Aren't you the Egyptian who started a revolt and led four thousand terrorists out into the wilderness some time ago?"[39] Paul answered, "I am a Jew, from Tarsus in Cilicia, a citizen of no ordinary city. Please let me speak to the people."* The Roman commander remembers Paul as being an Egyptian terrorist leader. Yes, a terrorist LEADER, not just a terrorist. Paul was like Rome's version of the Kharijite Osama bin Laden. This Paul truly is quite a character, why doesn't the bible explain Paul's Egyptian terrorist organization and history of revolt against the Roman government? Why don't they mention it in church? Sounds like Paul is someone who has a history of using terrorism in order to gain political power and fame. Keep in mind that Paul wrote in Romans 15:20, "[20] *It has always been my ambition to preach the gospel where Christ was not known"* So according to Paul it was Paul's ambition to preach the gospel while he was committing acts of terrorism in Egypt. Since Saul was a killing machine, we can be certain that Saul was the murderous criminal kind of terrorist and not simply one feared by the Roman government. In response to the commander Paul doesn't deny his terrorist activity, Egyptian connections, or ability to speak Greek, but instead claims that he is a Jew.  If Paul were such a good Christian preacher confirmed with the Spirit, then why doesn't he preach to this commander?  Instead, this supposed champion of Christianity tells this disbelieving gentile that he's a Jew.  Paul ignores the commander's comments about his past and claims to be Jewish admitting he is from Tarsus in Cilicia, which is the home of the cult of Mithras, which truly is no ordinary city as Paul claims.  If Paul really had such an amazing conversion story and talked to God which inspired his change of heart then this would have been the perfect time to tell it and it would explain why the Jews were upset and possibly get Paul off the hook for the charges of terrorism that were still on his record.  Instead, Paul completely denies Christ the moment he is saved by the pagan Romans from the Jews. Acts 22:23 continues: "As *they were shouting and throwing off their cloaks and flinging dust into the air, 24 the commander ordered that Paul be taken into the barracks. He directed that he be flogged and interrogated in order to find out why the people were shouting at him like this. 25 As they stretched him out to flog him, Paul said to the centurion standing there, "Is it legal for you to flog a Roman citizen who hasn't even been found guilty?" 26 When the centurion heard this, he went to the commander and reported it. "What are you going to do?" he asked. "This man is a Roman citizen." 27 The commander went to Paul and asked, "Tell me, are you a Roman citizen?" "Yes, I am," he answered. 28 Then the commander said, "I had to pay a lot of money for my citizenship." "But I was born a citizen," Paul replied. 29 Those who were about to interrogate him withdrew immediately. The commander himself was alarmed when he realized that he had put Paul, a Roman citizen, in chains.*"

    I skipped the 20+ verses of Paul's alleged speech to the Jews the commander is written to have let him make, because the bible verses indicate the commander had absolutely no idea why the Jews were mad at Paul. Had Paul actually made the speech the bible attributes to him to the Jews in front of the commander, then the commander would have had no doubt as to why the Jews were mad. Since the bible repeatedly states the commander didn't know why the Jews were mad at Paul, even after interrogating him, it reveals that Paul must not have made that speech the bible attributes to him because the commander would have known the reason for the animosity if Paul had preached. Rather than being the fearless "*soldier of Christ*", before he is even flogged once Paul claims he is a Roman citizen in order to save his skin. Paul didn't want any harm to come to him whatsoever and pulls roman citizenship out of his sleeve. Why didn't he say that sooner? Roman citizenship was very exclusive and rare, it was comparable to royalty, it was no small claim to make. Being a Roman citizen meant you had the right to vote, the right to make contracts, the right to marry and most importantly you were guaranteed safety from the death penalty. The commander knowing roman citizenship meant safety from the death penalty doubts the claim citing how expensive his own citizenship cost him. Paul replies that he was born a citizen. This reveals that somewhere along the way Paul has told a lie. First, he said he was a Jew from Tarsus, while I didn't include the alleged speech Paul gave to the Jews it started with him saying in Acts 22:3 "*I am a Jew, born in Tarsus of Cilicia, but brought up in this city. I studied under Gamaliel and was thoroughly trained in the law of our ancestors. I was just as zealous for God as any of you are today.*" Biblically Paul told the Jews during his speech that he is a Jew born in Tarsus, but raised in Jerusalem. I will give Paul the excuse that he was a Jew, because a Jew is an ethnic group as well as a religious group, technically speaking Paul was a Jew ethnically so that part is true. I have no issue with accepting Paul being Jewish and telling others he is Jewish. Although it is very misleading to say the least, especially for a

Christian to say. But then Paul says he was born in Tarsus. In order to get roman citizenship by birth you had to be born in the city of Rome, or have both parents be roman citizens. Tarsus is not Rome. Therefore, Paul lied when he said he was a Roman citizen, or he lied when he said he was born in Tarsus, and if the commander really let Paul make this speech as the bible says then he never would have believed Paul when he was told that Paul was a roman citizen by birthright. Yet historically Tarsus was a special Roman city where the inhabitants were granted citizenship in the first century BCE, so it is plausible to believe Paul's parents were legally married Roman citizens and that is how Paul got Roman citizenship, maybe. But then why didn't the commander know Paul was born a roman citizen as soon as Paul told him he was born in Tarsus? Historically Paul was executed by Nero once he had been taken to Rome. Had Paul truly been a Roman citizen he could not have been executed under any circumstances, not for terrorism, heresy or anything. Nero could not have executed Paul if Paul were a Roman citizen. If Paul were a Roman citizen, then Nero could have still killed him through other means, such as the gladiator's arena, or by just dropping him in the ocean, or using him as catapult ammunition. Although the historical fact that Nero executed Paul is evidence that Paul was not a roman citizen and either the bible is lying when it says Paul said he was a citizen, or Paul was lying. Nero was a bad guy and did many unpopular things, but he could not have gotten away with executing a roman citizen, no emperor had done that, not even the crazy ones. Emperors might have murdered romans, but never sentenced a roman citizen to death, unless it was for treason. The bible states the commander was afraid of punishment for having put a roman citizen in chains, the guy was afraid he would lose his job for that minor offense, to think that Nero would execute a roman citizen is irrational. You might be thinking well then obviously Paul must have been charged with treason and then beheaded perhaps because of his terrorist revolutionary activity in Egypt, which he didn't deny. The problem with this theory is that Nero specifically didn't behead roman citizens guilty of treason, other emperors did, but Nero had his own twisted punishment for the treasonous in which those sentenced as guilty would be stripped stark naked and with their head held up by a fork they were then whipped to death. This is not the way Paul died; Christians are relatively united in their belief that Nero had Paul beheaded. Therefore, if Paul were beheaded by Nero, then it means he was not a roman citizen, because Nero executed roman citizens by whipping them to death. This causes a dilemma because if Paul were born in Tarsus, then he likely would have had roman citizenship, but because he was executed then it means he didn't have roman citizenship. Either Paul was lying when he said he was a roman citizen in order to get saved from a flogging or the bible is lying when it says that Paul said he was a roman citizen, citizenship couldn't be stripped or lost in the ancient world. Without a doubt something about the biblical Paul is false. Yet Paul still maintains he was born in Tarsus, and raised in Jerusalem. The city of Tarsus is in modern day Turkey whereas the city of Jerusalem is in modern day Palestine. These two cities are not close to each other, they are very far away. Since it is improbable Paul's family would have moved to Jerusalem from Tarsus, then what exactly does Paul mean when he says he was *"born in Tarsus"*? When a Christian is baptized, they claim to be *"born in Christ"* or *"born again"* they don't mean that literally they were born in a land called Christ, they mean their doctrine purportedly comes from Christ and they subscribe to what they believe his doctrine to be. When we remember that Paul was a heavy proponent for Christian baptism then it may well be figurative when Paul says he was *"born in Tarsus"*. If so then

Saul/Paul is publicly admitting that Tarsus was where his religious doctrine originated, Saul/Paul wasn't born in Christ, he was "*born again*" in Christianity with his spiritual rebirth being a revamping of the Mithraic faith. To him Christianity was a means of going back to his own theological roots from the Mithraic cult of Tarsus. Paul said he was Jewish thereby betraying his ethnicity and true geographical birth location. Typically, whenever people talk, if they were born in a different place than they were raised they will say, "*I was raised in ____ but was born in ____*" which is why it is revealing that Paul says in his alleged biblical speech "*I am a Jew, born in Tarsus of Cilicia, but brought up in this city.*" because this makes no grammatical sense, unless being born in Tarsus means that is where Paul got his religion from. If he were physically born in Tarsus and was of Jewish ethnicity, he would have said "I am a Jew brought up in Jerusalem but born in Tarsus", especially since he was in Jerusalem at the time he allegedly spoke these words. Also, if Paul was born in Tarsus, it would be quite damning evidence that he borrowed from and was influenced by the Mithraic religion which is so similar to Pauline Christian teachings. If Paul was not physically born in Tarsus, he would not have been a roman citizen and thus Nero could legally put him to death, which he did and Paul wouldn't have been whipped to death, which he wasn't. By saying he was "*born in Tarsus*" Paul is essentially telling Jews that he was spiritually dead as a Jew in Jerusalem, and that Judaism is death while his religion is life. As the bible demonstrates Paul is repeatedly depicted as rejecting the Jewish laws and prophets, saying life is only available through Christ and Paul's doctrine. Now that would have been very offensive to the Jews living in Jewish Jerusalem, while at the same time not necessarily being understood by a gentile unconcerned with religion or figurative language. This would explain why the commander had so much trouble trying to find out why Paul incensed the Jews so much. Personally, I incline to believe that Paul was not actually born in Tarsus, but that the phrase meant his spirituality and religion was from there. However, I fear slandering Paul despite his heresy and saying something which is false, which would earn the displeasure of the Creator, so I want to make it clear that this is just my opinion based on my own observations. I hope God will forgive me if anything I've written was wrong or defamatory about Paul or anyone else, I've mentioned in this book. The difficulty in determining the birthplace of Paul is that the only source we have to use to determine the birthplace is the bible. Believing Paul was born in Tarsus is not a historical belief it is a biblical belief. The bible and Christian writers who based their history on the bible are the only sources that place the birthplace of Paul in Tarsus. I have not met Saul/Paul so I do not know the complete truth about him, just like Paul did not meet Jesus so Paul did not know the truth about Jesus. You do not have to agree with my theory, but whether Paul was physically born in Tarsus or not the fact that Paul's teachings about Jesus (whom he never met) were so similar to the Mithraic religion whose base was Tarsus shows that any way you look at it Paul was deeply influenced by the pagan religion of the city of Tarsus. Many of the same beliefs and practices of that false religion were taught by Paul under the brand Christianity and continue to be believed in and practiced today mistakenly being thought of as original, or stemming from Jesus. Also, it is suspicious that never does Saul/Paul say why he was persecuting Christians before his "conversion" and what it was about them or their belief that repulsed him and drove him to violence. Also Paul himself never claims to have had the vision of Jesus on the road to Damascus as is widely believed to be the reason for his conversion, only the book of Acts has this account in 2 different versions; but Paul didn't write the book of Acts and never mentions his conversion story in any letters that he writes. It is suspicious that Paul didn't write about the vision if it actually happened. Typically, when someone changes their religion, they tell you what they thought of the religion before they adopted it, for example in my biography I wrote about what I thought about Islam and Muslims while I was a Catholic and why I previously hated them, yet Paul never mentions his reasons for previous persecution. This is because the followers of Jesus that he was persecuting didn't believe Jesus was God or the son of God or that he was crucified, or died for their sins. They were Christians in the sense that they followed Jesus' teachings, not people who worshiped, deified Christ or prayed to him. That is also why when Paul started preaching to them all the followers of Jesus, with the sole exception of Barnabas, rejected Paul and wanted him killed for his blasphemous doctrine. Yet Barnabas eventually changed his mind too and Paul was denounced as a deviant liar in the gospel of Barnabas. One thing that is an undisputed fact regardless of one's religion is that Paul did not meet Jesus in the flesh and that Paul was "put to death" by Nero. Since Paul was "put to death" and his prophecies did not come true then it means that according to the biblical criteria in the book of Deuteronomy Paul was false and lied about being inspired by God. With that being the case anyone who bases their religious beliefs, or practices on what Paul taught is not following the religion of God, nor do they have the correct belief about God. This is not just the opinion of a former Catholic seminarian, ex-Christian rapper turned Muslim. This is based strictly on biblical criteria which classify the religion of Paul as false. But just what is the true doctrine that Paul actually preached to people? Well in the bible's letter Romans 8:14-29 explains: _"For those who are led by the Spirit of God are the children of God._ [15] _The Spirit you received does not make you slaves,_ so that you live in fear again; rather, _the Spirit you received_ *brought about your adoption to sonship.* And by him we cry, "Abba, Father." ¹⁶ *The Spirit himself testifies with our spirit that we are God's children.* ¹⁷ *Now if we are children, then we are heirs – heirs of God and co-heirs with Christ,* if indeed we share in his sufferings in order that we may also share in his glory. ¹⁸ I consider that our present sufferings are not worth comparing with the glory that will be revealed in us. ¹⁹ For the creation waits in eager expectation for *the children of God* to be revealed. ²⁰ For the creation was subjected to frustration, not by its own choice, but by the will of the one who subjected it, in hope ²¹ that the creation itself will be liberated from its bondage to decay and brought into the freedom and glory of *the children of God.* ²² We know that the whole creation has been groaning as in the pains of childbirth right up to the present time. ²³ Not only so, but *we ourselves, who have the first fruits of the Spirit, groan inwardly as we wait eagerly for our adoption to sonship,* the redemption of our bodies. ²⁴ *For in this hope we were saved.* But hope that is seen is no hope at all. *Who hopes for what they already have?* ²⁵ *But if we hope for what we do not yet have, we wait for it patiently.* ²⁶ In the same way, the Spirit helps us in our weakness. *We do not know what we ought to pray for,* but *the Spirit himself intercedes for us through wordless groans.* ²⁷ And he who searches our hearts knows the mind of the Spirit, because the Spirit intercedes for God's people in accordance with the will of God. ²⁸ And we know that in all things God works for the good of those who love him, who have been called according to his purpose. ²⁹ *For those God foreknew he also predestined to be conformed to the image of his Son, that he might be the firstborn among many brothers and sisters.*" Paul taught that every Christian is a "child of God" the same way Jesus is and that the "Spirit" turns people into "adopted children of God". This "Spirit" also testifies that all who receive him are God's kids and that they are co-heirs with Jesus. Meaning you have the same sonship as Jesus does, the only difference was the order in which you were all adopted. Paul taught that God has many children and that he is one of them sharing co-status with Jesus entitled to all that Jesus is entitled to because Jesus basically opened the door so everyone can get adopted and become God's kid whom he loves and takes care of in his mansion in paradise. This is also what Paul wrote in Ephesians 1:5 *"he predestined us for adoption to sonship through Jesus Christ, in accordance with his pleasure and will"*. Although in his letter to the Romans Paul backtracks and says the adoption papers basically haven't been finalized yet but they eagerly wait for God to raise the rest of his kids up as he did to Jesus and in this hope, Christians are saved from having to follow the law since there are different rules for God's kids than for the Jews who were "God's chosen people". Meaning to be a saved Christian according to Paul is to hope God adopts you and raises you up to paradise the same way he did to Jesus and that as a child of God you won't have to follow the laws God decreed for others to follow. Then unwittingly he admits they hope for what they don't have, referring to salvation and immunity from the law and that according to Paul's letter Christians aren't actually saved but are patiently waiting for God to adopt them so they are saved via Jesus' referral which carries weight due to the alleged sacrifice. Paul also admits *"We do not know what we ought to pray for,"* yet no prophet ever said such a thing. Even whenever the bible says Jesus told people to pray, he gave specific instructions to pray so they don't fall into temptation or for forgiveness or for safety from the hellfire etc. Paul plainly states that the "Spirit" intercedes and prays for them and that this "Spirit" knows best what to pray for on behalf of each individual prospective child of God. This is clearly nothing at all like what Jesus taught and neither is it what most Christians think Christianity teaches, but it is what Paul believed and taught according to what the bible says he wrote. Personally, I suspect Paul's "Spirit" was Satan because I've experienced as a Christian, and as a Muslim talking to Christians, how on the spot Christians can get satanic justifications for their false anti-biblical beliefs. Many times, they are all the same instantaneous responses which each one thinks they themselves thought of, yet since so many have told me the same satanic excuses thinking it's original, I realize when it happens that I'm not just talking with them but that Satan is whispering things for them to say without them knowing he is their source of "inspiration". Paul got his inspiration in this manner and knew it wasn't his own but incorrectly attributed it to God and misled many as a result. Paul associated "the Spirit" with "wordless groans" yet the prophecies about "the Prophet" and the "Spirit of Truth" are both adamant "he will speak" in words that are audibly heard and guide people "into all truth" yet Paul's "Spirit" has not informed them what to pray for and even when it "intercedes" it does so through "wordless groans". Paul tops his letter off by saying that all these "Children of God" will be brothers and sisters of Jesus who was God's first kid, thereby explicitly implying God will in the future gain more children both male and female. According to Paul God keeps on getting more and more kids as time goes by. Paul also implied God will adopt the kids of his adopted kids, thereby adopting his grandkids to be his own direct kids. So, Paul teaches that you could be a grandson of God if your parent was a Christian and also be a son of God if you yourself were a Christian. It's no wonder the pagans embraced Paul's new version of Christianity. The pagans believed the gods could have kids but they were few and far between. Saul/Paul essentially taught the pagans, *"you don't have to be Hercules to be a son of a god, if you accept my religion then God will adopt you as a son of God just like his first son the miracle working Jesus."* What polytheistic pagan would refuse to be a son of a deity who was adopting people? This is why the tolerant polytheists suddenly became intolerant, because now their deity was family so not following their religion was like insulting their clan and parent. Propagating their religion suddenly meant increasing tribal membership. When you talk about easy religions, Paul basically said God adopts people to be his kids and used up all his fatherly punishment on his first kid Jesus who opened the door to God's mansions in paradise for us after he took our beating for us on our behalf. Thus Paul taught God was like a Dad who sent Saul/Paul to give us the message, *"instead of beating all of ya for everything bad each one of you does, I'll just beat my first born favorite to death even though he happens to be the only innocent one among ya and then I'll bring him back to life, and because he's innocent it'll balance out and nobody else will ever have to be punished for doing wrong so I won't have to forgive anybody for making mistakes"*. The "love" Paul attributed to God is the tyrannically tough love of an abusive idiot, certainly not the kind of God the prophets told us about. Yet it's exactly the type of God pagans already believed in and it's the type of family values the Roman emperors lived with, such as Constantine who ordered that his beloved firstborn begotten son Crispus be executed in 326 CE for the sake of the empire. (The year after the famous Council of Nicaea) I'm inclined to think the Trinitarians inserted the "only begotten son" bit into John 3:16, because originally and biblically Paulinians thought every Christian was a son or daughter of God so they had to specify what distinguished Jesus from them, since they considered every Christian to be a child of God who was a prophet who had the "Spirit" in them/inspiring them. Which was another aspect of faith that attracted pagans to Christianity, because as the graphs showed Trinitarians technically think God dwells in them and are part-God. Paul's Christianity was beyond any pagan's wildest dreams, it was so pagan and polytheistic that some tribal pagans today reject it citing that it's too crazy of a pagan doctrine even for them. Seriously if your God loves Jesus who is his literal son and a great kid who never did anything wrong, yet God punished him so severely because of other people's crimes who aren't related to him then why would anyone think that's a loving God? That's like an abusive parent who beats up their kid because they're mad at everyone else in the world. It sounds psychotic, why wouldn't God just punish the bad people who weren't family, or be merciful and forgive them? The Christian idea of God is not loving, merciful or just, he's a bully insanely harming the only one in the world who hasn't offended him. People criticize the Old Testament depiction of God as being harsh, but at least the Old Testament God punishes guilty people instead of an innocent whom he "loves" for the sake of guilty people whom he "loves". Answer me this, if God loves both Jesus and Christians then why do they say he punished him and not them? Wouldn't that mean Christians think God loves them more than he does Jesus? In a real sense Christians actually do think this, just as a sibling who didn't get punished would think they were better than the one who did get punished. That's why Christians say Jesus had to follow certain laws which they don't have to follow because they subconsciously think they're better than their prophet. Thus, Paul taught that if you thought following the laws Jesus followed was obligatory then you weren't Christian, because Paul understood the implications of his teachings meant that he was leading Christians to think they were better than Jesus. Which is worse than what he did when killing them as Saul. Although later after Christians saw how illogical such a notion was, they had to turn prophet Jesus into God himself as part of the trinity, which further helped in spreading the paganesque doctrine. All I can say is, all thanks and praises be to God that Christianity today is watered down and diluted from what the bible says that Paul believed and taught. If Christians actually believed what the bible says Paul taught, they'd be even worse. Which may be why people were forbidden to read or have bibles in the past, under penalty of death.  Because what kind of a society would we have if everyone thought God loves everybody and they're God's kid with a "Spirit" of God within, inspiring them what to say and do?  Certainly not civilization, we'd be in a crazy chaotic circus.

      As extreme as Paul teachings were, the bible has him beat in the verses saying God declared in Deuteronomy 14:1, "Ye *are the children of the LORD your God*" and Psalms 82:6 "*I said, 'You are "gods"; you are all sons of the Most High.'* Which actually is a contradiction and polytheism in that it says the sons of God are gods themselves.  Meaning biblically, one literally becomes like part of the family as if God was merely a family name.  Now you tell me, does the phrase "You are gods" sound like something God would say to anything?  Also keep in mind that in Hebrew there are no uppercase and lowercase letters so God and god were spelled the same.  Although to make it less ungodly of a verse modern translators put a lowercase g on it.  Because it is clear that God stated many times before that he alone is the only God and this is what all the prophets taught, so they can't in good conscience let people read the bible say God said "You are Gods".  Although even more shocking is that the bible says Jesus quoted this in John 10:33-36, " *"<u>We are not stoning you for any good work,"</u> <u>they replied, "but for blasphemy,</u> because you, a mere man, claim to be God." ³⁴ Jesus answered them, "<u>**Is it not written in your Law, 'I have said you are "gods"'**</u>? ³⁵ If he called them 'gods,' to whom the word of God came – and Scripture cannot be set aside – ³⁶ what about the one whom the Father set apart as his very own and sent into the world? Why then do you accuse me of blasphemy because I said, 'I am God's Son'?*"  Now before you go join the 5%ers thinking you are God on earth because of these bible verses, calm down.  Take a breath.  And try not to get too emotional as you read this book.  Yes, some stuff is crazy, but you can't let learning about the craziness of the world make you go crazy yourself. Having crazy emotional reactions leads to crazy beliefs and deeds. First, we should note that Jesus was nearly stoned by the Jews, yet he was saved from death by God on this occasion just as he always was. They said they were going to stone him for claiming to be God, which the Trinitarians will quickly say "*See Jesus must be God because the bible says the Jews said he said so!*". Yet first of all the bible may not be true. Second of all Jesus never says that was what he meant or said at all. Thirdly they never did stone him for this alleged crime the biblical Jews accuse him of which the Christians say he was guilty of, yet since the Christian thinks that Jesus could do no wrong, they think if he said it then it must not have been a crime but must've been true based on their circular logic used to justify their beliefs in any way possible. The response of Jesus is important because he says " *Is it not written in your Law, 'I have said you are "gods"*" notice he did not say this was God's law. He was doing what I do when I address Christians saying "If X is wrong then what about how your bible says God said X?" Thus, the Jews were put in a tight spot of either admitting they changed God's words and are lying about God, which is what we can presume since Jesus clearly says their law and not God's whereas Jesus followed God's law, or that they had no valid charge against Jesus since their allegedly divine law said worse than what they claimed he had said. Jesus explains that their "Scripture" which can't be ignored if it truly is Scripture says God called previous prophets "gods", which in Hebrew would have said "Gods", thereby proving to them that they either changed God's Scripture and made it blasphemous or the words don't mean what they say; or both. Which in biblical context also alludes to Exodus 7:1 which says "*And the Lord said to Moses, See, I have made thee a god to Pharaoh*". So that's another verse where one could confidently say Moses was a god according to the bible, yet everyone knows Moses wasn't really God (keep in mind there are no lowercases in Hebrew). So, when biblical Jesus says he didn't claim to be God but God's Son and Christians quickly say "There he must be God's literal son, the bible said he said so!" You can say if they believe Jesus is God's son then they must believe Moses is God and that therefore Jesus must be the son of Moses and Moses must be the "Father" part of the trinity, as evidenced by the fact that Pharaoh didn't believe in Moses or God thus biblically, they must be the same. Whereas again the bible might not be true, but more importantly Jesus was simply making a point that if he is guilty of blasphemy then so are they and so is God if their book really is from God. Then by saying he said he was "God's son" the biblical Jesus is actually telling them: "You say God said prophets were Gods, I think that's blasphemous and am too humble to claim such a thing. So as a prophet I simply said I am God's Son, which since you say the prophets are Gods, and since we know Adam and our other ancestors were prophets, then if they are Gods based on your book saying God said they were Gods then we are all technically God's Son and that's what the verse in your book even says right after the bit about God saying people are Gods". So, this was actually theological wordplay and not a divine upgrade nor blasphemy. The problem is the language which has been mistranslated and our incorrect understanding of what words meant thousands of years ago in context. If Jesus actually told the Jews this then it meant, " If your Law is really from God then before you stone me for this charge you say I said then you better stone God for blasphemy and every single prophet for blasphemy too, or else you better stone yourselves first for changing God's law and inserting blasphemy claiming God said it when he didn't, or admit that you are trying to play linguistic games twisting the meaning of words in your attempts to kill me and not playing these same games when they would cause you to get killed too. So, either you stop playing these games with me, and/or stop lying about what God said, or you kill yourselves first, because your books say the same thing you say I said so are you saying it's blasphemy to read your book? If so then kill yourselves first for reading it and learning blasphemy merits death." Obviously, the Jews should've just shut their mouths after this, but the bible says they tried to arrest Jesus but he escaped. Jesus basically meant that such titles written in religious books which may or may not be from God if taken literally are indeed blasphemous, but they have never been interpreted that way unless someone was fooling themselves to justify what they wanted to believe or do, such as killing him; or as how Christians do to justify their entire religion. Jesus allegedly saying he claimed to be God's son means he is God's friend just as it meant every time that phrase was used in the Old Testament. In fact, if he even said such a thing it might've solely been said to trap the Jews into admitting they corrupted the book of God and inserted blasphemous words or didn't understand it. Also, Jesus had no forefather but simply a foremother. So in that patriarchal society, where the dominant male would dictate the role the rest of the family members would play in society, since Jesus had no dominant male forefather because Mary's father Imran was dead and he had no human father and since as a prophet God commanded Jesus and told him what to do with his life, in patriarchal terms Jesus would be God's son because that is who he lives for, gets his manners from and obeys. It's the same thing with how the phrase "Founding Father" just means the leader or inventor of. In that sense God is the "Founding Father" of Jesus because God created him and gave him his orders, but God is not his literal father at all. In America they also had this same understanding with the patriotic "Sons of Liberty". Those Americans weren't thought to have been biological offspring of

"Liberty" but they were just dedicated to "Liberty" in every aspect of life with their chief purpose being to serve "Liberty" as though they were devoted sons constantly fulfilling their father's orders. Even Paul himself used the word "son" in such a manner in his own biblical letter of Philemon, or at least Christians should hope he did. But if Paul used the word "son" metaphorically meaning follower then why interpret his claims that Jesus is a "son of God" to be literal? I'm referring to the biblical book of Philemon 1:8-22, "Therefore, although in Christ <u>I could be bold and order you</u> to do what you ought to do, <sup>9</sup> yet I prefer to appeal to you on the basis of love. It is as none other than <u>Paul – an old man and now also a prisoner of Christ Jesus</u> – <sup>10</sup> that <u>I appeal to you for my son Onesimus, who became my son while I was in chains</u>. <sup>11</sup> Formerly he was useless to you, but now he has become useful both to you and to me. <sup>12</sup> <u>I am sending him – who is my very heart</u> – back to you. <sup>13</sup> <u>I would have liked to keep him with me</u> so that he could take your place in helping me while I am in chains for the gospel. <sup>14</sup> <u>But I did not want to do anything without your consent</u>, so that any favor you do would not seem forced but would be voluntary. <sup>15</sup> Perhaps the reason he was separated from you for a little while was that you might have him back forever – <sup>16</sup> no longer as a slave, but better than a slave, as a dear brother. <u>He is very dear to me</u> but <u>even dearer to you</u>, both as a fellow man and as a brother in the Lord. <sup>17</sup> So <u>if you consider me a partner, welcome him as you would welcome me</u>. <sup>18</sup> <u>If he has done you any wrong or owes you anything, charge it to me</u>. <sup>19</sup> <u>I, Paul, am writing this with my own hand. I will pay it back</u> – <u>not to mention that you owe me your very self</u>. <sup>20</sup> I do wish, brother, that I may have some benefit from you in the Lord; refresh my heart in Christ. <sup>21</sup> Confident of your obedience, I write to you, knowing that you will do even more than I ask.<sup>22</sup> And one thing more: <u>Prepare a guest room for me, because I hope to be restored to you in answer to your prayers</u>.

Few Christians know of this biblical letter to Philemon, which is only 25 verses long, and about this Onesimus who Paul wrote "became my son while I was in chains". In 1 Corinthians 7:8 Paul wrote, "*Now to the unmarried and the widows <u>I say: It is good for them to stay unmarried, as I do</u>.*" Paul was not married, taught that it was good not to marry and historically Paul never married. Yet somehow Paul got a son, you know what that means right? Some may say that of course Paul didn't mean Onesimus was literally his son, but remember this letter isn't written in English. The Greek word translated as "became" in the NIV and "begotten" in other bibles is γεννάω (ghen-nah-o) which is defined as follows: *1) of men who fathered children 1a) to be born 1b) to be begotten 1b1) of women giving birth to children 2) metaph. 2a) to engender, cause to arise, excite 2b) in a Jewish sense, of one who brings others over to his way of life, to convert someone 2c) of God making Christ his son 2d) of God making men his sons through faith in Christ's work.* Notice that this word originally refers to literal biological children, but later it came to refer to the Christian/Jewish definition as religious followers or converts. Now if the same exact word can be used to refer to a biological/literal son as well as a follower or convert then why do Christians adamantly insist that Jesus is God's literal son but every other son is always metaphorical? The first reason people claim Onesimus is a convert is because "Onesimus" itself means beneficial or useful, however if this guy merely converted and changed his name then Philemon to whom this letter was written wouldn't have known this name. Yet Christians then claim this Onesimus was Philemon's runaway slave whom Paul kindly tells to return to his master as a useful Christian slave/brother. Yet that's not kind, that's actually sinful according to the bible in Deuteronomy 23:15-16, "*If a slave has taken refuge with you, do not hand them over to their master. 16 Let them live among you wherever they like and in whatever town they choose. Do not oppress them.*" So, when it comes to slavery the biblical loophole which is a hindrance to slavery and promotes liberation is disobeyed/rejected by Paul and rather than obey the law as he should and let the slave be free Paul prefers that Christian slaves remain slaves. Yet Christians today refer to Paul with reverence and claim he is a saint despite the biblical Old Testament "strict law of Moses" saying Paul is an oppressor. At least Paul is semi-consistent in rejecting the Jewish laws, he even rejects the good stuff. However, think about the reality if Onesimus was Paul's real son, how would Paul have written differently? Paul offers to pay for anything Onesimus owes, says he would've liked to keep him with him, he is his "very heart" and "very dear to me". Paul also says this guy became his son while in chains, but in the verse prior Paul said he was a "prisoner of Christ", which means this kid became Paul's son after Paul became Christian. Yet Paul never married, so this kid if Paul's would be the result of illegal sexual intercourse. But who was the mother? Well since Onesimus was Philemon's slave and Paul tells Philemon he owes him and that they are "partners", then it seems likely Paul had sinful sex with one of Philemon's female slaves who gave birth to Onesimus who then ran off to meet his father, after which Paul sent him back to Philemon. That Paul refers to Philemon as a "partner" is unusual because typically Paul referred to all other Christians as brothers or sisters, and even referred to Philemon as such. Thus, it may be that Paul meant Philemon was his partner in crime, maybe from his terrorist days or when Paul was robbing churches or maybe Paul was bisexual and sodomous too since he did write Philemon that "*I prefer to appeal to you on the basis of love*". Greek men were known to have sex with other men for fun, especially older men. Note Paul referred to himself as "*an old man and now also a prisoner of Christ Jesus*" thereby signifying that Philemon knew Saul before he became the Christian Paul but when he was Saul this Philemon knew him as "*an old man*" yet Saul was young then, so perhaps "old man" means sodomous man. Paul wrote Philemon " *I did not want to do anything without your consent"* so they were "consensual partners" as we'd say today. Oh, and on top of that Paul writes telling Philemon to prepare a room for him since he plans on coming to live with him and Onesimus, believing that their prayers will cause his release. Paul thought they will pray as he taught them and he will get released, then go live with his "partner" Philemon and his "son" Onesimus happily ever after; waiting a few more days for Jesus to come out of the sky and lift them up to heaven without them ever dying. Well despite Paul prophesying and anticipating the Christian prayers would be answered so he could live with his "son" and "partner", Paul ended up getting beheaded soon afterwards. So, this biblical prophecy of Paul's was false too. But the story gets better, because Paul wrote this letter while in captivity as an enemy of the state. Obviously, Paul's not going to write to a person using their real name, since the Romans will check the letters and kill his accomplices. So, Philemon is a pseudonym, but it's not just any type of pseudonym. The suffix "mon" means man but what does Phile mean? Some might think it refers to fellatio but they'd be mistaken, "Phile" comes from "Philia" which is "an unusual or abnormal sexual urge or feeling for someone or something". Linguistically "Philemon" means someone who desires abnormal sex with men. Yet Philemon also has a mythological usage too. Ancient Greeks believed in a female Bacuis and male Philemon who lived together in a cottage. One day the god Jupiter and his son Mercury came to earth in human form and looked for a place to stay, only Philemon's house showed hospitality. After which the god Jupiter and his son Mercury told Philemon and his wife that all the people of the village will be destroyed except for them. So, Philemon and his wife ascended a hill as the gods instructed them to see the destruction, during which their house became a luxurious temple, after which the god Jupiter and his son offered

Philemon and his wife anything they wished for. They consulted and asked to be made young so they could serve the gods as priests in their temple and that both of them wanted to die at the same time so they didn't have to spend a second without each other. Allegedly the pagan gods granted their wish. Now if Paul were a sodomous Christian writing his boyfriend, telling him about his bastard child who was his boyfriend's runaway slave and his plans to live with them happily ever after until Jesus comes to take them to heaven destroying all the rest, then how would Paul have written any differently? Onesimus himself might've been a secret sodomite and that's why he ran to his father Paul for advice, who then might've surprisingly revealed how his master "Philemon" was actually his "consensual partner" and Paul would patch things up in a letter advising how Onesimus who was formerly useless to "Philemon", now as a known sodomite is *"useful to you and me"*. Although Paul wished he could keep him with him so *"he could take your place in helping me while I'm in chains"*. Just go back to page 366 and reread what Paul wrote and tell me if this sounds like an apocalyptic sodomite's pornographic love letter or not. Also note that Paul wrote in 1 Corinthians 7:1 *"It is good for a man not to have sexual relations with a woman."* and in 2 Corinthians 12:7-8 about a thorn in the flesh given to him. Some speculate this "thorn in the flesh" given to him was "homosexuality", but let's see 2 Corinthians 12 in context from verses 1-16, "<u>I must go on boasting.</u> *Although there is nothing to be gained, I will go on to visions and revelations from the Lord.* ² <u>I know a man in Christ who fourteen years ago was caught up to the third heaven.</u> *Whether it was in the body or out of the body I do not know – God knows.* ³ *And* <u>I know that this man</u> *– whether in the body or apart from the body I do not know, but God knows –* ⁴ <u>was caught up to paradise and heard inexpressible things, things that no one is permitted to tell.</u> ⁵ *I will boast about a man like that, but* <u>I will not boast about</u>

*myself, except about my weaknesses.* *6 Even if I should choose to boast, I would not be a fool, because I would be speaking the truth. But I refrain, so no one will think more of me than is warranted by what I do or say, 7 or because of these surpassingly great revelations. Therefore, in order to keep me from becoming conceited, I was given a thorn in my flesh, a messenger of Satan,* to torment me. *8 Three times I pleaded with the Lord to take it away from me. 9 But he said to me, "My grace is sufficient for you, for my power is made perfect in weakness."* Therefore, *I will boast all the more gladly about my weaknesses*, so that Christ's power may rest on me. 10 That is why, for Christ's sake, I delight in weaknesses, in insults, in hardships, in persecutions, in difficulties. For when I am weak, then I am strong. 11 *I have made a fool of myself*, but you drove me to it. I ought to have been commended by you, for *I am not in the least inferior to the* **"super-apostles,"** *even though I am nothing.* 12 I persevered in demonstrating among you the marks of a true apostle, including signs, wonders and miracles. 13 How were you inferior to the other churches, except that I was never a burden to you? Forgive me this wrong! 14 Now *I am ready to visit you for the third time, and I will not be a burden to you, because what I want is not your possessions but you.* After all, children should not have to save up for their parents, but parents for their children. 15 So I will very gladly spend for you everything I have and expend myself as well. If I love you more, will you love me less? 16 Be that as it may, I have not been a burden to you. *Yet, crafty fellow that I am, I caught you by trickery!* **"Now** honestly do these sentences seem like the "Word of God" to you? Clearly Paul is arrogant pretending to be humble by saying he's humble and not arrogant. Yet at the same time angrily stating "*I am not in the least inferior to the "super-apostles" even though I am nothing.*" So, Paul says he's humble because he says he's "nothing" but despite being "nothing" the "super-apostles" aren't better than him in any way at all. Who are these "super-apostles"? They were the real apostles of Jesus who went around teaching Paul was wrong and false. Despite Paul saying they were "super" their stuff didn't make it into the bible and Paul got a big 52% slice of the New Testament. How did that happen when Paul contradicts himself saying he would not be a fool, then saying he made a fool of himself because other people forced him to make a fool of himself? Then Paul writes that he is going to visit again making it clear that he doesn't want their possessions, but them instead. Although why would he have to clarify that he doesn't want their possessions if they met him twice before? Did he rob their church too? Then Paul calls them his children, how many did he have? While he probably means it metaphorically here it does seem odd that he then writes he is so crafty he caught them by his trickery. Is the "inspired word of God" tricky and crafty, or is that just Paul? Did the prophets ever use trickery when preaching and make fools of themselves? I can't imagine Jesus saying people forced him to make a fool of himself because of the Pharisees influencing people, yet Paul says these "super-apostles" who were the apostles of Jesus taught the people a contrary doctrine that drove Paul to make a fool of himself. But in the end trickery, not God, made Paul succeed, or so Paul thought, claimed and wrote in his letters which he didn't know would one day be mass-published. Whereas I completely agree, Paul fooled none but himself, unfortunately Christians got fooled by this self-described fool. But why did Paul make a fool of himself? Because of these *"super-apostles"*. Well, what were they teaching that made Paul so foolishly foolish? Paul explains in 2 Corinthians 11:1-13,

> *"I hope you will put up with me in a little foolishness. Yes, please put up with me!* ² *I am jealous for you with a godly jealousy.* <u>*I promised you to one husband, to Christ, so that I might present you as a pure virgin to him.*</u> ³ *But I am afraid that just as Eve was deceived by the serpent's cunning, your minds may somehow be led astray from your*

*sincere and pure devotion to Christ. ⁴ For <u>if someone comes to you and preaches a Jesus other than the Jesus we preached, or if you receive a different spirit from the Spirit you received, or a different gospel from the one you accepted, you put up with it easily enough.</u>⁵ <u>I do not think I am in the least inferior to those "super-apostles." </u>⁶ <u>I may indeed be untrained as a speaker</u>, but I do have knowledge. We have made this perfectly clear to you in every way. ⁷ Was it a sin for me to lower myself in order to elevate you by preaching the gospel of God to you free of charge? ⁸ <u>I robbed other churches by receiving support from them so as to serve you.</u> ⁹ And when I was with you and needed something, I was not a burden to anyone, for the brothers who came from Macedonia supplied what I needed. I have kept myself from being a burden to you in any way, and will continue to do so. ¹⁰ As surely as the truth of Christ is in me, nobody in the regions of Achaia will stop this boasting of mine. ¹¹ Why? Because I do not love you? God knows I do! ¹² And <u>I will keep on doing what I am doing in order to cut the ground from under those who want an opportunity to be considered equal with us</u> in the things they boast about. ¹³ For <u>such people are false apostles, deceitful workers, masquerading as apostles of Christ.</u> "*

  Now we are starting to get a clearer picture. Paul admits his foolishness and asks us to tolerate it. I guess he thought that's how Jesus talked to people. Paul reminds them of his promise to the pagans that Jesus would be their "husband" and Paul hoped to present them as virgin brides of Christ. Now seriously did Jesus ever teach that all the believers are going to be his wives and Jesus is going to be their husband? I don't think so. Paul told pagans they would marry into God's family and be God's in-laws, and since Jesus is depicted by Paul as the Lord basically he says he taught pagans they could marry God and become a wife of his. Whereas not only has nobody before Jesus was born taught such a doctrine, neither biblical Jesus nor John the Baptist taught the things Paul taught; and on top of that they certainly didn't teach pagans. So, Paul taught pagans something no prior prophets taught. However, all of the prophets taught the same religion. Thus, can Paul's religion be the prophetic one? Consider whether the prophet John, who is perhaps the single closest person to Jesus, ever considered Jesus to be his "husband ". Paul preached pure pagan philosophies.

Also contrary to what Paul writes in 2nd Corinthians about God giving him a thorn in the flesh, religiously God doesn't make people sinful or give them a messenger of Satan in order to torment them and keep them humble; as Paul says God did to him. Satan fled from Jesus, but Paul says Satan was assigned to be his companion as a result of his "surpassingly great revelations". Oh, and when Paul prays to God to remove this affliction, God denies his request 3 times. Therefore, Paul's prayers weren't answered, yet people call him a "Saint"? Not only may Paul not have been a "Saint" but he might've been a sodomite. To be clear I don't know if he was and based on Islamic Shariah there isn't enough evidence to say, but I thought the possibility is interesting nonetheless and I hope God and Paul forgives me if such speculation is slanderous. Regardless either Paul had a bastard child out of wedlock via sinful sexual intercourse or else when Paul says someone is a "son" he doesn't mean they are an actual son, but if that's the case then Jesus couldn't be the son of God either. Yet just because Jesus isn't God's son doesn't necessarily get Paul off the hook, because based on this letter Paul clearly was attached to this "son" as a father would be and why else would Onesimus return to be a slave unless his father told him to do so because of a "special relationship" with "Philemon"? Unless of course one wants to say that slavery was and is a sacred Christian institution Paul adamantly promoted and endorsed advocating that his own "son" be a slave. Anyways no matter what you think of Paul, or his letter to "Philemon", he clearly led people astray by teaching pagans a distorted version of Jesus which he learned from a Satanic "Spirit", with translations of words pagans didn't understand the meaning of; despite the biblical Jesus expressly saying his teachings were only for the nation of Israel and not gentiles.  Next Paul warned in 2nd Corinthians about people preaching a different version of Jesus than he did and a different type of "Spirit" based on a different gospel.  Who was doing this?  The very next verse refers us to the "super-apostles" and Paul again maintains he is their equal if not better, despite being untrained as a speaker.  However, why would Paul be untrained if these "super-apostles" supported his message and he received the "Spirit"?  Then Paul boasts of preaching free of charge, but then says he was able to do that because of robbing other churches.  Which churches?  Probably those made by the "super-apostles", then Paul elaborates that folks from Macedonia supplied him so he didn't have to burden them.  Although whether these Macedonians voluntarily supplied him or supplied him the way the Church's he robbed did isn't specified.  He also says some people are "masquerading as apostles of Christ" but they are false.  However biblically speaking Paul is the only to have called himself an "apostle of Christ", no other biblical character told people they were apostles, thus those the people of Corinth thought were apostles could have only been the real apostles.  Regarding the "thorn in the flesh" some say that is the same thing Paul referred to in Galatians 4:12-20 when he wrote:  "*I plead with you, <u>brothers and sisters</u>, <u>become like me, for I became like you</u>. You did me no wrong.* ¹³ *As you know, <u>it was because of an illness that I first preached the gospel to you,</u>* ¹⁴ *and even though <u>my illness was a trial to you, you did not treat me with contempt or scorn. Instead, you welcomed me as if I were an angel of God, as if I were Christ Jesus himself.</u>* ¹⁵ *Where, then, is your blessing of me now? I can testify that, if* *you could have done so, you would have torn out your eyes and given them to me. ¹⁶ <u>Have I now become your enemy</u> by telling you the truth? ¹⁷ <u>Those people are zealous to win you over, but for no good. What they want is to alienate you from us</u>, so that you may have zeal for them. It is fine to be zealous, provided the purpose is good, and to <u>be so always, not just when I am with you</u>. ¹⁹ <u>My dear children</u>, for whom <u>I am again in the pains of childbirth until Christ is formed in you</u>, ²⁰ how I wish I could be with you now and change my tone, because I am perplexed about you!"*

In this authentic letter Saul/Paul relates the reason he began preaching to these people was because of an illness. Mental, Sexual, Spiritual? It's anybody's guess, but it was clearly a trial for them, yet Paul says they welcomed him as if he were an angel or Jesus himself. Thus, indicating they were pagans totally enchanted by Paul, but now that Paul left others came to teach them and he is now their enemy. Who were these "people" who wanted to alienate them from Paul? The "super-apostles". Paul once more plays the daddy card calling them his children, even though verses earlier he referred to them as brothers and sisters. Yet when Paul says children, we are told he doesn't really mean literal children, except for Jesus, or so the Christian would claim. However, I didn't quote the beginning portion of this 4th chapter of Galatians, let's see what Paul said before he called these people his "dear children" in verses 1-7, *"What I am saying is that as long as an heir is underage, he is no different from a slave, although he owns the whole estate. ² The heir is subject to guardians and trustees until the time set by his father. ³ So also, when we were underage, we were in slavery under the elemental spiritual forces of the world. ⁴ But when the set time had fully come, <u>God sent his Son, born of a woman, born under the law, ⁵ to redeem those under the law, that we might receive adoption to sonship</u>. ⁶ <u>Because you are his sons, God sent the Spirit of his Son into our hearts</u>, the Spirit who calls out, "Abba, Father." ⁷ So <u>you are no*

<u>*longer a slave, but God's child; and since you are his child, God has made you also an heir.*</u>" Keep in mind 12 verses after Paul says they are God's child he calls these same people "*My dear children*". So if they are God's child and Paul's child, doesn't that mean Paul is claiming to be God? He just kidnapped those he said were God's kids and took them for himself. Or is Paul God's husband and God is the mother? Or is Paul the mother since in Galatians 4:19 he mentioned being in the pains of childbirth and maybe that's where the term "Bride of Christ" comes from. But wait just a minute does this sound like anything that Moses or Jesus taught people? Do you really think Paul was inspired by God to write such crazy confusing contradicting verses? This is why the "super-apostles" were refuting Paul's nonsense. How do we know it was nonsense? Because every time Paul left people would stop believing in his faith and he had to constantly monitor the very churches he founded because that's how brainwashing works. If you aren't exposed to it, it wears off, whereas the truth never wears off. Since Galatians is one of the few 100% authentic letters known to be written by Saul/Paul let's see what else Saul/Paul said in the biblical verses of Galatians 1:6-20 "⁶ *I am astonished that <u>you are so quickly deserting the one who called you to live in the grace of Christ and are turning to a different gospel</u> — ⁷ which is really no gospel at all. Evidently <u>some people</u> are throwing you into confusion and are trying to pervert the gospel of Christ. ⁸ But even if we or an angel from heaven should preach a gospel other than the one we preached to you, let them be under God's curse! ⁹ As we have already said, so now I say again: <u>If anybody is preaching to you a gospel other than what you accepted, let them be under God's curse!</u>¹¹ I want you to know, brothers and sisters, that <u>the gospel I preached is not of human origin.</u> ¹² <u>I did not receive it from any man, nor was I taught it; rather, I received it by revelation from Jesus Christ.</u> ¹³ For you have heard of my previous way of life in Judaism, how intensely I persecuted the church of God and tried*

*to destroy it.* <u>14 *I was advancing in Judaism beyond many of my own age among my people and was extremely zealous for the traditions of my fathers.* 15 *But when God, who set me apart from my mother's womb and called me by his grace, was pleased* 16 to reveal his Son in me so that I might preach him among the Gentiles, *my immediate response was not to consult any human being.* 17 I did not go up to Jerusalem to see those who were apostles before I was, but I went into Arabia. Later I returned to Damascus.</u>18 *Then* <u>after three years, I went up to Jerusalem to get acquainted with Cephas</u> *and stayed with him fifteen days.* 19 <u>I saw none of the other apostles</u> *– only James, the Lord's brother.* 20 *I assure you before God that what I am writing you is no lie."*

First of all, Paul admits there is a different gospel that pertains to Christ, albeit he says it's a perversion, this is evidence that multiple gospels existed. Heck multiple gospels are in the bible today so any who say there is only one gospel is a fool. Yet the bible didn't exist when Paul was alive and this gospel of Paul never made it into the bible. Paul says even if an angel from heaven preaches a different gospel than what Paul preached let him be cursed by God. Now angels have no freewill so they can only do what God commands, yet Paul says let God's curse be upon an angel? Let's not forget Angels told Abraham things, Angels told Lot things, an Angel told Zachariah about the birth of John and an Angel told Mary about the conception and birth of Jesus. No prophet ever said to not follow revelation brought from angels, yet Paul does. Now in theory if Paul knew he was corrupting the religion of Jesus and an angel would be sent with revelation to correct his corruptions, don't you think Paul might've made this statement to prevent people from accepting the truth? Angels can't lie, now maybe a devil can pretend to be an angel and fool people but if you curse any angel then you are cursing those whom God loves and thereby become a disbeliever. Also, Paul goes further to say anybody preaching a gospel other than what they "already accepted" is under God's curse. This is interesting because the gospels of Mark, Matthew, Luke and John were not written until long after this letter was written so they couldn't have already accepted those gospels. In fact, if you look at what dates Christians say the books of the New Testament were written, which aren't the correct dates, but for the sake of argument this letter to Galatians was the first book of the New Testament ever written. Therefore, Paul is saying if anyone believes in any of the 26 books of the New Testament that accompany his letter to the Galatians then they are under the curse of God because they'd be accepting a gospel different to that which the Galatians accepted. Meaning ironically Paul is cursing everyone who believes in the New Testament of the bible. <u>Thus, any who believe in the 4 biblical gospels of Matthew, Mark, Luke or John are under God's curse according to Paul since it's not Paul's gospel nor "Christ's gospel" and they weren't accepted or even written at the time he wrote condemning all gospels to come in the future. And keep in mind Paul said even if those 4 gospels came from angels one would be accursed to accept anything of them.</u> So biblically Paul curses those who believe in the 4 biblical gospels. Where did Paul's gospel come from? Not God but allegedly Jesus Christ. But how does Paul know this when he never saw Jesus, never heard Jesus and his immediate response to this revelation was "not to consult any human being"? Paul was not qualified to spot Jesus in a crowd, so he wouldn't recognize him even if he bumped into him. Paul gets an alleged message from someone he never met before and doesn't know and Paul decides not to verify if it is really from that person by checking with those human "super-apostles" that actually knew Jesus. Think about it, Saul is persecuting Christians, gets an alleged revelation from Jesus and decides not to consult a single Christian about his "revelation". Instead, he goes to Arabia. Why there? He went there to see if "*the Prophet*" had come yet, because if he had then Paul would've fought him, if not then he had a chance at successfully spreading his own deviant ideology which would later combat the truth when "*the Prophet*" did come. Next Paul says he went to Damascus for 3 years. After that Paul went to Jerusalem to meet Cephas (which is Peter) and James, also Paul swears to God that what he wrote, which is the biblical book of Galatians, is no lie.

Let's check the story Paul told in comparison to the English translation of the New International version of the bible's story in Acts 9:3-29, <u>As he neared Damascus on his journey, suddenly a light from heaven flashed around him.</u> 4 He fell to the ground and heard a voice say to him, "Saul, Saul, why do you persecute me?" 5 "Who are you, Lord?" Saul asked. "I am Jesus, whom you are persecuting," he replied. 6 "**<u>Now get up and go into the city, and you will be told what you must do.</u>**" <u>The men traveling with Saul stood there speechless; they heard the sound but did not see anyone.</u> 8 <u>Saul got up from the ground, but when he opened his eyes, he could see nothing. So they led him by the hand into Damascus.</u> 9 <u>For three days he was blind, and did not eat or drink anything.</u> 10 <u>In Damascus there was a disciple named Ananias.</u> The Lord called to him in a vision, "Ananias!" "Yes, Lord," he answered. 11 The Lord told him, "Go to the house of Judas on Straight Street and ask for a man from Tarsus named Saul, for he is praying. 12 In a vision he has seen a man named Ananias come and place his hands on him to restore his sight." 13 "Lord," Ananias answered, "I have heard many reports about this man and all the harm he has done to your holy people in Jerusalem. 14 And he has come here with authority from the chief priests to arrest all who call on your name." 15 But the Lord said to Ananias, "Go! This man is my chosen instrument to proclaim my name to the Gentiles and their kings and to the people of Israel. 16 I will show him how much he must suffer for my name." 17 Then <u>Ananias went to the house and entered it. Placing his hands on Saul, he said, "Brother Saul, the</u>

*Lord – Jesus, who appeared to you on the road as you were coming here – has sent me so that you may see again and be filled with the Holy Spirit." ¹⁸ Immediately, something like scales fell from Saul's eyes, and he could see again. He got up and was baptized, ¹⁹ and after taking some food, he regained his strength. Saul spent several days with the disciples in Damascus. ²⁰ At once he began to preach in the synagogues that Jesus is the Son of God. ²¹ All those who heard him were astonished and asked, "Isn't he the man who raised havoc in Jerusalem among those who call on this name? And hasn't he come here to take them as prisoners to the chief priests?" ²² Yet Saul grew more and more powerful and baffled the Jews living in Damascus by proving that Jesus is the Messiah. ²³ After many days had gone by, there was a conspiracy among the Jews to kill him, ²⁴ but Saul learned of their plan. Day and night they kept close watch on the city gates in order to kill him. ²⁵ But his followers took him by night and lowered him in a basket through an opening in the wall. ²⁶ When he came to Jerusalem, he tried to join the disciples, but they were all afraid of him, not believing that he really was a disciple. ²⁷ But Barnabas took him and brought him to the apostles. He told them how Saul on his journey had seen the Lord and that the Lord had spoken to him, and how in Damascus he had preached fearlessly in the name of Jesus. ²⁸ So Saul stayed with them and moved about freely in Jerusalem, speaking boldly in the name of the Lord. "*

Now what the heck is this story? In his authentic letter to the Galatians Paul didn't say nothing about any blindness, nor any Ananias, nor any preaching in Damascus, nor any Baptism, nor any Barnabas. Paul said he went to Arabia before Damascus which he stayed in for 3 years, before going to Jerusalem to meet only Peter (Cephas) and James, not Barnabas or anyone else. Yet Acts says Paul was blinded went to Damascus, was healed and baptized by Ananias then spent several days with the disciples immediately preaching his doctrine. Then the Jews (it doesn't specify whether they were ethnic Jews (Christians) or religious

Jews) allegedly plotted to kill him so then he came to Jerusalem and met everybody where Barnabas testified to this version of events, allegedly.  However, according to what Paul wrote in Galatians the book of Acts is a bunch of lies and anyone who accepts it is cursed by God.  So that's where the bible tells lies about everybody, even Paul himself!  Yet the Christian tells us it's the "word of God", textually speaking Paul himself would be considered a disbeliever by Christians for saying Acts was a book of lies.  Although Christians insist, we must believe in the bible or else, even though the biblical books themselves say that the other biblical books are lies.  Yet who is this Ananias whom inducted Paul into his new faith according to Acts?  Perhaps it was the very same from Acts 5:1-11 *"Now a man named Ananias, together with his wife Sapphira, also sold a piece of property. ² With his wife's full knowledge he kept back part of the money for himself, but brought the rest and put it at the apostles' feet. ³ Then <u>Peter said, "Ananias, how is it that Satan has so filled your heart that you have lied to the Holy Spirit</u> and have kept for yourself some of the money you received for the land? ⁴ Didn't it belong to you before it was sold? And after it was sold, wasn't the money at your disposal? What made you think of doing such a thing? <u>You have not lied just to human beings but to God." ⁵ When Ananias heard this, he fell down and died.</u> And great fear seized all who heard what had happened. ⁶ Then some young men came forward, wrapped up his body, and carried him out and buried him. ⁷ About three hours later his wife came in, not knowing what had happened. ⁸ Peter asked her, "Tell me, is this the price you and Ananias got for the land?" "Yes," she said, "that is the price." ⁹ Peter said to her, "How could you conspire to test the Spirit of the Lord? Listen! The feet of the men who buried your husband are at the door, and they will carry you out also."¹⁰ At that moment she fell down at his feet and died. Then the young men came in and, finding her dead, carried her out and buried her beside her husband. ¹¹ Great fear seized the whole church and all who heard about these* *events."* Keep in mind just because this Ananias dies in Acts 5 for being a satanic Lier who lies to people doesn't mean he isn't the same Ananias mentioned with Paul in Acts 9, because the Acts weren't necessarily written in chronological order. Also, that the whole church was afraid is a clue, perhaps they were afraid because it was this same Ananias who let Saul into their ranks. But there is another Ananias mentioned in Acts 23:1-10, "*Paul looked straight at the Sanhedrin and said, "My brothers, I have fulfilled my duty to God in all good conscience to this day." 2 At this <u>the high priest Ananias ordered those standing near Paul to strike him on the mouth. 3 Then Paul said to him, "God will strike you, you whitewashed wall! You sit there to judge me according to the law, yet you yourself violate the law by commanding that I be struck!" 4 Those who were standing near Paul said, "How dare you insult God's high priest!" 5 Paul replied, "Brothers, I did not realize that he was the high priest; for it is written: 'Do not speak evil about the ruler of your people.'"</u> 6 Then Paul, knowing that some of them were Sadducees and the others Pharisees, called out in the Sanhedrin, "<u>My brothers, I am a Pharisee, descended from Pharisees.</u> I stand on trial because of the hope of the resurrection of the dead." 7 When he said this, a dispute broke out between the Pharisees and the Sadducees, and the assembly was divided. 8 (The Sadducees say that there is no resurrection, and that there are neither angels nor spirits, but the Pharisees believe all these things.) 9 There was a great uproar, and <u>some of the teachers of the law who were Pharisees stood up and argued vigorously. "We find nothing wrong with this man," they said. "What if a spirit or an angel has spoken to him?"</u> 10 The dispute became so violent that the commander was afraid Paul would be torn to pieces by them. He ordered the troops to go down and take him away from them by force and bring him into the barracks.*" Like I said before, Paul really is a character. Paul insults the Jewish high priest then he apologizes because he "didn't know he was the high priest". Then Paul proclaims he is a Pharisee and the descendant of a Pharisee.

Now every Christian knows the Pharisees were the bad guys, and Paul publicly biblically said *"My Brothers, I am a Pharisee"*(note he calls Pharisees his brothers) and that he's descended from Pharisees. This can be interpreted 2 ways, either Paul's dad and grandfathers where also Pharisees or else he was the son of Pharisees just as he said those he wrote where his children in that he followed the Pharisees' religion. This is what Christians ignore, Paul was a Pharisee! According to the bible that is. Basically, to believe in Saul/Paul would be like believing in Pharaoh if he outlived Moses and then claimed God made him a prophet after Moses. Anyone would be suspicious in such a scenario, especially if the later person's teachings contradicted the prior prophet's teachings as Paul's do and the "super-apostles" of that prophet refuted this *"Satan in Saint's clothing"*. Whereas some may say Paul was just lying in public when the bible says he claimed to be a Pharisee and the descendant of a Pharisee, yet keep in mind the Pharisees said *"We find nothing wrong with this man."* Meaning they knew that was true and wasn't a lie and the Pharisees had no issue with Paul's religious teachings. So, who's team was Paul really on? Now consider what the Pharisees said of Jesus and how they consistently would find fault with him, yet with Paul they can't find any problems. Why is that? Because Paul was one of them and didn't teach what Jesus taught and was corrupting Jesus' religion from the inside. However, didn't Barnabas, Cephas (Peter) and James vouch for Paul? Well at first Barnabas was fooled but guess what Paul later said about these "super-apostles" of Jesus? Paul wrote in Galatians 2:11-14, "11 *When Cephas came to Antioch, I opposed him to his face, because he stood condemned.* 12 *For before certain men came from James, he used to eat with the Gentiles. But when they arrived, he began to draw back and separate himself from the Gentiles because he was afraid of those who belonged to the circumcision group.* 13 *The other Jews joined him in his hypocrisy, so that by their hypocrisy even Barnabas was led astray."* Paul himself writes that he opposed Peter straight to his face and condemns him, as well as men who came from James and says they and Barnabas were hypocrites who were led astray. Keep in mind Jew may mean ethnicity and not religion in this instance. Astray in this context means disbelief. Paul said the "super- apostles" of Jesus became disbelievers and he knew better than them even though he never had one conversation with Jesus or even knew what he looked or sounded like. Now which do you think is more likely? The apostles of Jesus were wrong or that the Pharisee who was killing the apostles relentlessly who then joined the group, who began teaching gentile pagans despite Jesus' instructions not to and then denounced the apostles as disbelievers was wrong? Unfortunately, we only get to hear Paul's version of events because all the other gospels and letters from those who disagreed with Paul's doctrines were destroyed. Also note that only 22 times is Paul ever called an apostle in the New Testament, 20 of those 22 times it's Paul who calls himself an apostle and the other 2 times it was Luke who was Paul's physician and believed in Paul. Yet <u>not one apostle of Jesus ever called Paul an apostle, and Paul denounced them all</u>. Unfortunately, the Roman might said Paul was right and compiled a collection of texts to support their understandings and tried to destroy all things/persons that opposed their crazy falsehood. Thus, Paul's religion ended up finishing the war Saul so zealously waged throughout his life. As Samiri was to Moses, Saul/Paul was to Jesus. Both Samiri and Saul claimed to have visions and formulated their doctrines based on "inspiration", the main difference is Jesus hasn't come back; yet. While even to this day some Christians use the same excuse as those who worshipped the golden calf, by saying "We'll just have to wait until Jesus () comes back to see who's right." That's actually what some Christians tell me when I prove them wrong, they tell me to shut up leave them alone and wait until Jesus comes back and if he tells them Islam is right then they'll change. Yet this is exactly the same thing the disbelievers who worshipped the golden calf said to Aaron when he told them to stop worshipping the golden calf, they said they wouldn't stop until Moses came back and told them otherwise. Yet who ever said they all lived to see Moses come back? And how did the plan of those who waited for Moses to tell them they were wrong turn out for them? Did Moses tell them "Good choice, you did the smart thing"? But today it's even worse because people say they'll just wait til they die and then see which was right and choose the right religion on the day of judgement. By saying this they think they are clever but they doom themselves, because they are saying that even if Jesus came back in their own lifetime they would still wait until they died until changing religions. This plan is the plan of many and it's the worst of all because for it to work nobody could ever possibly get punished in the afterlife. Realistically if they can pick a religion after they die then so can Goliath and Pharoah and even the anti-christ. What makes them so special they can pick after death and others like Pharoah couldn't even change religions in his last moments before death? Also, if they are so special to get this privilege of picking after death then why doesn't God just let them know the truth while they are alive? Doesn't God want them to worship him now? Yet if God doesn't help them accept the truth in this life, what makes them think he will help them or allow them to accept it in the next? The whole reason believers get paradise is because they choose to believe the truth before they die and before they get judged despite not visually seeing paradise or hell. That's called belief in the unseen, if you wait til you see it until you believe it then that's not believing that's just waiting until the correct answers to the test of life are shared and all the tests are graded with the rewards distributed. So, for anyone thinking they will just wait til Jesus comes back or they find out after death, that's not a valid option. Jesus came and did his job, Muhammad came and did his job, the messages have been conveyed we can either accept the truth, reject it, or study more; to wait being content with ignorance or blame dead folk for making things confusing is to believe the prophets failed to do their job to pass the truth to us. Also, such a belief is a religion in itself where one believes the truth isn't available, whereas if the truth is available then the person who thinks or says it's not is labeling the truth as false. What do you think God will do to one with such a plan as to tell God after they die, they didn't believe in the true religion because they didn't believe it was true and decided to find out after death? If that were possible then what is the point of life, is it just for fun; why not just kill themselves so they can find out faster? Honestly how do they even know that they'll know after they die? Well, they'll say the prophets said so, but then no prophet ever taught that people could intentionally choose to choose after death. No prophet said, "Accept my religion now, or after you die then you can accept it." So, who taught this post-death plan? None but the accursed Satan. This plan is Satan's very own personal plan, since Satan asked God to give him respite until the Day of Judgement before punishing him. So, such Christians and others are literally in Satan's ship, except Satan isn't going to be surprised with his destination; and they shouldn't be either. When it comes to religions, if you don't know the truth then find out. To say "I don't know which is right" means you got a problem to be solving.

    Yet we have yet to hear the other side of the story from the "super-apostles"? Maybe things would be clearer if we knew their side so that we could compare Paul's message vs. his enemies the "super-apostles"?

Sadly about 52% of the New Testament is allegedly written by Paul and the other texts are heavily influenced by his teachings because he wrote his letters before the gospels were written. In fact, there are more words of Paul in the bible than there are of Jesus. Therefore, a dilemma is created where because the bible contains the New Testament, anyone trying to practice the religion of the New Testament would be upon a false religion according to the Old Testament. This is why many Christian preachers will say that the Old Testament is just history and doesn't have to be followed. Most Christians despite their belief that the Old Testament may not have to be followed 100% still believe in the commandment that *"Thou shalt not steal."* But Paul was a thief after he became a Christian, according to the English translation of the New International Version of the bible in 2 Corinthians 11:6-8 where he writes, *"Was it a sin for me to lower myself in order to elevate you by preaching the gospel of God to you free of charge? ⁸ <u>I robbed other churches by receiving support from them so as to serve you</u>."* These verses explain to us how Paul was able to pay for such extensive traveling and church construction. The bible says he robbed other churches in order to serve his own constituents. Whether it means he literally robbed them at knife point, by breaking and entering, or by getting paid to preach and then running off without fulfilling the duties of his paid position; anyway, one looks at its Paul knowingly and unashamedly conducted his operations with stolen money. Is that what Jesus told him to do? Maybe Paul stole from the Christian churches who taught different things than he did and justified his crimes that way. Now it's easy to see why he rejected the law of Moses, because according to the Old Testament Paul is a crook. Thus, it's rather coincidental that bishops today walk around with a "crosier" shaped like a shepherd's crook. Don't they also take money from churches fleecing their flock and then serve others with those funds? Paul was a man who believed in using any means possible to create customers for his doctrines. Most of the Christian leaders of today believe the same and they quote a letter from Paul in the bible to justify using any means possible from 1 Corinthians 9:22 where Paul confessed: "*To the weak I became weak, to win the weak. <u>I have become all things to all people </u>so that<u> by all possible means</u> I might save some.*" If Christians don't believe "all possible means" are justified to convert someone to their faith then they don't believe in the bible or Paul. The true eternal Christian goal is to convert anyone they can by using all possible means in order to convert everybody. Although using all possible means includes violence, lies, rewriting the bible, etc. However, no prophet of the true religion ever endorsed using "*all possible means*" to spread the truth, only the purveyors of falsehood and bad guys like Paul advocate using "*all possible means*". Yet Jesus never said people were allowed to follow Paul or the Bible, and even Paul didn't tell people to follow the Bible because it didn't exist until long after Paul died. So instead of being called "Christians" the titles "Paulians" or "Bible thumpers" are more accurate. However most "Christians" don't really follow Paul or their Bible either, but typically have their own religious beliefs specific to them, which is different from all the other "Christians", and follow their desires. It's really frustrating sometimes because most Christians don't know or believe what Christianity teaches, or what Paul teaches, or what the Bible teaches; but the problem is that most of them think they do and they get offended if you tell them they don't. Personally, I've yet to meet two Christians who believe the same religious doctrines as each other, even if they're married to each other.

  Why else did Paul reject the Law of Moses? Because the Old Testament and the religion of Moses is in opposition to and irreconcilable with the religion of Paul and the New Testament. For example, take the verses of the English translation of the New International version of the bible of Deuteronomy 25:5-10, *If brothers are living together and one of them dies without a son, his widow must not marry outside the family. Her husband's brother shall take her and marry her and fulfill the duty of a brother-in-law to her.* ⁶ *The first son she bears shall carry on the name of the dead brother so that his name will not be blotted out from Israel.* ⁷ However, *if a man does not want to marry his brother's wife, she shall go to the elders at the town gate and say,* "My husband's brother refuses to carry on his brother's name in Israel. He will not fulfill the duty of a brother-in-law to me." ⁸ Then *the elders of his town shall summon him and talk to him. If he persists in saying, "I do not want to marry her,"* ⁹ *his brother's widow shall go up to him in the presence of the elders, take off one of his sandals, spit in his face and say, "This is what is done to the man who will not build up his brother's family line."* ¹⁰ *That man's line shall be known in Israel as The Family of the Unsandaled.* Biblically speaking God wants some guys to marry their dead brother's wife whether they want to or not, and if they don't, they will forever be disgraced and dejected by the community. Also notice this biblical command isn't just if the guy doesn't want to marry his sister in-law, the widow has no choice. The bible is clear she "must not marry outside the family". So, imagine that being a woman or if you have a daughter, sister, mother or aunt, biblically speaking there could be a situation where legally she would be forced to remarry someone in the family or else remain a widow forever. Don't be judgmental that's just what the bible teaches. Yet the bible continues with some other divinely revealed or inspired "wisdom" or "guidance" as Jews and Christians proudly call it. Coincidentally in the very next verses following the law about widows being forced to marry inside the family and have the brother in-law become her new husband, or else.

Deuteronomy 25:11-12, *"If two men are fighting and the wife of one of them comes to rescue her husband from his assailant, and she reaches out and seizes him by his private parts, 12 you shall cut off her hand. Show her no pity."*

What Christian man today if he were attacked in the middle of the night at his bedside in danger of losing his life, would cut off the hand of his wife for having rescued him by grabbing his attacker's private parts? Most Christians would say that is crazy, barbaric and criminal; but this is a command from the bible which people say is the "word of God". If one believes the bible to be the "word of God" then this is a command from God and a believer would be obligated to sever the hand of his wife that saved him, without showing her pity. According to the bible this would be considered a good deed for the husband to do. To say that this is crazy is to say God is crazy for having made such a command, or else this verse is not from divine origin and the crazy one is the person who thinks this biblical verse is the "word of God". This is just one example of how it is impossible to live according to the bible and believe it to be the "word of God". I've tried to demonstrate this in the least offensive way possible, but deep down every Christian knows that it's impossible to follow both the Old and New Testament because of the differences in doctrine and laws. If they don't know then if they read the bible, they will find out for themselves how it is impossible to live in accordance with both and believe the doctrines contained in both the Old and New Testaments. If you were to follow 100% of the teachings of the Old Testament today, you'd be locked up as a criminal. If you were to follow 100% of the teachings of the New Testament today, you'd be locked up for being insane. Someone who tells you that they believe in and live according to the bible today is a liar because it's impossible.

Whereas it is not impossible to live in accordance with the wishes of the Creator, God would never punish people eternally for failing to do the impossible. A believer in the bible is required to believe multiple contradictory beliefs simultaneously thinking them all to be true despite belief in one amounting to disbelief in the others. This is why many don't read the bible and rely on Christian leaders to tell them what the bible means. I'm not saying the religion of the Old Testament is true, or that it is 100% authentic, Jesus was sent because of the fact that the Jews had corrupted the religion of God. Neither do I say the New Testament is 100% true or authentic. The point is that the bible teaches more than one religion. There is only one God and he has only legalized one religion, since the bible teaches multiple religions, it cannot all be from the same one true God. The bible itself says in Jeremiah 8:8, "*How can you say, "We are wise, for we have the law of the* LORD*," when actually the lying pen of the scribes has handled it falsely?*" The bible itself says the pen of the scribes were lying when they wrote religious texts saying it was divine revelation, yet today we don't even know the names of the biblical scribes nor do we have what they transcribed, so we can only have bigger lies in the bible today than the bible says the scribes wrote in the past. However, a few kernels and bits of truth could still be in the bible so the book itself could in theory be beneficial, but one would have to critically analyze the bible in order to learn the truth from it. Although even then it could still lead us into error and the hellfire. Fundamentally we would need a prophet's ruling about the contents of the bible and what we should think of it and how or if we should read/learn from it.

    The Pauline dilemma is another instance of where when people read the bible they fail to read between the lines, misunderstanding the metaphors and allegories contained within it. Christianity is rich with symbolism as is the bible, but even if one were to take a strict literalist interpretation of the bible, as I used to, they still would find discrepancies and contradictions which are impossible to reconcile. Many of these misunderstandings stem from people not reading what they believe in and being brainwashed long before they read, that is if they even bother to read the bible at all. It is because most people only read or hear a few select verses that they are able to believe the bible is of divine origin and completely uncorrupted. Whether it is a figurative, literal, or mixed viewpoint the reader uses to interpret the bible, if they read it in its entirety, they will find that it is of a split personality throughout having many different authors and conflicting viewpoints. God doesn't inspire contradictory Scriptures. When we look at Paul for who the bible says he is then clearly he was a dishonest guy if the bible is truthful. If the bible is not truthful then that means the bible is not 100% divine revelation and if the bible is not 100% divine revelation, then Christianity is not 100% correct and a new prophet must be sent by God so that the 100% true and correct religion can be practiced. This brings us back to "*the prophet*" and we still have another prediction of Agabus to see whether he is a prophet according to biblical criteria. Acts 11:27-30,

> "During this time <u>some prophets</u> came down from Jerusalem to Antioch. <sup>28</sup> One of them, named Agabus, stood up and <u>through the Spirit predicted that a severe famine would spread over the entire Roman world.</u> <sup>29</sup> The disciples, as each one was able, decided to provide <u>help for the brothers and sisters living in Judea.</u>"

Surprisingly this biblical passage doesn't just say that Agabus was a prophet after the time of Jesus, but that there was more than one, there were "some". However, that is the first and last that we ever hear of these other prophets. If they were real prophets, it is inconceivable that this would be the only time and place, they are mentioned. It seems they are only mentioned in order to include Agabus along with them. This verse is important nonetheless because it demonstrates that biblically there were lots of "prophets" immediately after the departure of Jesus. However, the criteria for prophethood in the New Testament is different from the criteria of prophethood in the Old Testament. Traditionally a prophet is someone who calls people to worship God alone without partners and is supported by God with miracles. Attributes of a prophet include: being trustworthy, keeping kinship ties, never lying, helping others, being generously charitable, feeding guests abundantly and having a mole on a certain part of the back as a further indication of prophethood. All the prophets avoided major sins from the time they were born until their death. The prophets might have made a minor sin which they then repented from and were forgiven, but none of them ever committed a major sin. God specially chose these people to be role models for all mankind, had they done major sins then nobody would have followed them. The fact that people followed the prophets shows they didn't commit the major sins that have been falsely attributed to them, it's difficult enough to follow the prophets, if they were sinful hypocrites' people would have a justifiable excuse not to follow them. Since there is no excuse for not following and obeying the prophets, then it is impossible for them to have been major sinners, God is not going to give us a sinful example to emulate. A Messenger of God is a prophet who was ordered to convey a Message or revelation from God such as Moses, David, Jesus, or Muhammad. Not all prophets are Messengers, but all Messengers are prophets. In matters of religion, they were infallible, but in matters not pertaining to religion they were human and could err. Messengers could receive 3 types of revelation, either through a dream, through inspiration, or through talking to God or an angel. Some rare instances of revelation occurred to people who weren't prophets such as Mary talking to the angel Gabriel, or the mother of Moses being inspired to put her baby in the river. In Christianity it is believed that the authors of the gospels were inspired and received divine revelation along with those who translated the gospels. This means, whether they acknowledge it or not, Christians believe that bible authors and translators are Messengers of God similar to how Moses was. According to the criteria of prophets, the Catholic Church identifies all Popes as Messengers since Vatican dogma states Popes are infallible and the representative of God on earth, which is practically the very definition of a prophet. While the "saints" canonized by the Popes essentially take the place of God since they are prayed to, which is a level higher than Messengers because Moses isn't prayed to, yet some random "saint" who's standing with God isn't known is. Theologically speaking whatever you pray to is your God and on the Day of Judgment those who pray to other than God when they expect to be rewarded by God will be told to go to who you prayed to for your reward, since you didn't pray to God alone then don't expect God to reward you. On that day people will learn the "saints" they prayed to weren't so saintly, have no power to help them and weren't even aware of the prayers which were said to them. When people pray to Jesus, he is whom people expect to get rewarded from since they are not praying to God, even by their own claim that he is a "son of God" they admit that praying to Jesus is not the same as praying to God. Jesus never asked people to pray to him and the bible says he instructed people to worship their Creator alone. Jesus never taught any prayer directed towards him, or his mother and none of the "saints" did either. These prayers to people are just like the prayers made to statues or animals and it is depressing that such idolaters do not realize this, God-willing they will know and pray to God alone before their death. Trinitarians believe that they are confirmed with the "Holy Spirit", who they think is part of God and that they are inspired by the "Holy Spirit", with that part of God filling them, technically thinking on a metaphysical level that God is inside of them. Trinitarians fundamentally consider themselves to be on an elite level as Messengers of God since they are "inspired". Although since they rarely know what they are "inspired" to do, say or write this "inspiration" is not like the inspiration of revelation. Rather it is more like the inspiration of a movie that's "inspired by a true story". If you research such movies many times you find out that the plot of the movie is actually false and never happened. Instead, the movie producers were actually inspired by other movies that were very profitable and that success story was the true story that inspired them to make a fictional movie. Unfortunately, the way they present their inspiration is misleading and many think a fictional movie which says it was inspired by a true story actually contains a plot that is rooted in factual occurrences, whereas in reality the movie plot has nothing to do with facts at all. Today's movies that are "based on a true story" are the things that create myths. Many Christians then read or hear how Paul and others were "inspired" by the "Holy Spirit" and since they believe the same doctrines they think they are "inspired" as well. In actuality they are just "inspired" to think they are "inspired", but unlike the movie producers who were inspired by a true story, these Christians are inspired by Christian propaganda. As a side note the very word "propaganda" was invented by the Catholic Church in 1622 CE by Pope Gregory XV in order to describe what his new "*Office of the Propagation of Faith*" would use to counter the Protestant Reformation. While Pope Urban VIII created a "*College of Propaganda*" at Rome in 1627 CE for training missionary priests which still exists today, it was just renamed in 1982 CE by Pope John Paul II as the "*Congregation for the Evangelization of People*". It is very significant that from all the information we have about Jesus, he never instructed people to write down what he said, taught or did. Thus, we can conclude that Jesus never provided inspiration for anybody to write about him in the bible. If Jesus were God, then that would mean God never provided inspiration for anybody to write about him in the bible, therefore the bible cannot be inspired by God unless you say the inspiration came only after God left earth. But that makes little sense because if God were to become a human and inspire people to write about him, he would probably inspire such authors onsite so he could be certain everything was written correctly and it would give extra authority to the text if Jesus had personally overseen its compilation. The point is that when the bible says "some prophets" the New Testament criteria of a prophet is not necessarily the same as God's criteria of a prophet. As has been previously shown to be the case with Agabus' other false prophesy, a New Testament prophet is someone who claims to have talked to God and their word tends to be believed at face value as long as their beliefs are in accordance with what biblical authors considered correct. This is why these numerous prophets are not mentioned by name and all details of them and their teachings are omitted. Some Christians such as the Jehovah's Witnesses even applied these biblical definitions of prophets to themselves and stated in their "Awake!" publication of June 8, 1986 CE on page 9, "<u>All True Christians ARE Prophets</u>. *The New American Bible correctly states: "Prophet means 'one who speaks for another,' especially for God. It does not necessarily mean that he predicts the future!" You will be interested to learn that <u>God has on earth a people, all of whom are prophets</u>, or witnesses for God. In fact, they are <u>known throughout the world as Jehovah's Witnesses</u>.*" But ironically the bible actually does say that prophets predict the future and says that's how to identify a false prophet. Maybe they simply don't know of those bible verses, or don't want to know about them because of their numerous false predictions about the future biblically makes their founders, leaders and bible translators false prophets. In comparison to true prophets like Noah, Abraham or Moses, these biblical and Christian post-Jesus "prophets" are not real prophets at all and are mislabeled. If there were prophets after Jesus, we would be obligated to follow them and their teachings, since the bible completely ignores them, aside from Agabus, it would be complete irresponsibility and blasphemous for the "prophets" to have not been mentioned in depth by the gospel authors. It would be akin to a Jew deleting all the details of the prophets after Moses. It means destroying the religion of God if these "prophets" were truly prophets! These unknown "prophets" in the New Testament were likely just people like Agabus who claimed to be "inspired" by the Holy Spirit. Which leads us at last to the second prophesy of Agabus. So, you don't have to look back, I've included his prophesy again: "*One of them, named Agabus, stood up and <u>through the Spirit predicted that a severe famine would spread over the entire Roman world.</u> 29 The disciples, as each one was able, decided to provide <u>help for the brothers and sisters living in Judea.</u>*" Some readings of these verses include "*(This happened during the reign of Claudius.)*" after the 28th verse, but because this is in parenthesis it shows that it is not a part of the original document and is a commentary later inserted, biblically that is what words in parenthesis tend to mean. Many are frequently misled into thinking that the text in parenthesis in the bible is part of the text but this is not the case. The prediction itself says a famine would spread over the entire Roman world and that the disciples who heard this then helped the believers living in Judea. However, if in this case the text in parenthesis is a part of the text then it would show that the writing of the text took place long after the events described thereby giving us a clue. During the reign of Claudius four famines occurred over the course of 11 years. There actually was a famine that plagued Judea in around 45 CE which is likely the one alluded to in the text. However, despite this famine taking place it doesn't fulfill the criteria because the prediction states it would spread over "*the entire Roman world*" whereas the famine of 45 CE was isolated to Judea. In fact, all four famines that happened during the reign of Claudius were isolated incidences, first in Rome during 41-42 CE, then Judea in 45 CE, then Greece in 50 CE and again in Rome in 52 CE. None of these famines were spread over "*the entire Roman world*". Even if you combine them all into one famine, a vast expanse of the Roman Empire remains unscathed such as Gaul (France), Germany, Spain, Turkey, Britain and Africa. Since the parenthesis commentary, which may or may not be part of the original text, directs us to the reign of Claudius we can safely say that this prediction of Agabus, just like his other prediction, did not come true and it nullifies his alleged prophethood. It also disqualifies "*the Spirit*" who gave Agabus his information from being God dispelling the trinity theory which the verses were intended to support.

    Before reading this book, you may never have heard of Agabus and I'm sure you have now learned more than you ever wanted to know about him. Let's now go to a different prophet of the New Testament and see if the prophecy of Jesus is true. In the English translation of the New International Version of the bible Matthew 16:28 attributes Jesus as saying: "*"Truly I tell you, some who are standing here will not taste death before they see the Son of Man coming in his kingdom."* This bible verse allegedly claims Jesus told people they would not die before the "Son of Man" came in his kingdom. First "Son of Man" must be defined because Jesus was not the son of a man in a literal sense, he was the son of a virgin woman, which was why his birth was a miracle. In the three main Semitic languages Hebrew, Arabic and Aramaic the phrase "Son of Man" means human being. In the gospels "Son of Man" is mentioned 85 times and Jesus refers to himself as the "Son of Man" 28 times. The expression "Son of Man" is a unique Aramaic term, the word for which is "bar-nasha" with "Bar" meaning "son" and "Nasha" meaning man. If translated literally it would mean "Son of man" however when "Bar" is joined to a word, as is the case here, the words change meaning and cannot be translated literally. For example, "Bar-agara" literally means "son of the rooftop", but translated correctly means "lunatic". "Bar-zauga" literally means "son of the yoke", translated correctly is "friend". The word "bar-hila" literally means "son of power", but properly translates to "soldier". The word "bar-yolpana" literally means "son of learning", but is correctly translated in the New Testament as "disciple". This is a double standard of translation found in the bible where "bar-nasha" is literally translated, but "bar-yolpana" is not. If "bar-nasha" were correctly translated it would not read "Son of Man" but "human being", obviously very few Christian translators would be motivated to correctly translate a bible that has Jesus calling himself a "human being" 28 times. This is a problem rampant in biblical translations. Too often the words are translated to fit the faith of the translator, rather than translated for what they actually mean regardless of whether they agree with the translator's personal beliefs or not. While Christians like to translate "Bar-nasha" literally they never translate Beth-lehem literally but instead treat it as a name. Literally the word "Beth-lehem" means "House of Bread", but when Christians say Jesus was born in Bethlehem, they never literally take it to mean he was born in a physical "House of Bread". That's the kind of nonsense that occurs when translating all things literally, or mistranslating all things literally. Now that we understand what the alleged words actually mean we can see if this prophesy came true. There are two possible ways to interpret this depending on if we use the correct translation of "Bar-nasha". It says Jesus said to his disciples" some who are standing here will not taste death" before they see the human being coming in his kingdom. Keep in mind that Jesus knew that every soul must taste death at one time or another, even so this verse is allegedly directly from him to his disciples, if we translate "bar-yolpana" correctly. With "Bar-nasha" translated as human being, it seems to directly refer to the Romans entering Jerusalem during the riots that occurred after Jesus departed and seems like a true prophesy foretelling the roman governor Herod Agrippa II. Herod Agrippa II had spent a personal fortune in constructing buildings in Jerusalem and entered it between 65-66 CE trying to prevent Jews from revolting in the territory he ruled over. This was a momentous event because typically the governor didn't come to Jerusalem and tended to remain in the capital, as governors do today. Despite the symbolic gesture the Jews pelted Herod Agrippa II with stones and revolted anyway. It is very likely that some of those whom Jesus was speaking to were still alive to witness Herod Agrippa II coming into Jerusalem which would technically be considered his Kingdom. Since elsewhere the bible has Jesus saying that his kingdom is not of this world, we understand this "Son of Man" means human being and "his kingdom" cannot be alluding to Jesus, or the entire planet. Thus, Jesus is a true prophet based on this prophesy if we translate "Bar-nasha" as human being. On the other hand, some will refuse to believe that Jesus would call himself a human being 28 times in the bible, so they incorrectly translate "Bar-nasha" literally as "Son of Man" and claim "Son of Man" must refer to Jesus even though he was the son of a woman only. According to their translation the verse would mean that the disciples of Jesus would not die before the Second Coming of Jesus. Clearly, they all died and we are still waiting for the Second Coming so it would be a false prophesy according to their translation and understanding. I do not believe Jesus to be a liar, or a false prophet as such a translation indicates. Some bibles contain this incorrect translation that portrays Jesus as someone who told false prophesies and therefore would be put to death, such a bible contains libel. This is a manifest slander against Jesus and I repeat that such a bible contains libel. The only reason I haven't labeled every bible as libel is because I have not read every bible. Although of all the bibles I have read thus far, I have found them all to contain libel in one place or another. Whereas while most people today are not directly responsible for inserting the libel into the bible, they are liable for the consequences of spreading libel if they promote their bible.

Depending on how many times your bible has been translated it will have a completely different portrayal of Jesus than a different bible. According to the bibles with the correct translation of "Bar-nasha" Jesus says he is a human being 28 times. According to the incorrect translation of the bible Jesus is a false prophet and liar. Although the English bibles we read today are not just translations, they are translations of translations of translations of translations of translations; some are translated even more times over. Every edition of the bible has a different portrayal of Jesus; sometimes these different versions of Jesus are irreconcilable and contradicting to each other. Depending on which translation of the bible you use, or believe in, you will have a completely different religion than someone who uses a different translation than you. It is impossible to believe in them all because the different translations say completely different things.

For instance, I was going to explain how people are wrong to say that every time the "Son of Man" is mentioned in the bible it refers to Jesus because if that's the case then Psalms 146:3 and Job 25:6 must be about Jesus too. Incidentally when I looked up verses in the New International Version of the Bible, I saw that they were missing the words "Son of Man". Job 25:6 says the "Son of man" is a worm, but in the NIV bible they used the words "human being". I was certain Psalms 146:3 spoke about the "Son of Man" so I was confused that perhaps I had the wrong numbers for the verses. I checked other bibles and saw the deception; I was furious that they had changed the words in the verses I planned to use to prove a point. This type of thing happened more than once while I wrote this book. They are actually changing the bibles faster than I can write about the verses of the bibles. I read a verse, I write about it, then I go back to check making sure I didn't misquote it, to discover that the verses changed before I could publish my refutation. So, I decided to expose them and demonstrate how the bibles differ. The following are all Psalm 146:3 from some English bibles:

### Psalms 146:3 New International Version
*Do not put your trust in princes, in human beings, who cannot save.*

### Psalms 146:3 New Living Translation
*Don't put your confidence in powerful people; there is no help for you there.*

### Psalms 146:3 English Standard Version
*Put not your trust in princes, in a son of man, in whom there is no salvation.*

### Psalms 146:3 New American Standard Bible
*Do not trust in princes, In mortal man, in whom there is no salvation.*

### Psalms 146:3 King James Bible
*Put not your trust in princes, nor in the son of man, in whom there is no help.*

### Psalms 146:3 Holman Christian Standard Bible
*Do not trust in nobles, in man, who cannot save.*

### Psalms 146:3 International Standard Version
*Do not look to nobles, nor to mere human beings who cannot save.*

### Psalms 146:3 NET Bible
*Do not trust in princes, or in human beings, who cannot deliver!*

### Psalms 146:3 Aramaic Bible in Plain English
*Do not trust a prince or upon a son of man, for there is no salvation in his hand.*

### Psalms 146:3 GOD'S WORD Translation
*Do not trust influential people, mortals who cannot help you.*

### Psalms 146:3 Jubilee Bible 2000
*Put not your trust in princes, nor in the son of man in whom there is no salvation.*

Another bible verse often mistranslated is Job 38:7 when it conflicts with publishers' beliefs about Jesus being the only "*son of God*".

### Job 38:7 New International Version
*while the morning stars sang together and <u>all the angels</u> shouted for joy?*

### Job 38:7 English Standard Version
*when the morning stars sang together and <u>all the sons of God</u> shouted for joy?*

<u>Job 38:7 King James Bible</u>
*When the morning stars sang together, and <u>all the sons of God</u> shouted for joy?*

<u>Job 38:7 International Standard Version</u>
*while the morning stars sang together and <u>all the divine beings</u> shouted joyfully?*

These brief examples show just how different the bibles are from each other in words and meaning. Yet some still will maintain that there is only 1 bible. You have seen with your own eyes that the different bibles say different things in the same exact place. How then can they all be the "Word of God" when they all have different words for the same verses? Even the gospels within the same bibles say completely different things than other gospels just a couple pages away. Thus, there are some people with different bibles who believe very different things about Jesus yet they incorrectly think that both of them are considered "believers in Jesus", or "believers in God". While they may consider themselves to be "believers in Jesus" their idea of Jesus is specific to their version of the bible, with some overlapping beliefs between the different versions. At the time of this writing there are over 450 different English translations of the bible, and each one promotes a different version of Jesus; and that's just with English bibles. Technically speaking all bible readers can say they "believe in Jesus", but realistically there is only 1 Jesus, therefore only one type of belief about him can be correct. There is a huge difference between believing in Jesus according to what your bible says about him and in having the correct belief about Jesus that remains accurate to who he was and what he taught. Because if your bible is the truth then that means all the other bibles are false because they say different things than yours and if you are going to make such a bold statement then rock-solid proof is required to substantiate such a claim. Whereas because one bible being true means all the rest are false some even destroy all other bibles just because they aren't the one they personally choose. With my own eyes I have even witnessed Christians burning 2 different bibles which were different than the ones they read and get told to believe in. Yet not only do the bibles say different things they don't even have the same verses! I've found this out the hard way when I tried to use a "smoking gun" verse in a talk with a Christian to show how the bible has crazy advice that they don't believe should be followed, they opened their bible up and told me *"Oh well it turns out those verses aren't in my bible, you see the publishers took it out because it wasn't authentic but were added at a later time."* At first, I was slightly embarrassed because I had taken a risk assuming the verses would be in their bible and I was wrong, but then I said something like: *"Well that's good it's not in there because it shouldn't be, but that's the whole problem. Every bible has and says different stuff. There is no such thing as "THE BIBLE", they're all different. So, since you admit stuff has been taken out of your bible that wasn't true, and that the other bibles which still have these verses in them contain false information that isn't the word of God or inspired by God, then how much stuff is still left in your bible that's false which they didn't take out yet? The problem is the bible publishers stopped short before all the false and unverifiable information was removed, because if they didn't, they were afraid they wouldn't have anything left in the bible to publish at all."* What each Christian denomination does when they don't believe in doctrines which other Christians believe in is they print their bible without the verses that support those doctrines and say those verses aren't found in the "ancient manuscripts". Which is actually correct, because those verses aren't in the ancient scraps but the problem is that if there are verses that do support their doctrines, they leave those verses in their bible and say they are found in the "ancient manuscripts" but when they say "ancient manuscripts" referring to the verses they kept their definition is not "most ancient" and it's not the same as when they said "ancient" referring to the verses they didn't include. It's a complete double standard where if they disagree, they'll take it out of their bible saying it's not old enough to be authentic but if they agree with it, they keep it in and change their definition of old so that way they can say it's authentic. All bible publishers I know of do this, every single one of them. It's actually the only way a bible can be made because the originals which would be the "oldest most ancient manuscripts" don't exist. Yet they all say "Everyone else does that but not us, we're different." Whereas the only reason they're "different" is because they have different beliefs because their bibles have different words in them, their methodologies are exactly the same and they are just as unreliable as those they criticize. However, they will swear they are trustworthy and all this stuff is true but it just doesn't apply to them. Why is that, why them? They actually do have an answer to this. Do you know what it is? Can you guess why they say we can trust them and their special bible but not the other Christians and their corrupted bibles? It's all because of the "Holy Spirit". Seriously that's what they'll say, if they're advanced, if not then they'll have to ask another Christian how to respond and get rid of the nagging feeling they've been bamboozled by their bible. Since those who will say this actually believe it, you have to be serious with them. So, ask them where did they learn about this "Holy Spirit", that lets them know they can trust their bible? What source of information told them this "Holy Spirit" even existed? The bible. I say "the bible" because all bibles say this, even the ones the Christians themselves will say are corrupted books. Thus, it is a continuous cycle of Christians saying: *"The Holy Spirit says our bible is right. And we can trust the Holy Spirit is right because our bible says so."* But how do we know the bible is trustworthy when it tells us to trust in a Holy Spirit who tells us to trust the bible? Because of the Holy Spirit. But who ever said the Holy Spirit was right to begin with? The bible. And thus, it goes on and on in circular crazy logic ad infinitum until eventually someone exposes the truth that their bible is not trustworthy and got changed with things being added and deleted. Then to do damage repair Christians rapidly make their own new bible edition or blame it on mistranslations. However, the problem is not just the transmission and translations, the problem is the biblical source materials themselves. Scholastically the bible can't even be used to teach a religion, unless one were to say it was a modern religion created many centuries after Jesus. Yet since most Christians are too emotionally attached and mentally fragile to contemplate their beloved bible may not be divine revelation or "inspired" then I tend to use the bible to show how the bible teaches Christianity is false and that it actually teaches multiple contradictory religions. If one believes in a bible, they must believe in multiple religions which contradict each other in which belief in one means disbelief in the others. Usually, this status quo is achieved by Christians simply not reading the bible or by having some external non-biblical source for interpreting the bible according to their whims and desires. Ex. Catholics interpret the bible according to the Pope, Jehovah's Witnesses according to the WatchTower, Mormons according to whoever they believe their current prophet is. With all Christians changing their doctrines and beliefs throughout time going against their self-made bible and then claiming the Holy Spirit guides them to change their beliefs and practices, and that it's only them who is truly guided by the Holy Spirit even though everyone claims to be guided by it. And how do they know it's only them who is guided by the Holy Spirit and they aren't one of the many who incorrectly thinks they are guided? Because the bible says so and they think it's talking about them because they read it casually and get told by their peers that they are the "true believers" following Jesus; and they just "feel right" you know? Although they rarely will say they "just feel right" but usually claim they "know they are right" and even though all Christians say they know, they know that those other Christians just feel it and don't really know even though they say they do. And why is that? Because their religious leaders and peers told them so. Or if they are advanced, they can quote a couple of bible verses proving those Christians don't follow the bible and haven't eliminated the same false verses which their bible publishers did. Yet they get upset when I do the same thing to them with their own special bible edition. But it can be useful because when I interact with advanced Christians frequently they will bring verses to my attention which disprove other Christians and then the other Christians show me the verses that disprove those who proved them to be wrong. Sometimes the Christians will even show me a bible verse and it proves them wrong but they didn't know it and then they get really mad that you are using the verses they quote against you as weapons against them. Yet sadly most Christians simply cannot accept that they are wrong according to their bible because they practically have a Santa Claus Bible in that it says what they believe it says, even though they didn't read it, and it means what they believe it means, and it was written when they believe it was written and by those they believe it to be written by and they believe it was translated by those they believe it was translated by, and they believe it's correct because they believe it's correct. Sometimes you just have to tell them that it seems to you that they got one of those special "Santa Claus Bibles". Be serious too, tell them some types of bibles going around are "Santa Claus

Bibles" which have been mislabeled and you are worried they might have a copy of such a Santa Claus Bible and don't even know it. Although they might think of it more as a "Holy Spirit Bible", because for Christians the "Holy Spirit" is like a spiritual Santa Claus prophet type of ghost/2nd consciousness/their own thoughts/their excuse for anything good they think they do, which guarantees they are right because they have faith in their false faith. They'll admit they've never seen this "Holy Spirit" which allegedly inspires and motivates them but then they claim it's not blind faith. Technically it's more of "a feeling" faith. Christians think this "Holy Spirit" is a substitute for an isnad and can just make translations possible without any loss of meaning. How does that work? Well because the bibles got translated then it must work because the Holy Spirit guarantees their bible is right, so if it happened then it must be possible because they think it's impossible, they and so many others could be so very wrong. Why is that? Because of the bible which says the Holy Spirit says so and they have personally experienced it. I've experienced this "Holy Spirit" too as a Christian, his other more popular name is Satan. Fundamentally the Christian religions' "Holy Spirit" is their doctrinal Santa Claus and they think Jesus is their physical Santa Claus who is going to give them gifts when he comes back to earth or take them to paradise on his cross if/when they die. Although it might not a good idea to tell them they think Jesus is like Santa Claus. Instead, when a Christian tries to claim they have the Holy Spirit in them or guiding them or their organization or that it inspired the authors of the bible just ask them to prove it. Ask them to prove to you that they have a Holy Spirit in them or that a Holy Spirit is guiding their leaders or inspired their books in any way. They truly have absolutely no proof for their claim and tell them you think so. Then they may try to use the bible, that's the only card they can play. So, then you can say all

Christians have bibles and they all use their bibles to say they got the Holy Spirit's favor and such. Now their religious doctrines teach that only their specific sect is truly guided by the Holy Spirit and all the rest are wrong and lying when they say the Holy Spirit is on their side. So, ask them to prove that they personally have the Holy Spirit in them or guiding them in a scientific manner or if they can't do it scientifically because Christianity is anti-Science then ask them at the very least to prove to you, they have it AND all the other Christians don't. If they are one of those types who have a bible with Mark 16:18 in it (not all bibles do) then you can tell them to prove they are a believer by picking up deadly snakes without getting harmed and drinking poison as those bible verses says is one sign of proof. Typically, only snake handlers will dare to try this and some Christians don't have these verses in their bible. Yet even if you are talking to snake handling Christians and they try and survive then tell them to drink the poison in front of you for 40 days in a row, since biblically Jesus had the Spirit in him for 40 days you want to see if they have the Spirit for at least 40 days. If for some reason they do this and survive then you can use other things to prove they don't have the Holy Spirit in them as they claim, but I don't think any would try nor survive this 40-day challenge. Now if their bible doesn't have Mark 16:18 in it because it's not in older bible editions and is not authentic then you can still use this against such Christians. When they tell you it's not in there for the reasons I said you can ask them 1. *"How do you know it's not in the ancient manuscripts? Did you read these manuscripts yourself and see these verses weren't there or do you just have blind faith and believe the footnotes and commentary you read in your bible or hear from your leaders?"* 2. *"Did the Holy Spirit tell you or your leaders that these bible verses weren't authentic? Or was it human archaeologists who have a different religion than you and don't have a Holy Spirit in them or guiding them? If people had the Holy*

*Spirit in them or guiding them then how come for centuries people believed these verses were divine revelation and said they were inspired by the Holy Spirit to say they were just as you are saying about other bible verses today? Why didn't the Holy Spirit make the truth of the biblical falsehood known sooner? Why do you accept the Archaeologist's data when they say these verses are not authentic but reject Archaeologist's data when they say most of the other verses in the bible are not authentic either?"* Then sincerely ask them for their advice on how you can prove to those deviant Christians who belong to other sects, which you and they both agree are disbelievers, that they don't really have a Holy Spirit in them or guiding them even though they'll claim they do and will quote their bibles to say they do.  Finally ask them *"How can I convince a heretical Christian who is brainwashed that they are brainwashed and both their bible and religion is false leading them to hell?"* I guarantee if you applied the same fundamental criteria they give, if they give any (even if they say by using the bible), that they will also fail their own criteria for determining whether a Christian is upon falsehood or not.  The trouble is being patient and kind while struggling to prove to them they are upon falsehood even according to their own faith which is also false according to their own faith's criteria of truth.  None of them ever take a scholarly approach to religion or religious texts, especially their own.

      To put it in perspective the people who publish bibles today are merely making their own book with their own spin based off of the bibles written in the past, which also had their own spin based on bibles written earlier than that which had their own spin, which were based on writings by people unknown who lied about their names and wrote in a language not spoken by the characters depicted in the stories that are written.  Basically, the bibles are books that evolve over time as people change them to suit their changing belief systems, but everybody pretends that their bible is original and everyone else's is evolutionary. The advanced one's will prove the other bibles are corrupted but they don't apply the same methodology to their own bibles. Unfortunately, the consumers of these bibles don't know how their bibles came to be translated and published but just believe the false advertisement in the appendix, preface or commentary. To this day I've yet to meet one person who can provide solid evidence saying why their bible is the truth to the exclusion of all others. At best they will tell me, "It's more true than the others", which is the same exact thing as saying that, "it's less false than the others". Less false is still false and the divine revelation of God does not contain an iota of falsehood. This means that unfortunately billions of people who think they "believe in Jesus" or "believe in God" don't have an accurate belief that is correct and will be considered disbelievers in the actual Jesus and God, or slanderers of Jesus and God if they publicly or privately share their incorrect beliefs. Technically and linguistically, they do "believe in Jesus" and God, but they believe lies and in a Jesus that did not exist and a false version of God. Mainly because of their bible, of which no prophet of God ever said they had to believe in, but because their religious leaders say to believe in it they do and in doing so turn their modern leaders into prophets and by extension God without knowing it. This is because the bible prohibits things God didn't and allows things which God forbid, thus to follow the bible is to take humans as their God and the worst part is that they don't even know who really wrote those biblical books. It would be difficult for them to recognize the real Jesus because he doesn't match what they believe him to be. With all this confusion about who Jesus was and what we are required to believe about him, we need another prophet to clarify who the prophet Jesus was. Seriously, it's such a mess that we need a prophet of God with divine revelation to let us know just who the prophet Jesus really was because there is so much confusion. It's sad but true.

Do we have enough proof to say who "*the Prophet*" is? Muhammad claimed to be "*the Prophet*" so his claim must be taken seriously and not easily dismissed. Much research has been done with the Hebrew and Greek biblical texts and many have made cases that Muhammad is mentioned in the bible as the final prophet and written books on that subject. However, I leave that for the reader to research themselves. Personally, I don't like using the bible to prove Muhammad's prophethood because he never did, he came with the Quran and other miracles to prove his prophethood and the bible today is not the same as those that existed in his time. In his time the Jews and Christians like Abdullah ibn Salam, Sa'd ibn Muad, Salman Farsi, Adi ibn Hatim and others who did convert to Islam said Muhammad was mentioned in their bibles. However in between that time and ours those bibles got changed by those who didn't like what they said. The fundamental point of this book is that 1. The bible is not 100% revelation. 2. Christians don't follow the bible. 3. The bibles are impossible to follow even if one tried. With the 4th minor point being that another post-Jesus prophet is required to lead mankind according to the bible. I'm sorry if it's a cliffhanger ending that I don't mention who "the Prophet" is according to the bible but I don't think the bibles today says who it is definitively and even if they did then they would change the bibles soon afterwards in the future so that they didn't. Personally, I believe it's Muhammad  but I got that belief from the Quran not the bible, even though I read the Quran because I learned those 3 points about the bible. The point is that if you want to follow "the Prophet" for our time you are going to have to read another book or maybe more than one. Be certain "that book" is NOT the bible or any of the biblical books. I believe that prophet will come with a new book since the bible is flawed and needs to be abrogated.

It might seem hypocritical to have declared that the bibles are not divine revelation yet demonstrate how the bibles anticipate the prophethood of Muhammad. Let me clarify that I do not believe the bibles are 100% true in everything that is written in them; neither do I believe they are 100% false. My belief in Islam and Muhammad is not based on what the bibles say. However, there are some people who base their beliefs on the bibles believing them to be true 100%. Despite Jesus never asking people to worship him, or claiming to be God, or the son of God inside or outside of the bibles, there are some who believe such things about Jesus and justify this anti-Jesus blasphemous belief with the retort *"because the bible says so"*. In reality much of what some Christians believe is not in the bibles, such as the doctrine of original sin, the trinity, confession, purgatory, the "Holy Spirit", and the list goes on. In actuality these doctrines are contrary to what biblical verses teach, so such beliefs are anti-bible. Many think they believe something *"because the bible says so"*, but it's actually *"because the priest or preacher says so"* and they think the Christian religious leaders are using the bible, or divine sources to get their information. Many who identify themselves as Christians practice Churchianity rather than Christianity. In the bibles nowhere does Jesus claim to be more than human, other humans claimed he was and he rebuked them publicly. There is never any direct quote from Jesus making such a claim of divine relationship in all recorded history, only flimsy misinterpretations. The only things that even come close are alleged visions that cannot be substantiated. Regardless if you read only what Jesus is alleged to have said in the modern bibles you would see that he did not teach anything resembling what we today know as Christianity. On top of that 90% of the information in the New Testament is not even alleged to have been said by Jesus. Whereas even with the stuff that is alleged to have been said by Jesus in the bible, there is absolutely no way to prove that he actually said any of what the bible attributes to him, in fact there is a 100% certainty that he didn't say any of it because he spoke Aramaic and Hebrew whereas no text from the bibles New Testament originates from anything said in that language. So, while a meaning could potentially be accurate, literally there is not one bible in the world which has recorded an actual statement of Jesus unless it was put in there by accidental probability. Aramaic and Hebrew forms of the New Testament didn't even exist until very recently when Christians began to translate bibles into those languages attempting to deceive other Christians into thinking they were the original texts, with some even forging hoax manuscripts pretending they "found" such alleged Aramaic texts that preceded the Greek texts which they don't have. Yet these so-called Aramaic manuscripts have been exposed as being translated into Aramaic from the distorted Greek copies of copies of copies of copies. What happened was that when Christians found out that the first Greek manuscripts of the gospels (which no longer exist) were translations and the alleged gospel authors couldn't have written them, then Christian enthusiasts translated what they had into Aramaic artificially aging the texts to make them seem ancient. Later they "found" these texts in staged archaeological digs, like those staged during the Crusades which "found" many "relics", in order to claim they're the original Aramaic text but they aren't and have been exposed as forgeries according to the majority of Christian Biblical Scholars. Thus, many Christians returned to the Greek and now try to say how all the Jews spoke Greek and the Greek originals (which don't exist) aren't translations at all and that their modern era translations are based on the originals. Yet historically very few Jews in 1st century Palestine spoke Greek, the Jewish historian Josephus even wrote in 37 CE that he only knew of 1 or 2 Jews who were fluent in Greek. Jews viewed Greek as the language of their Gentile enemy occupiers and even the Greek texts themselves confirm that they are translations. Jews tended to treat those who learned Greek as traitors collaborating with their Hellenistic oppressors and some rabbis even forbid Jews from learning Greek. Many Jews believed it was sinful to even learn Greek. So, for the followers of Jesus to come out with Greek books is one of the most unrealistic notions because it would mean those whom Jesus preached to would not be the target audience but the pagans would be. The texts in Greek were written in Greek to be read by Greeks and not the Jews to whom Jesus preached. What better way to corrupt the religion of Jesus than by teaching a religion in the name of Jesus to the enemies of Jesus in a language which the followers of Jesus didn't know and couldn't speak or write? And who best to use than a Jewish enemy of Jesus named Saul to make the Greeks think the Jewish followers were upon the same things they were being taught? Whereas to cover his tracks Saul even changes his name to Paul so if the Jewish followers heard that a Paul was preaching about Jesus they wouldn't know and warn the Greeks that it was their archnemesis intentionally corrupting the faith lying to the Greeks. The problem today is twofold in that most Christians don't read the Greek texts but just believe in their own translations in their native languages thinking they came from the original Greek texts, not knowing those originals were translations and their modern translations aren't translated from those originals. When Christian Biblical Scholars publicly state there are absolutely no original Aramaic gospels or Greek translations, that's not something they are saying for fun because it damages their faith and makes them seem stupid for being

Christian when they know such things. So, there is no incentive at all for them to lie and say they don't have anything if they do. Yet because there is significant incentive for Christian ministers and Bible publishers to lie and tell people that their bibles are reliable, they preach such lies and put such fiction in the bible commentaries and then Christians believe it because it's what they want to believe. Then those with Crusader mentalities will say the Christian Biblical Scholars must not have read the bible because the bible commentaries clearly say it's reliable, so all those Biblical Scholars must be fake Christians trying to discredit Christianity and the bible from the inside and they're all paid off by Satan. Some may not express this notion verbally yet still believe it. For instance, sometimes I tell Christians this and in response they open up their bible and start quoting the appendix or what the Bible Publisher wrote, and I actually have to tell them that what they are reading isn't part of the biblical text but a commentary written by the publisher/book seller and it's not the word of God even if you think the bible is. So, there is a gulf between Biblical Scholars and Christian laity who place their trust in ministers, publishers and popular personalities instead of the Biblical experts who refute their religious misconceptions. Once a Christian of a certain denomination even suggested that I read the appendix of their latest edition of the bible online telling me that it explains why I can trust that their edition is reliable to the exclusion of all the rest. I reluctantly went on to their own website that they told me to visit and read it as they said to, bracing myself for a swath of lies, yet to my surprise in between the lies even their own bible's appendix said: "*The Greek manuscripts we possess today are not the originals. Of the thousands of copies in existence today, most were made at least two centuries after the originals were composed.*" While in another section of their appendix their bible said: "*no original Bible manuscript of the Hebrew and Aramaic*

<u>*Scriptures or of the Christian Greek Scriptures has survived to this day.*</u>"
I even took pictures to show them that their own bible on their own bible publisher's website says that their bibles are not based on original source documents and that the original documents and the copies of them do not exist. Keep in mind this means both the Old and New Testament originals do not exist, the Hebrew and Aramaic refers to the Old while the Greek refers to the New. Since the bibles themselves say they are based on documents copied many times over that were translated many times over with the oldest manuscript being hundreds of years older than the originals which don't exist then why don't Christians believe this when it's in their own bibles? Sadly, they are brainwashed and they brainwash each other so they don't grasp the significance of what they learn when it contradicts their beliefs. Blind faith can't be shaken by proof if the person chooses to keep their eyes, ears, mind and heart closed to any possibility they could be wrong and that to be right or good they may have to drastically change themselves. Satanic forces, a corrupted heart and lack of sincerity all play a role. Also, there are many lies and unauthentic mistranslated verses taken out of context which are provided to them so as to keep them in error. Yet regarding the "blind faith" just look at the following chart of all the "*thousands of Greek New Testament manuscripts*".

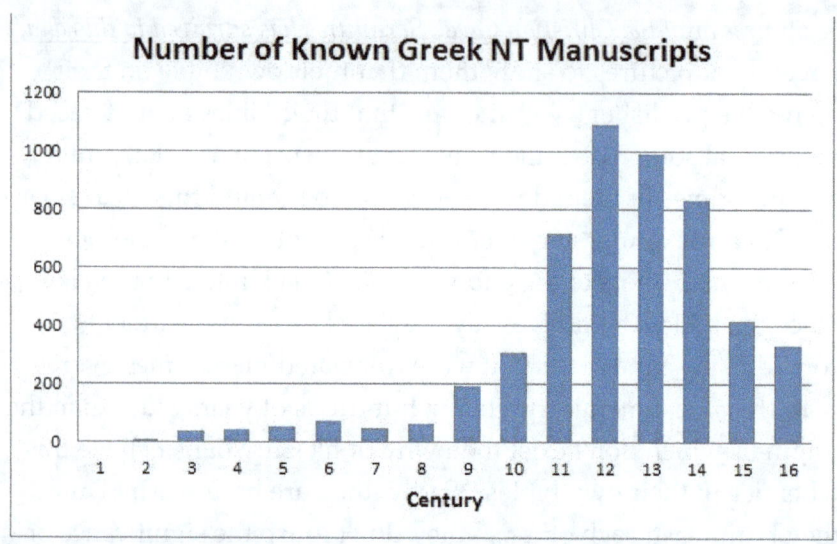

The case Christians always make is that because there are thousands of Greek manuscripts then surely you can't have thousands if they were all false. Whereas first of all having a lot of texts doesn't mean anything, we have thousands of old Buddhist and Hindu texts too but that doesn't mean they are true just because there are so many. Secondly these thousands contradict each other. However most importantly these "thousands" didn't exist until recently. They are only "old" to us because we are thousands of years after the time of Jesus. As the chart shows the thousand marks wasn't even reached until hundreds of years after Muhammad came in the 6th century. Then they multiplied in the 11th to 15th century, do you know why that is? The Crusaders were in the holy land during that time and used their presence as an excuse to write new manuscripts. They actually did write them too and didn't "find them" because this chart is based on the carbon dating of the manuscripts and the date such documents were written, it's not based on when they were "found". After the 15th century the printing press came about so Christians figured they could just print their new material into the bibles and it would get accepted as Scripture and it was. Today Christians see the post 15th century stuff was added and are taking it out, if it goes against their own doctrines or is too embarrassing or contradictory for them to keep included. Yet perhaps the most important aspect of this chart is the 1st century. Not a single Greek manuscript has been found that was written in the 1st century. Also, these manuscripts are not really manuscripts at all but they are scraps as I explained before. <u>The first century is between the years 0 CE and 100 CE.</u> Whereas Jesus is thought to have went to heaven around 30 CE. <u>We have nothing that was written from the first century, and nothing in the bible comes from stuff written during that time. This includes Paul's letters.</u> Of course, Christians will claim the originals were written during the first century but they have zero proof for this claim. Nothing, there is not one scrap of evidence to prove that anything in the New Testament today was written by anybody until after 100 CE. They'll say what they say but academically one is not allowed to say that stuff. Such a belief has zero proof. It is a purely religious belief without a shred of evidence to support it. Where there Christians during that time? Yes. What did they believe? We don't know because no writings from that time exist. Or rather some writings do exist, but those "Christian" writings are not included in the New Testament because they were considered heretical by the Catholic Church during the 4th century CE. To put that in perspective it'd be like Americans in about 225 years from now saying the U.S. Constitution first drafted in the 1780s is not really American and is a not an authentic document because it doesn't agree with what they believe about America or American laws. Anyone would say such future Americans don't have a valid opinion to say such a document isn't really American just because they believe differently. If they want to believe differently then that's that, but they can't just say that earlier

Americans didn't write what they wrote or believe what they believed because future Americans believe differently. Yet that's what 4th century Christians said and the Roman Empire sided with the Church and the Church killed those who said the Church was wrong and burned their books and fooled the world so thoroughly that even after many found out the Church was corrupted and false they still take their book and use it thinking it's reliable or true. The Catholic Church wrote the bible AFTER it became corrupt and upon falsehood, not before. Christianity was corrupted before the New Testament was made. It's sad and bad but that's the facts. Fortunately, God sent a new prophet but sadly many don't want to accept that Christianity could've been so thoroughly corrupted and instead think the religion was corrupted but the book remained perfect. Yet logically since literacy rates were so low for so long, the easy part would be to change the book the hard part is corrupting the religion. If the Catholic Church so thoroughly corrupted the religion, as they did, then they aren't going to keep the book the same. Yet people will say "the word of God never changes". Well, the bibles have and still do change. Even the Jews change the Taurat and the Zabur so don't think the Christians can't, especially when I've just thoroughly proven that they have. Afterall Catholics today still use the bible because it can be used to teach Catholicism as well as any other religion in the world. So, Christians thinking the bible is a test for truth are fools because Catholics use their bible to support themselves as does every Christian of every doctrine. The bible practically supports every religion if you want to make it support it. I could actually use the bible to support Hinduism or Atheism if I wanted to because it's such a pliable book that can be used to say whatever one wants. Yet in reality it doesn't support any religion aside from disbelief and polytheism because it teaches many contradictory religions. In my opinion the bibles are the worst books available on earth today, the only books that may be worse are the books of deeds which humans are having written for them by their angels who record all their deeds good and bad, big and small, private and public. Now is it possible that pieces of the New Testament were written in the first century? Yes. It's also possible that dragons existed too, haven't you seen what old maps look like? However, nobody can say, "*Dragons existed in the first century because we all have these old maps from later centuries that have dragons on them and people who read those maps when they were made believed such dragons existed in the first century. So therefore, we know dragons existed in the first century AND they were exactly what we today believe they were like.*" Everyone knows such a doctrine is false insanity that cannot be promoted even if there is a tiny highly improbable possibility it could be true. Yet just replace the word Dragons with Gospels/Epistles and maps with "manuscripts" and it's the exact Christian belief they have about the Gospels and Epistles. But did I just say there is a tiny possibility "it could be true". What is "it"? It in that context means the possibility that a gospel could have existed in the first century that is the same as a gospel today. Was it written by God? No. Was it written by Jesus? No. Was it read by Jesus? No. Was it in a language the followers of Jesus knew? No. So even if such a thing did exist and then 27 of those things did ever exist, which all 27 didn't for a fact since some New Testament books are known and proven not to have existed, then this only can apply to some gospels and some letters possibly; but none of them are the Injeel given to Jesus and none of them were approved by any prophet of God. Yet today we don't have them and don't know if they existed. Thus, we must move on. First of all, it's a nearly impossible if and the if is irrelevant to having divine revelation. Were the "if" of an existent biblical book to be true it still isn't the word of God anyways so what's the point of it? The main problem is that people confuse "following the bible" with following Jesus and equate belief in one to be belief in the other when neither have anything to do with each other despite the fact one is mentioned in the other.  The modern newspapers are as close to Jesus as the biblical documents are.  It all comes down to sincerity, if someone truly wants to worship God they will be guided away from falsehood into truth, if not then they'll use the excuses Satan gives them to justify disbelief.  Every new edition of the bibles that get printed is a public testimony that all previous versions had errors and flaws.  At what point will they stop and say: *"we finally got rid of all the mistakes, this is the last version ever"*? Why trust them this time to produce something authentic when every other bible printed has always been revised because of defects?  They tell us yesterday's bibles are unreliable because a new bible edition came out today, well tomorrow when the next edition is printed then they'll admit today's bible is unreliable too. It's a lucrative sales pitch.  Sadly, Christian bible consumers can't see the marketing cycle and think their version is sacred or reliable even though it's been thousands of years and they still haven't stopped changing the bibles in word and meaning.  Any company who did this with instruction manuals would be emphatically shut down and punished for constantly lying to the public and repeatedly selling a defective dangerous product.

      In summary the New Testament consists of what other people who never met Jesus said about him long after he left earth.  It doesn't contain the actual teachings of Jesus.  Instead, it contains teachings about what Greek-speaking Christians, some who were likely former pagan Gentiles, thought and believed Jesus did and taught.  The New Testament includes accounts written by people in names other than their own giving their opinions about Jesus and what they allege he taught even though none of them were eyewitnesses, despite some of the authors claiming to have been (that's why some books are forgeries). Jesus could have taught some of what the bibles say but there is no chain to link Jesus to anything in the bibles. We would need a prophet or a new revelation from God to tell us what Jesus actually said word for word. The accounts of the New Testament contradict history, contradict accounts of other gospels that were excluded from the New Testament, contradict the other gospels found in the bibles, contradict the Old Testament and the famous gospels of the New Testament even contradict themselves. On top of that both the Old and New Testaments in the bibles contradict Christian beliefs, attitudes, behaviors and morals and even basic math. Whilst the Christian's personal beliefs even contradict what Christianity teaches them to believe. The bibles are the most contradictory books I have ever read! How can such books possibly be considered divine revelation? Because people don't read the bibles, they don't read critically and if they do read critically, it is only to confirm what they already believe, not so that they can learn what the different bibles actually teach. Christians have never in all of history followed any edition of any bible because the Christian faith does not originate from biblical teachings. The Christian faith existed long before the biblical texts were conceived, translated, written, mistranslated, re-written, mistranslated and rewritten again and again continuing to change up until the present day. The bibles and the verses within them were written with the express reason to bolster Christianity. Christians are told and believe that their religion is based on the bibles, but in reality all the past and present bibles were based off Christianity. This is why Christians don't need the bible to be a Christian. The bibles were originally written to reinforce one's Christianity, yet ironically today the bibles are destroying Christianity. That is the backlash of lies. The later lies which get told to support earlier lies end up eventually destroying those earlier lies they were intended to support. Just as a spider web is weak because the various ends are held up only by pulling the web in opposite directions, it can only last a limited amount of time before crumbling on its own; sticky though it may be to trap things in. Once the fresh breath of truth comes the web of lies are blown away. The truth has come and falsehood has perished, but even if the truth hadn't come the falsehood would have perished due to its conflicting nature anyways, just as a spider web decomposes. Thus, Christianity must always rebrand and modernize in order to survive just as a spider must always spin a new web. Except their web is a sticky ticket to hell. Just as the spiders web it looks harmless and incapable of trapping anything, creature after creature falls into it. Whereas Christians will never stop making new bible editions because if they ever do then the game will be over and everyone can expose their final edition as false, whereas then what would they do? That's actually why they keep making new editions because people keep exposing their bibles as false and Christianity Inc. loses customers. While since the religion changes, they always will stress that Christians "go back to the bible" but in reality they mean "go follow the new bible", and you can verify this by asking any Christian if you can use an old bible printed 1,000 years ago and they will say no; or at least they should if they are smarter than average. Yet since Christians can't follow their own bibles even when they make them then they say "go back to the teachings of Jesus " and that basically means "*do what you feel like as long as you feel Jesus loves you and would approve*". Or Christians get a new idol in the form of an organization or "saint" or "inspired preacher" or special bible interpreters. So, one sorrow I have for this book is that since Christians are always changing doctrines in a few hundred years some of the stuff I say may no longer be useable or considered to be Christian or biblical teachings. Yet the more they change the harder it will be for them to hide the changes as long as people continue to observe and expose them until the Almighty ends it. Whereas the trap of Satan is that he gets many to use man-made tools against the falsehood instead of the weapons God gives us. While the best way to destroy falsehood is with the weapons God has provided us with and instructed the believers to use. I've just used the Christian weapons against Christianity because I used to be Christian and have more experience with their weapons than I do with using the weapons God has provided. Although when using God's weapons it must be done how God desires, for God's sake, according to how the prophets taught us.

      According to the modern and ancient bibles, Jesus is not God, or a literal "son of God". The trouble is that people don't base their beliefs on the bible they claim to believe in, but they base their beliefs on what people say the bible means and only use select bible passages to support their preconceived beliefs, ignoring how the bible itself came to be while neglecting to follow any of the laws the bibles say must be followed in daily life. The vast majority of Christians don't even pray bowing down with their face on the ground the way the bibles say every prophet including Jesus prayed, yet they claim to follow the teachings of Jesus just the same. Plus they will consume usury and eat pig and many other infractions which biblical Jesus himself prohibited. Paul is really the one Christians follow. Most Christians will take the words of biblical Jesus and interpret them within the context of Paul's doctrine, but none take the words of Paul and interpret them according to the words of Jesus because Paul's teachings conflict with the religion Jesus taught. If one reads a bible properly and lets it speak for itself one will realize that even with all the contradictions, which disqualify it from being 100% divine revelation, on the whole the bible teaches that Jesus is not God, there is no trinity, God doesn't have children in any literal sense and that there is another prophet coming after Jesus. Even with all the new versions, editions and translations there still isn't one verse to support most of what Christians believe. Bible publishers are literally writing their own book and they still don't have any verses in them to support Christian doctrines. This is because Christian doctrines don't need and never had support from the bible. Christianity is spread through emotionalism, media, tradition, social pressure, "visions", dreams, violence, brainwashing and apologetics. Even the word used to describe justifying Christianity, apologetics, comes from the word apology which means to acknowledge regret and sorrow for doing something wrong. Sadly, some evangelists actually know that Christianity is corrupted and false.

If someone doesn't believe in the bibles 100% then they cannot believe the parts about Jesus being divine or related to God, because those are the weakest parts of the bibles and should be the first parts a person would doubt because they are so foreign to the rest of the book. If the bibles aren't 100% divine revelation and have been corrupted then a new prophet must be sent. Muhammad claimed he was that prophet and has strong supporting evidence backing up that claim. On the other hand, someone who does believe in a bible 100% must believe in "*the Prophet*" who will come after Jesus and the bibles make a strong case for Muhammad being "*the Prophet*". Whether you believe in the bibles, a bible, or not, another prophet is necessary. There is no other person after Jesus who has made as significant of a religious impact on earth as Muhammad. Muhammad also claimed to be the last prophet so circumstances alone indicate that his religion must at the least be very special without even looking into it. However, only a fool blindly follows and God created us with many faculties so we should look into things before we subscribe to them. The blind follower doesn't see where they are going or whether what they are doing is right or wrong. How are you going to avoid the many slippery slopes to hell if you blindly follow? Without a doubt Muhammad and the religion of Islam definitely deserve serious research because the process of elimination already indicates its potential to be a true religion taught by a true prophet. The Deuteronomy 18:19 prophesy says God said, "*[19] I myself will call to account anyone who does not listen to my words that the prophet speaks in my name.*" Thus, if Muhammad is "*the Prophet*" anyone who doesn't listen to the words of God relayed by "*the Prophet*" Muhammad will be held accountable for ignoring his message and/or not accepting it. If the mail carrier comes to the door with a book for you and asks you to sign for it thereby testifying that he delivered it and you refuse because you don't like the mail carrier, then what does that mean? That means by refusing the messenger (mail carrier) and rejecting him, you are also rejecting the message (book) they have been sent to you with. By rejecting the message that was sent to you it means you have rejected the one who sent the book to you through the messenger. Since Muhammad has been sent to mankind and jinnkind with the book of Allah (aka God aka the Creator of all) and has been appointed to explain and teach it to us, if you are going to close the door in his face and refuse to testify that he is a valid messenger of God, then this means you are rejecting the book of God, the religion of God and God. To reject a messenger of God is to reject the messenger sender, God. That's why it is so dangerous to reject Islam without studying it. If Islam is true and you reject it just like that, or at all, then what do you think God is going to do to you after you have enjoyed all the things God has given you throughout your life? Do you think God will give you more pleasure in the next life for eternity after you slammed the door in his face when he sent you a messenger? God takes it personal when his friends are rejected or attacked and is the enemy of the enemy of his friends. You do not want God as an enemy. So, you better make sure you know God's friends and don't pick and choose a few to follow and reject others because rejecting any one of them implies that God chose bad friends or messengers. When you insult God then friendship and reward is not to be anticipated, rather torture and punishment should be expected and dreaded. Muhammad spoke words in the name of God perfectly fulfilling the prophesy in Deuteronomy. Therefore, if he is not the prophet and we fail to research his message then we will be held accountable for not researching one who claimed to be "*the Prophet*". Which would mean that we didn't care about "*the Prophet*" and wouldn't have accepted "*the Prophet*" no matter who it was, whether he came in our time, or after our time, because we would have proven ourselves negligent. The fact that other than Muhammad there is no alternative candidate who fulfills the criteria of "*the prophet*" means either Muhammad is "*the prophet*" as he claims, or "*the prophet*" is yet to come. Islam is the only major religion besides Christianity that mandates a belief in Jesus as a prophet of God who is a role model to follow. So, for someone who believes that Jesus was a prophet of God, they have 3 options to believe in. Either they believe in Christianity, or they believe in Islam, or they must believe that everybody is wrong and they are waiting for God to send "*the Prophet*" to clarify who Jesus was and guide mankind once again to the true religion since nobody has been worshipping God right for the last 2,000 years. Regardless of which option a person chooses to believe in, if you don't research Muhammad and his religion it means you don't want to know whether the prophet came or not and are rejecting the prophet, no matter who it is. Since "*the Prophet*" will speak the words of God such a person is fundamentally rejecting God. Any creature whether jinn or human who rejects God and the true religion is a disbeliever. A disbeliever is someone you and me do not want to be on the day when mankind is judged and the disbelievers are cast into eternal dungeons of fire therein to remain forever and ever. When we are talking about being punished forever that means this is something to pay very serious attention to and devote some significant time to research. If you were taking a trip that was to last for 2 months you would likely spend a lot of time preparing. When we are talking about staying in a location forever then you want to be sure you like where you're staying. Nobody wants to be on fire, especially not forever, yet this is indeed what can and will happen to us if we don't spend time to research this Muhammad's religion. This is because of the principle of abrogation. For instance, when God sends a Messenger of God to mankind it is like having a new coach appointed to a sports team. A new coach comes with a new playbook that makes the previous playbook obsolete. For example, when Jesus was sent to mankind with the Injeel the Torah was no longer acceptable to use as a guide for how to live life because the Injeel abrogated parts of the Torah. Thus, even if Jews had the complete original Torah at that time, which my studies indicate they didn't, they would not be allowed to simply follow the Torah and be ok with God. Just as someone playing for a sports team can't be following the playbook of the old coach. Despite the believers still having the same religion one must use the playbook God has decreed for you to use for the time you are living in, nobody can pick and choose. If you want to be a part of the believer's team today, you have to use the playbook God has given them to live by today. Thus, if Muhammad is a Messenger of God who was sent with divine revelation in the Quran, that means the previous revelations are no longer viable for a person to follow. This means if Moses were alive today, he would not be preaching the Torah to people, he would be following the current revelation and would not follow the divine revelation he was sent with because it's no longer applicable. Although it's important to stress with this coach analogy that the playbook for the believers doesn't change with the times as team playbooks change, it's God's playbook. The last Messenger must be sent with a final playbook fit to be followed ever after. The last prophet and the last book must make it clear that they are the last prophet and the last book must make it clear that nothing else will come after it. Whereas Jesus made it clear that he was not the last prophet and another would be sent after him. Also, it was clear that the next one to follow Jesus would be "sent", it wasn't someone currently alive at that time who would be appointed or "inspired" by some "holy ghost". The principle of abrogation also means that even if any bible were divine revelation, of which none of them are, it still would not be fit to be followed or used to derive religious rulings from today if God sent another book to mankind; since the most recent book carries the most precedent and abrogates the previous books. This means that all the bible verses I quoted in this book cannot be used as a source for which to base one's religion on today. Please don't misunderstand me quoting bible verses and think they are usable to formulate beliefs or to live one's life today. That's a disclaimer and warning. I just mentioned bible verses to show what the bibles actually say and teach, because so many don't know, particularly those who claim to base their religious beliefs and lifestyles on said bibles; which they refer to as being singular instead of being a continuously evolving or devolving plethora. I quoted bible verses so that you would know the information, I did not quote them for you to follow them. Me saying that X bible says__ is simply me saying what X bible says. I do not agree with, nor believe in the bibles that I quoted from. I simply relayed what they said, God informed mankind of what disbelievers said in the past but he doesn't agree with what they said and he hates what they said. I just wanted to make that clear so that you don't have any misunderstandings. Another purpose served by me quoting the bible is that it proves both Christian doctrines and the bible are innovations not having come from God or any of God's prophets. How can you tell? Because nearly everything that a person of religious innovation cites as evidence to prove their religious innovation is true/good, is actually evidence against their innovation that proves it to be false. Sadly, though most people of bida (religious innovations) fail to see how their "evidence" proves them wrong. This is because there is no authentic genuine proof for any type of falsehood, and there never ever will be proof that supports falsehood or anything of innovation whether big or small, new or old. Proof for the truth comes from the true prophets of God. The problem is we don't look for proof, and that was a mistake which Adam made, he never asked Satan to prove his claims about the forbidden fruit and the effects it would have but Adam just believed in the conviction of Satan's conjecture. The lesson of Adam is that he and Eve were removed from paradise and sent to earth due to making a decision about religious beliefs/deeds without authentic proofs. Anyways looking into Muhammad and his claims of being the final Messenger of God is very important. If he is then his religion is the only ship that floats, so if you want safety then you better be on board. There is only 1 ladder to paradise. This is something that is more important than everything else in life, if God sent "*the Prophet*" you better be following him because if you aren't then you are a malfunctioning human being that is not fulfilling the purpose for which they were created. Now if you had a major health problem, you'd drop everything and go to a hospital or doctor until it was fixed. Well, a religious problem, uncertainty or emergency is a matter of even more importance and urgency. It is completely irresponsible to not spend some of our God-given time looking into Islam, just on the basis of its potential alone. If it does happen to be true then woe to those who ignored it and used their time for trivial things that will cause them regret in the afterlife.

Since I expounded in detail what the Christian views and the biblical views about Jesus where it seems appropriate to mention some Quran verses about how Mary was born, how John was born, how Jesus was born as well as some of what the Quran says about the life and departure of Jesus along with the attitude Allah tells Muslims to have towards Jews and Christians. Don't worry I'm not going to quote very much as I did with the bible(s), just a few passages. In the Quran verses 3:31-73 Allah says what means:

*Say (O Muhammad to mankind): "If you (really) love Allah then follow me (i.e. accept Islamic Monotheism, follow the Qur'an and the Sunnah), Allah will love you and forgive you your sins. And Allah is Oft-Forgiving, Most Merciful." Say (O Muhammad): "Obey Allah and the Messenger (Muhammad)." But if they turn away, then Allah does not like the disbelievers. Allah chose Adam, Nûh (Noah), the family of Ibrahim (Abraham) and the family of 'Imran above the 'Alamîn (mankind and jinn) (of their times) Offspring, one of the other, and Allah is the All-Hearer, All-Knower. (Remember) when the wife of 'Imran said: "O my Lord! I have vowed to You what (the child that) is in my womb to be dedicated for Your services (free from all worldly work; to serve Your Place of worship), so accept this, from me. Verily, you are the All-Hearer, the All-Knowing." Then when she gave birth to her [child Maryam (Mary)], she said: "O my Lord! I have given birth to a female child," - and Allah knew better what she brought* forth, - "And the male is not like the female, and I have named her Maryam (Mary), and I seek refuge with You (Allah) for her and for her offspring from Shaitan (Satan), the outcast." So, her Lord (Allah) accepted her with goodly acceptance. He made her grow in a good manner and put her under the care of Zakariya (Zachariya). Every time he entered Al-Mihrâb to (visit) her, he found her supplied with sustenance. He said: "O Maryam (Mary)! From where have you got this?" She said, "This is from Allah." Verily, Allah provides sustenance to whom He wills, without limit." At that time Zakariya (Zachariya) invoked his Lord, saying: "O my Lord! Grant me from You, a good offspring. You are indeed the All-Hearer of invocation." Then the angels called him, while he was standing in prayer in Al-Mihrâb (a praying place or a private room), (saying): "Allah gives you glad tidings of Yahya (John), confirming (believing in) the Word from Allah [i.e. the creation of 'Isa (Jesus), the Word from Allah ("Be!" - and he was!), noble, keeping away from sexual relations with women, a Prophet, from among the righteous." He said: "O my Lord! How can I have a son when I am very old, and my wife is barren?" (Allah) said: "Thus Allah does what He wills." He said: "O my Lord! Make a sign for me." (Allah) said: "Your sign is that you shall not speak to mankind for three days except with signals. And remember your Lord much (by praising Him again and again), and glorify (Him) in the afternoon and in the morning." And (remember) when the angels said: "O Maryam (Mary)! Verily, Allah has chosen you, purified you (from polytheism and disbelief), and chosen you above the women of the 'Alamîn (mankind and jinn) (of her lifetime)." O Maryam! "Submit yourself with obedience to your Lord (Allah, by worshipping none but Him Alone) and prostrate yourself, and Irkâ'i (bow down) along with Ar-Râki'ûn (those who bow down)." This is a part of the news of the Ghaib (unseen, i.e. the news of the past nations of which you have no knowledge) which We revealed to you (O

Muhammad). You were not with them, when they cast lots with their pens as to which of them should be charged with the care of Maryam (Mary); nor were you with them when they disputed (Remember) when the angels said: "O Maryam (Mary)! Verily, Allah gives you the glad tidings of a Word ["Be!" - and he was! i.e. 'Isa (Jesus) the son of Maryam (Mary)] from Him, his name will be the Messiah 'Isa (Jesus), the son of Maryam (Mary), held in honor in this world and in the Hereafter, and will be one of those who are near to Allah." "He will speak to the people in the cradle [as a baby] and in manhood [after returning to earth as an adult thousands of years after leaving], and he will be one of the righteous." She said: "O my Lord! How shall I have a son when no man has touched me." He said: "So (it will be) for Allah creates what He wills. When He has decreed something, He says to it only: "Be!" - and it is And He (Allah) will teach him ['Isa (Jesus)] the Book and Al-Hikmah (i.e. the Sunnah, the faultless speech of the Prophets, wisdom), (and) the Taurat and the Injeel And will make him ['Isa (Jesus)] a Messenger to the Children of Israel (saying): "I have come to you with a sign from your Lord, that I design for you out of clay, a figure like that of a bird, and breathe into it, and it becomes a bird by Allah's Leave; and I heal him who was born blind, and the leper, and I bring the dead to life by Allah's Leave. And I inform you of what you eat, and what you store in your houses. Surely, therein is a sign for you, if you believe. And I have come confirming that which was before me of the Taurat, and to make lawful to you part of what was forbidden to you, and I have come to you with a proof from your Lord. So, fear Allah and obey me. Truly! Allah is my Lord and your Lord, so worship Him (Alone). This is the Straight Path. Then when 'Isa (Jesus) came to know of their disbelief, he said: "Who will be my helpers in Allah's Cause?" Al-Hawâriyyûn (the disciples) said: "We are the helpers of Allah; we believe in Allah, and bear witness that we are Muslims (i.e. we submit to Allah)."

Our Lord! We believe in what You have sent down, and we follow the Messenger ['Isa (Jesus)]; so, write us down among those who bear witness (to the truth i.e. Lâ ilâha ill-Allah - none has the right to be worshipped but Allah) And they (disbelievers) plotted [to kill 'Isa (Jesus)], and Allah plotted too. And Allah is the Best of those who plot. And (remember) when Allah said: "O 'Isa (Jesus)! I will take you and raise you to Myself and clear you [of the forged statement that 'Isa (Jesus) is Allah's son] of those who disbelieve, and I will make those who follow you (Monotheists, who worship none but Allah) superior to those who disbelieve [in the Oneness of Allah, or disbelieve in some of His Messengers, e.g. Muhammad, 'Isa (Jesus), Musa (Moses), etc., or in His Books, e.g. the Taurat , the Injeel , the Qur'an] till the Day of Resurrection. Then you will return to Me and I will judge between you in the matters in which you used to dispute." "As to those who disbelieve, I will punish them with a severe torment in this world and in the Hereafter, and they will have no helpers." And as for those who believe (in the Oneness of Allah) and do righteous good deeds, Allah will pay them their reward in full. And Allah does not like the Zâlimûn (polytheists and wrong-doers). This is what We recite to you (O Muhammad) of the Verses and the Wise Reminder (i.e. the Qur'an) Verily, the likeness of 'Isa (Jesus) before Allah is the likeness of Adam. He created him from dust, then (He) said to him: "Be!" - and he was. (This is) the truth from your Lord, so be not of those who doubt. Then whoever disputes with you concerning him ['Isa (Jesus)] after (all this) knowledge that has come to you, [i.e. 'Isa (Jesus)] being a slave of Allah, and having no share in Divinity) say: (O Muhammad) "Come, let us call our sons and your sons, our women and your women, ourselves and yourselves - then we pray and invoke (sincerely) the Curse of Allah upon those who lie." Verily! This is the true narrative [about the story of 'Isa (Jesus)], and, Lâ ilâha ill-Allah (none has the right to be worshipped but Allah, the One and the

Only True God, Who has neither a wife nor a son). And indeed, Allah is the All-Mighty, the All-Wise. And if they turn away (and do not accept these true proofs and evidences), then surely, Allah is All-Aware of those who do mischief. Say (O Muhammad): "O people of the Scripture (Jews and Christians): Come to a word that is just between us and you, that we worship none but Allah (Alone), and that we associate no partners with Him, and that none of us shall take others as lords besides Allah. Then, if they turn away, say: "Bear witness that we are Muslims." O people of the Scripture (Jews and Christians)! Why do you dispute about Ibrahim (Abraham), while the Taurat and the Injeel were not revealed till after him? Have you then no sense? Verily, you are those who have disputed about that of which you have knowledge. Why do you then dispute concerning that of which you have no knowledge? It is Allah Who knows, and you know not. Ibrahim (Abraham) was neither a Jew nor a Christian, but he was a true Muslim Hanifa (Islamic Monotheism - to worship none but Allah Alone) and he was not of Al-Mushrikûn (polytheists, pagans, idolaters, disbelievers in the Oneness of Allah). Verily, among mankind who have the best claim to Ibrahim (Abraham) are those who followed him, and this Prophet (Muhammad) and those who have believed (Muslims). And Allah is the Wali (Protector and Helper) of the believers. A party of the people of the Scripture (Jews and Christians) wish to lead you astray. But they shall not lead astray anyone except themselves, and they perceive not. O people of the Scripture! (Jews and Christians): "Why do you disbelieve in the Ayat (Signs/Verses) of Allah, while you (yourselves) bear witness (to their truth)." O people of the Scripture (Jews and Christians): "Why do you mix truth with falsehood and conceal the truth while you know?" And a party of the people of the Scripture say: "Believe in the morning in that which is revealed to the believers (Muslims), and reject it at the end of the day, so that they may turn back(apostate). And believe no one except the one who follows your religion." Say (O Muhammad): "Verily! Right guidance is the Guidance of Allah [Do you fear] lest someone be given [revelation] like you were given or that they would [thereby] argue with you before your Lord?" Say (O Muhammad): "All the bounty is in the Hand of Allah; He grants(prophethood) to whom He wills. And Allah is All-Sufficient for His creatures' needs, the All-Knower."

Elsewhere in the Quran 2:75-82 Allah says what means:

"Can ye (O ye men of Faith) entertain the hope that they will believe in you? Seeing that a party of them heard the word of Allah, and perverted it knowingly after they understood it. Behold! when they meet the men of Faith they say: "We believe" but when they meet each other in private they say: "Shall you tell them what Allah hath revealed to you that they may engage you in argument about it before your Lord?" Do ye not understand (their aim)? Know they not that Allah knoweth what they conceal and what they reveal? And there are among them illiterates, who know not the Book, but (see therein their own) desires, and they do nothing but conjecture. Then woe to those who write the Book with their own hands, and then say: "This is from Allah" to traffic with it for a miserable price! Woe to them for what their hands do write and for the gain they make thereby. And they say: "The fire shall not touch us but for a few numbered days"; Say: "Have ye taken a promise from Allah, for He never breaks His promise? Or is it that ye say of Allah what ye do not know?" Nay those who seek gain in Evil, and are girt round by their sins- they are Companions of the Fire. therein shall they abide (forever). But those who have faith and work righteousness, they are Companions of the Garden therein shall they abide (forever). "

Then in the Quran 2:90-101 Allah says:

"Miserable is the price for which they have sold their souls, in that they deny (the revelation) which Allah has sent down, in insolent envy that Allah of His Grace should send it to any of His servants He pleases; thus, have they drawn on themselves wrath upon wrath. and humiliating is the punishment of those who reject Faith. When it is said to them: "Believe in what Allah hath sent down" they say: "We believe in what was sent down to us"; yet they reject all besides even if it be Truth confirming what is with them. Say: "Why then have ye slain the prophets of Allah in times gone by if ye did indeed believe?" There came to you Moses with clear (Signs); yet ye worshipped the Calf (even) after that, and ye did behave wrongfully. And remember We took your Covenant and We raised above you the mount (Sinai): (saying): "Hold firmly to what We have given you, and hearken (to the Law)"; they said: "We hear, and we disobey"; and they had to drink into their hearts (of the taint) of the calf because of their faithlessness. Say: "Vile indeed are the behests of your faith, if ye have any faith!" Say: "If the last Home with, Allah, be for you specially, and not for anyone else, then seek ye for death, if ye are sincere." But they will never seek for death on account of the (sins) which their hands have sent on before them. And Allah is well—acquainted with the wrong-doers. Thou wilt indeed find them, of all people, most greedy of life-even more than the idolaters; each one of them wishes he could be given a life of a thousand years; but the grant of such life will not save him from (due) punishment, for Allah sees well all that they do. Say (O Muhammad): "Whoever is an enemy to Gabriel-for he brings down the (revelation) to thy heart by Allah's will, a confirmation of what went before and guidance and glad tidings for those who believe. — Whoever is an enemy to Allah and His angels and prophets to Gabriel and Michael-Lo! Allah is an enemy to those who reject faith (Islam)." We have sent down to thee manifest signs (Ayat); and none reject them but those who are perverse. Is it not (the case) that every time they make a Covenant some party among them throw it aside? - Nay most of them are faithless.

*And when came to them a Messenger from Allah (Muhammad), confirming what was with them, a party of the people of the Book threw away the Book of Allah behind their backs, as if (it had been something) they did not know!"*

In the Quran 4:163-174 Allah says what means:
*We have sent thee inspiration (O Muhammad) as We sent it to Noah and the Messengers after him; We sent inspiration to Abraham, Ismail, Isaac, Jacob, and the Tribes to Jesus, Job, Jonah, Aaron, and Solomon, and to David, We gave the Zabur. Of some Messengers We have mentioned to you before, and Messengers We have not mentioned to you, - and to Moses Allah spoke directly. Messengers as bearers of good news as well as of warning in order that mankind should have no plea against Allah after the (coming of) Messengers. And Allah is Ever All-Powerful, All-Wise. But Allah bears witness to that which He has sent down (the Qur'an) unto you (O Muhammad), He has sent it down with His Knowledge, and the angels bear witness. And Allah is All-Sufficient as a Witness. Verily, those who disbelieve [by concealing the truth about Prophet Muhammad and his message of true Islamic Monotheism written in the Taurat and the Injeel] and prevent (mankind) from the Path of Allah (Islamic Monotheism), they have certainly strayed far away. Verily, those who disbelieve and did wrong [by concealing the truth about Prophet Muhammad and his message of true Islamic Monotheism written in the Taurat and the Injeel], Allah will not forgive them, nor will He guide them to any way, Except the way of Hell, to dwell therein forever, and this is ever easy for Allah. O mankind! Verily, there has come to you the Messenger (Muhammad) with the truth from your Lord, so believe in him, it is better for you. But if you disbelieve, then certainly to Allah belongs all that is in the heavens and the earth. And Allah is Ever All-Knowing, All-Wise. O people of the Scripture! Do not exceed the limits in your*

*religion, nor say of Allah aught but the truth. The Messiah Isa (Jesus), son of Maryam (Mary), was (no more than) a Messenger of Allah and His Word, ("Be!" - and he was) which He bestowed on Maryam (Mary) and a spirit (soul)created by Him; so, believe in Allah and His Messengers. Say not: "Three (trinity)!" Cease! (it is) better for you. For Allah is (the only) One Ilâh (God), glory be to Him (Far Exalted is He) above having a son. To Him belongs all that is in the heavens and all that is in the earth. And Allah is All Sufficient as a Disposer of affairs. The Messiah will never be proud to reject to be a slave of Allah, nor the angels who are near (to Allah). And whosoever rejects His worship and is proud, then He will gather them all together unto Himself. So, as for those who believed (in the Oneness of Allah - Islamic Monotheism) and did deeds of righteousness, He will give their (due) rewards, and more out of His Bounty. But as for those who refused His worship and were proud, He will punish them with a painful torment. And they will not find for themselves besides Allah any protector or helper. O mankind! Verily, there has come to you a convincing proof (Prophet Muhammad) from your Lord, and We sent down to you a manifest light (this Qur'an).*

People of different religions tend to heatedly argue back and forth with each claiming their religion is the only true divine religion and all others are false or corrupted. The problem is most of them always use the same reason for why what they believe is true, their reason being *"because their scriptures said so!"* Usually that ends the argument and no further debate can be considered because no one wants to consider that their beloved scripture may not be entirely divine or true. Of course, they are quick to explain why the other's book isn't of divine origins, but they never offer a chance for their own book to be proven false and refuse to hear the other side's argument. Just because someone says the bible is the word of or inspired by God doesn't automatically make it so.

Proof needs to be provided, or else why not believe the Hindu, Buddhist or Aztec scriptures just because they say to? In this case we have the Muslim hypothesis that "The Quran is the word of God", but that's just a hypothesis, if it's not proven then it's just an opinion. The true religion is not a matter of opinion it's a matter of truth and the truth always has proof. In the scientific method there is something called a *"burden of proof"* which means that when a hypothesis is created there is a criteria presented along with it where if A, B and C are true then it means the hypothesis is false. The Quran presents such a *"burden of proof"* for anyone who doubts that it is the word of God. The Quran offers a challenge to those who doubt and gives a criterion which if met then it would mean the Quran is not from God. This is something special that no other book in the world contains. This challenge is significant because it puts the entire religion of Islam on the line. If anyone wants to destroy Islam and make Muslims leave their religion all they would have to do is meet this challenge and every Muslim in the world, including myself, would leave Islam because it would mean the Quran is not from God. This challenge is actually a part of Islam and Muslims are commanded to challenge people, devils and false deities to disprove the Quran. What is this challenge?

In chapter 11 verses 13 and 14

أَمْ يَقُولُونَ افْتَرَاهُ قُلْ فَأْتُوا بِعَشْرِ سُوَرٍ مِّثْلِهِ مُفْتَرَيَاتٍ وَادْعُوا مَنِ اسْتَطَعْتُم مِّن دُونِ اللَّهِ إِن كُنتُمْ صَادِقِينَ ﴿١٣﴾

*"Or they may say, "He forged it," Say, "Bring ye then ten chapters forged, like unto it, and call (to your aid) whomsoever ye can, other than Allah! - If ye speak the truth!"*

فَإِلَّمْ يَسْتَجِيبُوا۟ لَكُمْ فَٱعْلَمُوٓا۟ أَنَّمَآ أُنزِلَ بِعِلْمِ ٱللَّهِ وَأَن لَّآ إِلَٰهَ إِلَّا هُوَ فَهَلْ أَنتُم مُّسْلِمُونَ ﴿١٤﴾

*"If then they (your false gods) answer not your (call), know ye that this revelation is sent down (replete) with the knowledge of Allah, and that there is no god but He! will ye even then submit (to Islam)?"*

These verses, respond directly to the claims people had in the past about Muhammad having forged the Quran and it challenges them to prove their claim. If Muhammad, an unlettered man who worships Allah, could forge the Quran then they should call what they worship for help in order so that they can make 10 chapters like it. This is a challenge the Arab pagan critics tried to complete and failed. Ironically people still make the same claim that Muhammad wrote the Quran, or copied it from other sources. What is amazing is that the Quran says disbelievers will say this and if that is true then they can bring 10 chapters like the Quran with the help of anything they worship and prove the Quran to be forged. Many who claim the Quran to have been made by Muhammad and not divine revelation don't even know they are mentioned in the Quran and challenged to back up their claim. They don't even have to come up with the 114 chapters of the Quran, only 10 chapters like the Quran are needed for them to prove their point and make every Muslim disbelieve in the Quran and the prophet Muhammad. For over 1400+ years no one has been able to bring 10 chapters like the Quran because they can't make it, yet they foolishly claim that "He forged it". Those who say this should read what they are talking about before they make such a statement, because if someone makes such a statement then the Quran is challenging that person to back it up. The Quran says when those false gods do not help people to make something like 10 chapters of the Quran then we should know that the Quran is divine revelation and that Allah is the only deity deserving of worship.

In Chapter 2 verse 23 of the Quran, it says:

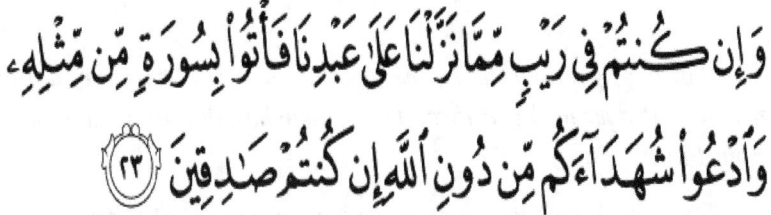

"*And if ye are in doubt as to what We have revealed from time to time to Our servant, then produce a chapter like thereunto; and call your witnesses or helpers (If there are any) besides Allah, if your (doubts) are true.*"

This verse makes the challenge easier reducing it from 10 chapters to just 1 chapter. The shortest chapter in the Quran is chapter 108. It has 3 verses with only 10 words. Only 10 words! That is the challenge. If anyone can produce 10 words like the Quran then it will disprove Islam, the Quran and the prophet Muhammad to all the Muslims on the planet including myself. Islam would cease to be a religion overnight, all that is required is for a person to produce 10 words like the Quran. It sounds simple right? Well, the second word of each verse ends with the Arabic letter form of K while the last letter of the last word of every verse is the Arabic form of R. This is a very specific and rigid structure; does the chapter even make any coherent sense? Let's examine the shortest chapter of the Quran to see how easy this challenge is.

Chapter 108 of the Quran:

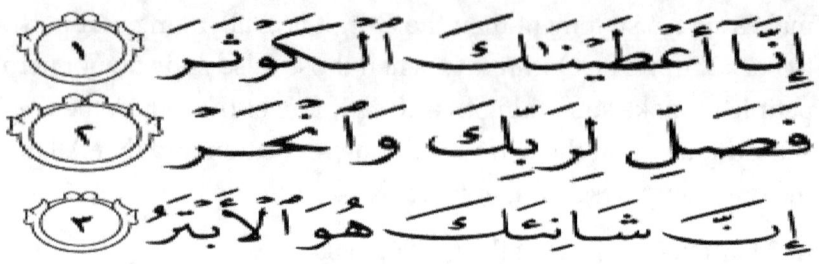

*"To thee have We granted the Fount (of Abundance). Therefore, to thy Lord turn in Prayer and Sacrifice. For he who hateth thee, he will be cut off (from Future Hope)"*

    The word thee is referring to Muhammad, to whom this verse was revealed. Remember the Quran is exactly as it was revealed to Muhammad, he did not recite it in the third person, but recited it in exactly the way it was recited to him by the Angel Gabriel, so the reader or reciter is actually put into Muhammad's perspective. The word "We" does not mean Allah is plural or a trinity, but is the English "We" as is used in the royal pronoun form, just the same as any King or Queen would refer to themselves as "We" even though they are just one person. This chapter actually makes quite a lot of sense for having such a rigid structure and is foreboding in that the last verse pronounces he who hates the prophet Muhammad will be cut off (from future Hope). It's significant that this would be the shortest chapter and the standard for those who want to disprove the Quran or the prophethood of Muhammad, because they are those who hate Muhammad since they reject his prophethood and would be the very people whom the chapter itself discusses. That's no coincidence. In fact, this chapter was one of the earliest chapters revealed when Muhammad was in Mecca, during the first 13 years of his 23 years of receiving revelation. When Muhammad's son died in infancy, a hate filled disbeliever taunted Muhammad making fun of him because his infant son died, just like all his sons did, saying he would be "cut off" from posterity and nobody would even know that "Muhammad" ever existed. This chapter of the Quran was a reassurance and retort to his opponent and continues to be a warning against all opponents who fail to produce a chapter like this.

Not only does the Quran offer a challenge and then make the challenge easier, but it also tells what the results will be for all who try to complete the challenge before they even try. In the verse after the easier challenge in 2:23 verse 2:24 says:

$$\text{فَإِن لَّمْ تَفْعَلُوا۟ وَلَن تَفْعَلُوا۟ فَٱتَّقُوا۟ ٱلنَّارَ ٱلَّتِى وَقُودُهَا ٱلنَّاسُ وَٱلْحِجَارَةُ ۖ أُعِدَّتْ لِلْكَافِرِينَ ﴿٢٤﴾}$$

*"But if ye cannot- and of a surety ye cannot- then fear the Fire whose fuel is men and stones, - which is prepared for those who reject Faith."*

These are strong words. Immediately after posting a challenge Allah says that all who try will fail. Who would be able to have the confidence to make such a statement unless they knew the results beforehand? Who would know except the All-knowing Creator of All things? Imagine if I claimed my book was the best book that will ever be written and that no one will be able to even bring 10 words that are like it. This would be a very stupid and arrogant challenge for me to make and it would likely be met within 10 minutes and expose the claim as false destroying all my credibility. The pagan Arabs were masters of Arabic, it was their specialty and pride, their poets were the most esteemed of society because of their linguistic abilities. They were the best equipped to meet such a challenge in all of history and they tried to come up with 10 words similar to the Quran in eloquence, sound, content, conciseness, rhetorical devices, grammar and literary form; however, they all failed and could not even come close. The Quran also rhymes with various diverse rhyme schemes present throughout. Although don't think that it is some kind of poetry, or rap, because as a former rapper and rap addict, I can testify that rap, or poetry, cannot even be compared with the literary achievement that the Quran is. That is how superior the Quran is to music, that you can't even compare the two. All thanks and praises be to Allah that I was guided away from music and discovered the Quran. Even from an objective point of view, atheist Arab linguists maintain that the Quran is the most advanced piece of Arabic that has ever existed. Everyone who has tried to meet the challenge of the Quran has failed and for over 1400 years people have been trying to meet the challenge to no avail. One Jewish man a few hundred years ago spent 6 entire months in a garage solely devoting himself to trying to produce a verse like the Quran and came out a mad man saying it is impossible to meet the challenge. More recently Reverend Abraham Phillips tried to disprove the Quran in his thesis for a doctorate degree but he found it impossible to refute and as a result embraced Islam and became a Muslim. Millions of failed attempts have been made, most of the challengers just use the Quran and change one word or two trying to pass that off as their attempt since they can't make anything original that can be comparable because only the Quran can be compared to the Quran; that is because it is the only revelation of God, we have access to today. However, the Quran doesn't just say all challengers will fail, but it says that those who try to disprove the Quran, by accepting the challenge instead of accepting the Quran to be the word of Allah, then such should *"fear the Fire whose fuel is men and stones"*. Again, this is a severe warning and who but the creator of Hell would know what the Fire uses as fuel? What a fire it is if stones are its fuel.  If you put stones on earthly fire the fire would likely be put out, but the hellfire devours and feeds off of stones and people, growing in intensity the more it burns.  Meaning the more people in hell the hotter it is and the longer they burn the hotter it gets.  It gets hotter and hotter and hotter and hotter and hotter increasing in heat forever.  That is the place promised to those who reject the Quran or try to imitate the Quran and fail in replicating it.  One would think after reading such a terrible fate awaiting certain people that such a person would be cautious about claiming the Quran is made by man or false.  The fact that people burn the Quran saying it's not from God proves that they haven't even read it, because if they did, they would know about the challenge in the Quran and try to disprove it by meeting the challenge.  If they really wanted to destroy the Quran and Islam then they would bring 10 words like it and it would prove Islam to be false, then presto everyone would burn the Quran and Islam would vanish.  They claim this is what they want, but they really just want to cause corruption and mischief to spread throughout the land instigating violent reactions which can be used to justify further violence against Muslims.  Their primary goal is to legally kill Muslims and stop Islam from spreading throughout the world.  It's really simple, if you don't believe the Quran is the word of God even though it says it is and that a human(s) authored what none can make 10 words like, then just bring 10 words like it to prove your point.  Anyone who doesn't try to do this and says the Quran is not divine revelation must not have read the Quran and therefore they cannot say whether it is divine revelation or not because they don't even know what they are talking about.  Ironically such people tend to quote the attempted translations of the meanings of the Quran out of context distorting the meaning yet the Quran quotes their quotes about the Quran.  Truly it is amazing to learn from the Quran what people will say about the Quran and then to hear those very people say exactly what the Quran said they would say. The Quran has quoted the enemies of Islam and what they say about the Quran before they were even born. By saying what they say about the Quran they prove it to be true revelation. Also, this challenge was given to the Jews and Christians while Muhammad was alive as well, they never met this challenge and it still stands. Yet despite Jews and Christians claiming to have sacred divine revelation or "books inspired by God" they have yet to bring 10 words like the Quran. To this day none have been able to do it. So, you know what that means right? That means if you take all the Jewish religious texts and all the Christian religious texts including every bible and alleged Hebrew Torah in the world combining everything all together, in total out of all their texts the Jews and Christians combined don't even have 10 words of divine revelation with them. Jews and Christians may disagree and even some Muslims may not know that Ahl-Kitab have less than 10 words of revelation in their books but that is the Islamic and Scholastic position. Originally Jews and Christians had more in the Suhuf of Ibrahim, Taurat of Musa, Zabur of Dawood and Injeel of Isa. However, keep in mind that none of those were in Hebrew or Greek which the Old and New Testament consist of. Hebrew did not originate until about 600 BCE and neither Abraham, Moses, or David spoke Hebrew thus the Hebrew Old Testament bible books cannot be the same as the Suhuf, Taurat and Zabur simply because that language didn't exist when the books were revealed. While the New Testament bible books are Greek which is a language not spoken by Jesus and none of those Greek Gospels even portend to be by God but by alleged disciples of Jesus and Paul all of which was written long after Jesus left earth. For that reason, no scholars in academic circles even consider the bibles as historical documents. Yet the Quran refers to Jews and Christians by phrases which mean people of the Scripture and people of the Book. Do you know why? Because they used to have Scripture and they used to have a Book sent by God, thus God honored them for what they used to have. But God also disgraces them with this phrase and challenge as well because by the time the Quran was revealed they didn't even have 10 words.

      As amazing as that is, it actually terrifies me because there are other things the Quran narrates which disbelievers think, say and do which I have personally seen and heard members of my own family and species say, do and write to me which match word for word what the Quran describes certain people in the past as thinking, saying and believing who ended up being punished in this life and the next. Their statements are so exact that it leaves me speechless to read their letters or hear them speak because I've already read in English translations word for word their very statements to the point where it sends chills down my spine because they are practically quoting an English translation of the Quran, but they have no clue. Several nights I simply could not sleep because of this phenomenon that makes me realize the Quran is a script. It is the speech of the Creator telling us what happened in the past, what is happening in the present and what is happening in the future. The scary thing is that I cannot recall one non-Muslim which I've talked with for over an hour straight about religion without them saying exactly what the Quran says they think, believe and would say. I've found the Quran translations mentioning their statements word for word and refuting their specious arguments. I seriously want to just shake them sometimes and say, "*Are all you non-Muslims quoting the Quran on purpose? If you aren't then surely only God could've predicted 1400+ years ago that you would tell me exactly what you just told me. You and every other non-Muslim I've talked to at length about religion are either part of some massive global conspiracy to quote the Quran to me pretending that you aren't or else the Quran really is from God!"* It is beyond awe-inspiring for me now, it seriously terrifies me causing me to lose sleep because nearly every verse where the Quran quotes what the non-Muslims will say to the Muslims, I have heard countless people say them to me word for word for word and not one of them has a clue they all say the same exact things to me word for word for word and that the Quran informed me they would say it exactly the way they said it. It's scary because it means that since the Quran which was revealed 1400+ years ago was able to exactly predict what people would say today then it is just as accurate in its descriptions of what people will say in the afterlife, when resurrected, when judged and rewarded or punished. The Quran for me has now become like a movie script in which I'm witnessing the movie being performed in real life knowing how it's all going to end, yet not knowing which character I will die as. Yet sadly many haven't believed it or given it a chance to learn what it says so they can save themselves from the terrible ending so many will have. It actually made me cry before because the Quran is so truthful yet so many reject it without even wanting to know what it says, but Allah instructs us not to grieve for them. I don't know what I can even possibly write to encourage someone to read it, because the Quran explains many will vehemently refuse to hear it or learn what it says. Which again causes the same situation because the Quran describes people who will absolutely refuse to learn about what it says no matter what anyone says or does. The Quran tells the future and there is no doubt about it, I've witnessed in my own life the frightening accuracy of what it says. It's so truthful that it scares me unlike anything besides God ever could.

Although on the positive side it means that the paradise promised to those who believe and do good is just as true.

If someone still doesn't believe the Quran is from God and can't bring a chapter like it then they can ask for help in meeting the challenge of the Quran and don't have to try to meet it all by themselves. Chapter 17 verse 88 of the Quran says:

قُل لَّئِنِ ٱجْتَمَعَتِ ٱلْإِنسُ وَٱلْجِنُّ عَلَىٰٓ أَن يَأْتُوا۟ بِمِثْلِ هَٰذَا ٱلْقُرْءَانِ لَا يَأْتُونَ بِمِثْلِهِۦ وَلَوْ كَانَ بَعْضُهُمْ لِبَعْضٍ ظَهِيرًا ﴿٨٨﴾

"Say: "If the whole of mankind and Jinn were to gather together to produce the like of this Qur´an, they could not produce the like thereof, even if they backed up each other with help and support." "

This verse instructs Muhammad to say how even if every human who ever existed and all of the species of the Jinn worked together to produce something like the Quran, they could never produce something like it. That may be one of the strongest statements a book can ever contain. Meaning even if Abraham, Moses, Jesus and Muhammad got together they couldn't produce the Quran. What author could have the nerve to make such a claim? If Christians disagree and really are inspired by the "Holy Spirit" and have their prayers answered by Jesus, Mary, or any of their alleged saints then why haven't they been able to come up with something equal to the Quran? It is because their prayers are unanswered and unheard and they are praying to people who cannot benefit them neither in this life or the next. Only the Creator deserves prayers and the Quran could only have come from the Creator. Muhammad was an unlettered man who could not read or write, he did not make the Quran. It was revealed to him during a period of 23 years piece by piece, every time revelation would come he would memorize it and those he shared it with would also memorize it on the spot. There is not one contradiction in this entire thing, it's impossible for a normal person to have others memorize what they say for 23 years and not contradict themselves one time. Only for a prophet of God who was receiving divine revelation would this be possible. Had one contradiction been made the entire religion would have been abandoned as man-made and false. There are many things in the Quran which the disbelievers heard recited which they could've used to say the Quran was false thereby discrediting the Quran, but they didn't. I will bring your attention to one short specific chapter. The 111th chapter, "*Surat al Masad*" which translates to "*The palm Fibre*" or "*Flame*" says:

"*Perish the hands of the Father of Flame! Perish he! No profit to him from all his wealth, and all his gains! Burnt soon will he be in a Fire of Blazing Flame! His wife shall carry the (crackling) wood - As fuel!- A twisted rope of palm-leaf fibre round her (own) neck!*"

Many translate "*Father of Flame*" to be Abu Lahab, which was the name of the uncle of the Prophet Muhammad, his nickname "*Abu Lahab*" literally means "*Father of the Flickering Red Flame at the tip of Fire*". He had this nickname because of his reddish face and fiery temper. Since red cheeks were a sign of beauty in Arab culture Abu Lahab was a famous attractive well-known celebrity. Allah changes the perspective of his nickname, before it was considered a name of beauty, after the chapter was revealed, it was considered a warning of his destiny of burning. His wife was Umm Jamil which means "*mother of beautiful*" because she was the prettiest girl of her tribe. These two together were a powerhouse celebrity couple. This chapter was revealed while Abu Lahab was still alive and is explicitly about him and his wife. Keep in mind they were non-Muslims and were next door neighbors of the Prophet Muhammad in Mecca. If Muhammad had been making the Quran up himself this chapter would have been completely foolish for him to have created, especially considering at the time of the revelation of this chapter he was already being harassed and abused by his neighbors and relatives. This chapter strongly states that the uncle and aunt-in-law of the Prophet will never become Muslims and will spend eternity in hell. Both were bitter enemies of Islam; this chapter gave both of them the opportunity to destroy the credibility of the Quran. If either one of them had become a Muslim, then it would have meant the Quran was wrong and lied, which would have proven that it could not be divine revelation. A man called Tariq Muharibi reported that he saw Abu Lahab following Muhammad in the market, Abu Lahab was publicly shouting out that Muhammad was a madman, while doing this he was throwing stones at the prophet's feet causing them to bleed. Abu Lahab might have been the man who hated Muhammad the most of all time. Therefore, he would be the last person Muhammad would want to have the opportunity to destroy his religion, Abu Lahab was already trying to destroy Islam before the chapter was revealed. When this chapter was revealed 2 of Muhammad's daughters were married to 2 of Abu Lahab's sons and once Abu Lahab and his wife heard this chapter, they forced both their sons to divorce their wives on the spot because they hated Muhammad and his daughters were Muslims. These 2 daughters were the same who later married Uthman bin Affan. Umm Jamil, Abu Lahab's wife would slander and backbite as well as put thorns on the path outside Muhammad's house every single night hoping he'd step on them and get hurt whenever he left his house. She also had a very expensive necklace which she pawned and vowed to use all the proceeds solely to hurt Muhammad and harm Islam. People even told Abu Lahab that maybe he shouldn't be as mean to Muhammad because what would then happen to him if Islam turned out to be right? Abu Lahab replied that if Muhammad's religion was right he would simply bribe the angels when they tried to take him to hell and would buy a spot in paradise with his wealth, thus he didn't show an ounce of restraint in harming Muhammad because he thought he had it all figured out even if Muhammad and his religion of Islam were true. Abu Lahab lived for 10 years after "*Surat al Masad*" was revealed. All he or his wife had to do was pretend to become a Muslim and the Quran would be proven false. They wouldn't even have had to pretend to be Muslim for more than a day, had they become Muslim within one hour the entire religion would have crumbled, because it would have meant the Quran wasn't divine and Muhammad was a false prophet. This is exactly what Abu Lahab and his wife wanted to happen, on top of that they knew of this chapter and heard it recited many times. This was the opportunity of a lifetime for an enemy of Islam to deal a fatal blow to the religion. Yet during all those years that they lived, neither Abu Lahab nor his wife could even pretend to believe and pay mere lip service to the Islamic faith for even 1 minute. The Muslims even informed them that the Muslims knew they would never become Muslim because Allah told them so in the Quran, and that if they even pretended to do so it would mean Islam was false. They basically told them,

*"You 2 hate our religion and harass us more than nearly everyone else, if one of you pretended to accept our religion, which you should do because it's true and what God wants from you, then it would destroy our religion which you hate so much and all of us would stop being Muslims immediately; which is what you want to happen. Yet we know that neither of you will ever even pretend for 1 second because God said so in the Quran and it's true, even though you hate it."* And that's what happened. These two enemies of Islam continued saying it was false, bad and attacking Muslims in every way possible; until they died years later. The Quran has proven itself true because they both died and never believed and never even tried to pretend to believe, even though they were informed that if they did so it would destroy Islam which was what they wanted and had made as their life goal. So, while they hated the Quran, in a sense they lived according to it because they fulfilled its prophesy exactly and on top of that, they knew they fulfilled it despite their hatred of and rejection of Islam. Now only Allah the all-knowing could have confidently made such a statement while Abu Lahab and his wife were still alive. One would have thought staunch opponents of the Quran would gleefully take advantage of the chance to prove it false. Yet despite how much they hated Islam, Muslims and the Quran they physically could not even pretend to be Muslim even though if they did so it would've completely destroyed Islam. Clearly this is a sign that no person can deny, this short chapter proves that what the Quran says is true. I mean seriously nobody but a Messenger of God with authentic divine revelation from God would recite such verses in such circumstances. If those enemies of Islam, who were the staunchest opponents of the prophet Muhammad and Muslims, couldn't destroy Islam at that time when they were given such an easy way to do so, then what chance does any enemy of Islam have today?

The Quran actually gives the answer to that question as well, but you will have to look that verse from the Quran up on your own.

Another opportunity in which the Quran and Islam could have been deemed false presented itself in another verse in "*Surat Yusuf*", Chapter 12 verses 2 and 3, which says:

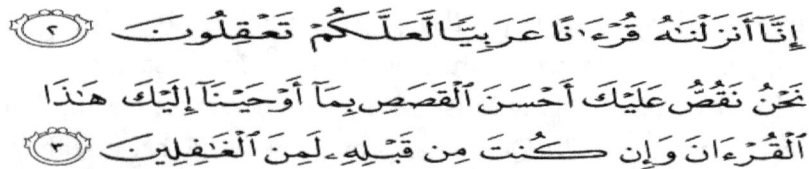

"*We have sent it down as an Arabic Qur'an, in order that ye may learn wisdom. We do relate unto thee the most beautiful of stories, in that We reveal to thee this (portion of the) Qur'an: before this, thou too was among those who knew it not.*"

Present in these verses is another special distinction that is unique to the Quran. The name of the "*Quran*" comes from the Quran. People did not name the Quran; the Quran names itself the Quran. No other religious book names itself. Nor does any other book we have access to today claim it has been sent down from the Creator.

In comparison if you read a bible nowhere in the bible does it say "*this is the bible*". The word "bible" itself is not found anywhere in the biblical text aside from outsider commentary or the cover. If you just took the "scriptures" and gave it to someone to read without a cover or commentary, they would never think to call what they read "*the bible*". If we call the Quran the Quran because the Quran names itself, then why do we call a bible a bible? The word "bible" actually originates from the word "Byblos", which was a city in Phoenicia. "Byblos" meant "*the city of the great Mother*". Bibles were named after this city because the earliest libraries were attached to the pagan temple of the goddess

Byblis who was the granddaughter of the pagan god Apollo who was a sun-deity. There was also a city in Egypt which bore the name Byblis. An alternate name for the Greek goddess Venus was Byblis. The year 400 CE was the first time anyone had ever used the word "Bible" to describe the Christian "scripture". Those who allegedly wrote the bible didn't call it the bible and Constantine didn't know of a bible either. In 399 CE if you were to ask a Christian if they believed in the bible, they would respond "*no I don't believe in that pagan goddess why would you think that?*" Today when Christians say, "*I believe in the Holy Bible*" they are linguistically saying they believe in the "*Holy great Mother, granddaughter of Apollo*". That is where the name "bible" comes from and what it linguistically means. So, the "bible" is actually a false pagan deity. The alleged authors of the book that is known as the bible today would have also said the bible is a pagan deity which only disbelievers believe in. Realistically Matthew, Mark, Luke and John would have all said "*if you believe in the bible you're going to hell*" because to them the bible was a pagan idol. Over time this word for a pagan idol came to be identified with a book and unfortunately people claim this "bible" is the word of God. This is why it is so important to know what words actually mean. It is even more important to know what words mean to God. Even if the book people call the bible is the word of God, to say that "the bible is the word of God" is blasphemous because it linguistically means that "the pagan deity is the word of God". What is even worse than that is that people today call it "the Holy Bible" just as the pagans of Byblos and Byblis would say, which is one of the reasons why many of those pagans will burn eternally in hell. Our tongues are very dangerous, before we speak, we should research what the words we are saying mean, because they may mean one thing to us but to others, such as God, they mean a completely different thing. Allah will hold us to account for every syllable our tongues utter. If people insist on calling the books bibles, then instead of spelling them "Holy Bibles" they should all be spelled "*Holey Bibles*" because they are full of literary, thematic, historical, mathematical, logical, chronological and theological holes, craters and fissures of religious fiction, leading its readers/victims to the chasm of disbelief in this life and the abyss of hell in the next.

    Whereas the Arabic word Quran linguistically means "*the recitation*" and since the Quran was a recitation of divine revelation from God to Gabriel to Muhammad to us, the Quran is an appropriate title. What is amazing is that "*the recitation*" calls itself "*the recitation*". It's quite a powerful thing which is able to dictate what we call it. The opponents of Islam and the Quran are unwittingly following the Quran by calling the Quran what it says to call it. Likewise, the name of the religion of Islam and the name of Muslims as its practitioners come from the Quran as well. We can only refer to the Quran by names it calls itself, we can't make up names for it. This is why the term "Holy Quran" is unislamic and wrong, because while the Quran is divine revelation and sacred neither God nor the prophet whom the Quran was revealed to referred to it as that, just as how Moses never called the Torah the "Holy Torah". Basically, some ignorant Muslims copied the Christian prefix they use for their "holey bibles" without realizing that it is not permissible to invent names for the Quran. The Muslim is forbidden to lie or exaggerate, adding "holy" is disrespectful to the Quran because to do so is to call it names which God hasn't given us permission to call it. Plus, linguistically it doesn't make sense because "Holy" is an English word and "Quran" is an Arabic word. There are some permissible Arabic prefixes and alternative names the Quran itself uses but we can't make up our own regardless of what our intentions may be.

Nor create a bilingual composite title for a book. Yet not only does the Quran name itself, but it also says what language it's in. The Quran says that it is Arabic, which means anything not in Arabic is not the Quran. If the book itself says it is an Arabic book, then no translation will ever be capable of conveying the same meaning as the original Arabic. This is why any attempted translation of the Quran into English is not actually a translation of the Quran, but is an attempted translation of the meanings of the Quran. The Quran is a divine revelation; in order to translate it correctly you would need a divine translation of the divine revelation for it to be comparable. No translations of any book can ever be said to be divine revelation because they are all done by human translators and humans are not divine. An English Torah, Bible, Bhagavad Gita, or Vedas is just an English interpretation, none of them can be considered divine revelation because they are not in the original language, but are in the English language. That doesn't mean that an attempted translation of the meanings of the Quran shouldn't be treated with respect, because it contains the colloquial meanings of the divine revelation. Even an English translation should be treated with respect, but it should be kept in mind that it is not actually divine revelation and only the original revelation in the language in which it was originally revealed would qualify as divine revelation and the respect a translation deserves is not the same as the respect the actual revelation deserves. For example, with the Arabic Quran a Muslim prostrates when they read certain verses because that's what Muhammad taught us to do and it's what the Quran teaches Muslims are supposed to do when reading certain verses of the Quran, but if Muslims read those same verses in a translated form they don't prostrate because they'd be reading a translation and not the actual Quran. To illustrate how translations are never the same as the original take this book I've written as an example. As the author I can say with certainty that no person will ever be able to translate this book correctly conveying 100% of the meanings I intended because only I and God know what I meant when I wrote something. You don't and will never know what I meant when I used every word, so to translate all of my words into another language you would need to know exactly what I meant to say with each word in order to translate all my words correctly. Thus, I am the only person who will ever be qualified to translate my book 100% correctly. Others could try but they could never claim to have accurately translated my book because they don't know what I really meant, they could only guess. Thus, anyone who tried to translate this book would be changing the book with their own ideas of my intended meanings and thus any translation that's not done by me personally would not really be "my book", but someone else's interpretation of my English book in another language. Whereas this also applies to the biblical books too, only Jesus is qualified to translate Jesus. Thus, in theory if the gospels were written by actual companions of Jesus, which they weren't, then they still would be corrupting his teachings by translating them since they wouldn't know if Jesus would've translated himself the way they allege to have done. The same applies to Paul's letters which get translated. The same even applies to hadith and the Quran. Translations done by 2nd parties can never be 100% the same thing as the original. But again, remember the biblical books aren't translations of the original sources, they are translations of translations of translations and only God knows how messed up they've gotten. Just as a fish cannot translate a human neither can a human translate God. By saying a translation is divine revelation then you are saying the translator was divine. To say a translation is "*the word of God*" it means you consider the translator to be God since it is their words you are referencing and not God's words even if they were translating

God's words, which typically isn't the case anyways. Truly if you have revelation of God get translated the only way it can be considered revelation is if God translated it himself. Simply claiming a translator was "inspired" doesn't count, just as nobody could say God inspired them to translate my book because accurate translations are not possible unless they are done by the original author themself. So, the common claim that the biblical passages are the "inspired word of God" is false for so many reasons. That a translation is done by a human is enough proof that translations are not divine revelations or 100% accurate because humans don't know every word in a language. God knows every word and knows the best word to use to convey the correct meaning, humans don't and thus can never ever translate another human 100% correctly, let alone God the Creator of the Universe. Honestly nobody can even translate me 100% accurately so it is impossible that anybody could translate God 100% accurately. That's why some Islamic Scholars passed legal rulings saying because the Quran is Arabic it is actually not permissible to print a translation of the Quran without also including the Arabic alongside the translation. There is great wisdom in this. For instance, how can someone know that the translation is accurate if the translator didn't show the reader the text they translated? This would amount to having blind faith in the translator. As a result of the religious books of other faiths being translated without the original text accompanying it, today the original texts are no longer accessible and adherents to such religions must simply hope their translations are accurate because they no longer possess the original revelation in its original language. Negligence caused them to lose the original divine revelation and thereby lose their way, become deviant and be led astray. Sometimes people modernize translations but then claim it's what was originally translated by someone else. So, when some Muslim scholars give a ruling saying how Quran translations must have the Arabic alongside, it's for a very important reason. Usually, Muslim strictness is for safety reasons, it's not to make things difficult. From my very limited experience the most reliable attempted English translation of the meanings of the Quran thus far is by Saheeh International or by Dr. Muhsin Khaan, and Taqi-ud-Deen Hilaali, but even those have some errors in that it incorrectly associates the Injeel with the word Gospel and Zabur with the word Psalms. Yet that grievous sacrilegious error stems from the translators forgetting we can only call God's revelations what God has said we can call them. The Injeel and Zabur are exactly that and can only be called that unless God says otherwise. The reason it is so important that the Quran remains in its original Arabic is because the previous revelations and their meanings were lost in translation. Concerning the bibles, the originals of the gospels, epistles and Jewish books don't exist. Any bible read today is not only named after a pagan deity, but is also disqualified from being divine revelation even if some teachings of a divine message still theoretically remained. For example, there are thousands of different translations of the bible today, which means thousands of different gospels of "Matthew". In reality there would only have been one gospel, today there are thousands of different translations of the gospel of "Matthew" and that is just counting the English translations. The original words of that gospel could never have had thousands of different meanings so these translations we know of today could not possibly even be considered comparable to the original. The original gospel doesn't exist, so how can someone translate what doesn't exist? Simply put they can't, instead they translate translations which most falsely allege are copies of the copies of the originals in the same language as the original. Yet even if such spurious hopes were true, even then the process of biblical copying, ignoring and denying the fact of translation, caused the gospels to become diluted through each translation of the Greek (translations, not copies) and the modern translations bear nearly no resemblance to the originals. This is why another prophet and further divine revelation was needed because the original revelations previously sent had been lost and the translations corrupted with the copies miscopied. A bible is not the revelation God gave Moses, David and Jesus as the Quran is the revelation God gave Muhammad. Instead the Old and New Testaments of the bibles would be comparable to a weak or fabricated hadith collection in which only translations are available and the original statements in the original language is unknown and the chain of narrators only includes Person C without anyone else in the chain listed for Persons A, B, D, E or F except it is known that the authors of the biblical books in reality aren't even Person C but are actually anonymous authors whose writings get changed with every new printing of their books. Sadly, Christians are led to believe that the authors of their texts are eyewitnesses and that what they consider to be an eyewitness account is divine revelation instead of a news report. The problem is the Judeo-Christian definition of divine revelation is wrong. A divine revelation is the verbatim speech of God revealed to a Messenger of God transmitted from that Messenger to us. Neither Moses, David nor Jesus taught any bible thus it cannot be divine revelation by definition, but since neither Jews nor Christians want to admit they don't have divine revelations they change the definition of revelation into being whatever they have and/or believe is an instruction manual for salvation. The Quran is the uncreated **Arabic speech of Allah that was revealed to the Prophet Muhammad both in word and in meaning.** The Ahl-Kitab (People of the book/Jew and Christians) have lost their Kitabs but they are still called Ahl-Kitab in Islam because they are descendants of those given Kitabs and a Kitab of Allah is a very big thing to have been given, even if one has lost it tis still an honor to have once been given one. Also, it's a type of shame for them and reminder to us that they're a people given books from Allah yet look at their evil and distance from Allah. This is why Jizya is ordained for them so they can exist as a constant reminder to us that just being given a book from Allah doesn't make you a believer or loved by God. One must believe in, learn, preserve, practice and apply that book to truly be considered a person worthy of that book. The book of Allah is a trust we must not violate. If Muslims become like the Ahl-Kitab then Allah will bring a new people to replace them who will love and hate for his sake whom he will love and help to establish Islam upon the earth no matter how much the Ahl-Kitab hate it (whether they be Ahl-Kitab of the Taurat, Zabur, Injeel or Quran). I'm not saying Muslims today are Ahl-Kitab legally as Shariah tends to classify Ahl-Kitab, but spiritually, methodologically and practically speaking there are characteristics among some claiming to be Muslims today that could make them be considered by God/Allah to be a Ahl-Kitab of the Quran unknowingly. Thus, in every prayer Muslims recite the last verse of fatihah praying/begging the Master of the day of Judgment that we do not become like or follow the paths of those he is angry with or those who have gone astray. Thus, it is that every deviant sect that's in and out of Islam resembles or shares a particular trait(s) and/or doctrine(s) of the traditional Ahl-Kitab of the Jews and Christians.

Now that you know what the Quran is we can discuss the other opportunity it gives for it to be proven false when it says, *"before this, thou too was among those who knew it not."* Keeping in mind that the Quran was revealed to Muhammad it is directed toward him in this instance. Today some level a charge that Muhammad copied "the bible" rebranding it in the Quran and that Islam is a copycat religion. One reason this charge is utterly false is because the Quran contains information about prophets who are completely absent from both the Old and New Testament such as the prophet Salih and Hud. These prophets are not mentioned in any record aside from the Quran and Sunnah, they would have been unknown to us today had Allah not mentioned them to Muhammad, so they could not have been copied from anyone. Muhammad was an unlettered Arab; he couldn't read or write let alone copy the bible because there were no Arabic bibles even alleged to have existed until the 8th century CE and Muhammad died in the 7th century CE. The earliest known Arabic version of the bible dates to 867 CE. Muhammad died in 632 CE. So how is Muhammad supposed to copy a book that didn't exist until 245 years after he died? He couldn't have copied the bible even if he wanted to because the world had no Arabic bibles that could've been read and even if it did, he was unlettered and couldn't read books. The Christians didn't even have Arabic bibles nor did the public at large, only the priests had access to bibles and none of them were in Arabic. Are we supposed to believe that Muhammad learned how to read both Hebrew and Greek when he couldn't even read his own name in his mother tongue on the peace treaty of Hudaibiyyah that he signed and had to have someone point it out to him? And just who is supposed to have taught Muhammad Hebrew and Greek and given him copies of a Hebrew bible and a Greek bible? Also how does one learn to read in a foreign language when they can't even read their native language? Imagine if the first language you learned to read was a language different than the one you spoke? To do that is practically impossible. Muhammad couldn't write his name to sign business contracts, loans, his marriage contracts or to sign the marriage contracts of his daughters. On top of that the Quran contains none of the scientific errors and impossibilities that plague the bible, nor those which were popularly believed in Arabia when the Quran was revealed. The Quran also contains an abundant number of scientific statements that are not present in the bible or in the scientific theories of the past, of which just a few decades ago could not be made by anyone. Of these statements in the Quran there is not even one which modern science disagrees with, in regards to all the statements modern science is able to comment on it has agreed with what the Quran says and scientists cannot find any human explanation for how it is possible for such statements to have been made in the Quran 14 centuries ago at the time when it was revealed to an unlettered middle-aged Arab. So, who taught Muhammad to be a scientific genius who knows more about the Universe and how everything works with greater accuracy and detail than the scientific genius' of the world today? Oh, and did I mention Muhammad was from Arabia which neither Rome nor Persia bothered to try to conquer because it was a desolate desert wasteland where the Romans and Persians deemed the Arabs too stupid to bother incorporating into their nation? Materially speaking, as a 40-year-old in the middle of the desert Muhammad was the least likely candidate to pick to be the leader of what would turn into a global religious movement that would span from Spain to China just a few decades after his death at the age of 63. Yet God knew it would happen and if any think God opposes Muhammad, then why did God allow it when all non-Muslims were against him and his religion? If Muhammad is not a true prophet of God, then how were his many accomplishments possible? Why has the Quran spread further across the world than any other religious book when the other religions were around centuries earlier? Why is it that those who don't believe in Islam have practically no clue at all what it is or what the Quran says?

When prophets came to mankind God supported them with signs and miracles to prove they were genuinely sent from God. Many of these signs and miracles were visual, which you had to see in order to believe such as Moses splitting the Sea, or Jesus healing the blind with God's permission. None of the prophets said "*just believe in faith alone, you got to have faith*", especially the type of faith as defined by Martin Luther when he taught: "<u>Faith does not require information, knowledge and certainty</u>, *but a free surrender and <u>**joyful bet**</u> on [God's] <u>unfelt, untried and unknown goodness</u>.*" Based on Martin Luther's explanation of Faith, we can sum up Christianity as: "*a joyful bet that does not require information, knowledge or certainty but is based on unfelt, untried and unknown goodness which is freely and consciously surrendered to in a manner that makes the Christian/gambler feel correct and content whilst oblivious to their own Satanic idiocy and outcome of guaranteed damnation.*" The prophets forbid people from gambling, especially regarding the afterlife. You don't get to paradise through a "*joyful bet that does not require information, knowledge and certainty*"! The prophets had solid undisputable proof to back up their religion and claim to prophethood. Yet people still rejected them. One of the signs of Muhammad was the Quran. He was unlettered and could not read or write, then for 23 years the Quran was gradually revealed piece by piece and memorized on the spot by him and his companions. Some Muslims wrote verses down on bone or parchment to study and help with memorization, these writings have been found and carbon dated and the verses are exactly the same as the Arabic Quran people read today. This is one difference between Islam and all other religions, Muslims have access to our prophet's miracle for all to witness and experience 1,440+ lunar years and counting. People didn't believe in Jesus so Allah helped him heal people as a sign and turned the staff of Moses into a serpent as proof that he was sent by the divine. Today no one can experience these signs or witness them firsthand and must just believe what they've been told, but you don't have to believe Muhammad is a prophet based on hearsay, one of his signs is the Quran and you can experience it today. The Quran was a miracle/sign to prove the prophethood of Muhammad and instruct all of mankind in guidance, this miracle has been perfectly preserved so that today we have the same access to the miracle as those who met Muhammad.

    Despite being known to man for over 1400+ years there is only one version/edition of the Arabic Quran. All over the world ancient manuscripts of the Quran have been found in Russia, Arabia, China, Africa, Europe and India with all of them having the same exact letters as the Arabic Quran we know of today. There are no different versions or editions of Divine Revelation. An Arabic book of the Quran from 646 CE contains the exact same letters, in the same order, as a freshly printed Arabic book of the Quran today and the same as the Qurans printed in any land at any time. But wait just one minute, didn't Muhammad die in 632 CE? How then can the earliest known physical copy of the Quran be dated to 646 CE, 14 years later? Shouldn't it be published earlier in Muhammad's lifetime? Well, that would be impossible. How so? Because Muhammad received revelation of the Quran until he died, so if a written book was published in his lifetime and then new verses were revealed to him then there would be a problem with incomplete Qurans and people who found those may think the later verses revealed after such a copy was published may not be part of the Quran since it wouldn't have been included in a copy published before Muhammad died or received that revelation. However, can't Christians claim the same about bibles to justify them not existing during the lifetime of Jesus? No. Why not? Because Jesus never read the bible or taught it to people and nothing in it was written during his lifetime. In comparison Muhammad taught the Quran and told people to write it down during his lifetime. A full compendium of every verse just wasn't compiled or published in his lifetime. Publicly Muhammad would recite the Quran to the masses on a daily basis as did all the other Muslims, when giving speeches, praying in congregation, talking or just as a hobby/good deed. Every Ramadan Muhammad would recite all that had been revealed of the entire Quran up to that point. After Muhammad died, it was known that no more verses of the Quran would be revealed by Allah since the prophet was gone and only prophets can receive revelation and Muhammad was the final prophet. Then the first Khalifh Abu Bakr ordered the complete Quran be organized into book form to be published. All of the Quran had already been written before Muhammad died but all the written verses just weren't collected in one written book. Thousands of people had memorized the whole Quran but the written pieces were the private property of the individual Muslims who had written them down. Thus, to publish the written book format of the Quran all these written pieces had to be collected. Also, since the publishing of the Quran effected the whole Muslim world, no individual wanted to just do it on their own because the consequences of making any error were too great and publishing costs were high during the 600s CE. To mass produce a book you needed quite a bit of money, the types that governments have and an Islamic State initially wasn't going to publish the first ever full written copy of the Quran because that was such an important religious deed the state figured it should make sure nothing goes wrong with such a project. Yet keep in mind the Islamic State was run by the companions of Muhammad, it wasn't a foreign state, the first 4 Khalifhs were not only the best friends of Muhammad but the first was his father in-law, as was the second and the third had married 2 of Muhammad's daughters (one at a time) while the 4th was his cousin and married Muhammad's favorite daughter. So, when the Islamic State worked on the written Quran project it wasn't some "shoddy state project" as we think of them today. Think of it as if it were Solomon composing the Zabur that was given to David in written form. Nobody would view Solomon as "some corrupt government official" who is unqualified to publish the revelation given to David. We'd agree Solomon would be the best one for the job after David himself, so rulership doesn't always mean anti-religious or unreligious sometimes good rulers can do great things for religion. The criteria for publication of the Quran was extremely strict. Zaid ibn Thabit was chosen for the task primarily because he was known to have heard the full Quran recited to him by Muhammad during the last Ramadan before Muhammad's death. Regarding the compilation of the Quran in its complete written form, not just any Muslim was able to say what the Quran said. A Muslim couldn't just come with a piece of paper and say it's a verse from the Quran and have it published in the book. They had to have heard it directly from Muhammad's mouth, AND they had to have written it down in the presence of Muhammad AND recited it to Muhammad; to verify they knew how to pronounce it and knew it exactly 100%. Also, aside from hearing it from Muhammad, writing it in his presence and reciting it to Muhammad, a person needed two trustworthy pious witnesses who could testify that person had heard, written and recited that particular verse or letter of the Quran during the lifetime of Muhammad to him/her directly before that person was qualified to testify to what a single letter of the Quran to be published said. Now Zaid bin Thabit had to have more than just 1 person who met these criteria for every letter of the Quran before he could compile the full written book, he needed a minimum 2 people who met these criteria for every letter, along with the 4 witnesses who could testify for those 2 people that they heard X letter from Muhammad, wrote it in his presence and recited X letter of the Quran to Muhammad. Every single letter in the written Quran had to have been written down at least twice in the presence of Muhammad by 2 different individuals with 4 different witnesses to that or else it would not be included in the Quran. Meaning every letter to be put into the written book format of the Quran needed a minimum of 6 people to testify it had come from Muhammad's mouth, was written in his presence and recited/verified by Muhammad. Fortunately, these criteria strict as they were did not cause authentic verses to be excluded. Why then was it done if in theory this strict criteria could have resulted in unabrogated authentic verses of the Quran not getting into the written version? For the sake of literary authenticity. Afterall you can't just say X is the word of God taught to us by a prophet of God, you got to prove that 100%. If you can't prove your book is truly from God via a prophet then there is no reason to believe in it at all. If X book is something which all people "need to believe in" this book needs to be proven to have come from the sources which it really came from. It's hard enough for people to believe in prophets, so the least a believer must do is prove that what they are telling people to believe in actually came from their prophet as they claim. Also, if you can't prove it then there is no justified reason for you to believe in it either, you'd just be blindly following what non-prophets told you without proof that it actually goes back to a prophet. The companions of Muhammad knew this and knew they needed to have an undisputable method for authentically preserving the teachings of the final Messenger of God because if they didn't then the religion of God would be lost and a "final messenger" means humanity cannot afford to screw it up and fail to keep the authentic information scholastically preserved. To not be able to prove the information preached after the final messenger of God is really from the final messenger of God is to delegitimize the true faith and to fail the test of life and give everybody a valid excuse to disbelieve in and disobey God. If the companions of Muhammad didn't painstakingly preserve the prophetic teachings and prove that they did so then everyone to come after them would not have to believe in or obey God and they would get blamed by God for every sin every person did after Muhammad died. They didn't want such blame from God so they decided to get super-scholastic and prove that the information they are passing on to people really is from Muhammad as they claim. If they didn't, they knew they would go to hell because Muhammad told them it was their duty to preserve the true religion after he died and that God wasn't sending any more prophets to fix things if they failed. Thus, the companions of Muhammad were put in a spot where they could either be the best of people if they succeeded in preserving the prophetic faith, when so many other peoples had failed, or they could be the worst for dooming everyone else if they didn't scholastically preserve and prove they preserved the authentic teachings of God's final prophet including God's final revelation, the Quran. Hence the companions of Muhammad knew they either preserved the Quran 100% or they would go to hell forever and whether you believe that would've happened to them or not, they did believe that and that's a fact. They knew the consequences of making mistakes and this is why Zaid ibn Thabit took so long to do the job and said how he wished someone else did it because for him it'd be easier to move a mountain than to bear the burden of the responsibility of publishing God's book in written form since the risk of making a mistake was so great and he didn't want to have that responsibility which the other companions forced upon him. All the Muslims were afraid of making a mistake unintentionally when the Quran was to be published. I mean just take my book for example, you've probably noticed hundreds of errors, spelling or grammatical or worse, and that's all from me with my own stuff. So, for a religious person to be burdened with publishing God's book is extremely hard to do, not impossible but it's perhaps the most stressful job one can have in life. A single spelling error and you go to hell forever, how would you like to publish a book like that considering all books at that time were written by hand? Thus, all the Muslims gave the job to Muhammad's companion Zaid ibn Thabit. Fortunately for him and us he succeeded with perfection. When he finished thousands of companions testified that his written compilation was 100% complete and accurate. This book was completed within 2 years after Muhammad's death, before Abu Bakr died about 2 years after Muhammad. This copy was kept with the Khalifh Abu Bakr, the Khalifh Umar kept it after Abu Bakr died, then Uthman bin Affan possessed it as Khalifh. Uthman bin Affan decided to make more than one copy and sent the various copies throughout the Muslim world. It is this Uthmanic copy that was published in 646 CE, 14 years after the death of Muhammad. But what about Abu Bakr's copy. Well, that doesn't have the dots. In Arabic the dots are diacritical marks that help one easily identify the letters since many letters in Arabic use the same root shape with only context or dots distinguishing them. For example, in English the letters, i and t both use the same exact root shape but the i has a dot and the t has dash. If the i wasn't dotted and the t wasn't dashed then one could mistake the two letters and misunderstand the text if you didn't know the letters from context or the English language well. The same applies to the letters l, d,

P, R, and b, they all look so similar sharing the l root shape that without the loops it'd be hard to identify each letter. In Arabia during the prophet's time nobody used the dots because they were that advanced linguistically because they lived in a desert and had nothing else to do but get good at language. However, Arabs and Arabia changed and since Islam was spreading to non-Arab lands where people could misunderstand the Quran if it wasn't dotted then Uthman included the dots so nobody could ever possibly make a mistake. The dots were added to the Quran in Uthman's time, though they existed in some of the individual written copies before that. Adding dots didn't change a thing regarding pronunciation nor meaning, but it just closed the door for misinterpretation. Uthman then gathered the companions of Muhammad and showed them his copy and Abu Bakr's and they confirmed they were identical to what everyone knew was the Quran. Uthman then said how he planned to burn the undotted copy because someone in the future might come and see the undotted copy and then wrongfully claim the Uthmanic copy did the dots incorrectly and then do their own dots incorrectly and get believed by ignorant people and thus the Quran could in theory be changed as long as that undotted copy remained. Because a thousand years later who is to say whether the dot should be above or below the line when all those who heard the verse from Muhammad directly are dead? Hence realizing the theoretical danger of the undotted copy for future generations and evil/ignorant people the companions agreed to burn Abu Bakr's copy though it was identical to Uthman's because it didn't have the dots, and if they simply added the dots in then future generations might say or learn somehow that they added the dots to Abu Bakr's copy years later and then accuse them of changing the Quran putting dots in the wrong places. To add the dots to Abu Bakr's copy years later would be forgery since Abu Bakr was dead, it could no longer then be called "Abu Bakr's copy" if it had the dots. So, they couldn't just add dots to "Abu Bakr's Quran copy" because that would be a type of forgery but if they left it intact and undotted then foolish or evil people might reject Uthman's correct copy that leaves no room for misunderstanding. Thus, Abu Bakr's copy was burned and replaced with the Uthmanic Quranic script in 646 CE. It was exactly the same, it was just non-Arab friendly and fool friendly. This way you didn't need to be a master in Arabic to read it in Arabic correctly. The Quran was memorized by the masses, the written copy was initially just a copy for safety reasons in case all those who memorized the full Quran died out. Over time to help with memorization of the Quran, copies were distributed to the masses as they are today. However, then people started translating them. This phenomenon of translation could lead to trouble down the road, if the Arabic is neglected or the translations get considered equal or 100% the same as the Arabic Quran. However, there is a benefit in the translations of the Quran in that non-Arabs can get some of its message, like me. Yet there is still a danger of losing the Arabic if the translations come to be treated in an extreme fashion as the trend seems to be going towards. However, because Muslims pray in Arabic and memorize the Quran in Arabic then the danger is much reduced. Anyways that in a nutshell explains why and how the oldest written copy of the Quran which exists today was published in 646 CE while Muhammad died in 632 CE and the first written copy was published between 632-634 CE. One could in theory allege Uthman changed the Quran but nobody ever said this against Uthman during his lifetime, Ali didn't say it either and thousands of Muslims memorized the Quran so it wasn't as though it was only a written copy. Plus, original scraps of undotted copies of the Quran exist and the verses are the same as the dotted

Uthmanic script, they just don't have the dots but contextually it means the same. For example, if I wrote "i did it" but didn't dot the i's and someone else came and said that it's supposed to be "t dtd tt", anyone who knows English would know that the claim "the dots are wrong" is foolish. So that's where theoretically one might think there is a tiny chance Uthman could've changed the meaning via the dots but if you know Arabic you know it is too hard to do and get away with. I've even seen English books written in the 1700s where the t is used for both t and f and you still understand contextually what is t and what is f even though the letters are messed up due to "wrong dots". So, the dot difference is theoretical, but even if it weren't that thousands of Muslims memorized the full Quran and never contested the dotted Uthmanic script during that era, nor have any ever contested it greatly implies no changes were made. Scholastically if one persists as a skeptic, they still must concede that since 646 CE all Muslims have had the same exact Quran without even a dot being changed. So, none can ever claim the written Quran has been changed from 646 CE onwards, even if they think it was changed before that, which no Muslim believes it was. Also, the written copies were meant to be backups primarily, just in case the world no longer has Muslims who have memorized the full Quran. Now people claim "the bible" is the same and just as authentic or historical. But answer me this? 1. Has a single Christian in all of history ever memorized any full bible in its original language including the original pronunciation (including the length which vowels are elongated and the spaces where the reader takes breaths when reading)? Seriously ask a Christian *"When you read the bible out loud at which points in the verses did Jesus or his companions teach you to take a breath while reading the bible?"* Because Muhammad and the companions of Muhammad taught the Muslims when to take a breath when they "speak the words of

God". Afterall, doesn't it make sense that if God is going to send you "God's word" to read and verbalize then God is going to tell you at which spots to pause for breath? God does know you got to breathe right? You can't just breathe in the middle of the word or sentence because that can change the whole meaning of the verse. Allah told Muhammad when to breathe when reciting the Quran. Do Christians actually think God doesn't care when they breathe when speaking God's word out loud? Why would God care when you breathe? Because God's book is unlike any other and if you read God's book aloud there are rules for breathing because it's a special book. That's one of the things that makes God's book special and unique in that there are rules for breathing when reading it aloud. Do Christians not think the word of God is special and unique or were they not "guided unto all truth" and "taught all things" as the bible says Jesus said the "Holy Spirit/Comforter/Holy Prophet" would do who would "speak only what he hears"? 2. Can Christians prove with physical documentation that the bible in their hand today is dot for dot exactly the same as the one that they allege existed 14 years after the departure of Jesus? But more importantly, 3. Did Jesus recite the New Testament to people during his lifetime, have it written down in his lifetime and have it recited to him in his lifetime and then have a minimum of 2 written copies of every verse in the New Testament that existed before he left earth? AND have 2 witnesses to witness each letter of the New Testament, meaning 4 trustworthy pious witnesses can testify for every letter in the New Testament that "Mark", "Matthew", "Luke", "John" and "Paul" wrote? Making a minimum of 6 total trustworthy pious witnesses who are companions of Jesus that approve of every verse in the New Testament and testify that Jesus taught it? Hell no! Paul and Luke even according to Christians never even met Jesus, heard him or saw what he looked like. Paul didn't even believe in the religion of Jesus while Jesus was on earth, according to his own admission. Thus, Paul is scholastically disqualified from saying a single word about Jesus, even if what he said was true, which it's not and is contradictory to Jesus, his disciples, other Christians (some whom Paul killed as Saul) and Paul's other versions of Jesus. The same applies to the books of the Hebrew bible and/or "Old Testament". None are traceable back to Moses and Moses; David and Solomon didn't even speak or write Hebrew. So, the bible is not only scholastically inauthentically transcribed but it's not even in the same language the prophets to whom such writings are alleged to have come from spoke. Just on that fundamental point alone, that the New Testament is written in a language Jesus never spoke and that the Old Testament is written in a language Abraham, Ishmael, Isaac, Jacob, Joseph, Noah, Job, Jonah, Adam, Moses, David, Solomon, Lot, Seth, Enoch and most biblical characters never spoke disqualifies them as authentic religiously useable texts. Forget translations, copies, forgeries, lack of chains of transmission. The books are in different languages than the prophets they purport to teach us about, hence they could never be from those prophets and could never be the divine revelation given to those prophets. There is absolutely zero connection between the biblical prophets and the biblical texts. A newspaper article written today has as much likelihood to have been written by Moses as the bible. Yet who would dare claim Moses is writing articles for the modern media outfits? This is how farfetched the claim of Jews and Christians are when they say that the books they read and preach today are the Taurat that was revealed to Moses or the Zabur revealed to David or the Suhuf revealed to Abraham (though most Jews/Christians don't even know about that book to even claim such a thing). Likewise, it's more reasonable to think Jesus wrote Mein Kempf than it is to think the New Testament is the Injeel that was revealed to Jesus.

Yet some people consider the Quran comparable to the bible? That's ludicrous insanity. Scholastically the bible is invalid and belongs in the fiction genre of libraries and bookstores. This is why the notion of Christian and Jewish "scholars" is an academic insult, it's an insult not a joke, but an insult, because scholastically speaking to believe in scholastic academia's methods of authenticity means to disbelieve in the authenticity of the alleged literary foundations of Judaism and Christianity. Nobody with academic integrity or credentials claims the bible has any connection with the prophets described in it. Not a single scholastic link exists. Zeus and Hercules have as much of a connection with the bible as Moses and Jesus do. Just because the bible has information about Moses and Jesus putting words in their mouth doesn't mean it has any connection to them at all. It's truly disgusting when religious scholastic minds examine the bible and then get told it's holy, sacred scripture, authentic or the "inspired word of God". It's utterly depressing to know of the deception Christians and Jews are under and the sheer lack of scholasticism amongst them regarding their claims. Put bluntly every Christian and Jew is a stupid fool. With Christians/Jews their claims about their texts is mainly all talk and tradition which contradicts genuine scholastic authenticity. Every "Scholar" they claim supports them is one of their own who just has a diploma. Sadly, though people think Muslims are just like Christians/Jews because we say we got a book from God too when scholastically our books are incomparable. It's the same claim but 2 totally different things, though many non-Muslim non-Christian non-Jews tend to unjustly judge the Quran the same as they do "the bible". Muslims beg them to just read the Quran knowing they will see the difference but since the bible is so damn long and Christians/Jews also say "Just read it then you'll see." they tend to arrogantly refuse not knowing you can read the whole Quran in a few hours. The bible may take years to read but the full Quran can be read within 1 days' time. The bible is nothing like the Quran it even addresses the reader in a different direct "God to reader" perspective while the bible is a boring contradictory historical monologue. Ironically evil cartoonish villains are known for monologues. In literary terms the bible has an "evil speech style" whereas God is not known to have ever monologed. In literary terms the Quran is unlike every other book, especially regarding style, worth of content/wisdom per length, historical authenticity and proof of preservation.

However, isn't it possible that somehow the Quran was corrupted in between Muhammad and us today? So that "our Quran" isn't the real Quran or couldn't the Quran be destroyed and lost and then someone invents a new one and tricks all the Muslims into thinking it was the same Quran as the original even though it wasn't? Imagine if we all agreed to destroy every book in the world, deleting every digital, audio and written copy by fire and/or other methods so that no book that we know of today existed in physical format. Within less than 24 hours mankind would be able to reprint the Quran from scratch without referencing any physical copies and have it turn out exactly the same as the original because millions have it entirely memorized in its original Arabic, no other book could be recovered as quickly as fully if at all. This is a vital detail because if God sends a final prophet with a final revelation, then that revelation has to be available, if it's not then people will not know how they are supposed to conduct themselves and will have an excuse for not living the way God desires them to. If you had no chance to know what God wanted from you then you would have had no chance to do what God wanted. In that case God would have no legal recourse to punish you if you had no chance to know the laws which you were supposed to obey. For someone to say that nothing today is divine revelation, it means that they think it's impossible to know what God's rules are for us, therefore it would be impossible for someone to go to hell no matter how evil they were, or what bad things they did. Obviously thinking that the evil mass-murdering, thieving, adulterous, disbelieving people will not be punished is preposterous. Thus, the divine revelation must exist and every religious text other than the Quran and Sunnah has been proven to be corrupted and changed from its original, as has been demonstrated with the analysis of the bibles. Some might say that "the bible" hasn't been corrupted (pretending there is only 1 version), but even they will agree that if all digital, audio and written bibles were destroyed then "the bible" would be lost forever. Now if something can potentially be lost then that is not the final divine revelation, because the final divine revelation cannot be potentially lost by definition. By default, that would make the Quran the only candidate for being the final divine revelation. Not only is it the only candidate, but it also says that it is the final divine revelation which will be preserved from distortion and corruption, which time has proven that claim to be true. The Quran is also the only religious Scripture that is impossible to be changed or lost. So many people have the Quran memorized completely in Arabic that it would be easier to change the multiplication tables than to change the Quran. It'd be easier to get people to forget or not think the sun and moon existed than to change the Quran. Little kids who can't even ride a bicycle have memorized the entire Quran in Arabic. Do you know how this is possible? Because Allah said in the Quran 54:17,

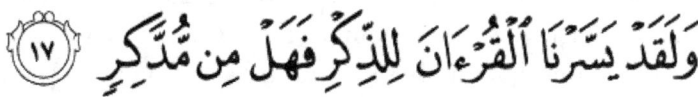

*"And We have indeed made the Quran easy to understand and remember, then is there any that will remember (or receive admonition)?"*

It's simply because the Quran said it was easy to remember and because it's true then it is. There is no other explanation one can have to say why a book which claims to be from God which says it is easy to remember is also the most memorized book in the history of all mankind in the original Arabic language which it was revealed in, being remembered by people who don't even know the meaning of the Arabic. If any book at all can be called "easy to remember" it's the Quran, it is the easiest to remember of all books. For example, Ibn Shihab Al-Zuhri is reported to have memorized the entire Quran when he was 7 years old in only 8 days. 8 days for a 7-year-old to memorize all 114 chapters of the Quran. Such things even take place in modern times with Rukkayatu Fatahu Umar being a 3-year-old girl in Nigeria who memorized the entire Quran in 2013 CE. She was 3 years old! For a 3-year-old in modern times to memorize a religious book of 114 chapters in length, totaling 600 pages in Arabic, is practically a miracle itself. Oh, and keep in mind she was a 3-year-old Nigerian and Arabic is not the common language in Nigeria, so most likely she didn't even know the meaning of the Arabic she memorized unless she also memorized the meanings in Nigerian or another language if she didn't know Arabic. Typically, it's hard to memorize things in a language you don't understand but not so with the Quran. What other 600-page religious book which has been on earth for thousands of years can be memorized by a modern 3-year-old child in a language they don't even know? So, when Allah says in the Quran how he has made it easy to understand and remember those aren't just words, it's miraculously easy to remember the Quran. It's not just some empty claim that any book could make. No book on the planet can even come close to being as easy to remember as the Quran.

The Quran is also the most popular and widely read book of all time. Christians may dispute this and say "the bible" is but they are pretending that there is only one edition of a bible and ignoring the fact that different languages constitute a different book and that until very recently only priests were allowed to even possess a bible, let alone read one. If any bible set any record, it's for being the most misunderstood least divine book of all time with the largest discrepancy between owners/readers. Out of all books that are bought or believed in "the bible' is the least read and least followed. Basically, if you consider the popularity of "the bible" it is technically the least impactful book known to man of all recorded history, any divine book if as widely known as the bible would've had much greater impact and created a much better world. Whereas case by case when one examines all the "Muslim regions" in the world their post-Quran history has always been better than their pre-Quran pre-Islamic pre-Muslim history, without exception. Every "Muslim nation" has historically been better off since becoming "Islamicized", regardless of whatever extent they were Islamicized. Even the regions which reverted to being unislamic, such as the Iberian Peninsula, have still been better off post-Islam than they were before, because of the blessings the Quran bestows on peoples and places wherever its obeyed. The reason the world is largely ignorant that the Quran is the most popular, most influential and most widely read book of all time is because most who read it become Muslims so their opinions get discounted and disbelievers ignore pro-Islamic facts. Even if one rejects Islam, they cannot deny the facts that what the Quran says about itself is true. It says it's in Arabic, true, it says it contains no discrepancies, true, it says it's easy to remember, true, it says exactly how different types of people will feel when they hear it or read it as well as exactly what they will say about it word for word even before they know that it foretold what they would say, it also says word for word what people will say to justify their false beliefs and sins and it is true word for word, the people physically cannot stop themselves from saying or doing what the Quran says they will say or do, but most importantly the Quran says it is from God. Do you think God would allow a book to exist on earth for as long as the Quran has which claims what the Quran claims if it wasn't truly from him? No other text available to the masses today says it's from God. Literally you cannot open up one book on this planet today except for the Quran where the book claims to be from God and everything else it says is true with such detail, accuracy and relevance today just as much as when the verses were initially made known. Actually, the Quran has more proof in its favor today because the more time which passes the more accurately the world recognizes the Quran to have been when first revealed and the less doubt there is that it could be anything other than divine revelation sent to us by the Creator of the Universe. That's why it's not even a matter of true or false, every rational intelligent person who genuinely examines it honestly concedes that it is true, even if they don't become Muslims. So, it's not about whether it's true or not, it's whether you believe it and obey, or take the disbeliever's attitude of "*I just can't believe/obey it, even though I know it's true and actually happened.*", or if you say/think, "*Screw it! I want to live my life the way I want and already am and I don't want to know what God wants me to think or do, and he's just going treat me the way I like to when I die because I'm not that bad compared to everyone else I know.*" Now let's be sensible, if there is only one thing that could be divine revelation and that one thing itself says that it is the one thing, then for a person to not even bother looking into that thing and continuing to look elsewhere is complete irresponsibility, bigotry and stupidity. Whereas to not look for/into the divine revelation is the very definition of a loser by default. Even from a basic literary standpoint a book that has stood the test of time, science, history and has been memorized by billions and only has one version deserves to be read just because of special uniqueness alone. I plead that you at least give the

Quran a read through, or a translation in a language that you understand if you can't read Arabic or understand the Arabic recitation. To reject it without reading it would be unjust even from a secular historically scientific standpoint. Let alone the fact that it says it's from the Creator which again makes it incumbent upon us to pay attention to it. When a book says it is from God that's something to look into for yourself, there is no text more important than God's. Honestly if you were trapped on an island and could only read one book and I got to choose for you between my book and the Quran, without hesitation I would prefer you read the Quran instead of my book. The only thing that separates my book and gives it any value compared to the billions of other books is that it contains verses from the Quran inside, it is an honor to include the speech of Allah in my book which elevates this book degrees above all others which don't have verses of the Quran within them. And that's also another reason why I don't profit from this book, and give any royalty above publishing cost to charity, because it has God's speech in it. The Quran challenges mankind to produce 10 words like it; I'm just asking you to read it. The Quran is the direct message from your Creator which guides you to the truth and paradise, which remains in the same form as revealed to God's prophet Muhammad in the first person. It is the final revelation that completes and perfects mankind's religion. I have researched every major religion practiced in the world today and many of the minor religions and found Islam to be the only true religion. But do not take my word for it, I simply ask you to do your own genuine research about Islam yourself, with an open mind. You have nothing to lose, absolutely nothing. If Islam is false then you will be able to tell and will be more confident in whatever religion you have right now, or at least one step closer to the truth whatever it is. If Islam is true then you will have the opportunity to obtain eternal bliss in the afterlife with inner peace and purpose in this life. At the minimum you would have a better understanding of nearly 2 billion people on the planet and be far less likely to believe a lie when it is told to you. What if Muhammad really is the final messenger of our Creator? Would you follow him and the rest of the prophets to paradise? Or would you reject it even if it was proven without a doubt to be the truth to you? What if the Quran is a direct message from your Creator and after me informing you about this fact you scoff at it and never bother to look into it, how do you think your Creator will treat you on the Day of judgment if you die in that condition? On that day you won't be able to say you didn't have time, or that no one ever warned you. You have time now. If you had time to read this book you definitely have time to read a translation of the meanings of the Quran more than once. Type "*Free Quran*" into any internet search engine and you can get a free Quran or a translation or the Arabic with a translation in electronic, audio or physical form.

www.ingramcontent.com/pod-product-compliance
Lightning Source LLC
Chambersburg PA
CBHW050249010526
44107CB00003B/242